INSIDERS' GUIDE® TO ANCHORAGE AND SOUTHCENTRAL ALASKA

Help Us Keep This Guide Up to Date

Every effort has been made by the authors and editors to make this guide as accurate and useful as possible. However, many things can change after a guide is published—trails are rerouted, regulations change, techniques evolve, facilities come under new management, etc.

We would love to hear from you concerning your experiences with this guide and how you feel it could be improved and kept up to date. While we may not be able to respond to all comments and suggestions, we'll take them to heart and we'll also make certain to share them with the authors. Please send your comments and suggestions to the following address:

The Globe Pequot Press
Reader Response/Editorial Department
P.O. Box 480
Guilford, CT 06437

Or you may e-mail us at:

editorial@globe-pequot.com

Thanks for your input, and happy travels!

INSIDERS' GUIDE® SERIES

INSIDERS' GUIDE® TO

ANCHORAGE AND SOUTHCENTRAL ALASKA

INCLUDING THE KENAI PENINSULA, PRINCE WILLIAM SOUND, AND DENALI NATIONAL PARK

DEB VANASSE

INSIDERS' GUIDE®

GUILFORD, CONNECTICUT
AN IMPRINT OF THE GLOBE PEQUOT PRESS

The prices and rates in this guidebook were confirmed at press time. We recommend, however, that you call establishments before traveling to obtain current information.

INSIDERS' GUIDE®

Copyright © 2007 Morris Book Publishing, LLC

Text design by Nancy Freeborn
Maps by Trailhead Graphics/Tim Kissel © Morris Book Publishing, LLC

Library of Congress Cataloging-in-Publication data is available for this title.

ISBN 978-0-7627-4028-4

Manufactured in the United States of America
First Edition/First Printing

CONTENTS

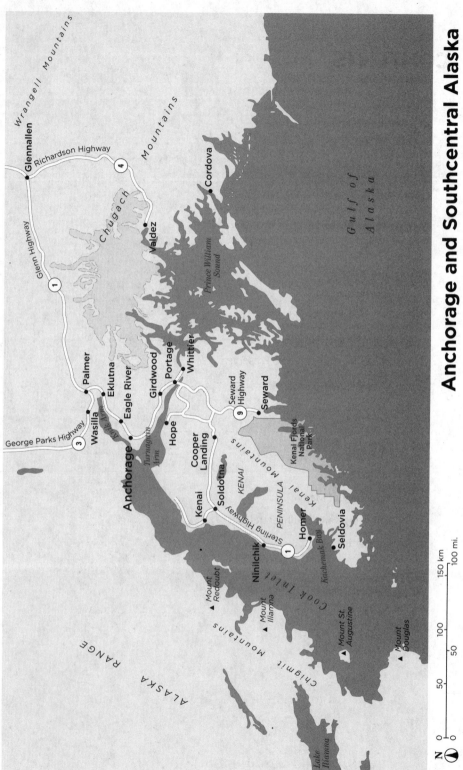

Anchorage and Southcentral Alaska

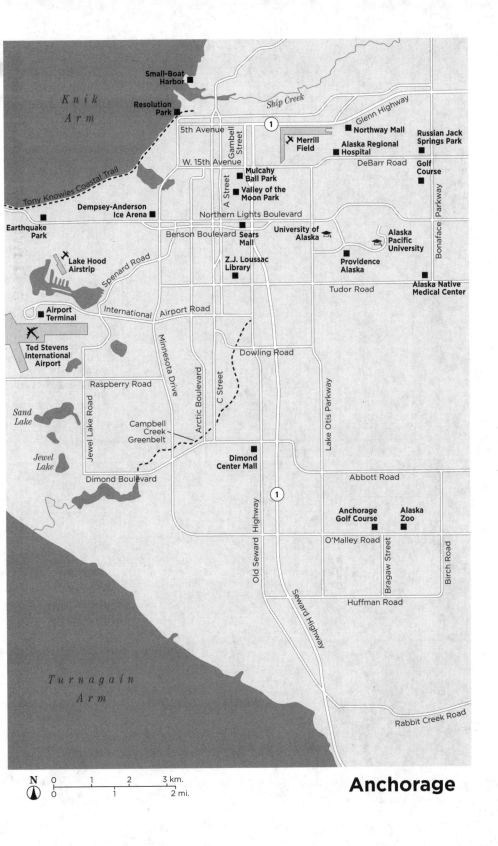

Anchorage

Downtown Anchorage

Knik Arm

Ship Creek

Merrill Field

GLENN HIGHWAY

Ship Creek Salmon Viewing

E. SHIP CREEK AVE.

Alaska Railroad Depot

E. 3RD AVE.
E. 4TH AVE.
E. 5TH AVE.
E. 6TH AVE.
E. 9TH AVE.

INGRA ST.

GAMBELL ST.

E. 15TH AVE.

SEWARD HIGHWAY

Resolution Park

Oscar Anderson House Museum

Elderberry Park

Ship Creek Center

Log Cabin Visitor Center

Egan Center

Post Office Mall

Center for the Performing Arts

5th Avenue Mall

Anchorage Museum of History and Art

Federal Building

City Cemetery

George M. Sullivan Sports Arena

Mulcahy Ball Park

Ben Boeke Arena

W. 3RD AVE.
W. 4TH AVE.
W. 5TH AVE.
W. 6TH AVE.
W. 9TH AVE.
W. 15TH AVE.

Delaney Park Strip

L ST.
K ST.
I ST.
H ST.
G ST.
F ST.
E ST.
D ST.
C ST.
A ST.

N

0   .5   1.5 km
0   .5   1 mi.

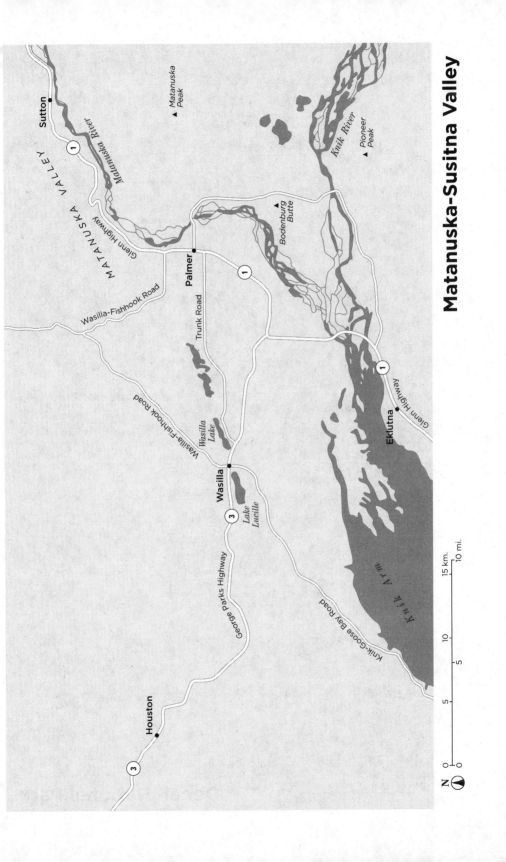

Matanuska-Susitna Valley

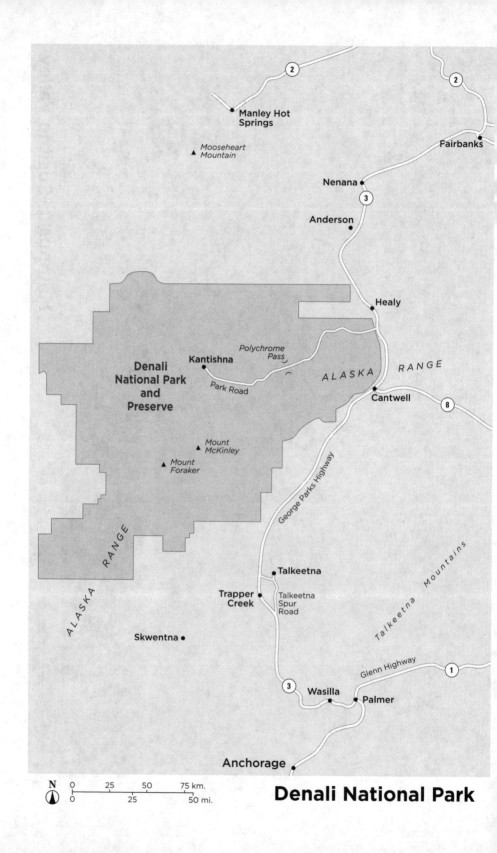

Denali National Park

PREFACE

It was nearly midnight. Sun streamed through the windows of the Hotel Captain Cook in downtown Anchorage, illuminating the cafe table where I sat with my companions. Energized by the long June day, we were in the midst of a lively discussion about Alaska's economy when one friend leapt to his feet. "Have to say hi to the governor," he announced, making his way to the door, where former governor Wally Hickel was on his way out.

That's how it is in Anchorage. Alaska's largest city is also in many ways a small town, where pretenses dissolve and people are drawn together by their love of the outdoors and the spectacular beauty of the place. Mountains rise up behind the skyline and the waters of Cook Inlet stretch along the western edge of town while lakes and creeks dot the city landscape. Head east to Prince William Sound, north to Denali National Park, or south to the Kenai Peninsula, and you'll encounter mile after mile of pristine wilderness that makes this country like no other.

It's a place that attracts rugged individualists, yet it's also a place where folks go out of their way to help each other. Native Alaskans, commercial fishermen, miners, oil company executives, construction workers, or white-collar professionals—it doesn't so much matter who you are. It's all about an independence of spirit, a sense of community, and a love of the land. It takes a certain something to call yourself an Alaskan, to know when you've moved from being a wet-behind-the-ears cheechako to a real sourdough.

Expect to be delighted. Expect to be charmed. Most of all, expect the unexpected, because Anchorage and Southcentral Alaska are full of surprises, from the double rainbows that span the expansive sky after a summer shower to the blanket of snow that glitters on a moonlit night to the northern lights that dance across a December sky. There's the surprise of finding world-class entertainment at the performing arts center in downtown Anchorage, of enjoying jazz in the park on a summer evening, of admiring the stunning landscapes painted by artists such as Sydney Laurence. There's the delight of watching your kids grin as they encounter their first moose, reel in a big salmon, or climb aboard a dogsled for a quick ride. And there's the sense of finding yourself all over again as you hike a wilderness trail into the mountains for an unforgettable view of the ocean and valleys below.

It's not easy to pack a place so vast into the pages of a book, but we've done our best to show you all of the best that this region has to offer. We hope you'll return again and again.

ACKNOWLEDGMENTS

Alaska is a big and humbling place. I couldn't have begun to do justice to such a vast region without a lot of help. Countless shopkeepers, bartenders, waiters, and business owners took the time to give me their insiders' perspective on their hometowns and their places of business. Of particular assistance were Bryan Zak, Jeff Huffman, Leeanne Mercier, Dorothy Johnson, Dr. Karen French, Jacqui Johansen, Jill Reese, Kelly Fisher, and Sharon Minsch. Sincere thanks go also to Kirsten Dixon and Janet Shafsky, two amazing Alaskan women who graciously shared a bit of their lives with me.

To my friends, colleagues, and family goes much appreciation for putting up with my long hours, my obsession with deadlines, and my enthusiasm about all the great things I discovered along the way. A special thanks to my longtime friend Karla Gleason, who checked, double-checked, and made lots of suggestions for the Anchorage portion of the book, and to Mike Ferency, who spent a whole lot of time driving me all over Anchorage and the Valley looking for just the right information and photos. You all made it good.

HOW TO USE THIS BOOK

Maybe you're arriving in Alaska independently or as part of a tour group. You could be traveling by plane, cruise ship, car, or RV. You might have plans to stay for a few days or for a lifetime. In any case, this book is designed to help you get your bearings and get to know this region the way those of us who love it well do. The vast landscape, the seemingly endless miles of wilderness, and the rich beauty of the Last Frontier can seem overwhelming at times. Many visitors leave feeling like they've only begun to discover all that Alaska has to offer. It's our hope that this guide will make your Alaskan experience richer, deeper, and more memorable than it would have been otherwise.

We've begun by giving you an overview of the region, followed by tips on how to get here and how to get around. From there, the book is organized geographically, beginning with Anchorage, Alaska's largest city. Subsequent chapters spin out from Anchorage the way our road system does—south to the Kenai Peninsula, north and east to Prince William Sound, and north and west to the Matanuska-Susitna (Mat-Su) Valley and Denali National Park. Though Denali is technically beyond what most folks consider to be Southcentral Alaska, it is such a key part of the Alaskan experience that we've given it full coverage in this guide. For the most part, we've focused on communities that are accessible by road or ferry, though we've also featured a number of fly-out adventures for those looking to truly get away from it all.

You can experience Alaska from the comfort of a cruise ship deck or a luxurious domed railroad car, or you can grab a pack and your hiking boots and head out into the wilderness. We've made every attempt to include information that will be helpful to all sorts of travelers with plans as diverse as the state itself. Almost all area chapters include sections on how to get there, how to get around, accommodations, restaurants, shopping, attractions, hiking, camping, fishing, parks, recreation, and tours. Where applicable, chapters also include information on nightlife, kidstuff, annual events, and the arts. Throughout the book we've included Insiders' Tips, indicated by an ℹ️ icon, which give you the sort of perspectives that come with sourdough status, the Alaskan measure of proving yourself in a place where it takes a certain degree of hardiness to get by. Our Close-up sections put you in touch with some of the fascinating people, places, events, and phenomena that make this place truly special.

If you dream of calling Alaska home, you're not alone. Never mind the long, cold winters and the top-of-the-world remoteness. There's a certain allure that draws folks here and won't let go. If your heart is calling you north, you'll want to check out our relocation section, with lots of useful information on real estate, education, child care, health care, worship, and even retirement. Our chapter on media will point you toward newspapers, magazines, and other resources to keep you in touch with all that's happening in the 49th state.

So dive in where you like, using the table of contents and the index as a guide. Use the book to plan and dream, bring it on your travels and, should you fall in love and decide to stay, keep it as a handy reference on your shelf. Welcome to the Last Great Place.

AREA OVERVIEW

CLIMATE AND SEASONS

No one comes to Alaska to bask in the heat, but you may be surprised to find that Anchorage and Southcentral Alaska are quite temperate considering their proximity to the Arctic Circle. The average high temperature in January is 21 degrees Fahrenheit, which is downright balmy compared to places farther north. July is typically the warmest month, with an average high of 65 degrees Fahrenheit. Summer temperatures generally climb as you travel north toward Fairbanks, but with those higher temperatures and drier conditions come the risk of forest fires that sometimes blanket Alaska's interior with smoke. For the most part, Anchorage and Southcentral Alaska still enjoy smoke-free summers, and their maritime setting means winter temperatures stay mostly above zero. Snowfall in Anchorage is typically heaviest in December, with an average of nearly 14 inches falling during that month. Valdez gets pummeled with an average of 27 feet of snow every winter, and Denali has its share as well, but in most of Southcentral Alaska, snowfall is about average for a northern climate.

While Alaska technically has four seasons, our spring and fall can be downright skimpy. On the highway between Anchorage and Denali, leaves will begin to turn in August, and a brief blaze of gold can be followed quickly by the first snowfall come September. Anchorage doesn't usually see significant amounts of the white stuff until late October or early November, with breakup arriving about six months later. Snow might fall in May or September, but it probably won't stick. June, July, and August are typically snow-free, except in Denali Park, where snow has fallen in every month of the year. Annual precipitation in Anchorage is close to 16 inches per

year, while annual snowfall is just short of 70 inches per year.

Though Anchorage is well to the south of the Arctic Circle, the city still enjoys 24 hours of functional daylight on the summer solstice, meaning that though the sun has set, there is enough light to get by without artificial illumination. It's the tilt of the earth on its axis that creates this phenomenon, with the Northern Hemisphere tipped toward the sun in the summer and away from the sun in the winter, so that Anchorage has approximately five and a half hours of daylight on the winter solstice. In the winter, some Alaskans suffer from Seasonal Affective Disorder, or SAD, which may be the result of higher melatonin levels in the blood as daylight decreases. Indoor light boxes that mimic natural sunlight can help those who suffer from this disorder.

NATURAL WONDERS

Describing natural wonders in a place that's almost synonymous with the term is tough. No matter what you read or hear about the incredible natural phenomena of Alaska, it ends up seeming like understatement when you cruise next to a calving glacier, gaze up at the northern lights leaping in the winter sky, or marvel at the beauty of mountains that press up against the sea.

When you look out across Cook Inlet, you'll see a string of volcanoes that are part of the Ring of Fire, where the Pacific tectonic plate is sliding beneath the North American plate. Approximately 10 percent of the world's active volcanoes are in Alaska. Occasionally eruptions disrupt air travel, as has been the case in recent years with Mount St. Augustine.

The Alaska Range and the Chugach Mountains are integral to the landscape of

From the Richardson Highway north of Valdez, you can walk to the face of Worthington Glacier. DEB VANASSE

Southcentral Alaska. The Alaska Range stretches 600 miles from the Canadian border into Southwest Alaska, creating a natural northern boundary of sorts for the Southcentral region. Mt. McKinley, also called Denali, is the highest peak in the Alaska Range as well as in all of North America. The Chugach Mountains form a natural backdrop for the city of Anchorage, offering abundant recreational opportunities and spectacular vistas. Along with the Wrangell and Aleutian Ranges, these mountains cause air to dry as it rises and moves north.

With northern mountains come glaciers, and Alaska has thousands of them. As snow accumulates beyond the amount that can melt in a summer season, it crystallizes into solid ice that may build for thousands of years. The most accessible glaciers are tidewater glaciers that extend into the sea, such as Columbia Glacier in Valdez, and valley glaciers such as Portage Glacier, south of Anchorage.

Some of the forests in Southcentral Alaska, particularly those of the Kenai Peninsula, are boreal forests, which include aspen, birch, poplar, cottonwood, and white spruce. Around Cook Inlet and Prince William Sound, you'll find coastal forests featuring primarily Sitka spruce. Where you see wet, treeless areas or stunted black spruce, you're probably looking at permafrost, where subsoils are frozen for two or more years. Farther north, there's continuous permafrost, while in Southcentral, the permafrost is discontinuous, meaning that it's found sporadically.

Beetle-killed spruce trees have turned parts of the Kenai Peninsula into kindling for wildfires that periodically plague the state. The year 2004 brought a record fire season as 6.4 million acres burned, though most of the activity was in Alaska's interior. Despite the

A young moose eats twigs near Sand Lake Road in Anchorage. DEB VANASSE

annoyance of smoke and occasional road closures, most of Alaska's wildfires are allowed to burn, as they provide a natural renewal for the landscape by burning off organic material that would otherwise keep soils from warming.

The northern lights, or aurora borealis, are the most famous phenomenon associated with Alaska's skies. You won't see them in the summer when the skies stay light, but from September to March, particularly between 10:00 P.M. and 2:00 A.M., you may be lucky enough to witness one of the most spectacular light shows in all of nature. Far away on the surface of the sun, solar flares create solar winds that blow a stream of particles toward us here on earth. As these winds hit the earth's magnetic shield, they create charged electrons that discharge electricity when they encounter gas particles. The result is a brilliant, dancing display of light. The most common color is green, but you also may see red when oxygen is struck at elevations of 150 miles or more, and blue or purple if nitrogen molecules are involved. Less exciting but still unique is Alaska's airglow effect, an atmospheric condition that makes our skies a little brighter and our stars a little dimmer than in most other places. During the day, you may also see sun dogs, little rainbows flanking the sun, caused by ice crystals in the air.

WILDLIFE

Uniquely adapted for life in the far north, wildlife has free reign over Alaska's mostly uninhabited lands. Moose, with long legs that help them forge through deep snow, are among the mammals you're most likely to see. They're not shy about coming into town or crossing roadways, so you'll want to be alert for them when you're driving. Though moose are normally docile creatures, they will charge and stomp when threatened, and a cow will do just about anything to protect her calves. Bears also have been known to frequent urban areas, so you'll want to exercise caution even when hiking on trails close to town, keeping trash in bear-proof containers and away from human habitation.

Wolves, fox, lynx, marmot, and a host of other smaller mammals are among those you may be lucky enough to see while you're here. Remember, though, that we've got a lot of land for these critters to call home. Some folks have been here for decades without spotting a wolf or a lynx in the wild. For the most predictable wildlife-viewing opportunities, try the Alaska Zoo, the Wildlife Conservation Center, or the bus ride into Denali National Park. If you'd love to see such marine mammals as sea lions, dolphins, seals, and otters, take a cruise out of the coastal towns of Valdez or Seward.

HUMAN INHABITANTS

It's thought that the first humans came to Alaska tens of thousands of years ago via the Bering Land Bridge, following the retreating ice. Eventually three distinct groups emerged. The Aleuts and Eskimos formed coastal cultures, while several tribes of Indians settled into the Interior and Southcentral regions. The Athabascans, who are perhaps related to the Navaho and Apache of the Southwestern United States, were the predominant group in Southcentral Alaska. They lived a migratory subsistence lifestyle, following food sources with spring, fall, winter, and summer fish camps. Today Alaska's Native peoples work hard to preserve their traditional cultures while meeting the challenges of surviving in a money-based economy.

GETTING HERE, GETTING AROUND

Part of the allure of Alaska is that it's so far from the rest of the country, a vast expanse of mostly wilderness set off by itself at the top of the world. But getting here need not be a struggle, and there are lots of ways to do it. Once you're here, there are all sorts of ways to get around. Some options, such as horseback riding, trolley tours, ATV rides, snowmobiling, and bicycle riding, are more about having fun than getting from point A to point B, so we'll discuss those in our Recreation and Attractions sections of the appropriate chapters.

BY AIR

There are plenty of nonstop flights offered by major air carriers from such cities as Seattle, Minneapolis, Denver, Chicago, and Salt Lake City, especially in the summer when tourists come and go in droves. Thanks to a major renovation, the Ted Stevens International Airport in Anchorage now offers a stunning point of entry for visitors, with gleaming marble floors and walls of windows opening up to striking mountain vistas. Most flights go in and out of the renovated portion of the airport, which includes a museum-quality exhibit of Alaskan native artifacts and a display of planes from bygone days. Some of the smaller carriers still use two of the older concourses, but the airport is small enough that you'll never be far from a nice assortment of shops and restaurants. A shuttle ride away is a second terminal used primarily by international carriers and Delta Airlines.

Once you're here, the fun in the air doesn't have to end. You can hop on small commuter planes to get from Anchorage to some of the more popular destinations in Southcentral Alaska, or you can get a bird's-eye view of the state's expansive beauty by taking a flight-seeing tour with one of the air services listed here. Prices, of course, are subject to change.

Alaska Flight Tours/Vernair
1704 East Fifth Avenue, Anchorage
(907) 258–7822
www.alaskavernair.com
For $195 per seat, you can opt for one of three two-and-a-half-hour tours. The Mt. McKinley trip will take you up the Matanuska Valley, where you'll see active gold claims and hopefully some impressive wildlife. From there you'll fly over Mt. McKinley's Tokositna and Kahiltna Glaciers, and then you'll get to see the stunning peaks of the Ruth Glacier Gorge. On the Columbia Glacier tour, you'll see your first glacier within 15 minutes, with up to 33 more glaciers to follow. Dall sheep and sea lions are commonly spotted on this tour, and you'll pass over Whittier, Portage, and Cook Inlet on your way back. The volcano tour will take you over two active volcanoes as well as offshore oil platforms in Cook Inlet, fish camps, commercial fishing boats, and the native village of Tyonek. Other tour options include Knik Glacier, Kenai Fjords, Prince William Sound, and a wildlife tour. Custom tours to more remote locations, such as Lake Clark, Lake Iliamna, Katmai National Park, and the Brooks Range, also can be arranged.

Ellison Air Seaplane Tours
4520 Wisconsin Drive, Anchorage
(907) 243–1959
www.ellisonair.com
From Lake Spenard, this family-owned and -operated business can send you off on a variety of airborne adventures. If you want just a glimpse of what's up there, opt for a $50, 30-minute local seaplane ride over the Anchorage Bowl, four mountain ranges, and the

The international airport, recently remodeled, welcomes visitors with high ceilings, skylights, and glass art.
DEB VANASSE

Susitna River drainage. If you have more time, you can take in a lot more wildlife and scenery on the Chugach State Park or Prince William Sound Tours, with prices ranging from $115 to $240, depending on the length of your flight. Ellison's most popular tour is the Wildlife Glacier Tour, with two hours of flight time for viewing massive ice fields and glaciers. Moose, bear, sheep, goats, caribou, and beluga whales are among the wildlife you may see. The tour includes a landing on a remote wilderness lake. Ellison Air pilots boast more than 20 years of Alaskan flying experience. There's a three-passenger minimum, with group and family discounts available.

Sound Aviation
Merrill Field and Reeve Boulevard, Anchorage
(907) 229–2462
Lifelong Alaskan Dan Easley promises premier tours at the lowest rates in town. Starting at $25 per person, you can take the Anchorage Scenic Tour, or you can opt for more expensive tours of Eagle, Knik, Blackstone, or Columbia Glacier. He also offers tours of Mt. McKinley, Kenai Fjords, and Prince William Sound. All tours include music and pilot narration as well as wildlife viewing. There's also the option of a 360-degree trips around Denali, weather permitting. Sound Aviation does personalized custom tours as well as offering statewide charter and air taxi service. They'll provide free shuttle service to Merrill Field, too. Tour rates are based on a minimum of three passengers.

Take Flight Alaska
1740 East Fifth Avenue, Anchorage
(907) 274–9943
www.takeflightalaska.com
Specializing in "earth and sky" experiences, Take Flight offers several excursion packages to maximize your flight-seeing adventure. Take a 90-minute flight through the Alaska

Private planes dock all around Lake Hood, east of the Anchorage airport. DEB VANASSE

Range to Denali, where you'll stay overnight at the Skyline Lodge and then travel 90 miles into the park by shuttle bus before returning to Anchorage on the Alaska Railroad. Another option is to head south on a one-hour scenic flight to Seward, where you'll board an all-day boat tour to see the abundant wildlife of the Kenai Fjords National Park, returning to Anchorage aboard the train in the evening. If you're looking for a river experience, try a 45-minute flight to Talkeetna and take a jet boat up the Talkeetna River on a fishing or natural history excursion with an experienced guide, returning to Anchorage by railroad.

Wings
Lake Hood, Anchorage
(907) 441–5736, (888) 389–4647
Ecotourism is the emphasis here, with everything from a $45 floatplane tour of Anchorage to a $299 bear-viewing tour with lunch (the lunch is for you, not the bear). Their most popular packages are the glacier tours, with your choice of Knik Glacier or the Neacola

Volcanoes. Wildlife and wilderness tours are another option, as are guided and unguided fly-out fishing trips that include fishing gear, lunch, and optional rafts. Their Expand Your Horizons flights will take you to all sorts of regional destinations. You can add a stop at a remote lake for a picnic lunch on most flights. For a real dining adventure, fly out to Call of the Wild Lodge for either lunch or dinner. Three-hour grand tours of Mt. McKinley, Prince William Sound, Kenai Fjords, or Lake Clark are also among the wide range of options at Wings. Rates run on a sliding scale depending on the number of passengers, with a four-passenger maximum, depending on weights.

i For road conditions, closures, construction, urgent reports, ferry information, weather, and other travel advisories in Alaska, dial 511, or go to http://511.alaska.gov. From out of state, call (866) 282–7577.

BY WATER

Cruise ships are another popular way of getting to Alaska. Cook Inlet is not suitable for cruise ship docking, so the luxury boats arrive at Whittier or Seward, with transfer service to and from Anchorage. The cruise companies offer a dizzying array of air, land, and sea packages, so you can arrive by one means of transportation and leave by another, with land tours by bus or rail in between. Alaska also has a state-operated ferry system that can get you to Southcentral Alaska.

The Alaska Marine Highway system offers ferry service from Seattle north to Haines, with stops at Ketchikan, Petersburg, Sitka, Juneau, and several smaller towns along the Inside Passage. You can fly from any of the larger towns to Anchorage, or you can drive to Anchorage from Skagway or Haines, though both towns are more than a day's drive from the city. The Alaska Marine Highway is about practical transport, not luxury, and like everything else it gets crowded in the summer, so make sure to plan ahead, especially if you want to book a stateroom or bring a vehicle. The system also offers more localized service between Cordova, Valdez, Whittier, Seward, Kodiak, and Seldovia. A cross-gulf schedule connects the local service with the Inside Passage service once a week.

BY CAR

For lots of people, driving the Alaska Highway, commonly known as the Al-Can, is part of the big adventure. Back in the day when the road was mostly gravel, driving up was a lot more adventurous than it is now. People still display "I survived the Al-Can" bumper stickers with a

i While nobody wants you to speed, be advised that Alaska has an impeding-traffic law. If you're on a two-lane highway outside an urban area where passing is unsafe and you're driving under the speed limit, you must pull over and allow vehicles to pass if five or more are backed up behind you.

i There are huge distances between services along most portions of Alaska's highways, so in addition to the usual flares, toolkit, jumper cables, and spare tire you keep in your vehicle, you should also have a first-aid kit, tow cable, flashlight, matches, drinking water and food, come-along, rope, and insect repellant. Try to keep your vehicle's gas tank at least half full at all times. In winter, make sure you have chains, a shovel, an ice scraper, a bag of sand or kitty litter, a blanket or sleeping bag, and extra warm clothing.

sense of pride and accomplishment, but now that the road is mostly paved, the main challenges are the long distances between services, prices that get higher as you go north, winding mountain roads, lots of road construction during the short summer season, and the overall length of the trip. Diehards have been known to get from the northern United States to the Alaskan border by driving nonstop for a couple of days, but most folks allow five to seven days so they can take their time, enjoy the scenery, and sleep once in a while.

RV traffic, including caravans, used to be thick during the summer, but with the rising cost of fuel, it has waned somewhat. RVers will still find Anchorage and Southcentral Alaska well-suited for accommodating their needs. Whether you're driving an RV, car, or motorcycle, you'd be foolish not to bring a copy of the *Alaska Milepost,* a detailed driving guide published each year by Alaska Northwest Books. Organized by highway name, the *Milepost* can be a bit cumbersome to use, but it's really the best way to navigate the state's roadways. By the way, you'll get some blank looks from locals if you ask for help finding a highway by number. No one knows who slapped those numbers on the highways a few decades ago, and no one cares. Alaskans refer to their highways by name—the Seward, the Glenn, the Richardson, and so on.

The Bill Sheffield Alaska Railroad Depot provides passenger service connections from the Ted Stevens International Airport. DEB VANASSE

i Soils in many parts of Alaska are wet, fine-grained clay or silt, which let in lots of water that expands when it freezes. Add some groundwater into the mix, and you get frost heaves, those jarring dips in Alaska's roadways that can eat axles and take out shock absorbers. Road authorities mark and repair these damaged roads in due time, but not all are marked right away, so beware. Watch for dips and valleys in the roads, and slow down before you encounter them. One advantage to gravel over asphalt is that frost heaves aren't an issue.

BY TRAIN

You can't get to Alaska by train, but you can get around using the state's top-notch Alaska Railroad system once you're here. From Anchorage, you can head out to Girdwood, Portage, Seward, Wasilla, Talkeetna, Denali, and Fairbanks, with special wilderness adventure stops at Spencer Lake and Grandview. Alaska Railroad cars have large picture windows, forward-facing reclining seats, dining service, and nonsmoking cars. Passengers also receive historical route maps and a complimentary *Alaska Railroad* magazine. From June through August, local high-school-students-turned-tour-guides offer professional commentary and assistance on board.

If you're looking for luxury, you'll want to upgrade to GoldStar Service on the Denali Star Train that runs from Anchorage to Fairbanks with stops at Wasilla, Talkeenta, and Denali. This first-class service includes seats in the railroad's new double-deck dome cars with custom-designed interiors and original Alaskan art, complimentary appetizers, and access to a private, one-of-a-kind outdoor viewing platform. There's even a spacious dining room and bar with big picture windows so you don't miss any scenery along the way. In addition to regular service, the Alaska Railroad offers several tour packages. Some service is seasonal. To get details on all your options, contact the Alaska Railroad at (907) 265–2492, (800) 544–0552, or www.alaska railroad.com.

BY BUS

If you don't want the hassles of driving and the train's not your thing, you can get around Southcentral Alaska by bus. Grayline of Alaska (800–628–3843, www.graylineof alaska.com) offers all sorts of tour packages in and around the region. Alaska Tour and Travel (907–245–0200, 800–266–8625, www.alaskacoach.com) offers daily service between Seward, Anchorage, and Denali in highway-quality motor coaches with onboard restrooms and informative narration by the driver/guide. Another option is the Alaska Express (888–488–8120, www.alaska shuttles.com), with scheduled and chartered service between Anchorage, Wasilla, Talkeetna, Cantwell, Denali, and any point en route.

i From mid-May to mid-September, you can ride one of America's last flag stop trains, the Hurricane Turn, on a route used by locals to reach their remote cabins since 1923. Starting in Talkeetna, you can get on and off where you please along 55 miles on the 115-mile route. To flag the train, stand 25 feet from the rail and wave a large white cloth until the engineer sounds the whistle to let you know he saw you. Now that's an Alaskan experience.

ANCHORAGE

Surrounded by six mountain ranges and the waters of Cook Inlet, Anchorage is awash in scenic beauty year-round. The maritime climate makes temperatures quite tolerable by Alaskan standards, and as the city has grown into itself, it offers plenty to do, whether you're looking for nightlife, culture, sporting events, shopping, or outdoor recreation. Like every city, it has its problems. Traffic bogs down at rush hour, and the city is just about out of raw land for residential development. But the inconveniences are small, and the quality of life is good. In fact, Anchorage has been recognized four times as an All-American city.

Anchorage is far and away the largest city in Alaska. A bit less than half of the state's residents, 260,000 people, live within the boundaries of the municipality that stretches from Eagle River to Girdwood. While the pace is less hectic than in many other cities its size, Anchorage still supports thriving retail and business sectors that serve Alaskans from the far-flung corners of the state. The Ted Stevens International Airport is uniquely positioned for top-of-the-world routing between Europe,

i Downtown at the corner of Fourth Avenue and F Street is a log cabin bustling with activity. Under the sod roof of the Anchorage Convention and Visitors Bureau Visitor Information Center (907–274–3531) are all sorts of great resources. It's open daily, with abbreviated hours in the winter. Both airport terminals have visitor information centers as well. Their Web site, www.anchorage.net, is another helpful planning resource. A special feature is the "Ask a Local" contact form, where you can get answers to questions about the Anchorage area.

Asia, and North America. On the northeast end of town, Elmendorf Air Force Base and Fort Richardson take similar advantage of the city's strategic location.

For visitors, Anchorage is a great place to get your bearings and launch into Alaskan-style adventures. Here you'll find everything from world-class restaurants and hotels to down-home cafes and bed-and-breakfasts, from downtown shopping malls to quirky secondhand shops, and from sprawling nightclubs to eclectic coffeehouses. No matter what your style, budget, or interests, Anchorage has plenty to offer.

GETTING AROUND

Anchorage is a small city, and while there's public transportation, the system is not extensive, so most people get around by private car or taxi. If you're visiting for just a few days and are content with limiting yourself to downtown destinations, you can take a taxi or a limo from the airport to your hotel and walk pretty much everywhere else. Otherwise, a car will be your best bet, though motorcycles are also available for rent for those with a yearning for the open road.

By Car

Finding your way around Anchorage isn't all that tough if you have a good map. Numbered downtown streets run east and west, beginning with Second Avenue, a short street close to the water. Fourth, Fifth, and Sixth Avenues are the main downtown streets, and of course they're one-ways. Cross streets running north and south are named by letter, with A Street being farthest to the east and closest to the mountains, while L Street is farthest west, closest to

Cook Inlet. Several downtown blocks are fused together with the Egan Center, the Town Square Park, the Alaska Center for the Performing Arts, and the Fifth Avenue Mall, so you can't count on all of the lettered streets to run the distance to Second Avenue. A Street, C Street, and L Street are your best bets for multiple lanes with minimal stops running the full span from north to south.

The Glenn Highway comes in from the northeast, where it splits into Fifth and Sixth Avenues heading into downtown, or you can dip south at Gambell Street and hit the Seward Highway, a main north-south artery along the east side of town. Many businesses are also located on the Old Seward Highway, which runs parallel to the New Seward Highway in south Anchorage and abruptly ends. Northern Lights and Benson Boulevards are important one-ways for making your way from east to west in midtown Anchorage, while Minnesota Drive is a major north-south artery moving traffic from the airport north to downtown and south to the busy Dimond shopping area, eventually connecting with the Seward Highway. Spenard Road cuts through older neighborhoods on a diagonal between the airport and downtown.

For a smaller city, the major thoroughfares can get surprisingly busy during rush hours, but you won't find any of those freeway standstills suffered in major urban areas. Even during times of peak traffic, it shouldn't take more than an hour to get from one end of town to the other.

As you might expect, there's ample parking at retail outlets, restaurants, and hotels outside of the downtown area. Anchorage retail stores tend to be fairly lenient about free overnight parking for RVs, but the policies get tighter every year, so don't assume anything without checking out the particular retailer's policy. Downtown parking is another story. There's metered parking along most streets, but it's tough to find a spot unless you're there early or late. Pay lots and parking garages are your best bet; just plan on

> **ℹ** There are more than 5,700 parking spots in downtown Anchorage. You can park for 75 cents an hour, with monthly permits available for lots and garages. Street-side parking is free after 6:00 P.M., on weekends, and on municipal holidays. For more information on parking in Anchorage, call (907) 276–PARK or (800) 770–ACAR, or go to www.anchorageparking.com.

walking a few blocks to your destination. The Fifth Avenue and JCPenney Parking Garages offer ample parking on the east end, and be sure to take your ticket with you if you're shopping, as most stores will validate it for two free hours. On the west end, the Sixth Avenue Parking Garage can accommodate quite a few vehicles, and there are side-street lots in between these larger garages.

Icy roads pose plenty of driving hazards from October all the way through April. If you're used to winter driving conditions, you'll be able to manage with front-wheel drive, but if you're at all hesitant or you're going to venture up into the hillside, a four-wheel-drive or all-wheel-drive vehicle is your best bet. Keep a safe distance between yourself and the vehicle in front of you, don't be in a hurry, and drive defensively when the roads are slick. Black ice, a sort of pavement sheen in hard-to-see patches, is especially dangerous. And don't count on locals to model good winter driving skills—Alaska is a transient state, and some of them won't be doing much better than you are, especially in the fall when everyone's making the transition to the challenges of ice and snow.

Public Transportation

The Anchorage People Mover is the local public transit system. It's a bus-only option, with no subway or commuter train service. One-way fares are $1.75, or you can opt for a $4.00 day pass. Bus Route 7 offers hourly service from the airport to the Downtown Transit Center, Spenard Road, and the

A log cabin with a traditional sod roof houses the Anchorage Visitor Information Center. DEB VANASSE

Dimond Center. Many buses have bike racks on the front. Check out www.peoplemover .org for more details on bus service, including shared-ride options and van service for senior citizens and the wheelchair bound.

Taxis and Limousines

You might be able to hail a taxi near one of the big downtown hotels, but for the most part you'll need to phone ahead, allowing approximately 20 minutes for pickups unless traffic is extra-heavy or bad weather is keeping people from driving themselves. Recent rates for taxis are $2.00 for the pickup and $2.00 per mile. Try Alaska Cab (907–563–5353), which has a taxi equipped with a wheelchair lift, Checker Cab (907–276–1234), or Yellow Cab (907–272–2422). Though they have different fleets, Alaska Cab and Yellow Cab have merged into one company. Most taxi services can deal with a phone call the

night before if you need to set up an early morning pickup.

You'll find some fun options if you want to treat yourself to a limousine ride, including popular Hummer and SUV limos that offer a real Alaskan take on the typical fare.

BAC Limousine and Bus Services
P.O. Box 243742, Anchorage, AK 99524
(907) 222–2600
www.baclimoandbus.com
With a large line of vehicles and 24-hour telephone reservations, BAC is one of the bigger players in the Anchorage limo market. They've got limos and mini-coaches to accommodate 1 to 20 passengers, with drivers well-versed in service and local knowledge. A nonrefundable deposit of 50 percent is required at the time of booking, and major credit cards are accepted. They offer Hummer and Lincoln Navigator limos as well as

mini-coach service and traditional Lincoln Towncar limousines.

Limousine of Alaska
P.O. Box 101186, Anchorage, AK 99510
(907) 350–9428
www.limousineofalaska.com
Impress your friends and enjoy some great Alaskan photo ops with an airport or cruise ship transfer in the Monster SUV limo, which holds up to 40 pieces of luggage and comes equipped with a full assortment of luxury features, including flat screen television, air-conditioning, and complimentary champagne. Limousine of Alaska guarantees the lowest rates for limo transfer service. For alternate rides, choose from the Hummer limo, a traditional limo, or a mini-coach. Vehicles are generally less than five years old, and groups will not be mixed without consent.

Rental Cars and Shuttles

Anchorage has the usual airport-based rental car companies, and thanks to the recent airport expansion, you most likely won't have to take a shuttle to pick up your car, though it is a bit of a hike across the uncovered lot. You may get better prices at some of the off-site rental outfits, but they're generally not as close to the airport as you might think, so allow some extra time for pickups and returns.

Don't count on landing at the airport during the busy summer season and just grabbing a car at the counter. Advance reservations are essential during peak travel months. As with hotels, you'll be paying top dollar in the summer but can get some great deals on cars in the winter. Most companies will have you sign an affidavit stating that you won't take the car on any gravel roads. Virtually all the roads in Anchorage proper are paved, but if you're staying at a bed-and-breakfast on the outskirts of town or planning on some adventure driving, you may end up having to take your chances. Gravel roads are hard on cars and especially on windshields.

Avis, Budget, Dollar, Enterprise, Hertz, and Thrifty all have counters at the Ted Stevens International Airport. Alaska Car and Van Rentals (907–243–4444, www.alaskacarandvan.com) has locations near the airport and also a downtown office in the Hilton Hotel. Denali Car Rental (907–276–1230) is another local company that offers lower rates, some on used vehicles. Denali has an off-airport location, so ask about pick-up service.

Feeling adventurous? You can rent a motorcycle at Alaska Rider Tours (907–272–2777, www.akrider.com), where both guided and self-guided tours on three different makes of cycles are available. They provide complimentary airport pickups as well as space to store your gear and change your oil. Along with information on road conditions, they offer free camping, showers, and coffee. If you get attached to your Harley, you can purchase one at the House of Harley right next door and drive it home. In fact, House of

Shuttle Service

Several attractions offer free or low-cost daytime shuttle service. Take "Lolly the Trolley" along Fourth and Fifth Avenues, compliments of the Ulu Factory. You can flag down the trolley or pick it up at one of the marked stops. The Ship Creek shuttle runs year-round, Monday through Saturday, from several downtown locations to Ship Creek for a nominal charge. The Alaska Native Heritage Center Shuttle, a free service during the summer, picks up at five downtown locations, including the Anchorage Museum and the Anchorage Convention and Visitors Bureau Log Cabin. The Alaska Zoo runs periodic shuttle service; for times, cost, and pickup locations, call (907) 346–1285.

Harley (800–248–5305, www.harleyalaska .com) has an adventure planner who'll set you up with a Fly-Buy-Ride package so you can fly up and ride home.

There are a few shuttle services in Anchorage, but for the most part they are focused on offering transfer service to and from such tourist destinations as the Alaska Railroad, the Seward and Whittier Cruise Ports, and Alyeska Ski Resort. Some shuttle companies also offer service between the airport and private residences, including bed-and-breakfasts, but depending on the location, a taxi may be cheaper. Try the Alaska Transportation Group (907–952–1249, 866–425–8687, www.alaskatransportation .net), Alaska Shuttle (907–338–8888), or the ever-fun Magic Bus (907–268–6311, 800–836–2006, www.themagicbus.com). Alaska Shuttle offers rides to Eagle River, Peter's Creek, and Eklutna, plus they'll go up to the Matanuska Valley upon request.

HISTORY

Human history in the Anchorage area doesn't go back as far as it does in some other places, but it has been a wild ride nonetheless. Evidence of the first indigenous people in the area dates from only 3000 B.C., when the first wave of Eskimos left artifacts discovered at the Beluga Point Site, not far from where downtown Anchorage stands today. Two additional waves of people of a similar background came through, one in 2000 B.C. and the other close to the turn of the millennium. Sometime between A.D. 500 and 1650, the Athabaskan Dena'ina people displaced the original inhabitants.

More displacement was to follow. Russians explored the general region in 1784, but it was famed explorer James Cook who reached the place now known as Anchorage and misnamed its flagship body of water "Turnagain River." A later explorer, George Vancouver, corrected the error by renaming it Turnagain Arm.

After the Russians sold Alaska to the United States for 7.2 million dollars in the famed "Seward's Folly" transaction of 1867, the Alaska Commercial Company moved in, setting up posts along Cook Inlet to outfit gold miners conducting explorations along Turnagain Arm and in the Kenai Peninsula. Though large fortunes eluded miners in the Anchorage area, President Wilson created another boom of sorts when he sanctioned the Alaska Railroad, with the Ship Creek landing as its headquarters, in 1915. A tent city sprang up, and on July 9 of the same year, 600 town-site lots were sold at auction, with a total of $150,000 put up in exchange for the land. Today those lots are valued at approximately $150,000 apiece. The U.S. Postal Service recognized Anchorage as the official name of the burgeoning community, and on November 23, 1920, the town was incorporated.

Eight years after it was begun, the Alaska Railroad project was finished, becoming a mainstay of both transportation and the Anchorage economy until Merrill Field opened in the 1930s. The airfield quickly became one of the busiest crossroads for civilian aircraft in the world, a distinction that continues today. The federal government gave another boost to the Anchorage area by sending colonists to the Matanuska Valley under the authority of the Depression-era Federal Relief Agency.

The threat of Japanese aggression, followed by the Cold War, made Anchorage a strategic military site. The population of Anchorage soared from 3,000 in 1940 to 47,000 in 1951. With the influx of people and military spending, Anchorage experienced one of several bouts with growing pains as both cost of living and crime rates skyrocketed.

In 1951 the Anchorage International Airport opened, connecting the city with the outside world, albeit on a slow and sometimes delayed basis. The Seward Highway linked Anchorage with the Kenai Peninsula at about the same time. On January 3, 1959, Alaska was admitted as the 49th state in the Union,

Outside the Alaska Railroad Terminal in Anchorage, this train car commemorates the railroad rehabilitation project from the Truman era. DEB VANASSE

causing inevitable changes that old-timers continue to lament.

But nothing changed Anchorage like the Good Friday Earthquake on March 27, 1964. The epicenter of this 9.2 trembler was only 75 miles from Anchorage. Streets buckled, buildings collapsed, homes slid down the hillside, and lives were lost. It took the rest of the decade for Anchorage and its sister cities of Seward and Valdez to rebuild.

In 1968, rumbling of a different sort began. Oil was discovered on Alaska's North Slope, and while the ramifications were slow in coming, the discovery changed the area forever. First was the Alaska Native Claims Settlement Act, commonly known as ANCSA, which settled land-rights issues with the formation of 12 regional Native corporations, plus 1 additional organization for Natives living outside the state. It's still too soon to judge the overall success or failure of this grand experiment that imposed a corporate structure on local Native groups, but most of the corporations are now turning a profit and creating economic opportunities for their shareholders.

In 1974, one year after the first modern Iditarod Sled Dog Race left from Anchorage, construction began on the trans-Alaska oil pipeline. Having served as a supply center when the Swanson River oil fields opened up in 1957, Anchorage was poised to be the hub of this huge project. Money flowed as freely as the oil did when the pipeline was completed in 1977, and you'll still hear folks talking about pipeline wages that were so extravagant they make even the tallest gold rush tales pale in comparison. "Please, God, send us another pipeline," reads a well-loved Alaskan bumper sticker.

There hasn't been another pipeline yet, but the boom continued well into the 1980s.

Close-up

Oil to Cash:
Alaska's Permanent Fund Dividend Program

PFD. It might stand for Personal Flotation Device in some circles, but Alaskans know it as an acronym for another sort of lifesaver: the Permanent Fund Dividend.

Each October since 1980, every eligible Alaskan man, woman, and child has received a check, courtesy of the Alaska Permanent Fund Dividend Corporation. The highest payout so far was almost $2,000 per person back in 2000. Even though the checks have dwindled to closer to $1,000 since then, Alaskans continue to look forward to the annual payout the way kids look forward to a visit from Santa.

Considering that most states collect money from their residents in the form of state income taxes, state sales taxes, and state property taxes (Alaska has none of these), it's quite the role reversal to have the state pay us. Don't even think about questioning the logic of it. Alaskans fiercely defend their PFDs.

That's exactly what former governor Jay Hammond had in mind when he came up with the concept as a way to get Alaskans on board with saving rather than squandering the state's windfall from North Slope oil production. The first $900 million in oil money the state received back in 1970 disappeared in three short years. Based on a program he developed as mayor of Bristol Bay, Governor Hammond pushed through a constitutional amendment mandating that at least 25 percent of the state's oil royalties be set aside in a permanent savings account. As of 2006, the unaudited value of this account was more than $33 billion.

A large portion of the earnings on the Permanent Fund principal is distributed annually to the state's residents, who must prove that they've lived in the state for the required number of days each year and that they intend to continue living here indefinitely. With the distribution of PFD checks each fall, retailers offer all sorts of enticements to get Alaskans to spend them, from airline ticket deals to "double your dividend" specials on big-ticket items such as cars and snow machines.

Certainly the free-flowing cash is good for the state's economy, but the bigger impact comes in the form of the voters' almost religious commitment to the state's savings plan. You can propose almost anything as a politician, but start talking about tinkering with the Permanent Fund, and you'll have a bunch of angry Alaskans on your tail.

That's not to say some haven't tried. Whenever the state's budget turns red, the healthy Permanent Fund is a natural place to look for extra cash. One proposal that

By then the population of Anchorage, at 184,775, was more than half that of the entire state, and the city and borough had merged into the municipality of Anchorage, covering an area from Eagle River to Portage that encompassed 1,955 square miles. From 1980 to 1987, almost a billion dollars of capital project money flowed into Anchorage, and the city came of age. Oil prices plunged in 1987, and a bust followed on the heels of

made the rounds a few years ago involved dissolving the fund and divvying up the pot, a whopping $42,000 per person, before the politicians got their hands on it.

Others worry that the program draws freeloaders to the state and encourages families to have more children that they otherwise would, since each means another check. And fighting dividend fraud becomes a bigger task every year. But every time talk of changing the program has gotten heated, oil prices have sky-rocketed, and the crisis is averted for the moment.

The trans-Alaska pipeline carries crude oil to Valdez. Earnings on the state's oil revenue fund are distributed annually to Alaskan residents. AMANDA BAUER

the big boom, but by the mid 1990s, the state's economy was flourishing again, with tourism playing no small part in the diversification and recovery efforts. We'd love another pipeline, with surplus North Slope natural gas as the new target fuel, but we're promising not to waste it this time around . . . at least that's what the bumper sticker says.

ACCOMMODATIONS

Like everything else in Anchorage, the options for overnight accommodation get better and better every year. From luxury hotels to budget motels to home-style bed-and-breakfasts and bare-bones hostels, there's an option to fit every traveler, as long as you plan ahead during the summer season. While the hotel industry is doing a good job of keeping up with demand, reservations should be made well in advance for visits from May through mid-September. Availability increases dramatically, with a corresponding decrease in rates, during the winter, except during such special events as the Alaska Federation of Natives convention in October, Fur Rondy in February, and the Iditarod in early March.

You won't find luxury inns or resorts in Anchorage, but we have included some exceptional fly-out options if you're looking for an all-inclusive wilderness resort experience. Likewise, keep in mind that bed-and-breakfasts in Alaska are not the specialty inns you'll find in the Lower 48. Most are run by friendly hosts renting out a few rooms in rather ordinary homes, and in many cases you'll share a bath. It's the chance to chat with longtime Alaskans and find out all about living in the 49th state that makes this option attractive to most visitors, not to mention the fact that prices tend to be significantly lower than at hotels during the peak tourist season. At hostels, you'll be bunking in rooms with strangers, but at bargain prices.

Most downtown hotels and motels do not offer airport shuttle service, but it's only a 10- or 15-minute drive from the airport to downtown, depending on traffic, so taxi fares are reasonable.

A unique Alaskan-style amenity available with some accommodations is the use of walk-in freezers for storing fish and game. You might not be thinking of air-conditioning when you visit Alaska, but it's not a bad feature to have if you're bothered by the heat—they may be few and far between, but there are some warm days in Anchorage in the summer. A few of the larger hotels offer air-conditioned rooms.

Price codes indicate the cost of a room for two during the peak season, generally May through mid-September. Some establishments offer attractive shoulder-season rates before Memorial Day and after Labor Day. You can assume that major credit cards are accepted and that the place is open year-round unless we note otherwise. Count on bringing the kids but not the pets unless the listing says differently. While hotels and motels generally have rooms with wheelchair access and rooms for smokers, we'll make a special note if these are available at B&Bs, hostels, guesthouses, and inns.

Price Codes

$ . . . . Less than $100
$$ . . . . $100–$149
$$$ . . . . $150–$200
$$$$ . . . . More than $200

Hotels and Motels

The Anchorage Downtown Hotel　　$$
826 K Street
(907) 258–7669
www.anchoragedowntownhotel.com
Here's a small family-operated hotel, almost like a B&B, right in the heart of the city. All 16 rooms have been freshly remodeled, and suites are available as well. Rooms come with coffeemaker, microwave, minifridge, hair dryer, iron, ironing board, and free continental breakfast. The Anchorage Downtown boasts a quiet location just 5 blocks from the city center and right across the street from a midtown park. Enjoy the ambience of an inn with the comforts of a hotel, including cable television, high-speed Internet access, free local calls, and free downtown parking. A family member is always on-site to provide assistance and information.

Anchorage Grand Hotel　　$$$
505 West Second Avenue
(907) 929–8888, (888) 800–0640
www.anchoragegrand.com

The Anchorage Grand combines the charm of the original 1950s building with the luxury of modern amenities and custom furnishings, thanks to a complete renovation in 2001. Known for its friendly service, this private boutique hotel is just off the Second Avenue entrance to the Tony Knowles Coastal Trail, 1 block from the train depot and 3 blocks from the convention center and the Fifth Avenue Mall. Their 500-square-foot suites come with queen- or king-size bed, fully-equipped kitchen, iron, ironing board, free morning paper, free continental breakfast, free high-speed Internet, two-line business phone, hair dryer, and same-day laundry service or in-house coin-op laundry. Their winter getaway specials include a one-night stay, a bottle of wine, dinner for two at Orso (see listing under Fine Dining in the Restaurants section), and late checkout. They've got great inlet and city views plus a business center for guest use. Two of the suites are wheelchair accessible.

Coast International Inn $$$
3333 West International Airport Road
(907) 243–2233, (800) 663–1144
www.coasthotels.com

Next to Lake Hood and minutes from the Ted Stevens International Airport, the Coast International has 141 newly refurbished rooms with lake or mountain views. Rooms come with spacious desks, dual-line speakerphones, in-room movies and Nintendo, irons, ironing boards, coffeemakers, and hair dryers. Guests can access the fitness center, sauna, fax machine, copier, high-speed wireless Internet, business center, and walk-in freezer for storing fish and game. There's round-the-clock airport shuttle service, too. Piper's Restaurant and lounge offers a full menu of Alaskan fare and an open-air deck overlooking the lake.

Days Inn $$$
321 East Fifth Avenue
(907) 276–7226, (800) 329–7466
www.daysinnalaska.com

Offering moderately priced accommodations in the heart of downtown Anchorage, the Days Inn has many of the amenities you'd expect from a larger hotel. They have 130 rooms with coffeemakers, irons, ironing boards, in-room movies, and Internet access. They also offer courtesy parking, banquet and meeting facilities, and a restaurant right across the street. As an added perk, they provide courtesy shuttles to and from the airport and the train station. They have both smoking and wheelchair-accessible rooms, and pets are allowed.

Dimond Center Hotel $$$$
700 East Dimond Center Boulevard
(907) 770–5000, (866) 750–5002
www.dimondcenterhotel.com

The Seldovia Native Association operates this modern hotel next to the largest shopping area in Alaska. The spacious rooms include plush beds, oversize soaking tubs with separate shower areas, televisions, microwaves, refrigerators, coffeemakers, and deluxe continental breakfast featuring Belgian waffles. There's also high-speed and wireless Internet access, an exercise area, coin-op laundry facilities, free airport shuttle, and seasonal downtown shuttle service. At the adjacent Dimond Center Mall, you'll find dining, shopping, bowling, ice skating, movie theaters, and a complete athletic club. Both wheelchair-accessible and smoking rooms are available. Ask about special rates for AAA, AARP, and Alaska residents.

Hilton Garden Inn $$$$
100 West Tudor Road
(907) 729–7000, (877) 782–9444
www.anchorage.stayhgi.com

The Hilton Garden Inn is a newer hotel in Anchorage's midtown area, within walking distance of several dining and entertainment options. Rooms include coffeemakers, microwaves, minifridges, irons, ironing boards, free morning papers, and free high-speed and wireless Internet access. Opt for either a king-size bed or two queen-size beds. The Hilton offers free airport transportation, fitness and business centers, a heated pool, and a whirlpool. The enthusiastic staff will help with your travel plans in the state, and there's a restaurant on-site. Smoking rooms are available.

Historic Anchorage Hotel $$$–$$$$
330 E Street
(907) 272–4553, (800) 554–0998
www.historicanchoragehotel.com

This elegantly restored boutique hotel, established in 1916, offers 26 charming rooms and suites in the heart of Anchorage. Just 1 block from the Egan Convention Center and within walking distance of just about everything downtown, the Historic Anchorage Hotel features European ambience with a friendly yet professional atmosphere. This is the only hotel in Anchorage that's on the National Register of Historic Places, with celebrities from Walt Disney to John Denver among those who've stayed there over the years. The hotel's comfortable, spacious, and well-appointed rooms include coffeemaker, microwave, minifridge, iron, ironing board, free morning paper, free continental breakfast, discounts at local attractions, and wi-fi Internet access. Book directly with the hotel and enjoy late-check-out privileges, too. Ask about their romantic "Night to Remember," which includes a tour by horse-drawn carriage and dinner for two at Orso (see listing under Fine Dining in the Restaurants section).

Homewood Suites Anchorage $$$$
140 West Tudor Road
(907) 762–7000, (800) 225–4663
www.anchorage.homewoodsuites.com

Operated by the same folks that run the Hilton Garden, the Homewood offers another new upscale option in midtown Anchorage. The hotel has 122 suites, most with a king-size bed plus a pull-out sofa bed. Each suite has a full kitchen plus separate living and sleeping areas. Irons, ironing boards, free morning papers, and free high-speed and wireless Internet come with the suites.

Guests enjoy a full breakfast buffet every morning, with light dinners offered Monday through Thursday. There's also a swimming pool and whirlpool for guest use. Free area transportation is provided, and smoking rooms are available, as are rooms with wheelchair access.

The Hotel Captain Cook $$$$
Fourth Avenue at K Street
(907) 276–6000, (800) 843–1950
www.captaincook.com

The Hotel Captain Cook is the only Alaskan property in the Preferred Hotels and Resorts Worldwide, a worldwide network of independent luxury hotels that sets high standards for detail and service. Relax on down duvets and pillows, lounge in a plush robe, and enjoy twice-daily maid service, including an evening turndown. The theme of exploration and discovery carries throughout the hotel, with solid teakwood decor and rich colors. Opt for a room on the private Captain's Deck in Tower II, and you'll enjoy a panoramic view, complimentary newspapers, continental breakfast, evening hors d'oeuvres, and a juice and soft drink bar. On-site you'll find 4 restaurants, 12 boutique shops, an athletic club with swimming pool, and wireless Internet access. On cruise ship days in the summer, the hotel is packed with people, but the courteous staff manages to keep everything running smoothly even on the busiest days.

Inlet Tower Hotel and Suites $$$
1200 L Street
(907) 276–0110, (800) 544–0786
www.inlettower.com

This apartment-complex-turned-hotel offers spectacular views of Mt. Susitna, Cook Inlet, and the Chugach Mountains at a convenient location midway between the airport and downtown. Amenities include ample free parking, free local calls, luxury linens, in-room movies, speakerphones with voice mail, on-site laundry facilities, and free shuttle service to the airport and the train station. Rooms have coffeemakers, refrigerators, microwaves, cable televisions, and free high-speed Internet access. It's a bit of a walk to shopping and restaurants, but Mick's at the Inlet offers fine cuisine on-site. Pets and smoking are allowed only on the third and fourth floors.

Long House Alaskan Hotel $$$
4335 Wisconsin Street
(907) 243–2133, (888) 243–2133
www.longhousehotel.com

With design and decor reflective of the Native heritage of Southeast Alaska, the Long House offers a convenient location near the airport with 54 spacious, comfortable rooms. Choose from a deluxe room, grand room, or personal suite. Opt for either a king-size bed or two queen-size beds with cable television, in-room movies, refrigerator, microwave, and telephone with voice mail and free local calling. Guests enjoy the use of the convenient laundry room, walk-in freezer space, and 24-hour courtesy airport shuttle. Enjoy an evening walk along the shore of Lake Hood, watching the floatplanes and waterfowl come and go. Pets are allowed, and smoking rooms are available.

Millennium Alaskan Hotel $$$$
4800 Spenard Road
(907) 243–2300, (800) 544–0553
www.millenniumhotels.com

There's a warm Alaskan ambience at this lakeside retreat, with decor featuring animal mounts and Native artifacts. Spacious rooms and suites, colorfully decorated, include refrigerators, coffeemakers, televisions with in-room movies, telephones with voice mail, modems, and 24-hour room service. There's a health club with whirlpool, steam bath, and sauna, or you can jog the path around Lake Spenard. The hotel is only a mile from the airport, with complimentary airport and downtown transportation. Gleaming wood and polished brass form the backdrop for casual dining at the Fancy Moose Lounge, or enjoy a meal at the Flying Machine Restaurant, with a great view of the floatplane base

right out front and patio seating in the summer. Smoking and wheelchair-accessible rooms are available.

Parkwood Inn $$
4455 Juneau Street
(907) 563–3590, (800) 478–3590
www.parkwoodinn.net

Tucked away in midtown Anchorage is a lodging option that's especially affordable for extended stays. Fifty 450-square-foot studio suites come with your choice of queen- or king-size beds, full kitchen, work area, private balcony, and cable television. The business center offers Internet access, and there's a barbecue on the landscaped grounds for guest use. The Parkwood is a short drive from the hospital and university, but it's not within walking distance of the usual tourist attractions and there's no shuttle service, so guests would do well to have their own transportation. Pet and smoking rooms are available. Ask about discounts for seniors, government employees, and long-term guests. There's a limit of five persons per room.

Puffin Inn $$
4400 Spenard Road
(907) 243–4044, (800) 478–3346
www.puffininn.net

The Puffin Inn has been an affordable favorite of Alaskan travelers for years. They've expanded and remodeled to offer 86 deluxe, boutique, moderate, and economy rooms to travelers. Rooms include refrigerators, microwaves, hair dryers, irons, coffeemakers, free local calls, free daily newspaper, and complimentary continental breakfasts. Guests also have access to the business center, fitness facility, guest laundry, freezer space, and 24-hour complimentary airport shuttle. Puffin guests also may reserve rooms at the nearby Chandler Inn, a classy 14-room boutique hotel just half a block away. Nonsmoking facilities and wheelchair-accessible rooms are available. Ask about early bird discounts for booking summer rooms before March 31.

Voyager Hotel $$$
501 K Street
(907) 277–9501, (800) 247–9070
www.voyagerhotel.com

Another favorite with Alaskans, the Voyager mixes the friendliness and ambience of a small hotel with service, style, and a fabulous location in the heart of downtown Anchorage. They have 40 nicely appointed guest rooms with hair dryers, makeup mirrors, microwaves, coffeemakers, refrigerators, filtered water taps, air-conditioning, and cable televisions. For business travelers, rooms have voice mail, broadband Internet, and dial-up modem ports. Guests have access to free overnight parking, same-day valet service, guest fax services, a health club, and complimentary continental breakfast.

Bed-and-Breakfasts

Aawesome Retreat B&B $$$
16528 Kings Way Drive
(907) 338–8873, (877) 226–9645
www.aawesomeworld.com

Surround yourself with original artwork in this stunning mountain retreat just 20 minutes from the Ted Stevens International Airport. You can walk the path to the meadow pond or simply enjoy the beauty of the 13-acre grounds with mountain and inlet views from your private deck. This unique B&B has three spacious suites with king-size beds and either one or two twin beds, marble tub surrounds, satellite television, microwaves, and refrigerators. Guests have full use of the guest kitchen and the Vortex Lounge, which has sunset views. The kitchen is stocked with continental fare for self-serve breakfasts. A full-view open room, the Penthouse, can be rented for group events. Two suites are wheelchair accessible, and pets may be accepted on approval. Rate discounts are available for consecutive-night stays.

All the Comforts of Home $–$$
12531 Turk's Turn
(907) 345–4279

Relaxation is the watchword at this custom-built cedar home on a mountainside just 20 minutes from downtown Anchorage. Soak in the outdoor hot tub surrounded by towering spruce trees, bask in the sauna, or curl up by the fireplace. Lodgings are furnished with antiques, Alaskan memorabilia commonly known as Alaskana, local art, and an extensive book and video collection. From your vantage point on the west veranda, at an elevation of 1,100 feet, you'll be able to see all of Anchorage with its surrounding mountains and spectacular sunsets, plus Mt. McKinley if the weather is cooperative. The Victorian and Sunset Rooms share a bath, but each room has its own sink and vanity. The Sourdough Suite is a romantic retreat with private bath, sitting alcove, television, VCR, refrigerator, and whirlpool tub. Your hostess, a lifelong Alaskan, serves a full breakfast including fresh brown eggs and reindeer sausage, or you may opt for a continental spread if it's more to your liking. Well-behaved children older than age 12 may accompany guests, and four-wheel drive is recommended if you're visiting after the snow flies.

Anchorage Lakeside Jewel B&B $$
8840 Gloralee Street
(907) 242–2126, (866) 539–3555
www.anchoragelakesidejewel.com

Only 4 miles from the Ted Stevens International Airport, you can enjoy lakeside serenity with fishing, swimming, hiking, and skiing right out this bed-and-breakfast's back door. Alaskan themes prevail, with rooms like the Fishin' Hole and the Loon's Nest, which include robes, television, queen-size bed, and shared bath with whirlpool tub. The Top of the World Suite sleeps four and includes private deck, sunroom with lake view, walk-in closet, washer/dryer, television, fireplace, and private bath with whirlpool tub. Household amenities include wireless Internet, guest telephone with private voice mail, video library, games, lakeside gardens, and full breakfast or buffet. The friendly hosts are longtime Alaskans who've lived and worked in Bush Alaska as well as in Anchorage.

Big Bear B&B $$
3401 Richmond Avenue
(907) 277–8189
www.alaskabigbearbb.com

Specializing in full breakfasts, comfortable rooms decorated with Alaskan art, and affordable rates, the Big Bear offers several accommodation options, all with private baths. Choose from the Glacier Room, decorated in blues with a polar bear theme, the yellow-hued Toklat Room, the elegant Grizzly Room, or the family-size Denali Room with whirlpool tub. The guest living room features Native crafts, a polar bear rug, and antique furniture, and here guests may use the cable television, a minifridge stocked with soda, and a microwave. Complimentary coffee, tea, and microwave popcorn are provided. The owner, a lifelong Alaskan, cooks up breakfasts featuring a variety of Alaskan treats, including sourdough waffles, blueberry coffee cake, and salmon quiche. Ask about discounts for seniors and weeklong stays.

Camai Bed and Breakfast $$
3838 Westminster Way
(907) 333–2219, (800) 659–8763
www.camaibnb.com

This award-winning B&B, the longest-operating one in Anchorage, offers three spacious suites in a quiet residential neighborhood with gardens bordering the Chester Creek greenbelt. Each tastefully appointed suite has a private bath, queen-size bed, and separate sitting room or second bedroom. Some suites have private entrances, and guests share an office area with computer and Internet access. Rooms come with coffeemakers, microwaves, minifridges, telephones, balconies, irons, and ironing boards. Full breakfasts are served in the summer, with continental breakfasts offered during the winter. Discounts are offered for consecutive-night stays.

Donna's Bed & Breakfast $
11335 Via Balboa
(907) 522–6025, (888) 421–6025
www.anchoragedonnasbandb.com

Families are welcome at this home away from home, approximately 10 minutes from the airport and downtown. The Forget-Me-Not, Iditarod, and Mt. McKinley Rooms come with cable televisions, VCRs, telephones, and refrigerators. Guests share kitchen and laundry privileges as well as use of the backyard barbeque and the family room, which includes books, magazines, microwave, and Internet access. Each evening, guests select a main course and a time for the next day's breakfast. In addition, bagels, toast, and a variety of cereals and juices are served each morning. Pets are allowed, and there's a cat on the premises.

**Frenchy's Adventure
Bed and Breakfast** $
3807 West Northern Lights Boulevard
(907) 344–4846, (800) 939–4846
www.adventurebnb.com

You'd be hard-pressed to find a friendlier or more accommodating hostess than Frenchy, a longtime Alaskan teacher and author who loves to help guests plan their Alaskan adventures. Conveniently located midway between the airport and downtown, Frenchy's serves a full breakfast with reservations, or a continental breakfast if guests prefer. There's cable television, telephone, iron, ironing board, free morning paper, and airport transportation upon request. The Musher's Retreat, Loon's Nest, and Tranquility Rooms are tastefully decorated with shared baths. Children are accommodated on a case-by-case basis.

Lake Hood Inn $$$
4702 Lake Spenard Drive
(907) 258–9321, (866) 663–9322
www.lakehoodinn.com

Watch the seaplanes come and go from this four-room inn on the shores of Lake Hood, the world's largest floatplane lake. The decor naturally includes aviation displays and other Alaskana, with sunsets over Mt. Susitna and local waterfowl providing more outdoor ambience. Located just minutes from the Ted Stevens International Airport, the inn provides coffeemakers, minifridges, in-room safes, hair dryers, televisions with VCRs, microwaves, irons, and ironing boards for guest use. Continental breakfast and airport transportation are also provided.

Mahogany Manor
Bed and Breakfast Inn $$$$
204 East 15th Avenue
(907) 278–1111, (888) 777–0346

Casual elegance is the watchword at the Mahogany Manor, which caters to discriminating guests with a combination of historical charm, hotel amenities, and Alaskan hospitality, re-creating the feel of a secluded lodge in downtown Anchorage. Huge fireplaces and a floor-to-ceiling waterfall grace the well-appointed lounge, while a private collection of museum-quality Alaskan art plus mountain and city views provide a feast for the eyes. There's free on-site parking, high-speed Internet, and cable television along with heated whirlpool swim-spa facilities. A hearty continental breakfast is available anytime. The Governor's Suite includes two private bedrooms, private bath with double sink, a large sitting area, and a spacious private deck. Three smaller guest rooms are also available. Minimum stays may apply during the high season.

Northern B&B $–$$
9431 Emerald Street
(907) 336–4248

Tucked away in a quiet neighborhood not far from the airport, Northern B&B offers comfortable accommodations with a full breakfast of eggs cooked to order, your choice of breakfast meats, potatoes, toast, juice, and coffee or tea. Guests share a spacious living room with large windows, vaulted ceiling, fireplace, and television. This property has a three-bedroom family suite, a room that shares a bath with the owner, and a sumptuous suite decorated in rich burgundy hues with a large private bath and whirlpool tub plus a private living room with fireplace. The owner is a longtime Alaskan who cooked at Land's End Resort (see the Kenai Peninsula chapter) back when it was just

a fisherman's hangout. Airport transportation is available, and guests have access to the kitchen and a free morning paper. Small pets are welcome.

Rabbit Creek Bed & Breakfast $–$$
P.O. Box 112842, Anchorage, AK 99511
(907) 345–0733, (866) 345–0733
www.arabbitcreekbandb.com

Nine miles from the airport, you can enjoy a panoramic view and the gentle sounds of the creek in this 3,000-square-foot home. Follow the hiking trails along the creek, relax in the outdoor hot tub, or browse the art and antiques, including some that are for sale. Choose from the Honeymoon Hideaway, Asian, Safari, and Antique Rooms, all with private baths and wireless Internet access. Morning brings a deluxe complimentary breakfast featuring fresh fruit, juices, cereals, bagels, coffee, and tea. Ask about discounts for seniors, ministers, and Alaska residents. They have a downtown location as well.

Sleeping Lady Bed and Breakfast $$$
548 Coastal Place
(907) 258–4455, (877) 705–4455
www.anchsleepingladybnb.com

Perched on a bluff overlooking Bootlegger's Cove and Cook Inlet, this state-of-the-art European-style home features spacious rooms and vaulted ceilings. It's only 2 blocks from downtown shopping and dining, yet there's peace and quiet here along with a great ocean view. Rooms with Victorian, Alaskan outdoors, mariner, and contemporary themes have coffeemakers, microwaves, minifridges, private baths, telephones, cable televisions, balconies, irons, and ironing boards. There's also a large outdoor deck, gardens, wireless Internet, free on-site parking, a fireplace, and a free morning paper. A full breakfast is served, featuring fresh fruit, yogurt, pastries, cereal, egg dishes, casseroles, sausage, and a selection of beverages. If you're leaving early, ask for a "to go" breakfast. The owner is a certified food sanitarian, so you can expect a high standard of cleanliness.

Reservations

A reservations service can be a big help when you want to book private lodging. The Anchorage Bed and Breakfast Association (907–272–5909, 888–584–5147, www.anchorage-bnb.com) inspects facilities with a wide range of amenities and prices. Anchorage Vacation Rentals, which is also known as 49th State Vacation Rentals, Lodging and Tours (907–242–6708, www.49thstatelodging.com), offers free concierge service and custom travel planning in addition to booking accommodations at B&Bs and vacation rental cabins, apartments, condos, and houses in Anchorage, Denali, Fairbanks, Homer, Kenai, Seward, and other cities upon request. At Alaska Vacation Rentals (907–278–1111, 888–766–2667, www.alaska-bnb-rentals.com), they have everything from budget rooms with shared baths to studios with minikitchens and larger units with full kitchens.

Susitna Place $$
727 N Street
(907) 274–3344
www.susitnaplace.com
Fabulous views of the ocean and mountains await you at this 4,000-square-foot bed-and-breakfast in a quiet spot near downtown Anchorage. Guests in each of the nine rooms enjoy cable television with HBO, a generous continental breakfast, unlimited local calling, and covered parking. Two of the rooms have private baths, and there's a luxury suite with king-size bed, sleeper sofa, master bath, private deck, and fireplace. The home, owned by local journalists, is decorated with a mix of contemporary and traditional furnishings peppered with antiques.

Guesthouses

26 Street Hostel $
1037 West 26th Street
(907) 274–1252
www.26streethostel.com
Simple, no-frills accommodations await the budget traveler at this hostel that's close to trails and accessible by bus from the Ted Stevens International Airport. Guests enjoy free Internet access, 24-hour check-in, use of cooking facilities, coin-op laundry, and access to television with video and DVD. Outside

there's a barbeque and garden area. Bike rentals are available, and breakfast is included with your stay.

Anchorage Guesthouse $
2001 Hillcrest Drive
(907) 274–0408
www.akhouse.com
Clean and comfortable rooms at bargain prices are available here, as long as you don't mind sharing your space with other travelers. The nearby Coastal Trail offers convenient access to downtown, especially if you rent one of the guesthouse mountain bikes. There's an Alaska library to help you plan your adventures, and you can stay in touch with friends back home with on-site Internet and fax services. There's no curfew, and laundry and storage facilities are available.

Anchorage International Hostel $
700 H Street
(907) 276–3635
www.anchorageinternationalhostel.org
Located in a no-nonsense building in the heart of downtown Anchorage, this is the grand-daddy of the local hostels. There are separate dormitory rooms for men and women with three to six beds in each, though mixed-gender groups may be accommodated by special

Within the Wild

Wisps of fog rise from the glassy waters of Lake Hood, backlit by the brilliant sun rising over the Chugach Mountains. The hour may be early, but the folks at Rust's Flying Service are already multitasking, checking with remote weather stations, doling out fishing licenses, and herding passengers toward the seaplanes that will transport them to their wilderness destinations.

"McKinley is out like a sore thumb," announces Warren, the bush pilot flying us to Winterlake Lodge. After we taxi around the lake and take off, we see exactly what he means. Some 250 miles to the north, the Great One dominates the skyline with its regal presence. We're lucky. Due to cloud cover, there's only a 1 in 10 chance of seeing North America's tallest mountain on any given day.

Warren is as skilled an entertainer as he is a pilot. Scooting our Beaver DeHavailland around Mt. Susitna, he recounts the legend of the Sleeping Lady for whom the mountain is named. Spotting a lone black bear galloping across the alpine tundra, he circles again and again until everyone onboard has had a look.

After an hour in flight, we touch down on Finger Lake, exhilarated by our journey, awestruck by the spot where we've landed. It's immediately apparent that Winterlake Lodge is a special place, an outpost of adventure nurtured by a family in love with the wilderness.

In the mid-1980s, Carl and Kirsten Dixon traded their city jobs for a remote lifestyle, starting a business from scratch and raising their two daughters where it's easy to remember what really matters. "We never once thought about failing," says Kirsten. "We were very naive, but we never looked back. We've been able to create our own lives here, and our own vision of what we want people who visit Alaska to experience."

It's a vision that's easy to embrace. With its soaring ceilings and open spaces, the lodge is the kind of place that inhabits the dreams of those who love the outdoors. It's comfortable but elegant, brimming with big windows and replete with cozy spaces. Pretty much by himself, Carl built not just Winterlake but also two other remote lodges for the couple's Within the Wild Adventure Company—no small feat, since all supplies must arrive by small plane as we just did.

Don't look for either Carl or Kirsten, a renowned chef, to dwell on their accomplishments. For them, it's all about their guests. "People are coming here for a broader experience, a lifestyle experience, exploring a little of this and a little of that," Kirsten says. "We befriend our guests. We have a rich relationship with them."

Today's experience begins with a hike down the famed Iditarod Trail, led by the Dixons' daughter Carly. We encounter beaver dams and bear scat, flush out grouse, and admire blazing red fireweed. If we'd been ambitious enough to trek to the top of the ridge, we would have been treated to a panoramic view of the valley and Mt. McKinley. After a gourmet lunch featuring glazed country ham and red lentils, there's time to check out the dog team, canoe among the loons, try a few practice casts, ponder a game of chess, or catch a nap. Other options include rafting, kayaking, massage therapy, and yoga. In Kirsten's words, it's all about offering "more of the best of what Alaska really is."

A lodge favorite is the open invitation to the kitchen, where we learn to make Gruyère puffs and fill them with cardamom salmon spread. "It's very rewarding for us to have people in the kitchen learning something," Kirsten says, speaking of the exhilaration she gets from sharing her love of cooking. Years ago, Kirsten made the grand leap from country cook to gourmet chef when some regular guests invited her to Paris to attend the famed Cordon Bleu cooking school. Many trips to France and a master's degree in gastronomy later, Kirsten has acquired a stellar reputation among her peers.

Like Carl with his building projects, Kirsten makes turning out gourmet meals with ingredients that must be grown on-site or shipped in by plane look easy, calling her kitchen "my playhouse all day long." Every dish that comes from Winterlake's massive kitchen features fresh, quality food, reflecting Kirsten's passion and that of her chefs. The author of two full-color cookbooks, Kirsten also hosts weekly

(cont'd)

An aerial view of Winterlake Lodge, one of the Within the Wild Adventure Company properties.
CARL DIXON

(cont'd)

cooking spots on an Anchorage television station and conducts cooking weekends at the lodge with instructors from around the world.

Winterlake is one of a handful of Alaskan lodges that is open year-round, except during breakup and freeze-up, when planes can't land on the lake. "It's really fun for us in the winter," Kirsten says. More Alaskans visit then, foodies as well as skiing and mushing enthusiasts. From mid-February to mid-March, there's a flurry of activity as the Iditarod Trail Committee sets up a race checkpoint at the lodge. In June, there's heli-skiing with world-class athletes, such as Olympic champion Tommy Moe. There are plans to keep the helicopter through the summer season to broaden the range of backcountry options for visitors.

Catering to the high-end crowd in the wilderness has its challenges. "Alaska is different," Kirsten explains. "It's more elusive to travelers. Some people don't get it." The "aha" moments come at special times. A guest relaxing on the deck spies first a moose, then a bear, then an eagle flying overhead. A visitor with a passion for mushrooms turns a 10-minute hike into a 2-hour foraging expedition, delighting his hosts by spotting more than 200 species. The edible finds make their way to the dinner table, of course.

It's this sort of intimate sharing of lifestyles, forged with outstanding service, that keeps Winterlake's guests coming back year after year. Winterlake and the other Within the Wild lodges don't advertise much; word of mouth and a few good agents keep them full. Kirsten admits that for the average traveler, finding a wilderness experience like the kind they offer can be something of a crapshoot. "One of the challenges of tourism in Alaska is a real gradient of quality in terms of backcountry standards," she says, suggesting that travelers connect with top agents who do site inspections and check references.

After sampling our crescent-shaped Gruyères, hot from the oven, we retire to the massive deck overlooking the lake, rocking and sipping tea as we watch the clouds roll in. The air turns cool, a reminder that fall is on the way, even though the gardens still abound with edible flowers. Content in body and soul, we wish for a storm strong enough to strand us here another day, away from the worries of the world, in the heart of Alaska's wilderness.

request. Small lockers are available in every room, but you must bring your own padlock. The hostel also has a limited number of private rooms and a second-floor common area with kitchen. There's no on-site parking, but if you're traveling without a car, you're well-situated here, just 1 block from the bus station and 6 blocks from the train station, with shuttles to outlying areas that stop right at the hostel. Guests enjoy use of the Internet, courtesy phone, and rented bicycles. Wheelchair access is available.

Duben Place, A Guest House $$
8307 Duben Avenue
(907) 351–2004
www.dubenplace.com
Duben Place offers private guesthouse

accommodations in a fully furnished two-bedroom duplex in a quiet east-side neighborhood. In addition to the queen-size beds in the bedrooms, there are two full-size futons in the living room, making this a great option for families or groups of travelers. Guests enjoy the feather beds, fully-equipped kitchen, and fresh vegetables and berries from the garden, in season. Pets are accepted on approval.

Off the Tracks Women's Guest House $
342 West 11th Avenue
(907) 272–6537
www.offthetracks.com
Here's a great downtown location providing a safe, convenient lodging option for women and children. The self-contained guest area has a private entrance, and the common area includes a kitchenette, shared bath, and private phone line. Breakfast foods are provided for a fix-it-yourself meal, and off-street parking is available.

Parkside Guest House $$$
1302 West 10th Avenue
(907) 683–2290
www.campdenali.com
Owned and operated by the Cole family of Camp Denali and North Face Lodge (see the Denali National Park chapter), the Parkside makes a convenient Anchorage add-on to your Denali adventures. Distinctively designed in the Arts and Crafts tradition, this downtown home features a spacious second-story living room with sweeping views of the inlet, mountains, and city. Laundry facilities are available, and a free continental breakfast comes with the room. Credit cards are not accepted.

Fly-out Lodges

Riversong Lodge $$$$
P.O. Box 191029, Anchorage, AK 99519
(907) 350–2392
www.riversonglodge.com
Seventy air miles northwest of Anchorage along the southern bank of the Yentna River, you'll find the peace and tranquility of River-song Lodge. They offer 10 cabins that accommodate a total of 44 guests, with a variety of all-inclusive packages that include transportation from Anchorage, meals, accommodations, fishing guide, and fishing equipment. The rustic lodge with its spacious decks, inviting living room, and tasteful decor serves as a gathering place for meals, activities, and relaxation. The grounds are lush with herbs, flowers, and gardens that contribute to the lodge's award-winning cuisine.

Winterlake Lodge $$$$
Within the Wild Adventure Company
2463 Cottonwood Street
(907) 274–2710
www.withinthewild.com
Pristine wilderness and warm Alaskan hospitality grace this lakeside lodge 198 miles from Anchorage on the historic Iditarod Trail. All-inclusive rates include accommodations, genuine gourmet meals, and a wide variety of activities, from hiking to fly-out fishing to cooking classes and bear watching at the sister property, Redoubt Lodge. Winterlake is a stunning hand-crafted lodge with soaring ceilings, large windows, and spacious decks for taking in the spectacular wilderness view. Hosts Carl and Kirsten Dixon cater to an upscale clientele with some of the most gracious hospitality you'll find anywhere.

RESTAURANTS

Twenty years ago the dining options in Anchorage were rather limited, but today you can satisfy just about any palate, whether it be for fresh sushi, eclectic vegetarian, a hearty steak, or home-style Alaskan fare. Fresh seafood is on just about every menu, so you don't have to make a special effort to find it.

Anchorage is just the right size for satisfying whatever cravings you have for lunch or dinner. No one thinks twice about driving across town to their favorite steak house or brewpub, and in fact folks head out to Girdwood in droves to check out the popular Double Musky restaurant, even though they don't take reservations. With that in mind, we've organized restaurants here by specialty rather than by location.

Compared to many other cities, Anchorage is a rather casual town when it comes to dress. Even in some of the fine dining spots, you may see folks in casual shirts and baseball hats, but in general attire for eating out is about the same as most places. While it's not exactly anything goes, you're less likely to feel uncomfortable about what you're wearing here than you might somewhere else.

Unlike restaurants in smaller, more remote towns, the eateries in Anchorage are generally open year-round. We'll note any that say they're open fewer than seven days a week, but be advised that those policies are subject to change. Assume major credit cards are accepted and wheelchair access is available unless we say otherwise.

The price codes indicate the average cost of a meal for two, excluding cocktails, wine, appetizers, desserts, tax, and tips. Most establishments that serve dinner have a license for beer and wine, and many also serve cocktails.

Price Codes

$. . . . . Less than $30
$$ . . . . $30–$39
$$$ . . . . $40–$50
$$$$ . . . . More than $50

All-American/All-Alaskan

The Alaska Salmon Chowder House $$
443 West Fourth Avenue
(907) 278–6901

If the patio furniture and lack of ambience doesn't put you off, there's reasonably priced seafood here along with an assortment of Asian specialties. Opt for the Alaskan Red Salmon, Alaskan Halibut, or the Boston Clam Chowder, or go for more hearty fare in the form of one pound of Alaska King Crab legs or the traditional Alaska Halibut or Salmon Olympia. Expect to find mostly tourists dining here, grabbing some quick Alaskan chow while sightseeing downtown. Beer and wine

are available with meals, and there's a selection of ice creams for dessert.

Arctic Roadrunner $
2477 Arctic Boulevard
(907) 279–7311

Classic burgers are the mainstay at this longtime Anchorage favorite. The walls are covered with photos of longtime patrons and historical trivia dating from the restaurant's beginning in the 1960s. In addition to hearty beef burgers, they offer salmon and halibut patties. Expect large portions, and don't forget the fries and milk shakes if you want the full experience. The place is not fancy, but the service is good, and it has plenty of character. The Arctic Roadrunner is closed on Sunday.

Gwennie's Old Alaska Restaurant $$
4333 Spenard Road
(907) 243–2090

Gwennie's is a perennial Alaskan favorite, famous especially for breakfasts so large that even the hungriest sourdough will be hard-pressed to clean his plate. They have gigantic omelets filled with all sorts of goodies, as well as whopping pancakes and towers of French toast. This is a fun all-Alaskan spot that's not a tourist trap; in fact, you'll find a whole lot of locals stuffing themselves on Gwennie's ample portions. It's always busy, especially on weekends, but even if you have to wait, you'll enjoy checking out all the Alaskan memorabilia that makes the place special. Even though Gwennie's is renowned for its breakfast fare, they're open for hearty Alaskan-style lunches and dinners as well. Located in the lower Spenard area, Gwennie's is a short drive from the Ted Stevens International Airport.

Sourdough Mining Company $$$
5200 Juneau Street
(907) 563–2272
www.alaskaone.com/aksourdough

Part of a little village replicating a gold rush–era mining operation, this restaurant is definitely geared toward tourists, bus loads of them, in fact. That being said, the ample lunch and dinner menu provides plenty of options for diners of all types, and the old mill-house atmosphere is fun for families. Favorite dishes include the Motherlode, an appetizer platter of potato skins, beer-battered halibut, and chicken strips; the Sizzling Sirloin; and Sourdough's Original Baby Back Ribs, sold by the rack. There's an all-you-can-eat Tent City Buffet, too. After dinner you can try your hand at panning for gold or check out the show at the Tent City Theater. Boxes and buckets of chicken, ribs, fritters, and other goodies are available for takeout and delivery.

Brewhouses and Pubs

Bear's Tooth Theatre Pub and Grill $
1230 West 27th Avenue
(907) 976–4200
www.beartooththeatre.net
Brought to you by the same folks who run the popular Moose's Tooth Pub and Pizzeria (see the write-up later in this section), the Bear's Tooth offers two dining options in the Spenard area of midtown, one with a movie theater and one with traditional casual dining. You can catch a movie in the 400-seat theater while enjoying food and beverages from their extensive menu, and there's a nondrinking, all-ages section for those younger than age 21. You'll get a whole lot more than the popcorn-and-candy fare served up at most theaters. At the Bear's Tooth, you can indulge in favorites such as Southwest Steamer Clams, Chicken Bomber Burrito, Habanero Chicken Skewers, Setting Sun Halibut, Lemon Beurre Blanc Salmon, and Seafood Enchiladas. It's a popular spot, but there's a large parking lot with street-side parking for the spillover.

Glacier Brewhouse $$$
737 West Fifth Avenue
(907) 274–2739
www.glacierbrewhouse.com
A great selection of microbrews, weekly menus with distinctive entrees, and a warm, inviting atmosphere make this a favorite downtown eatery. The lunch menu features such specialty sandwiches as the Chicken

Thai Chile as well as pizzas, entree salads such as the Cajun Duck and Spinach, and several seafood options. The dinner menu includes meats roasted over an Alderwood-fired rotisserie and pastas such as the Jambalaya Fettucine. Top it all off with a signature dessert such as the World Famous Bread Pudding, a classic apple and currant treat roasted in the wood oven and topped with caramelized pecans and Yukon Jack sauce. Chefs work in a gleaming kitchen in full view of diners, and vats of beer, including cask-conditioned real ale and specialty taps, are brewed in an adjacent, glass-fronted room. Brewery tours can be arranged through your server. Besides the great beers, there's a nice selection of wines and infused cocktails. All food, beverages, and service are unconditionally guaranteed, and substitutions are welcome. This place is always hopping, so reservations are a good idea.

Humpy's Great Alaskan Alehouse $$
610 West Sixth Avenue
(907) 276–2337
www.humpys.com
Humpy's lives up to its claim of being the ultimate watering hole with 44 draft beers, 20 Belgian ales, live music seven nights a week, and an expansive menu of seafood, burgers, and pasta. The casual alehouse atmosphere makes everybody feel at home, and while it's not usually the best choice if you're looking for quiet conversation, it's guaranteed to be a whole lot of fun. It's a favorite with both locals and tourists, known for its nightlife as well as casual dining. Check out the outdoor patio in the summer and the brunch on Sunday.

Moose's Tooth Pub and Pizzeria $
3300 Old Seward Highway
(907) 258–2537
www.moosestooth.net
If you're looking for great pizza, locals will point you toward the Moose's Tooth, an eclectic pub and eatery just off the Old Seward Highway in midtown Anchorage. In a casual atmosphere with warm, artsy, outdoorsy decor, they serve up such favorites as the Hal-

ibut Pizza, Oriental Chicken Salad, and Cheese Stix. The menu is chock-full of pizza selections, too. They brew their own signature ales, including Fairweather IPA, Pipeline Stout, and Klondike Golden. Open since 1996, they attract a diverse clientele, including families, adventurers, and professionals. There's on-site parking, and it's a popular "after play" spot.

Snow Goose Restaurant $$
717 West Third Avenue
(907) 277–7727
www.alaskabeers.com

From a three-story building overlooking Ship Creek and Cook Inlet, one of Anchorage's first brewpubs serves up great food and unique beers from their own on-site Sleeping Lady Brewery. Whether you're hungry for seafood, pizza, burgers, or salads, the Snow Goose offers some great options, including Borealis Blackened Mango Rockfish, Sitka Salmon Cheese Pizza with garlic cream pesto sauce, Old-English Prime Rib of Beef, and the Wasabi-Lime Halibut Cove Sandwich. If your timing's right, you can catch a concert at their theater, or book the whole thing for a private event. There's live music to celebrate the release of a new specialty brew on the first Friday of every month. Hand-crafted root beer plus top-quality wines and cocktails are also on the menu. In the summer, you'll want to get there early to grab a seat on the popular outdoor deck.

Cafes and Bistros

Alaska Bagel Restaurant $
113 West Northern Lights Boulevard, Suite L
(907) 276–3900
www.alaskabagel.com

Though the setting is nothing fancy, this is a great place to grab a bagel, salad, or sandwich from an extensive menu. Bagels are baked fresh daily, with more than two dozen varieties to choose from. With an equally extensive variety of schmears, it would take years to try all the possible combinations. Bagel sandwiches include The Pipeline, with roast beef, turkey,

lox, cheddar, Swiss, cream cheese, olives, pickle, and tomato on two bagels, and The Cook Inlet, with shrimp, avocado, and cheddar. They're open until 3:30 P.M. daily, with breakfast served until 1:00 P.M. on weekdays and until 3:00 P.M. on weekends. Call ahead for orders of six dozen bagels or more. Delivery and shipping are available.

Cafe del Mundo $
341 East Benson Boulevard
(907) 274–0026

The first coffee roaster in Anchorage, Cafe del Mundo set up shop in a converted greenhouse in 1975. Today they roast coffee for distribution throughout Alaska and to mail-order customers in the Lower 48 and even as far away as Antarctica. In addition to serving a full menu of specialty coffees, Cafe del Mundo offers fine teas and chai, specialty hot chocolate, fresh pastries, Italian gelato, and free wi-fi Internet access. They also have a south-side coffee shop at 2278 Abbott Road in the Fred Meyer shopping center.

Hogg Brothers Cafe and Watering Trough $
1049 West Northern Lights Boulevard
(907) 276–9649

This is a fun, casual eatery with a farmhouse atmosphere, complete with a "pig pen" that has small tables for the little ones in your group. Hogg Brothers features American food served Alaskan style, with Biscuits and Gravy, Hogg Trough, Polish Pork Omelet, Hogg McKinley (an in-house spin on eggs Benedict), and Hogg-Size Cinnamon Rolls among their popular menu items. For lunch, try the Kalif Burger, a huge burger smothered with cheese, fresh mushrooms, and avocados. Serving a diverse clientele for breakfast and lunch since 1977, they have ample parking in a great midtown location. You can count on huge portions, a great selection of omelets and burgers, and home-style cooking, right down to the homemade cheese sauce and gravy.

Middle Way Cafe and Coffee House $
1200 West Northern Lights Boulevard
(907) 272–6433

Its shopping-center setting may not provide much ambience, but there's plenty of parking plus a lot of great menu items at this midtown cafe. The Middle Way specializes in creative vegetarian fare, but they serve nonveggie items as well. Try a fresh gourmet sandwich, such as the Southwestern Turkey with low-fat turkey and cream cheese blended with jalapeño, sun-dried tomato and herbs, leaf lettuce, sprouts, onion, tomato, and avocado. The menu also features organic wraps, such as the Quantum, which is stuffed with organic pinto beans and brown rice, cheddar cheese, sprouts, red cabbage, scallions, carrots, avocado, and homemade salsa. As you might expect from a place that emphasizes fresh food, they also have great salads, such as the Italian Bruschetta Plate, with toasted sourdough, pesto, fresh tomato, provolone, and a hefty salad blend. Baked goods, such as the marion berry scones, come fresh from the oven daily. There's an espresso bar, organic juice bar, and selection of no-fat smoothies to complement your meal. They're open daily for breakfast, lunch, and dinner.

Mumbo Gumbo Cafe $$
2446 Tudor Road
(907) 770–1919

You'll think you've dropped about 3,000 miles south and landed in the savory kitchen of somebody's grandma when you step inside this quaint cafe serving up good food with lots of love and affection. There are three items on the lunch menu, and there's a different dinner entree each night of the week, with fried chicken and Gullah Gullah gumbo served daily, along with a choice of five sides. Owner and chef Patricia Dakota Grant brings patience to her kitchen, and it shows in dishes that Anchorage-ites, especially displaced Southerners, come back for again and again. The Mumbo Gumbo is open for breakfast on Saturday only, and they're closed on Sunday.

Roscoe's Catfish and Barbeque Cafe $$
3001 Penland Parkway
(907) 276–5879

For down-home Southern cooking way up north, it's hard to beat Roscoe's. Owner Roscoe Wyche III has been slow cooking and patiently seasoning southern specialties for appreciative patrons since 1988. Whether you're craving fried chicken, catfish, collard greens, gumbo, chitterlings, black-eyed peas, or peach cobbler, this is the place. In addition to a full menu, Roscoe's offers a buffet. The cafe is easy to find, right behind the Northway Mall.

Snow City Cafe $
Fourth Avenue and L Street
(907) 272–2489
www.snowcitycafe.com

One of the most popular breakfast and lunch spots in Anchorage is the Snow City Cafe, conveniently located downtown. Local art decorates the walls, and the place hums with a diverse clientele. There's a huge selection of egg dishes, including the Snow City Scramble with Black Forest ham, cheddar, sun-dried tomatoes, mushrooms, and onions, and the Heart Attack on a Plate, featuring hash browns topped with bacon crumbles, sautéed onions and mushrooms, cheddar, and sour cream. For another breakfast treat, try the Stuffed French Toast, packed with mandarin orange cream cheese and toasted walnuts. Among the sandwich choices are the Salmon Cake Hero and the Grilled Italian Classic. There's also a nice selection of fruit smoothies to go with your meal. The Snow City Cafe is open from 7:00 A.M. to 3:00 P.M. weekdays, and until 4:00 P.M. on weekends. They also host a First Friday evening art reception and Wednesday-night Traditional Irish Music Sessions.

Southside Bistro $$$
1320 Huffman Park Road
(907) 348–0088
www.southsidebistro.com

Enjoy lively European ambience with open kitchen, wine bar, gas fireplace, and French vintage posters in this popular American bistro serving fresh, fun food. You can opt for formal dining on the restaurant side or a more casual meal in the bistro area. An award-winning wine list, attentive waitstaff, and professional chefs keep their clientele, mostly a mix of local professionals and visitors, coming back. Try the roast rack of lamb with cilantro pesto, the fresh mussels in saffron cream, or the peach-raspberry cobbler with vanilla ice cream. Flat breads and unique pizzas are baked in the wood-fired brick oven, and desserts come with signature handpainted designs. In business since 1995, they've got ample parking and are open for lunch and dinner Tuesday through Saturday.

Ethnic

Aladdin's $$$
4240 Old Seward Highway, Suite 20
(907) 561–2373
www.aladdinsak.com
Here you can experience authentic Mediterranean cuisine in the heart of Anchorage with a full menu of meats, seafood, and vegetarian fare. Try their Vegetarian Mousaka with eggplant, mushrooms, zucchini, and tofu, or their Fesanjan Persian Style, featuring chicken breast cooked in walnut, pomegranate, and pistachio sauce. Meat dishes include Lamb Shiskabob and the Kefta Sandwich with grilled beef sauce in a pita served with yogurt mint. Desserts include favorites such as baklava, Chocolate Decadence, and Bread of Tunisia. Owner Rabah Chettfour opened his Anchorage venture in 1992 after studying culinary arts in London and working as a chef in various restaurants throughout Europe. The cozy restaurant has an upbeat family feel to it, with the chefs going out of their way to cater to vegan or other special dietary requests.

The Greek Corner $$$$
302 West Fireweed Lane
(907) 276–2820
At Greek Corner, you can enjoy an intimate

atmosphere with soft lighting and seasonal outdoor dining while sampling homemade Italian and Greek dishes. You'll find your waitstaff friendly and attentive, helping the customers feel right at home. Greek Corner favorites include scampi, lamb chops, gyros, and pistachio-mousaka pizza. Beer and wine are available with your meal. Open since 1981, the Greek Corner serves lunch and dinner seven days a week.

La Mex $
2550 Spenard Road
(907) 274–7511
www.lamexinalaska.com
La Mex has been an Anchorage favorite for great Mexican food since 1969, when they opened in a log cabin that had seating for 12. They now have seating for more than 600, and they're serving their second generation of loyal Alaskan clientele, who appreciate the comfortable atmosphere, colorful Mexican decor, tasty food, and generous portions. While the menu emphasizes such Mexican favorites as tostaditos, the Queen Tostado, chips and dips, and fajitas, there's standard American fare as well. Their famous Margarita Grandes are a great accompaniment to just about anything on the menu. They're the only Mexican restaurant in town that makes their own chips and tortillas fresh daily, and their salsa is so well-loved that they sell it by the gallon. Family owned and operated, La Mex welcomes families and longtime Alaskans as well as visitors looking for a well-prepared, affordable meal along with great service. They've got a second location at 8330 King Street, near the Dimond Center Mall, with high ceilings, a more hip decor, a fascinating tortilla machine, and patio dining in the summer. Both locations offer a full bar menu and ample free parking.

Peter's Sushi Spot $$
4140 B Street
(907) 562–5187
www.peterssushispot.com
This popular sushi restaurant boasts an

upscale location and a loyal following of fans. The menu offers plenty of fresh seafood options served up in a contemporary, fusion-style setting. For lunch, there are several sushi and sashimi combinations served with miso soup and salad, as well as donburi and noodle plates. Dinner options include an expanded array of combination plates plus special sushi and a huge selection of rolls with both cooked and uncooked fish. As you might expect, many of the special rolls incorporate Alaskan seafood such as crab, halibut, and salmon. Peter's is open daily for lunch and dinner except on Sunday, when dinner is the only option.

Pizza Olympia $$
2809 Spenard Road
(907) 561–5264
Fresh, healthy European-style cooking is the trademark here, where they offer free delivery and bookings for large parties. There's an extensive pizza menu, with dough made from scratch and homemade sauce. A favorite is Athena's Delight, with fresh garlic, feta cheese, onions, green peppers, fresh tomatoes, and artichoke hearts. Greek dinners include Olympia Roast Leg of Lamb served with oreganato potatoes and spaghetti, and mousaka, featuring layers of potatoes, eggplant, zucchini, and seasoned ground beef topped with béchamel sauce. For dessert, you can't go wrong with baklava.

Sorrento's $$$
610 East Fireweed Lane
(907) 278–3439
Sorrento's has a comfortable Italian-style decor accented in reds and greens to complement a full menu of pastas, pizzas, seafood, and other Italian dishes. Among the specialties are Tournedos Siciliano, featuring medallions of beef served with sautéed peppers, mushrooms, and fresh tomatoes, and the Taste of Sorrento's, a plate of lasagna, chicken a la Sorrento, and fettuccine. Seafood options include several tempting halibut entrees, including Halibut al Vino Blanco and Halibut

Almondine. All dinners are served with garlic bread and your choice of soup or salad. Conveniently located across from the Fireweed Theaters, Sorrento's makes a great before- or after-the-movie stop.

Touch of Russia Cafe and Deli $$
333 West Fourth Avenue
(907) 276–5907
For a dining experience that reaches beyond the ordinary at prices that won't break the bank, Touch of Russia offers Russian specialties such as pelmeni, borscht, and piroshkis in a quaint cafe in the heart of downtown. Russian-made shawls, porcelain, and artifacts decorate the dining area. Open for lunch and dinner year-round, Touch of Russia is a bit of a newcomer in the Anchorage dining scene, but they have a loyal clientele of folks who miss the cuisine of their home country as well as Americans who've acquired a taste for it. Alcohol is not served. There's no designated parking for the restaurant, so you'll have to scope out the usual paid lots and street-side parking downtown.

Fine Dining

The Crow's Nest $$$$
Hotel Captain Cook
Fourth Avenue at K Street
(907) 276–6000, (800) 843–1950
www.captaincook.com
Atop Tower 3 of the luxurious Hotel Captain Cook in downtown Anchorage (see our write-up under Hotels and Motels in the Accommodations section), you can experience some of Alaska's finest dining while taking in panoramic views of the city, mountains, and ocean. Decorated in rich wood tones and featuring alcove seating, the award-winning Crow's Nest serves New American cuisine with French overtones. Start your evening with nori-wrapped Hawaiian ahi, lightly breaded and served with Asian slaw and spicy ginger butter sauce, or try the seared foie gras with cinnamon sugar brioche, caramelized granny smith apples, sweet Alaskan onions, balsamic reduction, and apple syrup. Dinner favorites

include the potato herb–crusted Alaskan halibut, the Crow's Nest surf and turf, and the herb-crusted New Zealand rack of lamb. Desserts prepared at the table top off your meal. If you like, you can order from the monthly Chef's Tasting Menu, which features special starters, entrees, and desserts, each paired with a wine. The Crow's Nest has the largest wine selection in the state, with 10,000 bottles in its cellar and a sommelier on staff to assist with your selections. The service is impeccable, and if you're lucky, you might catch a glimpse of Alaska's well-known former governor Wally Hickel, a hotel owner and frequent guest.

Double Musky Inn $$$$
Mile 0.3 Crow Creek Road, Girdwood
(907) 783–2822
www.doublemuskyinn.com

The Double Musky is more than a great restaurant, it's a phenomenon. Press coverage from around the world has lauded the quirky decor and stunning food as among the finest in not only Alaska but in the nation. No one thinks twice about driving to Girdwood from Anchorage in hopes of getting a table—the Double Musky doesn't take reservations, and that's part of its charm. Nestled at the foot of the Chugach Mountains, the restaurant serves fabulous steaks and Alaskan seafood with New Orleans–style seasonings in a quaint, intimate atmosphere that showcases mirror art, stained glass, and "a million doodads." Pepper steak, jambalaya, étouffée, and gumbo are among the house favorites. The place is packed with tourists and locals in the summer and with fun-loving ski bums in the winter. Your fellow diners might be bush pilots, movie stars, governors, senators, or just plain old Alaskans and wannabe Alaskans looking for a truly memorable dining experience. In business since 1961, the Double Musky is open for dinner only. They're closed on Sunday and during the month of November.

Jens' Restaurant $$$
Olympic Center
701 West 36th Avenue
(907) 561–5367
www.jensrestaurant.com

Jens' serves new American cuisine with a French twist along with a lunch menu of Danish specialties in an elegant, light dining room enhanced by museum-quality art and a classy wine bar. The strip mall location may put off some visitors, but locals know there's great food to be had here, with a menu that changes daily to optimize the use of fresh ingredients. Favorite items on the lunch menu include Danish meatballs and chicken-fried steak. For dinner, try the Halibut Meuniere with wild mushrooms in garlic and herb sauce, or the popular pepper steak. Chef Jens Hansen is acclaimed for his ways with seafood, but everything here is tastefully prepared and served with style. Choose from more than 160 wine selections as well as beers from Alaska and around the world. In addition to the regular seating, there's a private dining room that can accommodate up to 20 guests. The wine bar serves appetizers from 4:00 P.M. to midnight Tuesday through Saturday. The restaurant is closed on Sunday.

Kincaid Grill $$$$
6700 Jewel Lake Road
(907) 243–0507
www.kincaidgrill.com

"Fine dining without the attitude" is the mantra at the Kincaid Grill, where you'll find fresh seafood, specialty meats and game, Alaskan regional cuisine, and hand-crafted desserts in an unpretentious setting just a few miles from the Ted Stevens International Airport. Everything is made in-house, from sauces and reductions to homemade dressings and accompaniments. Even the meats are carved on-site. Locals come back again and again for such favorites as the Seafood Fusion Soup, crab cakes, shrimp gumbo, and filet of beef served with fresh creamed spinach. The restaurant has a chic neighborhood feel, an extensive wine list, a friendly waitstaff, and ample on-site parking. Chef and owner Al Levinsohn, with an impressive track record featuring some of the most well-known restaurants in the area, hosts a weekly cooking show on a local television station. The Kincaid is open for dinner only Tuesday through Saturday. Reservations are recommended.

Marx Bros. Café $$$$
624 West Third Avenue
(907) 278–2133
www.marxcafe.com
Unlike most cafes, this place comes to life at night with an imaginative menu of contemporary cuisine featuring fresh Alaskan seafood, game meats, and other unique ingredients. Don't be fooled by this unassuming little 1916 house-turned-restaurant. Inside you'll find tasteful furnishings, a collection of original Alaska art, stained glass, and classic table settings to complement the innovative Northwest cuisine that's been drawing locals and visitors alike since 1979. Among the favorite dishes are the deviled crab cakes with Dungeness crab, chili aioli, and jicama-orange slaw; tableside Caesar salad; halibut baked in macadamia nut crust; and grilled Kodiak scallops coated with poppy and sesame seeds and served with salmon polenta, proscuitto, and mustard-shallot vinaigrette. Enjoy a selection from their extensive wine list, and top off your meal with a dessert specialty, such as the warm berry crisp or the chocolate truffle tart. The Marx Bros. serves dinner only, and it is closed on Sunday and Monday.

Mick's at the Inlet $$$$
1200 L Street
(907) 222–8787
www.inlettower.com
With an emphasis on fine-quality ingredients and creative presentation, Mick's offers fresh Alaskan seafood, North American game meats, and homemade pastas and pastries from its location in the lobby of the Inlet Tower Hotel on the south end of downtown Anchorage. The atmosphere is casual and relaxed, with polished black stone tables, brightly colored walls, and well-appointed lighting. Locals and visitors alike enjoy menu favorites such as the Blackened Alaskan Prawns and Chorizo or the Savory Mushroom Cheesecake, an appetizer served with bleu cheese, red wine syrup, and fried leeks. They also offer a unique pasta-less Spaghetti Provençale with squash noodles, yellow and grape tomatoes, fresh basil, and bleu cheese. There's a full bar menu featuring wines, local brews, and specialty cocktails. Ample parking is another plus. Mick's is open for breakfast, lunch, and dinner seven days a week.

Orso $$$
737 West Fifth Avenue
(907) 222–3232
www.orsoalaska.com
A relative newcomer to the Anchorage fine dining scene, Orso has quickly become a downtown favorite with its emphasis on global flavors with an Alaskan twist. Decorated in warm colors, seating includes an intimate loft level with fireside dining. The menu features fresh wild Alaskan seafood, seasonal Alaskan-grown herbs and vegetables, and locally made pasta. Popular dishes include the fennel-roasted clams in lemon-herb broth; the cashew-crusted halibut in golden raisin-caper sauce with spinach and roasted pepper couscous; the braised lamb Osso Buco with sweet and sour onions, kalamata olives, plum tomatoes, and creamy polenta; and the Molten Chocolate Cake, a dark chocolate flourless cake served with rich chocolate sauce and ice cream. Specialty cocktails, Glacier Brewhouse beers, and a selection of fine wines are available with your meal. Orso is open Monday through Friday for lunch and nightly for dinner. Validated parking is available, and reservations are recommended.

Sack's Cafe and Restaurant $$$
328 G Street
(907) 274–4022
www.sackscafe.com

A warm art deco atmosphere showcasing original creations provides the perfect setting for Sack's innovative cuisine. Locals and visitors alike enjoy Sack's extensive, eclectic menu that is new every day. Typical lunch fare includes a tiger prawn and avocado sandwich with herb cream cheese and Dijon mustard, or a Panzanella Bread Salad with buffalo mozzarella, capers, oven-roasted tomatoes, minced olives, and toasted pine nuts. For dinner you're likely to find fabulous seafood choices, such as oven-roasted halibut with chorizo drunken goat cheese, marinated artichoke hearts, and proscuitto-wrapped asparagus, along with pasta, Thai favorites, and such meat dishes as the organic free range chicken stuffed with proscuitto, spinach, caramelized onions, and manchego cheese. There's a huge wine list as well as draft and bottled beer to accompany your meal. Sack's is open Monday through Friday for lunch, with a brunch menu on weekends. The folks at Sack's will even graciously share some of their best recipes with you.

Simon and Seaforts $$$$
420 L Street
(907) 274–3502
www.simonandseaforts.com
Stunning views of Cook Inlet and an upscale saloon atmosphere provide the perfect backdrop for the fabulous food that keeps this nonsmoking restaurant on the list of Anchorage favorites. The friendly, professional waitstaff will help you choose from weekly specials that highlight fresh fish and seafood but also include original entrees, such as Grilled Elk Chops with Frangelico-Hazelnut Hollandaise and Smoked Reindeer Tenderloin with Blackberry Sage Sauce. The clientele include professionals, tourists, old-time Alaskans with their hallmark baseball hats, and families. The wine list and bar menu are extensive, and all the beer is draft. This place is so well-loved that they hardly need to advertise; in fact, the sign out front of the boxy building that houses the restaurant is so small you'll miss it if you're not looking

closely. There's free parking at the nearby Hotel Captain Cook for Simon and Seaforts patrons, and while reservations aren't required, they are a good idea.

Steak Houses

Club Paris $$$
417 West Fifth Avenue
(907) 272–6332
www.clubparisrestaurant.com
Serving up some of the best steaks in Anchorage since 1957, Club Paris is a perennial favorite with locals. Beyond its decidedly unassuming decor, you'll find a menu full of thick steaks individually cut and aged on-site as well as fresh Alaskan seafood. The 4-inch-thick filet mignon is a dinner favorite, as are the Australian lobster tail served steamed with lemon and drawn butter and the hearty clam chowder. Fresh ground filet mignon burgers top the lunch menu along with a nice assortment of sandwiches, homemade soups, salads, and lunch specialties. For a special treat, ask the chef to stuff your steak with bleu cheese. Desserts are also made from scratch, with Stan's Key Lime Pie, Crème Caramel, and New York Style Cheesecake topping the list of choices. Club Paris is open daily for lunch and dinner, and dinner reservations are recommended. Parking is available in the lot behind the restaurant.

Sullivan's Steakhouse $$$$
320 West Fifth Avenue
(907) 258–2882
www.sullivansteakhouse.com
Sullivan's sleek 1940s-style decor makes this a popular spot for the local business crowd. They often have live jazz music in the bar plus a variety of appetizers and bar menu specials. For lunch, choose from a selection of salads, seafood, steaks, chops, and burgers, with the 10-ounce charbroiled burger a perennial favorite. There's also a business lunch with choice of salad, entree, and side dish. Dinner entrees include the 20-ounce house special Bone-In Kansas City Strip, along with a wide selection of chops, seafood, and steaks.

Steaks and chops can be ordered Oscar-style, stuffed with crab meat. Entrees are served with a wedge of iceberg lettuce and blue cheese dressing; other side dishes are extra. Lunch is served Monday through Friday, with dinner offered seven days a week.

NIGHTLIFE

There's an upside to our long Alaskan winters: The nights go on and on, so there's plenty of time to get out and explore the nightlife. And summer nights? Truly magical. Even at midnight the day's still young and the party has just begun, with lots of open decks and patios available for revelers who want to soak up the light. Don't even think about sleeping.

Since the pipeline days, bars have been the mainstay of Anchorage nightlife. By law, there is one liquor license per 3,000 people, but some 70 establishments were grandfathered in when the municipality came into being, so there's really an abundance of options. In variety and quality, these places have come a long way. Fourth Avenue downtown used to be a red-light district, with one seedy bar after another. That has all been cleaned up. Now there are lots of fun, upscale bars downtown.

By municipal ordinance, establishments serving alcohol must be closed from 2:30 to 10:00 A.M. on weekdays, and from 3:00 to 10:00 A.M. on weekends and holidays. While restaurants are nonsmoking, bars are exempt from that regulation, and you'll find some of the smaller spots are pretty smoky, especially in the winter, when it's tougher to circulate fresh air.

If your blood alcohol level is .08 percent or higher, you're risking a DUI conviction in the state of Alaska. As in most states, this is a serious offense, resulting in confiscation of your license at the time of your arrest followed by a minimum of three days in jail, a $1,500 fine, and a three-month license suspension if you're convicted. And that's just for the first offense. It's best to play it safe and grab a taxi if you need it. Also, be advised that it is illegal to have an open container of alcohol in any vehicle except a chauffeured limousine.

Pubs and Clubs

Al's Alaskan Inn
7830 Old Seward Highway
(907) 344–6223
www.alsalaskaninn.com
Classy isn't the first word that comes to mind at Al's, but there's a lot happening here, with five bars, three levels, and a Plexiglas dance floor. The South Main Bar is packed with abstract iron art, with bicycle rims, mirrors, and signs protruding from the walls. To top off the unique atmosphere, the walkways, walls, and dance floors are diamond plated. For a more intimate setting, check out the North Cozy Bar or the New Orleans–style Voodoo lounge. Textured aluminum walls, a stainless-steel bar embedded with crop circles and life-size aliens—you can't expect anything much more unusual than Area 51. Head to the North Hollywood Bar if you'd rather have a life-size Marilyn Monroe watching you drink. And if you've had too much to drink, there's a motel conveniently located on the premises—no guarantees about sleep with the nightclub noise, though.

Bernie's Bungalow
626 D Street
(907) 276–8808
www.berniesbungalowlounge.com
A fun, friendly, relaxed martini lounge in downtown Anchorage, Bernie's features more than a dozen martinis plus 12 beers on tap. Wednesday is karaoke night, and you can learn to salsa on Sundays at 6:00 P.M. For more music and dancing, check out the DJ Thursday through Saturday. Comfy sofas, art on the walls, bright colors—this place will lift your spirits even before you have a drink. Bernie's is open for lunch at noon, too.

i Over three dozen clubs and pubs in Anchorage will pay for you and your car to get home if you've had too much to drink, so you may want to call ahead to see if the places you're headed to will oblige.

Blues Central
825 West Northern Lights Boulevard
(907) 272–1341

Voted the best blues joint in Anchorage, Blues Central brings in musicians from around the area as well as outside for live performances pretty much every night. It's just the sort of dark, funky place where you'd expect a good crowd and great music, including Blues Jam Sessions on Sunday and Jazz Jam every Tuesday. Pick up a free Blues Central music calendar for all the entertainment details. Food is served from 11:00 A.M. to 11:00 P.M. daily, with French dips on fresh-baked bread a house specialty.

Chilkoot Charlie's
2435 Spenard Road
(907) 272–1010
www.koots.com

Without question the most famous nightspot in Anchorage, Chilkoot Charlie's is pretty much always rocking with a wild and crazy crowd. Ten bars, four dance floors, a big long bar, padded tree-stump seats, sawdust floors—the character of this place just goes on and on. No wonder it made the list of *Playboy*'s top bars in America. DJs play top dance music on the bar's South Stage, while the North Stage spotlights house bands and acts from across the country. Try a custom martini to a backdrop of smooth music in the Swing Bar, or check out the famed Bird House, transplanted from Bird Creek—the panties hanging from the ceiling are your clue that you're in the right place. The bar has had some bad press over unfortunate incidents in their parking lot, including gun fights, but security has been beefed up and it's been relatively calm since. The windmill in the parking lot will let you know you've found the place. Expect a cover charge and a one-drink minimum to get in on the fun. Their motto: "We cheat the other guy and pass the savings on to you."

Club Soraya
Post Office Mall
333 West Fourth Avenue
(907) 276–0670

This Hispanic club offers up a whole lot of fun-filled dancing, including lessons, in a non-smoking environment. On Tuesday, there are East coast and Lindy lessons, while Wednesday is Argentine Tango Night followed by open dancing. Thursday brings reggae, R&B, and hip-hop, with ladies admitted free until 10:30 P.M. Learn your Latin basics on Friday and Saturday nights, followed by open dancing at 10:00 P.M. The cover charge ranges from $3.00 to $10.00, with a nominal charge for lessons except on Sunday, when swing lessons are free. Drop-ins are welcome, and you don't have to have any experience or even a partner to get started.

Darwin's Theory
426 G Street
(907) 277–5322

Young, old, regulars, the curious—you'll meet all sorts of people at this hole-in-the-wall bar with an upbeat reputation. Grab some free popcorn and a drink, edge your way to a seat, and do some people watching. It's eclectic, energetic, and interesting, but don't expect live music or anything really upscale here. There's wheelchair access, and in fine Alaskan tradition, they serve drinks from 10:00 A.M. to 2:00 A.M., 3:00 A.M. on weekends.

F Street Station
325 F Street
(907) 272–9196

The 40-pound block of cheese at the bar is one of the legends about this fun little bar

i For the latest on the Anchorage arts and entertainment scene, pick up a free copy of the *Anchorage Press*. Printed every Thursday, the *Press* is jam-packed with information on theater, live music, restaurants, and everything that's happening in the area. You can also access the *Press* online at www.anchoragepress .com. Another option for staying in the know is the *Anchorage Daily News*'s, Friday Play section, with great tips on what's happening over the weekend.

ℹ️ Looking for alternatives to the usual movie experience? Check out the Movies for Your Mind series at the Anchorage Museum, featuring great classic and contemporary films from around the world. Show times are at 6:00 P.M. every Saturday and Sunday, and admission is just $6.00, with discounts for seniors and museum members. Go to www.anchoragemuseum.org for a list of what's showing each month. And don't forget about the watch-and-dine fun at the Bear's Tooth Theatre Pub and Grill; see the complete listing in this chapter's Restaurants section.

and restaurant. Supposedly the health department complained, so the HELP YOURSELF sign had to come down. The cheese remains, with a FOR DISPLAY ONLY warning that everyone ignores. It's all in the Alaskan spirit of fun, as is the bar's aviator theme. In fact, the bar is a favorite after-hours hangout for pilots. There's a full menu of salads and sandwiches, along with a daily seafood special. Food is served from 11:00 A.M. to 1:00 A.M. seven days a week, but don't expect live entertainment here—it's mainly a great spot to wind down and relax with friends.

Humpy's Great Alaskan Alehouse
610 West Sixth Avenue
(907) 276–2337
www.humpys.com
Already featured in this chapter's Restaurant listings, Humpy's also earns a spot among the top places to have fun in Anchorage. There's live entertainment every night, with a casual, quirky, upbeat atmosphere with humpies, also known as pink or dog salmon, represented just about everywhere you turn. Great food, a big bar, and a reputation for being a happening place make this a gathering spot for all sorts of people looking for a good time. There's something for just about everyone here, from live music to the four big-screen plasma TVs. Humpy's is also a favorite watering hole for the after-theater crowd coming

from the nearby performing arts center. They don't take reservations, and as is the case for most everywhere downtown, you're on your own for parking.

Peanut Farm
5227 Old Seward Highway
(907) 563–2383
This newly expanded sports bar has something for everyone. Old-timers still flock to the original Peanut Farm, a dark, smoky, cabin-style bar with peanut shells on the floor and plenty of Alaskan character. If you prefer fresh air and lots of room, move on down to the 20,000-square-foot addition, a smoke-free spot with lots of big-screen TVs featuring your favorite sporting events. They also have table-top sets where you can choose from a selection of shows. In the summer the new addition offers outdoor seating. Besides the sports, the stage, and the dance floor, food is a big draw here. They serve big burgers, including a buffalo burger with pepper jack and barbeque sauce. Fresh shucked oysters, oyster shooters, or hot-hot-hot oysters are other bar menu favorites. From 6:00 A.M. to noon during football season, you can grab breakfast along with your game—remember, those East Coast games hit Alaskan screens pretty early in the morning. There's plenty of parking and plenty of room inside for you and all of your friends.

Platinum Jaxx
901 West Sixth Avenue
(907) 278–5299

ℹ️ During the winter, you'll find club-style boxing, complete with bikini-clad ring girls, every Thursday night at the Egan Convention Center. For more information, check out the listing in this chapter's Recreation section, or visit www.thursdaynightfights.com. Anchorage plays to Ultimate Fighting fans, too, drawing crowds of more than 3,000 to the Sullivan Arena for fights paired with heavy metal concerts.

i A handful of Anchorage nightspots, mostly those affiliated with upscale restaurants, have gone nonsmoking. If breathing secondhand smoke isn't part of your idea of a good time, check out Platinum Jaxx, Simon and Seaforts, Orso, and the Snow Goose. The Anchorage Assembly voted in 2006 to make all bars nonsmoking as of July 1, 2007, but a ballot referendum could change the outcome of that decision.

One of the newer clubs in town, Platinum Jaxx capitalizes on a prime location and spacious building formerly occupied by the popular La Mex restaurant, which relocated south of downtown. (See this chapter's Restaurants section for information on La Mex.) Decorated in silver, blue, and gray, this upbeat club offers music, dancing, food, and a low-key dress code. Downstairs you'll find a bar that has more than 50 beers and the usual assortment of drinks, seating at booths and tall tables, plasma TVs, a couple of pool tables, and a generally busy dance floor. Upstairs in the VIP lounge there's a smaller bar with leather chairs and walkways that look down into the main bar. The crowd is on the younger side. The dress code creates a bit of an upscale feel, but the restrictions are fairly loose—jeans are okay, but hats and grunge gear aren't. On the menu, there's chicken, burgers, ribs, and salads. Platinum Jaxx is one of a handful of nonsmoking clubs in downtown Anchorage.

Rumrunner's Old Towne Bar and Grill
Fourth Avenue and E Street
(907) 278–4493
www.rumrunnersak.com
One of the newer, larger downtown hangouts, Rumrunner's has a big menu, a lighted dance floor, and a lineup of fun almost every night of the week. Fuel up on your choice of burgers, sandwiches, ribs, or a full seafood dinner, with Rumrunner's own draft beers to go with your meal. Check out the Friday After Work Pre-Party Party with DJ music. The big party spools up at 10:00 P.M. on Friday and Saturday with more music and dancing. On weeknights there's karaoke, more music, and the perennial favorite, wet T-shirt contests.

Subzero Microlounge
612 F Street
(907) 276–2337
www.subzeromicrolounge.com
This is another nonsmoking place to be in Anchorage, with a fun club atmosphere and a disco ball to top it off. No sense lamenting Alaska's wicked cold—Subzero celebrates the Arctic in style, including a stainless-steel bar with a river of ice running through it to keep your drinks nicely chilled. And if you like Belgian ales, this is definitely the place to be, with more than 100 Belgian brews to choose from, many of which are on tap. They open at 7:00 P.M. Wednesday through Saturday. If you're looking for food, check out the Saturday Night Tasting Menu, pairing a three-course meal with chef-selected beers.

Coffeehouses

Organic Oasis
2610 Spenard Road
(907) 277–7882
This is a fun little place with lots of plants, about 20 wooden tables, and artwork on the walls. Organic Oasis hosts live entertainment every night but Monday, including regular open-microphone and talent show fare. As the name implies, everything's organic here, right down to the beer and wine selections.

i When you're looking for weekend activities, don't forget the First Friday Art Walk. Grab a map from the free *Anchorage Press* or the Play section of the Friday edition of the *Anchorage Daily News* and head to the downtown galleries for a host of receptions and art shows. For more about First Fridays, see this chapter's The Arts section.

Snow City Cafe
Fourth Avenue and L Street
(907) 272-2489
www.snowcitycafe.com
In addition to being a great place to eat, the
Snow City Cafe hosts an Irish folk jam on
Wednesday night, and there's no cover
charge. See the full description in this chapter's Restaurants section.

Snow Goose Restaurant
717 West Third Avenue
(907) 277-7727
www.alaskabeers.com
What better place than this popular downtown brewery to host live entertainment on
Friday and Saturday nights? Enjoy a view of
the inlet, sample some great house brews,
and order from a full menu while listening to
local musicians. See the full write-up in this
chapter's Restaurants section.

SHOPPING

When you live in the Alaskan Bush, those
regions inaccessible by road, Anchorage
seems like a shoppers' paradise. Outsiders
will undoubtedly have a different take on the
Anchorage shopping scene. Anchorage
might not be a true shopping mecca, but
between the big franchise stores and the
eclectic shops that cater to both tourists and
residents you can find pretty much everything you need and a lot of what you want.
And Anchorage is small enough that you
don't have to think twice about driving
across town to that specialty store you love
so much.

Anchorage residents do most of their
shopping at the Dimond Center Mall on the
south side of town just off the Old Seward
Highway, the Northway Mall on the northeast
end of town just off the Glenn Highway, and
the Fifth Avenue Mall downtown. The Dimond
Center Mall has seen some lean times, but
with a flood of such big box stores as Borders
and the Sportsman's Warehouse popping up
nearby, the mall has experienced a lot more

activity in recent years. The Fifth Avenue Mall,
anchored by Nordstrom and JCPenney, is the
most upscale of the three big malls.

Some items that are uniquely Alaskan have
entire shops dedicated to them. Beads, gold,
ivory, furs—these are treasures for tourists and
visitors alike. We've given these Alaskan specialty shops their own category, but be sure to
check the listings under Boutiques/Gift Shops,
Specialty Food Shops, and Souvenir Shops for
other places to buy Alaskan gifts and souvenirs.

Alaskan Specialty Shops

Alaska Bead Company
2217 East Tudor Road, Suite 7
(907) 563-2323
If you'd like to try your hand at creating some
of the gorgeous handiwork that Alaska's Native
beaders produce, here's a great place to get
started. Alaska Bead has beading supplies,
tools, books, wire, and classes, along with all
sorts of beads. Check out their Japanese seed
beads, Austrian crystals, cabochons, Czech
seed beads, and, of course, their uniquely
Alaskan beads. The shop is located at the corner of Lake Otis Parkway and Tudor Road.

Alaska Fur Exchange
4417 Old Seward Highway
www.alaskafurexchange.com
This is Alaska's largest fur pelt dealer, and the
place also carries a huge collection of
museum-quality gifts, including masks, horn
carvings, dolls, ivory, whalebone, jade, soapstone, and other Native arts and crafts,
including fur products, of course. They've got
a free wildlife exhibit (think taxidermy), and

i Due to the Marine Mammals Act,
contemporary ivory and baleen
must be crafted into art of some type by
Alaskan Natives before it can be sold.
Scrimshaw and carving are two common
art forms for these marine mammal products, though sometimes the work is as
simple as the scratching of initials on a
piece of baleen.

they ship products anywhere. Located at the corner of the Old Seward Highway and Tudor Road, they're closed on Sunday during the winter.

Alaska Ivory Exchange
700 West Fourth Avenue
(907) 272–3662
www.alaskaivoryexchange.com

A favorite with tourists, Alaska Ivory Exchange showcases all sorts of collectible ivory pieces in a small but inviting retail venue. They have pieces carved from ancient mammoth ivory, some of it 10,000 years old. In addition, you'll find walrus ivory carvings, whalebone carvings, scrimshaw, and soapstone carvings. If you want to whet your appetite before visiting the store, check out their online virtual gallery.

Alaska Mint
429 West Fourth Avenue
(907) 278–8414
www.alaskamint.com

There's so much to see at this retail outlet that it's as much a local attraction as it is a store. On display are the largest gold scales in the state, Native artifacts, and gold-mining artifacts. You can also watch as the mint's craftspeople make medallions with unique Alaskan designs. The Alaska Mint is the official manufacturer of the state medallion and boasts of longtime relationships with some of Alaska's oldest sourdough miners. Holiday medallions, Alaskan medallions, natural nugget jewelry, gold quartz jewelry, coin jewelry, charms, and a whole lot more are all part of their extensive inventory.

i Those huge black crescents that you see on some walls, with feathery tufts along the bottom edge? That's baleen, from inside the mouth of a plankton-eating whale. Baleen hangs from the upper jaw of a whale's mouth, with the hairy tendrils used to filter krill. Before modern plastics were invented, baleen was used in women's corsets. It's also called whalebone.

i If you want a real Alaskan creation, look for the Made in Alaska label. Products with the polar bear label have been manufactured or crafted in Alaska, using materials from Alaska whenever possible. The Silver Hand label authenticates original handiwork by Native Alaskans, while the Alaska Grown emblem showcases raw materials, such as food, fur, and wool, that are produced in state.

Alaskan Ivory Outlet
319 West Fifth Avenue
(907) 274–7748

Managed by Alaskan Natives, Alaskan Ivory specializes in scrimshaw, jewelry, artifacts, carving, and repair of ivory. Among the pieces for sale are mastodon, mammoth, and fossilized walrus ivory. Especially striking are some of the carved antler pieces, old-time totems, and baleen. It's not a fancy shop, but they've got some nice ivory plus large collections of jade and amber pieces for sale.

David Green, Master Furrier
130 West Fourth Avenue
(907) 277–9595
www.davidgreenfurs.com

Furs aren't for everyone, but they're a mainstay of Alaskan retail, and if you want a coat, David Green has a great reputation around town. Lynx, mink, fox, and beaver are all represented here, with a total inventory of more than 3,000 pieces. The store is a combination factory and retail outlet. The original David Green started it all in 1922, and his grandson carries on the tradition today.

Fifth Avenue Jewelers
345 West Fifth Avenue
(907) 258–3635
www.productsofalaska.com

This family-owned business offers five-year warranties and guarantees of authenticity on its gold nugget and gold quartz jewelry, the latter being the rarest of natural gold products. You'll also find a large selection of and

There's a great gift shop filled with craft items made by Alaskan Natives at the Alaska Native Medical Center (907–563–2662).

good values on diamonds, Alaska mint coins, watch bands, and a variety of Alaskan-made products. In addition, Fifth Avenue Jewelers provides a full range of jewelry services. They're conveniently located across from the Fifth Avenue Mall.

Oomingmak
604 H Street
(907) 272–9225, (888) 360–9665
www.oomingmak.com

This Alaska Native–owned cooperative, in business since 1969, is a great place to get *qiviut* (pronounced ki-vee-ute), an extraordinarily soft fiber made from the underwool of the domestic musk ox. Knitters in more than 150 isolated villages throughout Alaska create signature designs on scarves, hats, tunics, stoles, and the popular "smoke-ring," a sort of pullover scarf. Qiviut products are not cheap, but the unique grayish-brown yarn is light as air and coveted by Alaskans for its style and warmth.

Ulu Factory
211 West Ship Creek Avenue
(907) 276–3119, (800) 488–5592
www.theulufactory.com

Originally made of naturally curved slate, the traditional Native knife known as the *ulu* (pronounced *oo-loo*) is now formed from steel, but it's still as functional as ever for skinning, filleting, and sewing. You might not get the hang of using this clever tool for cleaning and cutting fish, but you can take one home to chop nuts, slice meats, and do other kitchen tasks. At the Ulu Factory, you can watch the knives being made or catch one of the weekly Native performances in addition to shopping for your own personal ulu.

Antiques

Antique Gallery
1001 West Fourth Avenue, Suite B
(907) 276–8986

In one of those "only in Alaska" combinations, you'll find both fine art and rare firearms at this downtown shop. American and European oils, watercolors, bronzes, and prints meet up with the work of such famed Alaskan painters as Sydney Lawrence and Fred Machetanz. There are also Russian icons, Fabergé, estate jewelry, and Indian art and basketry—in short, a little of everything.

Pack Rat Mall
5911 Old Seward Highway
(907) 522–5272
www.packratmall.com

Enjoy a complimentary cup of coffee and browse 23,000 square feet of antiques, gifts, and collectibles between this location and the north-side shop at 1036 East Seventh Avenue. Among the goodies you'll find are Alaskana, Fenton Art Glass, Fiestaware, and Tiffany lamps. With more than 75 dealers and 1,850 consignors, you can count on doing a whole lot of shopping here.

Sandy's Fab Finds
430 C Street
(907) 333–4637

This little hideaway, tucked upstairs on a downtown side street, is jam-packed with fun vintage clothing and accessories. Costume jewelry, purses of all shapes and sizes, shoes, and hats can all be found here. Be sure to give yourself plenty of time to shop, because there are literally thousands of things to look at. Owner Sandy Gottstein, from one of Alaska's pioneering retail families, shares her enthusiastic love of all things fun and eclectic, and her black lab gives customers a warm welcome. The shop is closed on Monday.

Bookstores

A Novel View
415 L Street
(907) 278–0084
www.homestead.com/anovelview
Located in a 1922 original town-site home across from the well-loved Simon and Seafort's restaurant, this charming shop is packed with new, used, and out-of-print books. They offer trading credit for used books and sponsor occasional Interactive Novel Dinners. Their Saturdays at 2 events showcase the talents of local performers. They also host First Friday art receptions. A Novel View is closed on Sunday during the winter.

Cook Inlet Book Company
415 West Fifth Avenue
(907) 258–4544, (800) 240–4148
www.cookinlet.com
This is Alaska's most well-established and revered independent bookstore. Owners Ron and Lynn Dixon, with more than 60 years of combined experience selling books in the far north, are passionate in their commitment to authors, readers, and Alaska. They have the largest collection of Alaskan books around, plus all of the usual bookstore fare. You'll find titles here that you can't find anywhere else, and their helpful staff will make you feel right at home. Cook Inlet Book Company is conveniently located downtown across from the Fifth Avenue Mall.

Title Wave Books
1360 West Northern Lights Boulevard
(907) 278–9283, (888) 598–9283
www.wavebooks.com
Book lovers won't want to miss Alaska's largest bookstore, with more than 33,000 square feet packed with more than a quarter of a million books. Despite its size, Title Wave is a friendly, relaxed place, and the staff is always at the ready to assist you in finding what you want. They offer a huge selection of used books and a great exchange program. They carry a wide range of Alaskan titles along with large print and audio books. With a great midtown location not far from Barnes & Noble, Title Wave hosts author events and musical performances, too.

Boutiques/Gift Shops

Alaska Glass Gallery
423 G Street
(907) 279–4527
www.alaskaglassgallery.com
Fluid lines and translucent colors abound in this shop's collection of handblown and sculptured glass art. Gallery director Cynthia England has been working glass since 1980 and has studied with some of the best glass artists in the world. Browse this downtown shop to find a unique gift for that special someone, or something special for yourself.

Anchorage Museum Shop
121 West Seventh Avenue
(907) 343–6163
www.anchoragemuseum.org
This attractive shop is one of the best places in the state to get Native art, because they

Native Arts

The Alaska Museum of Natural History offers pointers on selecting authentic Native arts and crafts. One is to check for quality work. Baskets should have a tight weave and symmetrical shape, while stitching on beadwork and skin products should be neat and regular. Check for authenticity by asking the artist's name and location as well as finding out about the raw materials used. In particular, the use of eagle and duck feathers is not in compliance with the Migratory Bird Act. Buy what you love, and make special note of traditions or innovations that reflect the cultural heritage of the artist.

guarantee its authenticity. They also carry fine jewelry by Alaskan craftspeople, distinctive apparel with the crests of North Coast cultures, and books about our state and its history. Besides picking up some quality merchandise, you'll have the added feel-good of knowing that you've supported the museum's exhibits and programs.

Cabin Fever
650 West Fourth Avenue
(907) 278–3522

Like its sister shop The Raven, Cabin Fever is one of the most tasteful Alaskan gift shops in town. They offer everything from traditional Native dolls and baskets to fun jewelry, hand-blown glass, ivory ulus, scrimshaw knives, and Alaskan books, all artfully displayed in a way that makes shopping a pleasure. Look for the purple banners at the corner of Fourth Avenue and G Street.

Celtic Treasures
4240 Old Seward Highway, Suite 2
(907) 333–2358

Take a trip back in time and to another land at Celtic Treasures while enjoying their charming atmosphere and friendly service. A cup of tea is always offered while you browse the unique imports from Ireland, Scotland, and Wales, displayed creatively for your shopping pleasure. The shop offers the state's largest variety of Celtic jewelry and gifts.

Downtown Co-op
320 West Fifth Avenue
(907) 277–5620

Owned and operated by a cooperative of local craftspeople, the Downtown Co-op has a large selection of arts, crafts, and collectibles. Whether you're looking for country or Victorian, stained glass or sweatshirts, rubber stamps or ornaments, there's a good chance you'll find a hand-crafted item to take home. The Downtown Co-op is on the first floor of the Fifth Avenue Mall, near the Sixth Avenue entrance.

The Raven
415 G Street
(907) 278–3522

What better place than Alaska to celebrate Christmas all year long? As whimsical as the legendary raven itself, this shop is filled with handmade Alaskan ornaments plus holiday creations from around the world. Get in the holiday spirit and shop ahead for gift baskets and other yuletide fare.

Style of Russia
333 West Fourth Avenue
(907) 276–5906
www.styleofrussia.com

The Russian influence in Alaska runs deep, and this little shop shows off some of the best of our sister country's art and giftware. Whether you're drawn to Lomonosov porcelain, Siberian shawls, hand-etched crystal eggs, miniature lacquers, Siberian birch bark crafts, Russian Baltic amber, or traditional Russian nesting dolls, they'll not only have something to show you but will also give you a card explaining the item's history, significance, and artistic highlights. If you work up an appetite while shopping, you can sample some authentic Russian cuisine at the adjacent Touch of Russia Cafe (see the full write-up in this chapter's Restaurants section). Style of Russia is closed on Sunday in the winter.

Tuliqi
410 G Street
(907) 272–4070
www.tuliqi.com

Tuliqi (pronounced *tooly-key*) is a bed and bath boutique with a focus on organics. This is a great place to shop for earth-friendly linens, sleepwear, and skin-care products. Beauty, wilderness, and home come together in a peaceful, spa-like setting.

Outfitters/Sports Shops

6th Avenue Outfitters
520 West Sixth Avenue
(907) 276–0233, (800) 276–0233
www.6thavenueoutfitters.com

For a small-time, general store approach to outfitting, 6th Avenue is the place to go. They have fishing tackle, arctic wear, rain gear, snowshoes, hip boots, camping gear, rods and reels, and outdoor gear.

Army/Navy Store
320 West Fourth Avenue
(888) 836–3535
www.army-navy-store.com

Since 1947, Alaskans have looked to the Army/Navy Store as a great source for government surplus and all types of outdoor gear. They offer a huge selection of Carhartts and Columbia sportswear along with a whole lot of other work wear and boots. Fishing licenses, gloves, rain gear, parkas—you name it, and Army/Navy probably has it. Located right downtown on the corner of Fourth Avenue and C Street, they also do in-house embroidery, if you're into that sort of thing. BP Exploration, Conoco Phillips, and Alyeska Pipeline Service Company all send their employees here for gear.

Mountain View Sports Center
3838 Old Seward Highway
(907) 563–8600

Fishing, camping, hunting, clothing—these are what Mountain View Sports Center is all

---

i Don't miss Alaska's largest outdoor market, the Downtown Saturday Market, held on summer weekends at the corner of Third Avenue and E Street. Look for the white tents housing more than 300 vendors, who offer everything from fresh seafood to Alaskan-grown produce to arts, crafts, and collectibles. There's also nonstop, live entertainment featuring local acts and groups from across the country, and great food to eat there or take home. Saturday and Sunday markets are open from 10:00 A.M. to 6:00 P.M., with an abbreviated Wednesday market from 11:00 A.M. to 5:00 P.M. at the Northway Mall.

---

about. They have a long-standing reputation as Alaskan outfitters. Anglers appreciate the large collection of fly rods and reels, fly-tying materials, and casting and spinning gear. You'll also find a large selection of knives, guns, and ammunition. Pick up a cup of free coffee and browse. You can get licenses and tags for hunting and fishing here, too.

Skinny Raven Sports
800 H Street
(907) 274–7222
www.skinnyraven.com

Specializing in running and casual shoes, the Skinny Raven offers such brands as Ibex, Kenneth Cole, Nike, and Patagonia. Try on a new pair of shoes and hop on the Gait Analysis Machine for a computerized opinion on how they're working for you. With the help of this technology, the Skinny Raven's friendly staff will compute the angle of impact and offer advice on how to improve your running gait. Across the street, the Skinny Raven's sister store, Her Tern, specializes in fine women's shoes and accessories.

Souvenir Shops

All Alaskan Arts and Gifts
427 West Fifth Avenue
www.alaskaonlygifts.com

You'll find no imports here—this unique shop sells only items made by Alaskans, in Alaska. They feature Native arts, carvings, dolls, soapstone, whalebone, baskets, wind chimes, jewelry, clothing, and food products. Among the special items are Yup'ik dance fans made with coiled grasses and trimmed with fox fur and beads as well as handmade soapstone carvings with inlaid ivory.

Once in a Blue Moose
547 West Fourth Avenue
(907) 276–2141, (888) 490–1898
www.onceinabluemoose.com

Besides the fun name, this sprawling gift shop carries just about everything you could want when it comes to souvenirs. T-shirts, sweatshirts, jackets, hats, gloves, books, videos, dolls, housewares, ulus, and gourmet food are all part of the big selection here. Free gifts are offered for purchases above $30 and $100, and there's free gift wrapping, too. They have a second location at the Fifth Avenue Mall, and the same owners operate several Remember Alaska gift shops.

Polar Bear Gifts
442 West Fifth Avenue
(907) 274–4387
There's a lot of fun kitsch here, right down to the player piano plunking away in the background. Everything's advertised at $9.99 or less, so if your pack of distant cousins are clamoring for Alaskan souvenirs, this would be the place to go. It's a huge shop with plenty of opportunities for browsing.

Trapper Jack's Trading Post
701 West Fifth Avenue
(907) 272–6110, (866) 272–6110
www.trapperjackstradingpost.com
With more than 7,000 feet devoted to souvenirs and gifts, Trapper Jack's has the potential to be your one-stop-shop for Alaskan stuff. It's a fun place with a lodge-style interior befitting the woodsy Alaskan items they sell. Don't miss the photo opportunities with the big stuffed moose and bear. Shop here for jewelry, jade, ulus, Native crafts, apparel, Russian gifts, soapstone, ivory, gold, totems, videos, hats, mugs, throws, and plush animals. There's a large kids' department, and they have all sorts of collectibles, including the popular Snowbabies and wildlife carvings by Big Sky Carvers. If you find you've over-shopped, ask about their shipping services.

Specialty Food Shops

Alaska Max Gourmet
737 West Fifth Avenue
(907) 274–0238
Featuring gourmet foods of all types with a good selection of Alaskan specialties, Alaska Max is a great place to treat yourself and your friends. Birch syrup, truffle oil, hot sauce, smoked salmon, chocolates, honey, and salsa

i Like to pick your own produce? Head north from Anchorage to Pyrah's Pioneer Peak U-Pick Vegetable Farm on Bodenburg Loop Road in the Matanuska-Susitna Valley, where you'll find prices that are about half of what you'd pay at the grocery store. Pyrah's is closed on Sunday. For more information, call (907) 745–4511. There are also several you-pick strawberry farms in the Mat-Su Valley.

are among the goodies you'll find here. The Made-in-Alaska baskets stocked with treats make great gifts. This is the perfect place to browse while you're waiting for a table at the nearby Glacier Brewhouse restaurant.

Alaska Sausage and Seafood
2914 Arctic Boulevard
(907) 562–3636, (800) 798–3636
www.alaskasausage.com
Since 1963, Alaska Sausage and Seafood has been making gourmet treats out of local fish and game. Bring in your own catch to be processed, or sample some of their pre-packaged fare. Salmon can be kipper smoked, smoked in strips, or cured into lox. They'll also cut, fillet, and vacuum pack fresh fish. Reindeer meat products are another specialty.

Alaska Wild Berry Products
5225 Juneau Street
(907) 561–9498
www.alaskawildberryproducts.com
This massive candy company and retail outlet is a favorite with tourists, and it's easy to see why. Who could resist the world's largest chocolate falls, the chance to see candies, jams, and jellies being made, or the yummy free samples of chocolates and truffles? Take a free kitchen tour and leave yourself plenty of time to shop, because they offer just about every Alaskan souvenir you can imagine. For added tourist fun, there's a Wild Berry Park and Village, complete with Holly the Reindeer.

Lasting Impressions

Birch, forget-me-not, yarrow, black currant, wild chive, rose hips, and chickweed. To Janet Shafsky, these are not just wild Alaskan plants, they're the foundation of a unique line of skin-care products and cosmetics made in Anchorage and distributed throughout the world.

It would be hard to find a more committed and energetic entrepreneur than the founder of Impressions by Janet. When she first moved to Alaska from Southern California in 1979, Shafsky says she cried all the way here. Formerly a makeup artist for Hollywood celebrities, she found herself in a place where she couldn't even get television newscasters interested in professional makeup services because they had no budget for it. Her friends placed bets on how quickly she'd move back, but she drew on her Alaskan heritage—her mother was born here and her grandfather was a territorial judge—and settled happily into a homestead off O'Malley Road in Anchorage. "It's a pretty awesome place to live," Shafsky says now. "The attraction of the people really did it for me."

As hard as she works at fine-tuning her products, people are still Janet's top priority. In fact, it was meeting the special needs of her clients and friends that got her to start using natural botanicals to counter the effects of the harsh Alaskan climate. The previous owner of their property, a master gardener who served on the Board of Directors for the University of Alaska Cooperative Extension program, had planted wildflowers and herbs across the homestead. Shafsky, a certified skin-care specialist, studied the medicinal properties of the plants growing in her own back yard and began incorporating them into the products she used while giving facials. Her customers kept bringing back empty jars and asking for more, prompting Shafsky to start her own line of cosmetics and skin-care products using Alaskan ingredients.

"You think of Alaska, and Alaska is pure. It's the most natural place left on earth," Shafsky says. "We boil a lot of extracts, and we tap our trees. It's a lot of hard work." Now that the homestead has been subdivided, the company also acquires ingredients from suppliers around the state, always with an eye to quality and purity.

Shafsky tinkers with her products until she gets them right. She went back and forth with Iditarod veteran DeeDee Jonrowe for six months in order to perfect her Ididacreme, designed to protect skin from extreme conditions like those on the Iditarod Sled Dog Race. "It acts like a little glove," Shafsky says of the creme, which has proven very helpful and soothing to clients with extra-dry skin and eczema. Given the severe lack of humidity in Alaska as well as in much of the Lower 48, Ididacreme is one of Shafsky's most popular products, along with Sleeping Lady Night Creme, Aurora Orange Cleansing Sensation, Gold Rush Toner, and the Forget-Me-Not Daily Exfoliator.

A distribution stint with a big-name box store robbed Shafsky of the satisfaction she gets from customer contact, so she has returned to distributing her products through boutique shops and over the Internet. "Customer service is the most important thing in the world to me," she says. "I love working with the Internet so I can still have the customer connection." How many other cosmetic manufacturers have photos of their customers on the walls of their shop or send personal thank-yous with each purchase they ship?

Birch trees are one of the natural botanical sources used in Impressions by Janet cosmetic and skin care products. DEB VANASSE

Even as she provides products to more than 5,000 customers, Shafsky achieves a sense of balance in her life. Perhaps it's due to the tranquil setting in which she works. The lower level of her 4,800-square-foot log home is replete with rock walls, candles, and waterfalls, making it a soothing place for her to give facials and do makeovers. Shafsky claims giving facials is almost as relaxing for her as it is for her clients. "A lot of times, that's when I think of new ideas," she says. More proof of the balance in this entrepreneur's life is that she has never let her business override her commitment to her family. Her husband, with a degree in biology and field chemistry, has been an invaluable resource in product devel-

(cont'd)

(cont'd)
opment, and her three daughters have grown up testing and modeling her cosmetics.

In Anchorage, you can find Impressions by Janet skin-care products and cosmetics at Bagoy's Home Store across from the Sears Mall on Benson Boulevard, or at Laura's Body and Soul in the Dimond Center Mall, or by appointment only at First and Lasting Impressions, Inc. (907–522–4506). You can also order products online at www.impressionsbyjanet .com, or by calling toll-free (888) 522–4507.

Kobuk Coffee and Tea Company
504 West Fifth Avenue
(907) 272–3626
www.kobukcoffee.com
Kobuk Coffee retains the 1915 charm of the original Kimball Dry Goods Store, with old-fashioned candy on display in glass jars and the smell of their spicy Samovar tea greeting shoppers as they come through the door. Sample a cup of tea while browsing the gift and coffee selections. The living quarters in the back of the store have been converted into a bakery with all sorts of treats to eat in or take out.

Women's and Children's Clothing

Blush
720 D Street
(907) 677–8967
www.boutiqueblush.com
Celebrating the individual, this new boutique offers hand-picked contemporary collections from New York and Los Angeles. They carry BCBG, Free People, Hudson, Trovata, Burning Torch, LaMade, Velvet, Puella, True Religion, and Meli Melo brands. Bringing chic urban style to Alaska, Blush is open Monday through Saturday, with shortened hours on Sunday.

Pia's Scandanavian Woolens
445 West Fourth Avenue
(907) 277–7964, (888) 274–9665
www.piasweaters.com
High-quality Nordic sweaters are the perfect apparel for Alaska's long cold winters, and Pia's is the place to get them. In this tasteful boutique, you'll find cardigans and sweaters for men and women, Icelandic jackets, children's woolens, lambskin slippers, and bulky-but-oh-so-warm-and-comfy Loebben boots. Nothing's cheap here, but it's all warm and colorful.

Rosita's Boutique
939 West Fifth Avenue, Suite Q
(907) 274–7143
Tucked among the shops in the Hotel Captain Cook, Rosita's is a stand-out boutique with a fabulous assortment of women's clothing and accessories. Artful without being trendy, you can count on finding something unique and well-cut for all sorts of occasions, from unique European fashions to wearable art accessories. And a thank-you note from your sales clerk? That's just another reason to feel pleased with your purchase. Ask about their discounts for Alaskan residents—they really mean it.

Spoiled
610 C Street, Suite 4A
(907) 743–3095
www.spoiledboutique.com
A sister store to Blush, Spoiled specializes in luxuries for little ones, with beautiful children's clothing from newborn to size 18. They also carry imported nursery furniture, BumbleRide strollers, Dwell bedding, and unique baby gifts. Moms are pampered here as well, with beautiful maternity clothes you won't want to part with.

ATTRACTIONS

A number of Anchorage attractions celebrate the rich cultural diversity, the colorful history, and the abundant wildlife of Alaska. As an added bonus, most admission charges are minimal, and you're guaranteed to walk away knowing a lot more about the 49th state than you knew going in.

Many attractions operate on abbreviated schedules or are closed completely in the winter, so be sure to pay attention to notes about winter hours in the listings below. The price codes show what you can expect to pay for one adult admission. Most places offer discounts for children and seniors, and some offer military discounts as well. Attractions with free admission will have no price code.

Price Codes

$. . . . . Less than $5.00
$$ . . . . $5.00–$10.00
$$$ . . . . $11.00–$15.00
$$$$ . . . . More than $15.00

Alaska Aviation Heritage Museum $$
4721 Aircraft Drive
(907) 248–5325
http://home.gci.net/~aahm
Alaska has always been on the cutting edge of what's happening in aviation, so it's not surprising that we have an entire museum devoted to aviation history. At the museum you'll see 25 rare bush planes plus photographs and memorabilia from some of the state's legendary bush pilots. You'll also get to see aircraft in the process of being restored. There's a theater where you can watch pioneer film footage and an observation deck where you can watch seaplanes taking off from and landing on Lake Hood. This is a great place to get a better appreciation for the incredible courage and pluck that put Alaskan bush pilots in a class by themselves. The Alaska Aviation Heritage Museum is just a short drive from the Ted Stevens International Airport, and shuttle service is available. The museum is closed on Monday and Tuesday during the winter.

Alaska Botanical Garden $$
P.O. Box 202202, Anchorage, AK 99520
(907) 770–3692
www.alaskabg.org
Alaskan summers are short by some standards, but our extensive daylight makes the growing season intense. The Alaska Botanical Garden is a great place to check out the beauty and diversity of the hardy plants, shrubs, herbs, and wildflowers that flourish here in spite of the long, cold winters and the rather rushed summers. Nestled among the spruce and birch in this 110-acre sanctuary, you'll find more than 1,100 species of perennials and 150 native plants. Hike the self-guided, 1.1 mile Lowenfels Family Nature Trail down to Campbell Creek, where you may be treated to a glimpse of the king salmon run. The Alaska Botanical Garden hosts many special events throughout the summer, and they offer free parking. The gardens are open from May 15 to September 15, with guided tours available for a nominal charge on Wednesday and Saturday.

Alaska Experience Center $$
705 West Sixth Avenue
(907) 276–3730, (877) 276–3730
www.alaskaexperiencetheatre.com
It's pretty much impossible to see all of this great state, but the Alaska Experience Center captures the highlights with two virtual film experiences. Enjoy planetarium seating as you watch *Alaska the Greatland* on a three-story-high, 180-degree screen. Digital surround sound, breathtaking photography, and the domed screen create an illusion of reality, transporting you to places you'd love to go if only you had the time and the resources. After your 40-minute tour of the greatland, you can go back in time and relive Alaska's famous 1964 earthquake, which registered 9.2 on the Richter scale. Your seat will shake and tremble during the film, simulating the earthquake experience. Giant wall murals along with science, history, and photo exhibits enhance your understanding of what happened on that fateful day.

Alaska's Native Cultures

Alaska's Native peoples enjoy a cultural diversity unmatched by any other state, with each group well-adapted to its own unique ecological and geographical landscapes. Eskimo groups include the Inupiaq in the north and the Yup'ik/Cup'ik cultures in Southwestern Alaska. Athabascan Indians traditionally inhabited the interior regions of the state, while the Alutiq are native to the Aleutian Islands. The Evak, Haida, Tlingit, and Tsimshian are peoples of the southeastern coastal region. Unlike American Indians, Alaska's Native peoples do not live on reservations. Under provisions of the Alaska Native Claims Settlement Act, they own land and are shareholders in 1 of 13 Native corporations.

Alaska Museum of Natural History $$
201 North Bragaw Street
(907) 274–2400
www.alaskamuseum.org
Two University of Alaska professors with a commitment to science education spearheaded an organizational effort that started in 1989 and culminated with the opening of this educational facility in 1994. In recent years the fledgling museum has acquired a 12,000-square-foot building to house exhibits featuring the geological, ecological, and cultural history of Alaska. The annual tally of 4,000 visitors is a drop in the bucket compared to what the larger, plusher Anchorage Museum takes in, but if you don't need a lot of fancy bells and whistles to pique your interest, you'll learn about Alaska's wildlife, rocks, minerals, dinosaurs, and artifacts here. The museum is closed Sunday through Tuesday during the winter.

Alaska Native Heritage Center $$
8800 Heritage Center Drive
(907) 330–8000, (800) 315–6608
www.alaskanative.net
Alaska is so big that it's almost impossible to see it all. Visitors rarely get to the more remote parts of the state where Alaska Native peoples live a more traditional lifestyle. In order to promote and share these traditions, the Alaska Federation of Natives established this nonprofit center in 1989. Spread across 26 acres, the center includes a Welcome House facility plus five traditional outdoor village sites surrounding Lake Tiulana. The center hosts demonstrations by artists and dance groups, films and exhibits, story-telling, classes in art, dance, and Alaska Native languages, and self-guided tours of the outdoor villages.

At the Welcome House, you'll find a timeline of significant historical and legendary events, as well as video monitors showing clips of contemporary Native life. An 18-minute film, *Stories Given, Stories Shared,* introduces the diverse cultures of the Alaska Native people and the unique places where they live. In the Hall of Cultures, you'll find exhibits and demonstrations featuring Athabascan, Yup'ik, Cup'ik, Inupiaq, Alutiq, Tlingit, Evak, Haida, and Tsimshian cultures and lifestyles. At the Gathering Place, you can watch traditional dancers or listen to stories that have been passed from one generation to the next.

The center hosts an Institute of Alaska Native Artists, youth programs, school visits, and adult education classes and workshops, with class schedules changing every four weeks. Two Heritage Gift Stores, one in the Welcome House and one downtown at 333 West Fourth Avenue, support the ongoing work of the center. During the winter the center is open on Saturday only, featuring special Celebrating Culture Saturday programs.

Alaska Public Lands Information Center
605 West Fourth Avenue
(907) 271–2737
www.nps.gov/aplic
The Public Lands Information Center is a great

place to orient yourself to the state and to plan your Alaskan adventures. They offer free natural history and cultural exhibits along with information on wildlife, camping, and recreational cabins on federal land. In the summer you can participate in a free special event almost every hour, whether it's a movie about the big earthquake or Alaskan wildlife, a Captain Cook Walking Tour, or a live animal program. You'll find the Public Lands Information Center downtown at the corner of Fourth Avenue and F Street, across from the Hilton Hotel.

Alaska State Trooper Museum
P.O. Box 100280, Anchorage, AK 99510
www.alaska.net/~foast
In a place known as the Last Frontier, you'd expect some hefty law enforcement challenges, and Alaska doesn't disappoint. At the Alaska State Trooper Museum, you'll get a free glimpse into the colorful history and excitement that are part of laying down the law in one of the most far-flung jurisdictions in the country. Exhibits include photographs, memorabilia, and historic police equipment, including a restored 1952 Hudson patrol vehicle. Located downtown off Fifth Avenue between B and C Streets, the State Trooper Museum includes a gift shop, with proceeds going to fund the activities of the Fraternal Order of Alaska State Troopers.

The Alaska Zoo $$
4731 O'Malley Road
(907) 346–3242
www.alaskazoo.org
Most newcomers to Alaska are anxious to see some of our wildlife, and even the most seasoned sourdoughs thrill at the sight of a grizzly, a moose, or an elusive lynx. But even though the wildlife is abundant, Alaska's huge wilderness areas provide plenty of room for animals to roam, so you may not see as many critters as you'd hoped. At the Alaska Zoo, there's guaranteed wildlife viewing that attracts both locals and visitors. The zoo is only 15 minutes from downtown Anchorage, and seasonal shuttle service is available.

Founded in 1968, the Alaska Zoo is a private nonprofit that houses arctic and subarctic wildlife for the joint purposes of education and enjoyment. Among the zoo favorites are Apuhn the polar bear and Maggie the elephant. Maggie, of course, is not native to the arctic, but she was rescued from Africa and enjoys a heated enclosure in her northern home. Among the zoo's summer programs are Tuesday family nights and Summer Naturalist Tours. The zoo has a gift shop, coffee shop, and education center, and it's open year-round.

Alyeska Tramway $$$$
Alyeska Resort
P.O. Box 249, Girdwood, AK 99587
(907) 754–2275

Aurora Borealis

What causes the aurora borealis, or northern lights? Solar winds from eruptions on the sun are drawn into the earth's magnetic field, where they show up as haunting, dancing fingers of green, red, and purple light. Legends about the northern lights abound. Some Alaskan Native children are taught to whistle when they see the lights so they won't be snatched into the sky, while in some Asian cultures it's believed that a child conceived under the northern lights will be especially gifted. The *Anchorage Daily News* includes daily aurora forecasts, and many hotels provide aurora wake-up calls for those who want them. You'll see the lights best on dark, clear nights, away from the light pollution of the city. When there's a stunning display, you'll see drivers pulling over left and right to watch.

At the Alaska Public Lands Center, located in the Federal Building in downtown Anchorage, you can learn about Alaska's national parks and other public lands. DEB VANASSE

The Alyeska Tramway whisks you from 306 feet above sea level to 2,334 feet above sea level in a matter of minutes. You'll have a spectacular view of mountains, glaciers, and streams en route, and when you reach the observation deck, you can hike, explore, pick berries, or even try some paragliding. The Swiss-built tram runs slower in the summer so you can soak up the view, and there are telescopes up top if you want to get a closer look. To catch the tram, head for the Alyeska Ski Resort in Girdwood, about 40 miles south of Anchorage.

Anchorage Museum of History and Art $$
121 West Seventh Avenue
(907) 343–4326
www.anchoragemuseum.org

It's the largest museum in Alaska, it's one of the 10 most visited attractions in the state, and it hosts more than 150,000 guests each year. And that's just as it sits now. After a major expansion project slated for completion in early 2010, the Anchorage Museum will add 70,000 square feet to its current 93,000 square feet of interior space, including a fourth-floor library and an Arctic Studies Center. The expansion also includes development of a two-acre urban forest, complete with a promenade, tidal pool, outdoor pavilion, and skating rink.

Making the museum bigger means more of what's already a very good thing for Anchorage. The Alaska Gallery, exploring 10,000 years of Alaskan history, is a great place to orient yourself to the state. There you'll see Alaskan Native artifacts, life-size renditions of pioneer and Native dwellings, and a slice of the Alaska Pipeline. The six galleries in the Art of the North section display sculpture and paintings from the days of early exploration through modern times, while three additional galleries house special exhibits on art, archaeology, and his-

One of the most visited attractions in the state, the Anchorage Museum contains exhibits on Alaskan history and art as well as hosting workshops, films, and other community events. DEB VANASSE

tory. There's also a Children's Gallery and adjacent Art Activity Room for hands-on family activities.

If all this exploring makes you hungry, don't despair. Anchorage's well-loved Marx Bros. Café operates a museum cafe that serves up dishes that rival museum food from anywhere in the world. On top of that, the museum's gift shop has one of the best collections of authentic Alaska Native art you'll find; see the complete listing on the gift shop in this chapter's Shopping section. In addition, the museum maintains a full slate of activities, including Historical Society lectures, First Friday jazz, crafts weekends, book signings, workshops, and weekend Movies for Your Mind, which feature classic and contemporary global cinema.

The parking garage is open for handicap parking during the week and for public parking on weekends. During the winter the museum is closed on Monday and Tuesday.

Aurora: Alaska's Great Northern Lights $$
Sydney Laurence Theatre
Alaska Center for the Performing Arts
Sixth Avenue and F Street
(907) 263–2993
www.thealaskacollection.com
When do they turn on the northern lights? Not in the summer, when almost endless daylight prevents us from seeing any heavenly attractions. But summer visitors can watch stunning digital images of this incredible phenomenon in the Sydney Laurence Theatre at the Alaska Center for the Performing Arts. Anchorage photographer Dave Parkhurst has been chasing and photographing rare auroral displays since 1981. You'll get to sit back and enjoy the fruits of his cold, midnight labors in comfort, complete with a background of original digital music. Shows run about 40 minutes, with 13 performances daily. Reservations are not required. This attraction is open only in the summer, so if you're here in the off-

season, you'll have to try your luck at seeing the real thing. If you'd like some help planning your aurora expeditions, the folks at the Alaska Collection offer winter Aurora Watch tours; for more information, check out the Web address above.

Crow Creek Mine $$
P.O. Box 113, Girdwood, AK 99587
(907) 278–8060
www.akmining.com/mine/crow.htm

Just a few miles past Alyeska Resort, Crow Creek Mine is a great place to try finding your own gold nugget to take home. Over the years the mine has produced more than 45,000 ounces of gold, and there's an estimated one million yards left to be tried. First-timers are given a bag of gold-bearing dirt from the creek to help them get started. Even if you don't get lucky, you'll enjoy the wilderness setting. Crow Creek Mine is on the Register of National Historic Places, with old mining buildings and artifacts scattered throughout. This area can be damper than Anchorage, so be sure to bring rain gear. There's no food for sale on-site, so you'll want to bring your own. You can camp overnight for a fee.

Eagle River Nature Center $
32750 Eagle River Road, Eagle River
(907) 694–2108
www.ernc.org

In response to drastic cuts in the budget for Chugach State Park, park administrators linked avid nature lovers with corporate sponsors to create a gateway destination. Open year-round, the center provides great opportunities for wildlife viewing along with weekly interpretive programs and daily guided walks in the summer. If you want to spend the night, an easy 2-mile hike will take you to one of the center's yurts or cabins. The center maintains several trails and operates a gift shop. To get there, take the Eagle River Loop Road exit off the Glenn Highway, turn right at the third light, and continue 12 miles to the road's end, where you'll find the facility. No admission is charged, but there is a parking fee.

Heritage Library Museum
301 West Northern Lights Boulevard
(907) 265–2834

For a museum experience with no admission charge, you can't beat the Heritage Library Museum, located on the first floor of the Wells Fargo Bank Building at the corner of C Street and Northern Lights Boulevard. Established in 1968, this is one of the largest privately owned displays of Alaskan culture and history that you'll find anywhere. The collection of Alaskan Native artifacts includes baskets, ivory carvings, household utensils, clothing, and hunting implements. The fine arts collection includes impressive landscapes by well-known Alaska painters Sydney Laurence, Eustace Ziegler, Magnus Heurlin, and James Belcher. The museum also maintains a 2,600-volume reference library on Alaska, along with photo archives featuring pictures from the gold rush era and beyond. The museum is open on weekday afternoons only. There is no admission charge, and parking is free.

Hullabaloo $$$
Fourth Avenue Theatre
630 West Fourth Avenue
(907) 257–5678

Alice Welling and Tim Tucker prove that history can be fun in this rollicking musical comedy that, unlike some of its competitors, is good family fare. The historic Fourth Avenue Theatre makes a great backdrop for the show. Hullabaloo opens nightly at 7:00 P.M. There are some nights with no shows, so be sure to phone ahead before you make your plans.

i If a little tourist mining whets your appetite for more serious stuff, check with Steve Herschbach, owner of Alaska Mining and Diving Supply (907–277–1741). He registered the first recreational mining business with the Alaska Department of Natural Resources in order to take groups to his claims at Moore Creek. The trip isn't cheap, but some takers have walked away with gold nuggets worth more than $2,000.

The Fourth Avenue Theatre in downtown Anchorage dates from 1947. DEB VANASSE

Indian Valley Mine $
Mile 104 Seward Highway, Indian
(907) 653–1120
www.indianvalleymine.com
Though the address is out of town, this family-run mining attraction is only about 20 minutes south of Anchorage. For a nominal admission charge, you'll get to see two of the oldest structures on Turnagain Arm and browse a small museum. If you want to buy a bucket of pay dirt, you can learn to pan for gold and find out about other places to try your luck. While you're here, the Cowles family will tell you the story of Peter Strong, the original prospector who did some small-time mining and built the assay office here. Even if you're not into gold, you can relax at the picnic tables, enjoy the gardens, and take in some fabulous views of Turnagain Arm. This isn't a big, showy attraction, but sometimes it's a relief to go where you don't have to fight your way past busloads of tourists to try something new. The mine is open only during the summer.

Native Village of Eklutna $$
26339 Eklutna Village Road, Chugiak
(907) 688–6020
Get a small taste of a traditional Native Alaskan village by driving just a half hour north of downtown, taking the Eklutna exit at Mile 26.5 of the Glenn Highway. This tiny Athabascan Village, inhabited for more than 800 years and now tucked into the Municipality of Anchorage, includes a Russian Orthodox church, Spirit Houses in the adjacent cemetery, a handful of homes, and a gift shop. The village may be accessed only by participating in a two-hour cultural tour. One tour highlights the traditional use of local animals and plants, while the other emphasizes village history and the subsistence lifestyle. Tours include some hiking, so dress accordingly. No wheelchair facilities are available.

The Oscar Anderson House Museum $
420 M Street
(907) 274–2336

i Catch a glimpse of local history at Historic City Hall at the corner of Fourth Avenue and E Street, where there's a free exhibit on Anchorage's pioneer days on the main floor. Or check out the Fourth Avenue Theatre, an art deco–style building dating from 1947. At the Ship Creek Center downtown, you might be lucky enough to catch one of two free daily summer performances of Alaska Native dancing.

Back in 1915 when Anchorage was still a tent city, Swedish immigrant Oscar Anderson built the first frame house. Restored with period detail and many of the original fixtures, this is now the only house museum in town. Guided tours take approximately 45 minutes. You also can opt for a combined ticket that includes a 2-mile walking tour of historic downtown Anchorage with a volunteer guide. The museum is open afternoons in the summer only, and it is closed on Sunday and Monday. For the first two weekends in December, the house re-opens for Swedish Christmas Tours.

KIDSTUFF

Kids, like their parents, will have a lot of fun getting outside and enjoying all the outdoor recreation opportunities in Anchorage. But there's lots of indoor fun to be had as well. From science explorations to rollicking water-slides, kids in Anchorage will find plenty to do even on those cold winter days that don't lend themselves well to the great outdoors.

Be sure to check the listings under this chapter's Parks, Recreation, and Tours section for additional kid-friendly adventures, but keep in mind that Alaska is more wild and rugged than what some folks are used to. If you're biking, hiking, or skiing with kids, be extra-sure to prepare for the unexpected, whether it might be a change in weather, a lack of facilities, or rougher trail conditions than anticipated. If you're participating in an organized activity such as river rafting or

horseback riding, ask about suitability for young adventurers.

Some of these kid-friendly spots are also discussed in this chapter's Attractions section. Many of them operate on an abbreviated schedule or are closed completely in the winter, so be sure to pay attention to notes about winter hours. The price codes show what you can expect to pay for one adult admission. Those geared to both adults and children tend to offer reduced admission for kids. Attractions with free admission will have no price code.

Price Codes

$	Less than $5.00
$$	$5.00–$10.00
$$$	$11.00–$15.00
$$$$	More than $15.00

Alaska Botanical Garden $$
P.O. Box 202202, Anchorage, AK 99520
(907) 770–3692
www.alaskabg.org
The self-guided, 1.1-mile Lowenfels Family Nature Trail down to Campbell Creek makes a great family outing. The reward at the end of the trail, in season, is the salmon run. On Wednesdays during the summer, there's a free story time for kids at the garden. The garden is open from May 15 through September 15, with guided tours available for a nominal charge on Wednesday and Saturday. See the complete write-up in this chapter's Attractions section.

Alaska Dance Theatre $$$
550 East 33rd Avenue
(907) 277–9591
www.alaskadancetheatre.org
Preschoolers have all sorts of fun in Discovery, a creative movement class especially for the youngest of aspiring dancers. Speed, size, shape, and balance are among the concepts kids learn as they paint rainbows, play butterfly, "swim" like swordfish, and pretend to be airplanes. Creative expression reigns supreme, and parents are bound to enjoy watching almost as much as the kids enjoy dancing.

Alaska Experience Center $$
705 West Sixth Avenue
(907) 276–3730, (877) 276–3730
www.alaskaexperiencetheatre.com
What kid doesn't like to rock and roll? The
moving and shaking of this simulated seismic
experience, based on the tremors of Alaska's
famous Good Friday Earthquake of 1964, is
sure to be a hit with youngsters. Even the
tremor-free companion film, *Alaska the Great-
land,* will awe viewers with its digital sound
and three-story-high screen. For more infor-
mation, check out the complete write-up in
this chapter's Attractions section.

Alaska Wild Berry Products
5225 Juneau Street
(907) 561–9498
www.alaskawildberryproducts.com
A chocolate waterfall and a huge candy store
are great ways to distract the kids while
you're busy hand-picking souvenirs for the
folks back home. Kids can watch their favorite
candies, jams, and jellies being made and
even indulge in some free samples. Don't
miss Holly the Reindeer in the adjacent Wild
Berry Park and Village. See the full write-up in
this chapter's Shopping section under Spe-
cialty Food Shops.

Alaska Wildlife Conservation Center $
Mile 79 Seward Highway, Portage Glacier
(907) 783–2025
www.alaskawildlife.org
Kids will love getting a close look at wildlife in
its natural habitat at this drive-through wildlife
park 48 miles south of Anchorage. They'll see
dozens of species, from big game to smaller
mammals and birds. All the animals here are
rescued in a nonprofit effort to rehabilitate
injured or orphaned animals while educating
visitors on Alaskan wildlife. Admission fees
are quite reasonable, and proceeds go
toward supporting the continued efforts on
behalf of the animals. The center is open daily
throughout the year, from 8:00 A.M. to 8:00
P.M. during the summer season, from 10:00
A.M. to 6:00 P.M. from April to mid-May, and

from 10:00 A.M. to 5:00 P.M. September
through March. See the complete listing in
the Portage/Whittier section of the Prince
William Sound chapter.

The Alaska Zoo $$
4731 O'Malley Road
(907) 346–3242
www.alaskazoo.org
Sure, most kids have been to the zoo, but the
Alaska Zoo is unique in presenting almost 50
native Alaskan mammals and birds in a natural setting about 15 minutes from downtown
Anchorage. None of these animals was simply
snatched from the wild; all were either
orphaned, abandoned, endangered, or
injured before being brought here. Among the
kids' favorites are Apuhn the polar bear and
Maggie the elephant. In the summer, Tuesday
is family night at the zoo, and there are also
Summer Naturalist Tours. Ask for the zoo's
Unguided Tour Supplement, which provides
lots of fun facts for kids. Children must stay
with adults during their visits to the zoo. For
more details, check out our complete listing
in this chapter's Attractions section.

Alyeska Tramway $$$$
Alyeska Resort
P. O. Box 249, Girdwood, AK 99587
(907) 754–2275
Short attention spans are welcome here,
where the ride from 306 feet above sea level
to 2,334 feet above sea level happens in
about eight minutes during the summer. It's
about twice as fast in the winter. At the top,
kids can hike, explore, or pick berries. See our
complete listing under this chapter's Attractions section.

i While downtown, take a look at the
   Alaska Statehood Monument, a
plaque and bust of President Eisenhower
commemorating the Alaska Statehood
Act. The life-size Captain Cook Monument
stands at the corner of Third Avenue and
L Street, where you'll also find great views
of Cook Inlet and Mt. Susitna.

Anchorage Museum of History and Art Children's Gallery $$

121 West Seventh Avenue
(907) 343–4326
www.anchoragemuseum.org

With an emphasis on art, the Children's Gallery features yearlong special exhibits designed for kids. Past displays involved such fun themes as Dogs in Art, Toys and Games in Art, and an exhibition of art made from found objects. Other kid-friendly events at the Children's Gallery include art classes for children and adults, Saturday Artventure Workshops, and Sunday Family Art with a local artist-guide. In the main galleries of the museum, kids will enjoy seeing Alaskan Native artifacts, life-size renditions of pioneer and Native dwellings, and a slice of the Alaska Pipeline. The parking garage is open for handicap parking during the week and for public parking on weekends. During the winter, the museum is closed on Monday and Tuesday. See the full write-up on the Anchorage Museum in this chapter's Attractions section.

Dimond Ice Chalet $$

Dimond Center Mall
800 East Dimond Boulevard, #3-30
(907) 344–7788, (907) 522–6790
www.dimondicechalet.com

This indoor rink on the bottom level of the Dimond Center Mall is perfect for beginning skaters or for families who want to take a break from shopping. You can rent either hockey or figure skates and set off around the rink. The atmosphere is generally more recreational than competitive, making it perfect for kids. If your youngster has a special event to celebrate, the Ice Chalet offers party packages. There's food-court seating around the

i Looking for playgrounds? The Anchorage Department of Parks and Recreation Web site (www.muni.org/parks) includes a map of 72 parks with playgrounds, color-coded to direct you to age-appropriate playground equipment.

rink, and there's also a bowling alley nearby if you're looking for another family-friendly recreational option. Skating lessons are also available. Also see the listing within this chapter's Recreation section.

H2Oasis Indoor Waterpark $$$

1520 O'Malley Road
(907) 522–4420
www.h2oasiswaterpark.com

Winters were a lot longer and colder for Alaskan kids before the H2Oasis came to town. No matter what it's like outside, you can count on 84-degree water and a whole lot of fun at this indoor water park. They've got a slew of kid-friendly water thrills, including the four-story Master Blaster Water Coaster, the Never Ending River, the wave pool, the Mushroom Water Drop, the Beached Boat Slide, the Enclosed Body Slide, the Children's Lagoon, and the Sea Dragon Pirate Ship. On the upper level, there's a food court and game arcade, too. If you're looking for structured activities, H2Oasis offers swim lessons, kayak lessons, water aerobics, and parent-toddler sessions. If you just go to play, parents may want to bring their ear plugs, as the screams of delight get a bit intense in the enclosed space.

Imaginarium Science Discovery Center $$

737 West Fifth Avenue
(907) 276–3179
www.imaginarium.org

With more than 50,000 visitors every year, Alaska's only hands-on science center must be doing something right. Here's a place where kids can touch exotic reptiles, fondle sea creatures, pet a life-size dinosaur, create giant bubbles, check out the aurora, and learn about physics by playing with specialized toys. In addition to providing fun science-based experiences for family, the Imaginarium runs workshops, school visits, and summer science camps. Monthly special events, including regular preschool science hours, make this a place that kids will want to return to again and again. The Imaginarium is located in the Glacier Brewhouse Mall, with parking available at nearby public lots, including the Sixth Avenue parking garage. It's open daily, with shortened hours on Sunday, and there's a science store on-site so kids can take some of their enthusiasm home.

Indian Valley Mine $
Mile 104 Seward Highway, Indian
(907) 653–1120
www.indianvalleymine.com
Perfect for a child-size attention span, this little mine 20 minutes south of Anchorage will give kids a taste of history and gold rush excitement without boring them to tears. Buy a bucket of pay dirt, and kids can try their hand at finding their own gold. Bring a picnic lunch and enjoy the views of Turnagain Arm. The mine is open only during the summer. For details, see the complete write-up in this chapter's Attractions section.

Tiny Tourist
(907) 696–2821
www.tinytouristalaska.com
As any parent knows, kids can require a lot of contraptions to keep them happy, and it's pretty much impossible to bring it all with you when you're traveling. Enter Tiny Tourist, founded by an Eagle River grandmother who got tired of making do when traveling with her grandchildren. They'll deliver cribs, swings, strollers, toys, booster seats, or high chairs wherever you need them. You can rent by the day or by the week, but there's a $25 minimum rental fee. You also can pay to have the equipment picked up when you leave. Be sure to reserve at least two weeks in advance during the busy summer travel season.

ANNUAL FESTIVALS AND EVENTS

Alaskans are famous for their go-out-and-get-it approach to life, so if there's any cause to get together and celebrate something, someone has probably organized an event to do just that. In particular, the months of late win-

i If you're driving around downtown, take a look inside the fenced yard at the corner of 10th Avenue and I Street, and you just might see a reindeer. Back in 1960, Oro Stewart, wife of the founder of Stewart's photography, asked her husband for an Alaskan pet. He presented her with the first Star, a reindeer from breeder Larry Davis in Nome, so named because of the distinctive white patch on her forehead. There have been several Stars since, and they've all been a big hit with Anchorage children, who enjoy seeing her on weekly walks along the Park Strip as well as at Fur Rondy and in Christmas parades.

ter and early spring are chock-full of activities designed to break the cabin-fever syndrome and get people out having a good time. Likewise, there are quite a few running, skiing, and dog-mushing events that capitalize on what Alaska does best: the outdoors.

Whether it's outdoors or indoors, you can expect a fun, low-key ambience at most of these affairs. Where else can you find a Duct Tape Ball or a Wilderness Women Contest and Bachelor Auction among the highlights for the year?

Wherever possible, we've given general indications about cost and dates for these events, but keep in mind that it's all subject to change, so your best bet is to check directly with organizers for specifics.

January

Anchorage Folk Festival
P.O. Box 243034
Anchorage, AK 99524-3034
www.anchoragefolkfestival.org
More than 120 acts from across Alaska and around the world grace the stage at the annual Anchorage Folk Festival. You can enjoy performances by dancers, singers, storytellers, and groups with both traditional and original compositions in bluegrass, jazz, folk, Celtic, and other musical styles. Concerts and

workshops are free, while dance admission fees go toward funding future events.

Great Alaska Beer and Barleywine Festival
Aurora Productions
3401 Denali Street
(907) 562–9911

Alaska's coldest, darkest month has proved itself perfect for sampling beers and strong, complex ales known as barleywines. Head to the Egan Convention Center, where you'll find more than 175 beers to try. The admission fee includes a souvenir glass and 30 beer sample tickets, so you can hunker down and make a night of it. There's a detailed program and a good crowd, from twentysomethings to families and older couples. Any festival that draws celebrities this far north to join locals in a celebration of beer in mid-January must be doing something right.

February

ACVB Torchlight Ski Parade
Nordic Skiing Association of Anchorage
203 West 15th Avenue, #204
(907) 276–7609

Here's a fun opportunity for families and folks who aren't necessarily hard-core skiers to get out and enjoy a group ski event. In conjunction with Fur Rondy, the Nordic Skiing Association hosts a 4-mile evening trek from the University of Alaska, Anchorage to Westchester Lagoon. At the end of the trail, there are door prizes, hot beverages, and even an optional motor coach ride back to the starting point. Seymour the Moose, official mascot of the Anchorage Convention and Visitors Bureau, joins in the fun. The event is dependent on trail conditions; admission fees are charged.

Anchorage Fur Rendezvous (Fur Rondy)
(907) 274–1177
www.furrondy.net

This classic event got its start back in 1935, when Anchorage was a little town of 3,000 people. It didn't take long for folks to figure out that everyone could use some fun to break up the winter months, and with that in mind, a three-day festival was coordinated, featuring basketball, skiing, hockey, and a children's sled dog race. A big bonfire and torchlight parade capped off the festivities. Over the years, Fur Rondy got bigger and bigger, bringing in a traditional Native Blanket Toss, the World Championship Sled Dog Race, a Grand Parade, the Rondy Carnival, the Grand Prix Auto Race, and the Alaskan Original Men's Snowshoe Softball game.

Rondy typically starts in mid-February and continues through the first Saturday in March, when the Iditarod Sled Dog Race has its ceremonial start in downtown Anchorage. These days, Fur Rondy is jam-packed with just about every form of fun you can imagine: fireworks, a parade, a masque ball, a Texas hold'em tournament, a train show, Rondy Bingo, storytelling, sled dog rides, ice bowling, helicopter rides, a snow-sculpture competition, pony rides, wine tastings, fashion shows, and even a Fur Rondy melodrama. In fact, there's so much to do that some folks complain the three-weekend event has been watered down, with attendance at some of the mainstay events dwindling. Still, Rondy is a good time, and even if you can sample only a few activities, you'll be glad you did. Many events are free.

Duct Tape Ball
(907) 646–8600

It's another only-in-Alaska function, with locals decked out in duct tape for a fund-raising dinner/dance event to raise money for various charities. It's amazing what a little duct tape can do, whether it's a funky hat, a black duct tape halter, or a full-length gown. Wear a little or a lot, but don't miss the fun. Even the table settings and decor are enhanced by the ubiquitous tape.

Miners and Trappers Ball
Egan Convention Center
555 West Fifth Avenue
(907) 349–2255

As one of the mainstay Fur Rondy events, this flamboyant ball is big enough to get its own billing. From its roots in the drafty ACS warehouse, the Miners and Trappers Ball has moved into plush digs at the Egan Convention Center. The atmosphere is wacky and fun, with a costume contest drawing revelers dressed in all sorts of outrageous attire, especially those competing in the newsmakers category. The charity fund-raiser includes live music, alcohol, and a big-beard contest. Attendance isn't what it used to be, but the party is still a whole lot of fun.

Ski for Women
Nordic Skiing Association of Anchorage
203 West 15th Avenue, #204
(907) 276–7609
www.alaskaskiforwomen.org
The largest women-only ski event in the nation is held each year on Super Bowl Sunday in Kincaid Park. The atmosphere is more fun than competitive as women pair up in teams for skate/freestyle and classic/diagonal events. Awards are given to top teams categorized by relationship: Friends, Relatives, and Mother/Daughter. No partner? No worries. Event organizers will match you with another skier. Refreshments, door prizes, and a silent auction are all part of the fun. A race fee is charged

Susitna 100
14424 Canyon Road
(907) 345–2282
www.susitna100.com
Want a taste of the Iditarod trail without the dogs? The Susitna 100 and the Little Su 50K provide an opportunity for you to ski, bike, or run a portion of the challenging Iditarod route. It's not an undertaking for those uninitiated to the harsh winter conditions you're likely to encounter along the way. If the chances of frostbite, hypothermia, unpredictable weather, navigational challenges, and river overflow don't scare you away, you'll enjoy the rewards of traveling one of the world's most famous trails framed by winter landscapes of striking beauty. The race organizers provide a wealth of information on their Web site. A standard fee is charged to enter.

Tesoro Iron Dog
7100 Old Seward Highway, Suite C
(907) 563–4414
www.irondog.org
Head to Wasilla to watch the start of one of the world's most grueling snowmobile races, a 2,000-mile trek from Wasilla to Nome and back to either Wasilla or Fairbanks. Temperatures down to 60 degrees below zero, speeds in excess of 100 mph, unpredictable trail conditions—it's all part of the fun. The race kicks off with a parade, followed by a fevered start the next day. There's no charge to watch the parade or the start of the race.

Winterfest
Alyeska Resort
P. O. Box 249, Girdwood, AK 99587
(907) 754–1111
www.alyeskaresort.com
Head down to Girdwood and take in the fun at this annual festival slated for the first weekend in February. Choose from a full roster of activities, including paragliding and skating exhibitions, tubing, the Mountain Bike Slalom, the Polar Bear Plunge, a telemark clinic, and World Cup demos. When you've exhausted yourself with watching and playing, check out the après-ski parties and wine-tasting events along with the Winterfest fireworks.

March

Iditarod Sled Dog Race
(907) 376–5155
On the first weekend in March, Alaska comes into the international spotlight with the start of the 1,500-mile Iditarod Sled Dog Race. On Saturday, more than 1,300 sled dogs along with their owners and handlers line up on Fourth Avenue downtown for the ceremonial start of this popular event. Expect lots of barking and tail wagging along with big crowds along a 1-mile stretch of Fourth Avenue. Crowds spill over into the side streets to watch the frenzied teams shoot out.

After a quick 11-mile run, the mushers pack up their teams and head north to Wasilla for the real start of the race on Sunday. Some

This commemorative sled dog sculpture marks the point of the ceremonial start of the annual Iditarod Sled Dog Race. DEB VANASSE

years the dogs must be trucked to Willow or even to Fairbanks, where snow is more plentiful. The race commemorates the famous 1925 diphtheria serum run from Nenana to Nome. The current trail takes mushers over the Alaska Range, across frozen tundra and rivers, and along the windswept coast of the Bering Sea, past 24 checkpoints at villages and wilderness cabins, to the finish line at Nome. The stakes are high in this grueling event: The first 30 finishers split a prize pot worth almost $800,000. But talk to these mushers, and you'll soon learn it's not about the money. These are folks who love their dogs, love their sport, and love the wilderness where they live and train. There's no charge to watch the start of the race.

Nordic Skiing Association of Anchorage
Ski Train
203 West 15th Avenue, #204
(907) 276–7609
www.anchoragenordicski.com
Hop aboard for a three-hour ride south to Grandview or a four-hour ride north to Curry, and enjoy backcountry skiing, touring, snowshoeing and snowboarding. Curry is the preferred destination for families and beginning to intermediate outdoor enthusiasts, while Grandview is more appropriate for intermediate to advanced wilderness sojourns. At both destinations, warming facilities are provided, either in the form of bonfires or on the train itself. These popular events sell out early, so be sure to get your tickets well in advance. The trips are on different weekends, with one typically in February and one typically in March, so you can do both if you like. Riding the train isn't cheap, but it's a fun, all-day adventure.

Tour of Anchorage
Nordic Skiing Association of Anchorage
203 West 15th Avenue, #204
(907) 276–7609
A premier ski marathon event that's part of the American Ski Marathon Series, this is actually a collection of four races: a 50K, 40K, or 25K freestyle, or a 25K classical race. The longer

races go from one side of Anchorage to the other, following bike trails, while the shorter races start in the middle of town. The finish line is at Kincaid Park, with transportation back to the start available and an informal banquet to follow. An entrance fee is charged.

April
Alaska Women's Show
George M. Sullivan Sports Arena
1600 Gambell Street
(907) 562–9911
Billed as the only trade show in Alaska for women, this event typically follows a week or two after the Sportsman's Show at the Sullivan Arena. More than 200 vendors display all sorts of products, including cosmetics, crafts, apparel, and outdoor gear. Typically 12,000-plus people attend. Wheelchair access is available.

Great Alaska Sportsman Show
George M. Sullivan Sports Arena
1600 Gambell Street
(907) 562–9911
Alaska has no shortage of outdoor enthusiasts, and most of them love their outdoor toys, so it's no surprise that this annual event draws crowds topping 20,000. More than 300 booths cater to the whims and wishes of anglers, hunters, snowmobilers, rock climbers, and golfers. Look for lots of equipment demonstrations, seminars, and plenty of ways to spend your money. Past favorites have included a bird-treatment learning center, an interactive shooting range, and an archery range. This trade-show event has been an Anchorage tradition since 1984. Wheelchair access is available.

May
Alaska Women's Gold Nugget Triathlon
(907) 868–3630
www.goldnuggettriathlon.com
Billed as a fitness event for women of all abilities and ages, the Gold Nugget includes a 500-yard swim at Bartlett Pool, a 10-mile bicycle ride, and a 4.1-mile run. Organizers recom-

Iditarod Sled Dog Race

In many parts of the country, March brings daffodils. In Anchorage, it brings dogs, lots of dogs, more than a thousand of them lined up along downtown streets on the first Saturday of the month for the ceremonial start of the internationally renowned Iditarod Sled Dog Race. You can feel the excitement as you walk the streets, looking for the best place to watch the teams take off. Dogs bark, mushers pose for pictures and sign autographs, and journalists from around the world jockey for position.

First run in 1973, the Iditarod was the brainchild of Joe Reddington Sr., known as the "Father of the Iditarod." The race commemorates the 1925 serum run to Nome, when a series of heroic mushers, including Gunner Kaasen and his lead dog Balto, rushed diphtheria vaccine from Nenana to Nome in a relay effort that managed to deliver the life-saving serum in only one week.

Mushers now follow either the northern or southern route of the Iditarod National Historic Trail for approximately 1,150 miles, through mountain passes, across frozen rivers, and over windswept tundra to reach their final destination in Nome. After the ceremonial start in Anchorage, they pack up their teams and

One day after the ceremonial start in Anchorage, the official start of the Iditarod Sled Dog Race is usually held in Wasilla. DEB VANASSE

head north for the official start of the race the following day, from Wasilla if trail conditions permit. The shortest finish time is just shy of 9 days, while the longest, acknowledged by the annual Red Lantern Award, was nearly 33 days.

The mushing life is hard for most of us to fathom. There's so much to consider: the science of breeding, the commitment to training, and the strategy of how to outmaneuver your competitors in a grueling long-distance race when factors like weather and trail conditions can change without warning. There's a big purse for the winner: more than $72,000 and a brand-new pickup truck, but as mushers will be quick to admit, there's no purse big enough to truly compensate for the dedication of time and money that they put into their obsession. More than anything, they agree that it's about the dogs. And these are dogs that love to run.

In Alaska, many of the Iditarod contenders are household names. Rick Swenson? He's the one who's entered 20 Iditarods and never has finished out of the top 10; in fact, he's the only five-time winner. Libby Riddles? She broke the gender barrier by becoming the first woman to win the Iditarod in 1985. Following on her heels was Susan Butcher, winner of four Iditarods until she retired in 1993 to raise a family of the two-legged kind; she's remembered as well for her courageous battle against the cancer that took her life in 2006. And then there's Norman Vaughn, who ran the race at age 88 and was planning a comeback when he died at the age of 100.

The excitement of the race's beginning carries right on through to the finish. Folks from around the world follow the progress of the mushers as they travel through checkpoints from the mountains of Finger Lake and Rainy Pass, then along the Kuskokwim and Yukon Rivers and through coastal villages to No Man's Land, the final stretch to the finish, where no one has to give up trail to their competitors. Everyone's still talking about the photo finish in 1978, when Dick Mackey came in one second ahead of Rick Swenson, leading literally by the nose of his lead dog.

Conditions along the way can be brutal. Temperatures dip far below zero in many spots, and winds can whip up snow into total whiteout conditions. Teams and drivers can get soaked by overflow along the rivers, creating an almost instant danger of hypothermia. Mushers lose their way or lose their teams. Encounters with belligerent moose or ill-placed trees have caused them to withdraw. It's not a race for the faint of heart.

Still, 80 mushers, give or take a few, return year after year to test their mettle. And though much of the world's attention turns on the top 10 contenders, the rest of the pack have their own stories to tell. From Rachael Scdoris, the first legally blind musher to compete, to the drivers testing out puppy teams for some of the more prominent contenders, they all share a love of the wilderness and a spirit of adventure that embodies the spirit of the Iditarod.

mend that you familiarize yourself with the course to enhance your chances of success. The event has been a fun fitness challenge for Alaskans since 1984. There's a standard entrance fee.

Native Youth Olympics (NYO)
Cook Inlet Tribal Council
(907) 793–3267

More than 400 finalists from around the state travel to Anchorage each year to show their stuff in skills related to traditional hunting and subsistence activities. The one-hand reach and the arm pull, for instance, traditionally strengthened arm muscles for seal hunting, while the high kick was a means of communicating across the tundra. Other popular events include the stick pull, the scissor broad jump, and the toe kick. The NYO is a three-day event sponsored by the Cook Inlet Tribal Council.

Visitor Industry Charity Walk
(907) 334–3550
www.alaskacharitywalk.org

You'll get some exercise, but don't expect to lose any weight on this 5K walk. Also known as "Graze to Raise," this annual event includes food villas along the route, with a grand finale at the Park Strip that includes a beer and wine garden, desserts, jugglers, clowns, face painting, door prizes, and carnival games. Individuals and teams walk to raise money in support of charities throughout Alaska.

June

Alaskan Scottish Highland Games
Eagle River Lion's Park, Eagle River
(907) 770–4967
www.alaskascottish.org

Since 1981, the Alaskan Scottish Club has been hosting this two-day event, which begins on a Friday night with bagpipe competitions at the Loussac Library. From there the festivities move out to Eagle River's Lion's Park, where on Saturday you'll find athletic events, more pipe and dance competitions, historic reenactments, storytelling, fencing demonstrations, wandering minstrels, and

vendors of all thing Celtic. Graze the food and refreshment stands, then head back to town for an evening of Celtic music and dancing at St. Patrick Cathedral.

AWAIC Summer Solstice
Town Square
Fifth Avenue and E Street
(907) 786–1230

The longest day of the year is cause for special celebration in Alaska, with the extra daylight making up for some very short days in mid-December. This fund-raiser for Abused Women's Aid in Crisis (AWAIC) focuses on fun family activities, such as the Boy Scout Obstacle course, an Imaginarium reptile touch tank, and demonstrations by wood-carvers, bead artists, and weavers. You can snack on such carnival foods as korn fritters, hot dogs, and kettle korn and pick up free balloons for the kids.

Blues on the Green Festival
6998 Raspberry Road (Kincaid Park Amphitheater)
(907) 272–1341

Performers come from across the country to entertain crowds of more than 5,000 people at this all-day event. Notable acts from past festivals include Otis Rush, Too Slim, Bo Diddley, the Backstreet Blues Band, and the Mighty Untouchables. Food and merchandise are on sale throughout the day. Admission is charged.

Mayor's Midnight Sun Marathon
c/o UAA Athletics Department
3211 Providence Drive
www.mayorsmarathon.com

Forty-five-hundred runners from around the state and around the world converge on Anchorage to compete in one of five simultaneous races. There's a 26.2-mile marathon, a 13.1-mile half-marathon, a recreational 5-mile event, a marathon relay, and a Youth Cup. The course spans from the Chugach Mountains on the east end of Anchorage to Cook Inlet on the west side. Shuttles run from major hotels to the start and finish lines. The race is a

National Leukemia and Lymphoma Society "Team in Training" marathon, and the course is certified so runners may use their results as part of the qualification process for the Boston Marathon. Expect a standard race fee to participate.

Spirit Days
6998 Raspberry Road (Kincaid Park Amphitheater)
(907) 258–2672
Celebrate the Alaskan Native traditions that lie at the foundation of the state's cultural heritage by taking part in this free event designed to promote understanding and foster awareness. Traditional Native sports, drumming, dancing, singing, foods, crafts, storytelling, and the famous blanket toss are among the many activities included in this three-day event. More than 250 performers and artists come from Alaska, Canada, Russia, and the Lower 48 to participate in Spirit Days. The event's location is subject to change, and there's typically no admission charge.

Three Barons Renaissance Fair
Tozier Track
3400 East Tudor Road
(907) 868–8012
http://3barons.org
Wander among barons, pirates, alchemists, and Celts as they transform a bit of Alaska into a faraway time and place. Artists and craftspeople showcase their talents and wares in this annual event, held on the first two weekends in June, with a mid-Fair Feast in between. Renaissance enthusiasts dress in costume and act out roles as citizens of three baronies in 16th-century England. Founded in 1996, the fair features 60 vendors as well as acts on six stages

July

Anchorage July 4th Celebration
Downtown Anchorage
(907) 279–7500
There's too much daylight for fireworks, but that doesn't stop around 30,000 Anchorag-

ites from celebrating Independence Day in style. Start off with a benefit pancake breakfast, then take in the community parade along Sixth Avenue from E Street to K Street. The afternoon brings the National Veteran's Wheelchair Games and a reading of the Declaration of Independence by Harvard Club members in period costumes. The day ends with a big picnic on Park Strip (Delaney Park) featuring lots of food and three stages of fun-filled music and entertainment. Most events are free.

Eagle River–Chugiak Bear Paw Festival
Chugiak–Eagle River Chamber of Commerce
(907) 272–5634
www.cer.org
First held in 1985, this four-day event celebrates all that's fun about the communities just to the north of Anchorage. Enjoy a whole host of festivities, including the Bear Paw Classic 5K Run, the Slippery Salmon Olympics, the Miss Bear Paw Pageant, the Bear Paw Chili Cook-Off, and a classic car show. There's an Eagle River Renaissance Village with food and fun as well as a Teddy Bear Picnic & Family Fun Day. Don't miss the Grand Parade, billed as one of the largest in the state, along with the carnival rides and games.

Girdwood Forest Fair
Girdwood
It's worth the 36-mile drive south of Anchorage to take in the unique art, crafts, music, and foods at this three-day event. Entertaining locals and visitors since 1975, the Forest Fair has developed a reputation for promoting some of the best entertainers and artists in the state in a venue that promises no politicians and no religious orders (no dogs or beer outside the garden, either, for practical reasons). The array of music has grown to two stages featuring 17 acts each day. You'll find the fair at Mile 2.2 of the Alyeska Highway, in the community park, but you can park at the Alyeska Resort and take the shuttle if you like.

August

Arctic Thunder
Elmendorf Air Force Base
(907) 552–7469

The Blue Angels, the premier flight demonstration team of the U.S. Navy and Marines, comes
to town with an annual air show that features
all manner of breathtaking rolls, dives, and
spins. In addition to watching the high-flying
daredevils, there's plenty to do on the ground,
as the hangars fill with everything from hunting
and fishing simulators to face-painting activities and clowns. Participants have a chance to
meet the pilots, too. The show's schedule may
change from year to year, but it's generally
held during one of the summer months.

Blueberry and Mountain Arts Festival
Alyeska Resort
P.O. Box 249, Girdwood, AK 99587
(907) 754–1111
www.alyeskaresort.com

If you had fun at the Girdwood Forest Fair in
July, you can keep the spirit alive by attending
the Blueberry and Mountain Arts Festival in
August. Look for more great music, with an
emphasis on folk fare, and lots of fun arts and
crafts. Of course there's food, too, and wine.

Humpy's Marathon
Humpy's Great Alaskan Alehouse
610 West Sixth Avenue
(907) 258–4964
www.humpysmarathon.com

Attracting upwards of 1,000 runners and
walkers in the marathon, half-marathon, and
5K events, Humpy's Marathon starts and ends
at one of Anchorage's best-loved ale houses.
The Anchorage Running Club charts a course
that includes less than 1 mile of roads, with
the rest of the event taking place on paved
bike paths. There's a dirt trail alongside most
of the route for those who prefer it. Lots of
great scenery and camaraderie plus a great
pasta dinner at Humpy's for the finishers
make this a popular event. A wheelchair category is included. Look to pay a standard race
fee to participate.

September

Alaska Railroad Blues Train
Alaska Railroad
(907) 265–2494
www.alaskarailroad.com

A relative newcomer among Alaska Railroad's
special events, the Blues Train first chugged
out of the station in 2005, with lots of happy
riders listening to one of their favorite local
blues bands while enjoying a spread of appetizers and a no-host bar in cars decked out by the
folks at Blues Central, one of the city's favorite
nightspots. The train pulls into Seward for
more music and a big barbeque. An overnight
stay in Seward is included in the ticket price.

Alaska State Fair
2075 Glenn Highway, Palmer
(907) 745–4827
www.alaskastatefair.org

Alaska is funny about its state fairs. Nearly
every town of any size claims to be a proud
sponsor of a "state fair." But the big fair is the
one in Palmer, about an hour's drive north of
Anchorage, held each year from the end of
August through Labor Day weekend. Here's
your chance to see those gigantic cabbages
and other vegetables that thrive in Alaska's
extreme summer daylight, as well as taking in
the usual state fair entertainment, booths,
rides, and exhibits. A daily admission is
charged.

October

AlaskaFEST
(907) 257–2375

Thanks to the timely arrival of the Alaska Permanent Fund Dividend checks (see the Close-
up in this chapter's History section), Alaskans
make predictable visits to Anchorage to
spend, spend, spend. Area businesses have
joined together to market all the special
events, services, and spending opportunities
in a themed package that includes the Nye
Frontier Classic and the Anchorage City of
Lights celebration. The particulars change
from year to year, but the concept stays the

same: Let's keep this money in the state and have fun while we spend it.

Great Alaska Beer Train
Alaska Railroad
(907) 265–2494
www.alaskarailroad.com
Here's a great way to chug some of Alaska's best microbrews to the backdrop of incredible views as the Alaska Railroad chugs its way around Turnagain Arm. Tickets include six half-pints of Glacier Brewhouse beer plus a selection of appetizers. This is typically a sell-out event, so sign up early. The admission is fairly hefty, but it's a great experience.

Make It Alaskan Festival
George M. Sullivan Sports Arena
1600 Gambell Street
(907) 279–0618
www.miafestival.com
Get a head start on your holiday shopping with this event featuring 250-plus vendors with great Alaskan-made products. Browse the booths with a backdrop of live music, or vie for prizes in the Natural Pantry Alaskan Food Safari. The Sullivan Arena offers wheelchair access.

November

Arts and Crafts Emporium
Egan Convention Center
555 West Fifth Avenue
(907) 563–8310
Didn't find gifts for everyone on your list at last month's Make It Alaskan Festival? Don't despair. November brings another great shopping opportunity in the form of the annual Arts and Crafts Emporium, featuring crafts, foods, and fun. This event is downtown at the Egan Convention Center, and unlike many of these shopping extravaganzas, there's no admission charge.

Downtown for the Holidays
www.anchorage.net/events
Start the holiday season in style on the weekend after Thanksgiving by taking in the Parade

of Lights and the Town Square Tree Lighting Ceremony. If you like, try some caroling or have breakfast with Santa. At the Anchorage Museum of History and Art, artisans display their wares in a holiday crafts weekend. The Cincinnati Ballet's annual performances of The Nutcracker are also this weekend. There's no charge for many of the events.

Great Alaska Shootout
George M. Sullivan Sports Arena
1600 Gambell Street
(907) 279–0618
Can't wait for basketball season to start? Here's a great opportunity to watch some of the nation's best college teams in preseason competition. Many years ago, former University of Alaska coach Bob Rachal conceived of this tournament as a great way to lure teams to Alaska, since the NCAA doesn't count games beyond the Lower 48 against a team's normal allotment. The loophole makes for fine viewing opportunities by Alaskans. Men's and women's teams compete in separate tournaments. Ticket prices are based on the number of games you want to attend.

December

New Year's Torchlight Parade and Fireworks Display
Alyeska Resort
P.O. Box 249, Girdwood, AK 99587
(907) 754–1111
www.alyeskaresort.com
End the year with lights, food, and a whole lot of Alaskan ambience at Alyeska's Torchlight Parade and Fireworks. Skiers light up the long night, with a big fireworks display following. Post fireworks, there's a big buffet and the usual New Year's festivities. Be sure to book a room well in advance if you don't want to drive back to town at the end of the evening. There's a charge for the buffet and for skiing.

Wilderness Women Contest and Bachelor Auction
(907) 733–3939
www.talkeetnachamber.org

It's a bit of a drive from Anchorage, about two hours north, but this legendary contest still draws a crowd. Single women compete in at least three timed events, demonstrating (more or less tongue in cheek) the skills that they think a bachelor from a woodsy town like Talkeetna would find most appealing. A 100-yard dash to fill water buckets from the "creek," gathering firewood, shooting ptarmigan, climbing a tree to escape a pesky moose, and delivering sandwiches and beer during Sunday-afternoon football are among these valuable skills. After the contest, the bachelors put on their own airs in a Bachelor Bidding Contest, with the lucky (?) bidders entitled to a drink and a dance with their eligible men. This all-in-good-fun event sponsored by the Talkeetna Bachelor Society put this little town on the map, and it manages to be a great fund-raiser, too.

THE ARTS

For a city its size, Anchorage enjoys a vibrant, active arts scene. Many residents transplanted from larger cities in the Lower 48 arrive with a love of the arts and a strong desire to see them flourish in the Far North. From such intimate venues as Cyrano's Off-Center Playhouse to the world-class theaters of the Alaska Center for the Performing Arts, Anchorage invites the best in live performances as well as encouraging the visual and literary arts through galleries and local arts organizations.

The First Friday Art Walks are great fun, drawing art lovers to dozens of downtown studios, galleries, and coffee shops for receptions highlighting art and music by

i For a free look at Alaskan Native arts, don't miss the working-artist demonstrations at Ship Creek Center every day from noon to 1:00 P.M. during the summer, followed by Alaska Native Dance Shows starting at 1:00 P.M. The center is located at the corner of Fourth Avenue and C Street.

some of the best local talent you'll find anywhere. Pick up a copy of the *Anchorage Press* for a complete list and map for this monthly event.

With their "Downtown Summer in the City" series, the Anchorage Downtown Partnership sponsors a full slate of free outdoor arts events. On every other Monday from noon to 1:00 P.M., there's Music and Magic at Peratrovich Park, with live outdoor theater at the same time and place on Thursday. On Saturday from 2:00 to 3:00 P.M., enjoy either Marionettes in the Park or a cultural faire of multicultural dance and music, also at Peratrovich Park. On Sunday from 1:00 to 3:00 P.M. at the town square, you'll find visual and performing arts classes as well as live music as part of the Art in the Park events. In addition, the Downtown Partnership sponsors live music events; see the Insiders' Tip in the Music section below. If it rains, you'll have to make other plans, as these are fair-weather functions only. For details on Summer in the City events, go to www.anchorage downtown.org.

Dance

Alaska Dance Theatre
500 East 33rd Avenue
(907) 277-9591
www.alaskadancetheatre.org
From its inauspicious beginnings in a World War II–vintage Quonset hut back in 1981, the Alaska Dance Theatre has become the biggest and best-known dance school and company in the state. Fall and spring concerts feature the company's 25 dancers, and the Alaska Dance Theatre also strives to make dance accessible to everyone by offering a full class schedule of ballet, jazz, hip-hop, modern, and social dance. In addition the organization provides choreography and dancers for various productions throughout the community. In 2006 the Alaska Dance Theatre moved into a new five-studio building with its own theater, offices, and ample parking.

Streetside art in Anchorage includes this whale sculpture outside the Carr-Gottstein Building downtown.
DEB VANASSE

Galleries

Arctic Rose Gallery
420 L Street
(907) 279–3911
www.arcticrosegallery.com
This unique gallery in front of the popular Simon and Seaforts restaurant supports local artists as well as displaying unique creations from around the world. Tucked into the main gallery and side rooms are original paintings, glasswork, Alaska Native art, jewelry, Russian art, and pottery. They'll be happy to ship your purchases if you like.

Artique
314 G Street
(907) 277–1663
www.artiqueltd.com
Among the oldest fine arts galleries in town, Artique features ceramics, prints, glass, original paintings, crafts, and jewelry by some of Alaska's best-known artists. Byron Birdsall Giclee prints, Lisa McCormick handmade silver jewelry, Roy Peratrovich Jr. bronze sculptures, Holly Gittlein metal and glass fish sculptures, and Barbara Lavallee books and prints are among the popular items here. The gallery is open daily throughout the year.

Aurora Fine Art Gallery
737 West Fifth Avenue
(907) 274–0234
The works of more than 400 artists are represented in this large downtown gallery at the corner of Fifth Avenue and G Street. Choose

i Some of the most fun and unique outdoor art you'll see anywhere comes to downtown Anchorage every summer with the Wild Salmon on Parade displays. Local artists decorate fiberglass salmon with riotous colors and humorous themes, and at the end of the summer these one-of-a-kind creations are sold at a charity auction. Pick up maps at the Log Cabin and Downtown Visitor Information Center on Fourth Avenue.

from handpainted furniture, original oils, whalebone, prints, sculpture, ivory, pottery, and glass. All art displayed here is made in the United States, and all Alaskan art is handmade within the state. For a selection of jewelry and other eclectic art, visit Aurora's sister gallery, ZoeZ Window Gallery, next door in the Glacier Brewhouse building.

Decker/Morris Gallery
621 West Sixth Avenue
(907) 272–1489
Specializing in contemporary creations by Alaskan artists, this gallery features monthly solo exhibitions as well as a wide range of sculptures, paintings, ceramics, photography, prints, and jewelry. Open daily, the gallery is conveniently located within the Alaska Center for the Performing Arts.

Stephan Fine Arts Gallery
Sixth Avenue and F Street
(907) 274–5009
Fred Machetanz, Rie Munoz, Charles Gause, and Ernest Robertson are some of the well-known Alaskan artists featured in this upscale gallery. You'll find original oils, giclee prints, photographs, and sculptures by some of the best artists in the region. There's a second Stephan Gallery inside the Hotel Captain Cook. The gallery offers shipping services for your purchases, too.

Music

Anchorage Concert Chorus
P.O. Box 103738
Anchorage, AK 99510
(907) 274–7464
www.anchorageconcertchorus.org
Founded in 1946 to promote choral music in Anchorage and Southcentral Alaska, this 160-member chorus hosts several concerts each year. Past performances include such classics as Beethoven's Symphony No. 9 and Handel's Messiah as well as more contemporary Holiday Pops and Chorale Concert series. In addition to community performances, this audition-only choral group promotes music

education through scholarships and a mentoring program. Season subscriptions may be purchased through CenterTix at (907) 263–2787.

Anchorage Festival of Music
P.O. Box 103251
Anchorage, AK 99510-3251
(907) 276–2465
www.festivalmusic.org

With the mission of providing a summer festival of classical music as well as promoting educational opportunities in music, the Anchorage Festival of Music was founded in 1956 as a nonprofit community organization and later consolidated with the Basically Bach Festival. Past Summer Solstice Series presentations have included A Tribute to the Boston Pops, an Unfolding of Romanticism series, and a children's concert, Boyz in the Wood. Performances are held in the Discovery Theatre of the Alaska Center for the Performing Arts, and season tickets are available.

Anchorage Opera Company
1507 Spar Avenue
(907) 279–2557
www.anchorageopera.org

From its beginnings as an all-volunteer group in 1962, the Anchorage Opera Company has become one of most highly acclaimed regional companies in the country. Judging from the growing demand for advance ticket sales and the popularity of the opera's annual fund-raising events, the Anchorage Opera is making good on its mission to bring world-class opera to the far north. Each year, they host three productions at the Discovery Theatre of the Alaska Center for the Performing Arts, showcasing world-class guest performers along with regional talent. Past productions have included Rossini's *The Italian Girl in Algiers* and Puccini's *Madame Butterfly*. There's also a Dark Night Recital Series celebrating the skills of local musicians. As the only professional opera company in the state, the Anchorage Opera serves as a resource for other arts organizations by sharing their large inventory of costumes, props, and lighting equipment.

Anchorage Symphony Orchestra
400 D Street, Suite 230
(907) 278–8668, (800) 478–7328
www.anchoragesymphony.org

Eighty professional musicians leave their day jobs behind to bring high-quality orchestral music to audiences throughout Southcentral Alaska under the auspices of the Anchorage Symphony Orchestra. The orchestra began in 1946 with 17 local musicians who met weekly to share their love of music. Concert seasons typically include six classical concerts, four Young People's concerts, and a Halloween Family Concert. The orchestra also sponsors outreach and education efforts, including equipment and music rentals.

Snow Goose Theatre
717 West Third Avenue
(907) 277–7727
www.alaskabeers.com

The theater at the popular Snow Goose Restaurant and Sleeping Lady Brewery hosts great live music, too. Thursday is open mic night, when lesser-known artists take the stage with music as well as stand-up comedy and poetry. On the first Friday of every month, you can enjoy singers and bands while checking out a new microbrew. Acoustic Saturdays bring an opportunity to hear a new singer-songwriter every weekend. The Snow Goose serves as a venue for special concerts as well.

Whistling Swan Productions
P.O. Box 773354
Eagle River, AK 99577
www.whistlingswan.net

Since the mid-1990s this production company has brought more than 150 acoustically-oriented singer-songwriters to the stage in Anchorage and Southcentral Alaska. From such smaller venues as Side Street Espresso to larger stages such as those at the Alaska Center for the Performing

i The Anchorage Downtown Partnership showcases Music in the Park all summer long. From noon to 1:00 P.M. on Wednesday and Friday, enjoy live music at Fourth Avenue and E Street and Peratrovich Park. On Thursday from 5:00 to 8:00 P.M. in the town square, you can catch the Live After Five series, featuring bands, food, and dancing.

Arts, high-caliber performers Allison Krauss, Bruce Cockburn, Leo Kottke, and Tom Paxton have ventured north thanks to the efforts of this family-owned business.

Theater

Alaska Junior Theater
329 F Street, Suite 204
(907) 272–7546
www.akjt.org
Since its inception in 1981, this nonprofit group has brought high-quality theater productions to more than half a million children and parents via field trips and public performances. Mime, dance, music, puppetry, and theater productions are featured in the Alaska Junior Theater's efforts to promote live performances throughout the Anchorage area. For their community shows, the group seeks out family-friendly theater, with a policy of never booking a performance that they have not previewed in live format.

Cyrano's Theatre Company
Cyrano's Off-Center Playhouse,
Bookstore, & Café
Fourth Avenue and D Street
(907) 274–2599, (907) 277–4698
www.cyranos.org
Formed in 1995 by a group of volunteers dedicated to fostering professional dramatic productions, Cyrano's offers an intimate theater experience in a venue that includes wine and a snack bar. Recipients of the Governor's Award for Arts Organizations, the company is dedicated to nurturing regional talent, with

the ultimate goal of creating endowments to support full-time actors. Past productions include classic works by Chekov, Tennessee Williams, and Shakespeare as well as world premier productions of original drama. Tickets may be purchased for individual productions or in 10-show punch cards.

Literary Arts

Alaska Center for the Book
3600 Denali Street
(907) 786–4379
www.alaskacenterforthebook.org
Affiliated with the Library of Congress Center for the Book, this organization serves to promote public interest in literacy by acting as a clearinghouse for the literary arts in Alaska. Writing workshops, author events, and book discussion groups are among the activities sponsored by the Alaska Center. They are developing *LitSite Alaska,* an online literary magazine, and Northern Letters, a 13-week radio program highlighting the work of Alaskan authors. Most years the Alaska Center for the Book, in conjunction with the UAA Department of Creative Writing and Literary Arts, sponsors the Writing Rendezvous, a spring conference featuring guest authors from the Lower 48 as well as Alaskan writers.

Alaska Sisters in Crime
P.O. Box 100382
Anchorage, AK 99510
www.alaskasistersincrime.com
This association of female mystery writers has been active in promoting the literary arts in Anchorage and throughout the state through such programs as Authors in the Schools and Young Writers Retreats. Author Dana Stabenow has led the group in sponsoring major writers' events, including a Left Coast Crime convention and International Boucheron. Alaska Sisters in Crime sponsors the Booktalk Alaska radio show, various writing workshops, and literary grants for local authors.

The Alaska Center for the Performing Arts contains four stages on which you can see everything from touring Broadway shows to concerts and guest lecturers. DEB VANASSE

Arts Organizations

Alaska Center for the Performing Arts
621 West Sixth Avenue
(907) 263–2900
www.alaskapac.org

Occupying a full block adjacent to the town square, the Alaska Center for the Performing Arts has become a vibrant hub of downtown Anchorage. With four high-quality performance spaces in the 176,000-square-foot building, this is one of only a few dozen multivenue arts complexes in the country. Here you'll find Broadway Series performances, jazz, ballet, comedy shows, and community social events. Though this costly venture opened to some grumbling in the wake of a statewide recession in 1988, the center now hosts annual audiences exceeding 240,000 people per year and is home to seven resident companies. For tickets to resident company functions, call

(907) 263–2787 or (877) 263–2787, or go to www.centertix.net.

The facility is owned by the municipality of Anchorage but operated by the nonprofit Alaska Center for the Performing Arts, Inc. The Atwood Concert Hall, with its starburst ceiling of gold, red, and green, captures the effect of the northern lights and provides stunning acoustics for musical performances. In the Discovery Theatre, audiences of up to 700 enjoy theater, opera, and musical performances from a large stage with "salmonberry" seat upholstery adding to the Alaskan decor. The Sydney Laurence Theatre, with seating for 340, is a great venue for film and smaller live productions, including Dave Parkhurst's popular Aurora show (see our complete write-up within this chapter's Attractions section). The Elvera Voth Hall, with its signature metal and neon sculpture

i Much of the art you'll see around Anchorage and throughout the state is thanks to Alaska's "1 percent for art" legislation, which requires any public buildings constructed or renovated after 1975 to include art, with 1 percent of state funding for such projects to be devoted to the design, construction, and display of these works.

Nature's Illumination, is a popular setting for lectures, recitals, and other special events.

Anchorage Concert Association
430 West Seventh Avenue, Suite 200
(907) 272–1471
Since 1950 the Anchorage Concert Association has been bringing top-notch performing artists to town with the help of a volunteer group of more than 75 associates. Typically the association sponsors a Classical Series; a BP Horizons Series, featuring musical influences from around the world; Family Performances, with acts such as the New Shanghai Circus; a Dance Series; and Broadway & Beyond productions. For discounted ticket prices, priority seating, and exchange privileges, order by the series, or create your own custom series.

PARKS, RECREATION, AND TOURS

Parks

One of the best things about Anchorage is the way you can access the wilderness almost from your back door. Take a 30-minute drive from just about anywhere in town, and you'll find a place where you can immerse yourself in trees and trails, often with spectacular scenic views to boot. Whether it's the massive Chugach State Park, one of the Bureau of Land Management (BLM) tracts, or one of more than 120 city parks in and around Anchorage, you won't have a problem finding a place to enjoy the outdoors even within the boundaries of the municipality. Space pro-

hibits us from discussing every park, but the more popular spots are described here.

Campbell Tract and Campbell Creek Science Center
6881 Abbott Loop Road
(907) 267–1247
On the east side of town, up against the Chugach Mountains, the 730-acre Campbell Tract provides space for all types of nonmotorized enjoyment, including biking, hiking, and horseback riding. Hemmed in by city parks on three sides, this BLM-maintained facility offers opportunities to meander along Campbell Creek through spruce and aspen forests. Fox, lynx, coyote, moose, and bear have been spotted within the tract boundaries. Also within the tract is the 10,500-square-foot Campbell Creek Science Center, serving as an educational resource with a library, greenhouse, and a variety of wilderness activities. You can access Campbell Tract either from the Smokejumper trailhead off Abbott Loop Road or from Campbell Airstrip Road off of Tudor Road.

Chugach State Park
Area Office
HC 52 Box 8999
Indian, AK 99540
(907) 345–5014
The third-largest state park in the country spreads out from the foothills on the east side of Anchorage, stretching south to where the Seward Highway crosses into the Kenai Peninsula and north to the Mat-Su Valley. You can access the half-million acres of parklands from several points throughout the Anchorage Bowl. As you venture into the park, you'll be treated to panoramic mountain views, the crystal-clear water of wilderness streams, a plethora of wildflowers in season, and perhaps a glimpse of a moose, bear, fox, eagle, or lynx. Within the park, you can enjoy hiking, camping, skiing, rafting, climbing, camping, and, in designated areas, snowmachining.

The Eagle River Nature Center is a great place to get an introduction to all that the park has to offer; see the write-up on the nature center in the Attractions section above. North of Eagle River, Eklutna Lake Valley is another popular place to get into all that the park has to offer, including picnicking and boating on the turquoise waters of Eklutna Lake.

Don't feel like driving that far? You can enter the park's Hillside Trail System from one of four access points on the east side of town. Take O'Malley Road east to Upper O'Malley Road, where you can go north on Prospect Drive to the Prospect Heights Access, or continue south to the O'Malley access. Another option is to take DeArmoun Road from the south side of town to Hillside Drive and Upper Huffman Road. From there you can choose either the Upper Huffman Access or the Glen Alps Access at the end of Tolsome Hill Road. From any of these points, you can set off on a myriad of trails; see this chapter's Hiking, Camping, and Fishing section for details on some of the most popular routes. Only the Upper Huffman Access may be used for snow-machining.

South of Anchorage you can venture into the park at the Turnagain Arm Trail, formerly called the Old Johnson Trail. You'll find trailheads at either Mile 112 or Mile 115 of the Seward Highway. Details on the Turnagain Arm Trail may be found in this chapter's Hiking, Camping, and Fishing section. In this southern section of the park, you'll also find

i Beware of the bore tides when exploring the coastline of Turnagain and Knik Arms. Unique to this part of the country, these 2- to 6-foot walls of water move at speeds of 10 to 15 mph. Caused by wide discrepancies between low and high tides, bore tides can come in sounding like a freight train. They're fun to watch from a distance, and Beluga Point in the southern part of Chugach State Park is a great place to see them, usually about 45 minutes after low tide in Anchorage.

the Potter Section House, a state historic site with restored buildings from a former railroad section camp. The park headquarters is located here.

Delaney Park (Park Strip)
A–P Streets, between 9th and 10th Avenues
Also known as the Park Strip, Delaney Park offers a broad, sweeping swath of green along the south end of downtown Anchorage. First cleared as a fire break and later used as an airstrip, the park is mostly wide open, but there are a few shaded and secluded spots to relax on a warm summer day. You'll find lots of fun flowers, including the Centennial Rose Garden, along with memorials to World War II vets and Martin Luther King Jr. There's also an antique train engine that attracts the attention of young and old alike.

Earthquake Park
4306 West Northern Lights Boulevard
When the infamous 9.2 Good Friday Earthquake struck Alaska in 1964, some of the most extensive damage occurred along Turnagain Arm on the northwest end of Anchorage, where the clay soils collapsed into the sea. Dozens of homes were lost, and six people were killed. Walking through Earthquake Park, established along this forever-altered stretch of coastline, it's hard to imagine the massive destruction that happened here only a few decades ago. An interpretive facility with kiosks, sculptures, signs, photos, and maps conveys the transformation from calm to chaos and back again. If you follow non-sanctioned footpaths down to the water to get a closer look at the way nature rearranged the bluff overlooking the inlet, be advised that the walkways are steep and the tidal flats are extremely dangerous.

Far North Bicentennial Park
6501 East Tudor Road
This 4,000-acre city park is bordered by Chugach State Park to the east, by Tudor Road to the north, and by Abbott Road and Abbott Loop Road to the south and west. You

Earthquake

Without a doubt, the geological phenomenon that most changed Anchorage and Southcentral Alaska in recent years was the Good Friday Earthquake of 1964. With an adjusted magnitude of 9.2, this shaker was slightly stronger than the 9.0 Sumatra event in 2004 that caused more than 280,000 tsunami-related deaths.

With more earthquakes than any other part of the country, Alaska is considered one of the most seismically active areas of the world. Registering 11 percent of the world's total quakes, Alaska has been the site of three of the eight largest

Memorial sculptures in Earthquake Park recall the impact of the 1964 earthquake.
DEB VANASSE

tremblers ever recorded. The 1964 earthquake was the second largest on record, with only the 1960 Chilean earthquake measuring higher on the Richter scale.

The big one started at 5:36 P.M. on March 27, 1964. During four to seven minutes of shaking, buildings toppled, landslides and avalanches rearranged the landscape, and 15 people died. Anchorage, about 75 miles west of the epicenter, sustained the greatest losses. Downtown, approximately 30 blocks of residential and commercial buildings were damaged, including the JCPenney store and the new Four Seasons apartment complex, which collapsed completely. Schools were especially hard-hit, including the Government Hill Grade School, which was pulled apart as the result of landslides. The Turnagain Heights residential area sustained huge landslide damage as more than 130 acres crumpled and collapsed, destroying an estimated 75 homes and disrupting all major services. Today, Earthquake Park stands as a memorial to the Turnagain Heights devastation.

In Seward, a 1,070-meter section of waterfront slid into the ocean, causing a local tsunami that took at least 11 lives and sent oil spilling from storage tanks into the water, where it went up in flames. A 67-meter wave was recorded in Valdez Inlet, where quake-related damage was so extensive that the entire town was subsequently moved to more stable ground. In all, 106 Alaskans died as a result of quake-related tsunamis. Statewide, property damage from the quake and tsunamis was estimated to be between $300 and $500 million.

Beyond Alaska, the big waves generated by the Good Friday Earthquake were the most disastrous to ever hit the west coasts of the United States and Canada. California suffered an estimated 13 deaths and $10 million in property damage, while Oregon saw 4 deaths and $7 million in damage. British Columbia also reported $10 million in tsunami-related damage. In 1967, the West Coast and Alaska Tsunami Warning System was established in Palmer in order to help avert future disasters.

When you travel from Anchorage to Portage, you'll see a forest of dead gray trees that were doused in salt water as a result of the 1964 Earthquake. Geologist Rod Combellick studied these soils for evidence of liquefaction, which results when earthquake activity causes sand to act as a liquid. In the process, he discovered patterns of sand layered with organic silt, revealing that earthquakes as big as the one in 1964 most likely have occurred in Southcentral Alaska every 600 to 800 years. Statewide, there's one earthquake measuring 8.0 or higher on the Richter scale every 13 years, with an average of 1,000 Alaskan quakes each month.

Since 1964 the state's population has more than doubled, and construction practices have been modified to prevent the extensive damage that resulted from the last big quake. Nevertheless, the Federal Emergency Management Agency estimates that Alaska has the second-highest possible earthquake loss ratios in the country. Earthquake insurance? Only about 20 percent of Alaskans carry coverage, and some companies have discontinued it. In earthquake-prone Alaska, it's just another example of living, literally, on the edge.

can enter the park either by driving east on Abbott Road to Hillside Park, or by heading east on Tudor Road to Campbell Airstrip Road. The park includes a vast network of trails for skiing, running, dog mushing, biking, hiking, and horseback riding through the woods and along streams. The park experiences heavy year-round use with downhill skiing and horseback riding concessions as well as two baseball fields. A users group meets monthly to promote efforts to protect this vast park from encroachment by roadways and other development.

Kincaid Park
9401 West Raspberry Road
(907) 343–6397

Acclaimed as the site of some the best running and ski trails in the country, this 1,400-acre park is a real treasure. Kincaid's 43-mile network of trails has served several major recreational events over the years, including World Cup races, North American Biathalon Championships, and a slew of national and international cross-country ski events. With access from the west end of Raspberry Road, the park intersects with the Tony Knowles Coastal Trail as well. From all around the park, you'll catch great views of Mt. Susitna, Mt. Foraker, the Chugach Mountains, Cook Inlet, and, on especially clear days, Mt. McKinley. Portions of the park's expansive Outdoor Center, which includes huge barbeque grills, a batting cage, and a climbing tower, may be rented for private functions.

i Mt. Susitna, the most visible peak as you look across Cook Inlet from downtown Anchorage, is nicknamed the Sleeping Lady because the shape of the mountain looks like a woman resting on her side. Legend has it that an Indian princess laid down to wait for her lover to return from battle, but he was killed as she slept, so she has never awakened.

Resolution Park
300 L Street

This small park is a fun spot for downtowners to eat a to-go lunch and admire the views of Cook Inlet, Mt. Susitna (the Sleeping Lady), and even Mt. McKinley on especially clear days. The Tony Knowles Coastal Trail cuts through the park, and there's also a statue of Captain Cook, whose ship the *Resolution* visited nearby waters in 1778. The park is located at the junction of Third Avenue and L Street.

Russian Jack Springs Park
5300 DeBarr Road
(907) 343–6992

Originally a homestead owned by an immigrant known as "Russian Jack," the land for this park was transferred from the Bureau of Land Management to the municipality of Anchorage back in 1948, making it one of the oldest parks in the city. Before the park was formally established, the city set up a minimum security prison there, with an adjacent prison farm. Today the park includes soccer and softball fields, a Girl Scout day camp, picnic and playground areas, tennis courts, the Mann Leister Memorial Greenhouse, the nine-hole Russian Jack Golf Course, and 9 miles of trails for biking, walking, and skiing. Also within the 300-acre park is the Lidia Selkregg Chalet, serving as a clubhouse for skiers in the winter and golfers in the summer. The chalet also may be rented for private functions. Access to the park is from Pine Street and DeBarr Road to the north and from Boniface Parkway and DeBarr Road to the south.

Town Square Municipal Park
E Street, between Fifth and Sixth Avenues

Part of a downtown revitalization effort, this lovely park is ablaze with color in the summer, when more than 9,000 plants plus a waterfall make it the perfect backdrop for concerts and other public events. In the winter, look for the annual tree-lighting ceremony and a fireworks display on New Year's Eve.

Kincaid Park in southwest Anchorage offers a myriad of world-class trails for skiers, hikers, and bikers. DEB VANASSE

Valley of the Moon
Arctic Boulevard and West 17th Avenue
This is a fun little park tucked in the heart of midtown. You'll find playground equipment for all ages here. Grab a burger at the Arctic Roadrunner just down Arctic Boulevard (see the All-American/All-Alaskan category in this chapter's Restaurants section) and have an impromptu picnic.

Recreation

If you can't find something to do around Anchorage, you're probably not looking very hard. The city is filled with recreation enthusiasts, and on evenings and weekends you'll find them out doing what they love best. Though much of the recreation centers on the outdoors, Anchorage has its share of spectator sports and indoor activities, too.

Berry Picking

A favorite Alaskan pastime, berry picking gives you a great excuse to get outdoors with the added benefit of savoring tasty souvenirs from your outing. Almost 50 varieties of berries grow in the state, and most of them are edible. Blueberries, salmonberries, and cranberries are among the favorites of avid berry pickers. Salmonberries ripen in late June, and blueberries are typically out by mid-July. Cranberries are generally best picked after the first frost. Aside from the great flavor of our wild berries, they're extra-healthy, with antioxidant levels much higher than those of berries from more southerly climes.

One popular berry-picking spot is the Flattop Mountain Trail, accessed from Upper Huffman Road. Just above the parking lot, you'll see Blueberry Hill. Another option is to take the Powerline Pass Trail and pick along the South Fork of Campbell Creek. North of town, the Rendezvous Peak Trail, next to Alpenglow Ski Area, will take you to a valley filled with blueberries, cranberries, and the less-popular crowberries. Or take the Highland exit off the Glenn Highway to South Fork Valley Trail for low-bush blueberries. There are also some berries to be had if you take the tram up to the top of Alyeska and walk down.

Bicycling

With more than 120 miles of paved multiuse trails maintained by the Parks and Recreation Department, Anchorage is a great place for biking. Among the recreational routes is the Chester Creek Greenbelt, a 4-mile trail from Goose Lake to Westchester that then turns east toward the Chugach Mountains. Another great option is the 8-mile Campbell Creek Trail, which runs through Far North Bicentennial Park and along the Campbell Creek Greenbelt, where you'll spot spawning salmon in season.

The 11-mile Tony Knowles Coastal Trail also makes for great biking. Starting from downtown Anchorage, this coastal trail will take you along the ocean past Westchester Lagoon, Earthquake Park, and Point Woronzof, then on to miles of adjoining trails within Kincaid Park. The views of Knik Arm, Mt. Susitna, and Cook Inlet from the coastal trail are nothing short of spectacular. On a clear day, you'll also see Mt. McKinley from points along the way.

Just south of town the bike trail from Indian to Girdwood runs through some of the most fabulous scenery you'll find anywhere. Hills are part of the terrain, but the ride's still accessible for most cyclists.

If your interest is mountain biking, check out the Far North Bicentennial Trails, the Hilltop Ski Trail System, and the Kincaid Park Trails. Within Chugach State Park, the Bird Creek Valley, Eklutna Lakeside, Middle Fork to Williwaw Lakes, and Powerline Trails all offer nice challenges and spectacular scenery.

A great local resource for biking enthusiasts is the Arctic Bicycle Club (907–566–0177, www.arcticbike.org), which began in the 1970s as a road-cycling club in Anchorage but now has expanded to include mountain biking and touring throughout Southcentral Alaska. The club hosts rides for cyclists of all levels and sponsors both competitive and noncompetitive racing events.

The Tony Knowles Coastal Trail begins in downtown Anchorage and ends 11 miles down the coast at Kincaid Park. DEB VANASSE

Thanks to a number of bike rental businesses, visitors can partake in all the biking fun in and around Anchorage. Pablo's Café and Bicycle Rentals (907–250–2871) rents Cannondale and Tandem adult bikes. Helmets, maps, and bike locks are included with each rental. Their convenient location 1 block from the Tony Knowles Coastal Trail makes Pablo's a popular option. They're open daily from May to September, with rentals starting at $15.00 for up to four hours, with an additional charge of $5.00 per hour after that. Downtown Bicycle Rental (907–279–5293, www.alaska-bike-rentals.com) offers similar rental services with 24-hour rental periods and a 10:00 P.M. return option. They also rent hybrid bikes, kids' bikes, tagalongs, mountain bikes, and trailers.

If you're interested in a backcountry bike tour, check out Mountain Bike Alaska (907–746–5018, 866–354–2453, www.mountain bikealaska.com). They specialize in day and multiday trips, including transportation to and from your Anchorage-area accommodations. The Ekluna Lake tour is a popular day trip for beginners, while the Johnson Pass tour provides more advanced single-track riding. Prices start at $95 per person and include lunch, snacks, beverages, helmet, and a souvenir water bottle.

Boating and Water Sports

An abundance of lakes and rivers within day-trip distance of Anchorage makes this a great place to play in the water. If you like canoeing, you can put in at Cheney, Campell, or Jewel Lakes, as well as Westchester Lagoon. North of the city, Mirror and Eklutna Lakes are popular spots for paddling.

For a little more excitement, try rafting. The Matanuska River and Sixmile Creek are popular destinations, with rapids ranging from Class I to IV. Borealis River Guides (907–783–0195, 877–525–7238) provides transportation to the Matanuska River King Mountain Run, less than half an hour from Anchorage. For a more challenging Class IV trip, they'll also take you to the Lions Head Run on the Matanuska River. A box lunch is included with both trips. Nova (800–746–5753, www.novalaska.com) offers both the King Mountain and Lions Head Runs as well as combo trips that pair mountain biking, glacier hiking, or a helicopter ride with your white-water adventure.

You can also head about 60 miles south of Anchorage to Hope, where you can raft the waters of Sixmile Creek, which plunges from high in the Chugach Mountains through three canyons. Chugach Outdoor Center (907–277–7238, 866–277–7238) offers three levels of adventure, from the more gentle Turnagain Pass Float Trip that's suitable for children as young as six years old to the wild and woolly Upper, Middle, and Lower Canyon Float that takes you through sections of river with such nicknames as "Suckhole" and "Jaws."

Kayaking is another great way to experience Alaska's rivers. Eagle River and Eklutna Lake are popular kayaking destinations near Anchorage. With the Alaska Kayak Academy (907–746–6600, 877–215–6600), you'll navigate either the Matanuska or Knik River in an inflatable kayak, accompanied by an experienced guide. All equipment, including dry suit, is provided, as is instruction.

It's not for the timid, but those not put off by the extreme tides and sometimes hefty winds have been known to sailboard in Turnagain Arm. If you prefer motorized boats, your best bet is to head for the Mat-Su Valley, where Nancy Lakes and other smaller lakes are open to motorboats and Jet Skis.

Boxing

From fall through spring, there's club boxing most Thursday nights at the Egan Center. This is your chance to watch amateurs, including some women, duke it out. Seating includes both drinking and nondrinking sections, and the bouts draw a pretty good crowd. For more information, contact Jim Patton Promotions at (907) 243–0106 or go to www.thursdaynightfights.com. If you're interested in getting in the ring yourself, check out the Anchorage Amateur Boxing Club (907–529–7057).

Curling

If you want to have fun on the ice but skating's not your thing, Anchorage is a great place to give curling a try. The Anchorage Curling Club (907–272–2825) on Government Hill is open from October to April with two sheets of ice for newcomers and experienced curlers. The club offers classes for beginners, league action, and bonspiels for a variety of experience levels.

Diving

With all sorts of coastline within easy reach, it's not surprising that diving is a popular recreational option in the Anchorage area. Though the ocean waters are a cool 55 degrees in the summer, with a proper dry suit you can see all sorts of marine life, including octopus, rockfish, sea lions, and whales. A great resource for divers is the full-service shop at Dive Alaska (907–770–1778, www .divealaska.net), where you can arrange dives, get certified, and rent equipment. Ask about their custom dive trips and packages.

Fitness

Fitness centers and athletic clubs are especially popular here, where the snow and cold make it difficult to get out and exercise if you're not into winter sports. The Alaska Club (www.thealaskaclub.com) has nine locations throughout the Anchorage area, including one express club and one club exclusively for women. You can expect the usual fitness options, including weights and aerobic training, at all of the locations, while some of the larger clubs have indoor swimming pools, saunas, steam rooms, and racquetball and tennis courts.

The YMCA of Anchorage (907–563–3211, www.ymcaalaska.org) is open until 10:00 P.M. Monday through Saturday. They have an indoor/outdoor pool, fitness center, weight room, sauna and steam room, aerobics studio, and outdoor track and field facilities. Programs include aquatics, health and fitness, child care, and activities for kids.

Golf

Golf might not be the first activity you think of in connection with Alaska, but there are plenty of avid golfers out taking advantage of the long summer days. Look for courses to open in May and stay open through September.

The Anchorage Golf Course (907–522–3363), known to locals as O'Malley's on the Green, features 18 holes sprinkled with water hazards, blind tee shots, and other challenges. There's also a driving range. It's a par 72 course, and you can get tee times as late as 10:00 P.M. in the summer. Lessons and club rentals are also available. If you're just looking for nine holes, the Tanglewood Lakes Golf Club (907–345–4600) is the place to go. They offer pull carts and club rentals, too.

You also can get civilian access to the Moose Run Golf Course (907–428–0056) on Fort Richardson. Moose Run is a challenging 18-hole creek course with trees, hills, bunkers, and, as the name suggests, an occasional moose. The old Hill Course is still available for play, and there's a driving range. You can rent clubs here as well. Another military course open to civilians is Eagleglen Golf (907–552–3821, www.elmendorfservices.com) on Elmendorf Air Force Base. You can up the ante with lots of par 5 holes and a fair amount of water.

To the north, Palmer Municipal Golf Course (907–745–4653) is a nice, flat course that still provides a challenge. In Wasilla, the Settlers Bay Golf Course (907–376–5466) offers great scenery and a variety of fairways. Another option in Wasilla is the Sleepy Hollow Golf Course (907–376–5948), known for its affordability. You can rent clubs at all three courses, and the Palmer course has a driving range.

Horseback Riding

You don't have to go far to enjoy great horseback riding adventures in Anchorage. Horse Trekkin Alaska (907–868–3728, www.horse trekkinalaska.com), on O'Malley Road, offers all sorts of trail-riding options, beginning at $55 for a ride lasting an hour and a half. Longer rides include picnic lunches. Custom wagon tours and pack trips also are available. One of the best things about Horse Trekkin is that they offer year-round riding, including sleigh rides that end with a cabin warm-up complete with hot beverages and optional fondue. For a special romantic getaway, check out their Great Alaskan Date package, combining a sleigh ride with an overnight stay at A Critic's Choice Bed and Breakfast.

You can also head for Hilltop Ski Area on the east side of town for small group rides with Turnagain Trails (907–336–4077, www.turnagaintrails.com). These personalized horseback adventures will take you up into the mountains for a scenic view of the Anchorage Bowl. One-hour rides are $50 per person, with full-day rides including lunch at $250 per person. Ask about their overnight pack trips. Turnagain Trails is open from mid-May to mid-October, and reservations are required.

Ice Skating and Hockey

If you're not a skater when you come to Anchorage, this is a great place to take it up. Whether you're looking for recreational skating or competitive ice hockey opportunities, you'll find plenty of options both indoors and out. Westchester Lagoon is a great place to enjoy casual and family-style skating. You can count on the ice being plowed for Saturday skating functions, which may include concessions and live music. For outdoor hockey, try the Chester Creek Sports Complex, where there's activity at both rinks day and night. Cheney Lake, Goose Lake, Jewel Lake, and Spenard Lake all have maintained outdoor rinks as well. You also may find recreational skating at several rinks connected with the Anchorage Public Schools.

Anchorage has all sorts of organizations for kids and adults who like to skate. For figure skating, there's the Anchorage Figure Skating Club (907–566–3743) and the Alaska Association of Figure Skaters (907–344–2233). Speed skaters will find company at the Alaska Speed Skating Club (907–349–4039) and the Eagle River/Anchorage Speed Skating Club (907–269–7900).

Ice Safety

The municipality of Anchorage requires at least 12 inches of solid ice before they begin plowing rinks. Ice that's 2-inches thick will generally support one person, while you'll need at least a thickness of 4 to 7 inches for small groups. Avoid ice with wet cracks, frozen slush, or overflow. If you're skating outdoors, always skate with a friend. In an emergency, the safest way to help someone who has fallen through the ice is to sprawl out on the surface and inch toward the opening with a stick or rope to offer the person in the water.

For recreational hockey, check out the Anchorage Hockey Association (907–227–1175), the Anchorage Neighborhood Hockey League (907–349–7465), and the Anchorage Outdoor Hockey Association (907–245–1860). Boys & Girls Club Hockey (907–249–5445), the South Anchorage Hockey Association (907–345–8502), and the Southcentral Alaska Hockey Association (907–337–9705) all promote recreational hockey as well. Competitive level opportunities can by found with the Alaska All Stars Hockey Association (907–522–3790), the Anchorage Junior Aces (907–349–8324), and the Mustang Hockey Association (907–694–7849). While women can play in any of these leagues, Anchorage also has two women-only leagues, the Alaska Firebirds (907–345–1196) and the Anchorage Women's Hockey League (907–566–3453).

Ben Boeke Indoor Ice Arenas
334 East 16th Avenue
(907) 274–5715
Here you'll find two indoor rinks owned by the municipality of Anchorage and operated by a private contractor. The facility includes six locker rooms and a concessions stand,

with seating for 1,000 at the larger rink and for 100 at the smaller rink. The rinks are used by various youth hockey associations, figure-skating clubs, and adult hockey associations. Public skating and learn-to-skate programs are available.

Dempsey-Anderson Ice Arena
1741 West Northern Lights Boulevard
(907) 277–7571

A sister facility to the larger Ben Boeke complex, the Dempsey-Anderson also offers figure skating, public skating, skating lessons, and ice time for several levels of hockey. Parties and special events can be booked at the rink.

Dimond Ice Chalet
Dimond Center Mall
800 East Dimond Boulevard, #3-30
(907) 344–7788, (907) 522–6790
www.dimondicechalet.com

This indoor rink on the bottom level of the Dimond Center Mall is perfect for enjoying a bit of skating without dealing with the cold temperatures at an outdoor rink. It's not a huge rink, and its overall atmosphere is more recreational than competitive. There's food-court seating around the rink. You can rent either hockey or figure skates, and skating lessons are also available. Also see our write-up in the Kidstuff section of this chapter.

Orienteering

If you're going to venture into Alaska's vast wilderness areas, orienteering will give you a fun and practical place to start. The Arctic Orienteering Club (www.oalaska.org) fosters the sport of navigating the woods with a compass and map. It can get competitive if you like, but many folks just like to get out and challenge themselves. Beginners are welcome. The club sponsors regular recreational and competitive events.

Paragliding

Certified instructors Pete Gautreau and Scott Amy of Alaska Paragliding and Hang Gliding (907–301–1215) will take you on tandem flights for a thrilling bird's-eye view of the stunning scenery in and around Anchorage. Instruction typically begins on a small hill or field and then graduates to Hatcher Pass, Eagle River, Flattop Mountain, Wasilla, or Alyeska, where the school is located. Equipment and instruction are provided; the courage is up to you.

Skiing and Snowboarding

With lots of mountains and plenty of snow, Anchorage is a skier's paradise. Nordic skiers have an abundance of trail options right in town. The 11-mile Tony Knowles Coastal Trail offers groomed, mostly flat terrain with great mountain and inlet views. Kincaid Park, where the Coastal Trail ends, has a system of 31 groomed trails certified for international competition. Russian Jack Springs, Hillside/Bicentennial Park, and Campbell Tract all offer trail networks, some of which are lighted. North of town, the Eagle River Nature Center is a great place to pick up trails through Chugach State Park, while Hatcher Pass offers challenging mountain skiing in a spot where Olympic athletes come to train.

The Nordic Skiing Association of Anchorage is a great resource and advocacy group for cross-country skiing. They offer maps of the various park trails within the city, with proceeds from map sales going to support the maintenance of these trails. Call (907) 276–7609 or visit www.anchoragenordicski.com for more information.

With mountains jutted up next to the ocean, Anchorage offers world-class downhill skiing conditions. Alyeska Resort in Girdwood is the premier alpine skiing venue in the area, while the slopes at Hilltop and Arctic Valley offer a more low-key, family-oriented ski experience.

Alpenglow at Arctic Valley
Arctic Valley Road
(907) 563–2524
www.skialpenglow.com

Originally designed as a recreational facility for the nearby military installations, Alpeni Looking for an affordable downhill rush? Check out one of the many sledding spots in Anchorage. Sunset Park at Government Hill, Conifer Park at Third Avenue and Lane Street, Connors Lake Park at Jewel Lake and International Airport Roads, and Kincaid Park at the west end of Raspberry Road are among several good locations. Kincaid has warm-up and restroom facilities, too.

glow is now operated by the Anchorage Ski Club. With two chair lifts and one T-bar, this is a family-friendly ski facility that capitalizes on great views of the Alaska Range, Mt. Susitna, and downtown Anchorage. For an all-volunteer operation, Alpenglow has a lot to offer the recreational alpine skier. Surrounded by the wilderness of Chugach State Park, the ski area stretches across 320 acres, encompassing 4,000-foot Rendezvous Peak. Ten percent of the terrain is appropriate for beginners, while 20 percent is considered expert territory. Alpenglow is open only on weekends, and the access road can be rough at times.

Alyeska Resort
P.O. Box 249, Girdwood, AK 99587
(907) 754–2111, (800) 880–3880
www.alyeskaresort.com

With an average annual snowfall of 631 inches and 2,500 feet of vertical terrain, it's not hard to see why skiers from around the world flock to Alyeska. Located 40 miles south of Anchorage, the resort makes all sorts of top lists for serious skiers and snowboarders, but they offer beginner classes and experiences as well. Toss in stunning scenery, awesome glaciers, and brilliant northern lights, and you have a mix that's sure to please everyone.

The season begins in mid-November and ends in mid-April, with weekend skiing through May as conditions allow. The resort features nine lifts and an aerial tram, with a total lift capacity of more than 10,000 skiers per hour. There are 86 runs, including open bowls, long top-to-bottom runs, and a fair

number of beginner slopes. Fifty-two percent of the terrain falls into the intermediate category, while 37 percent is best suited for advanced skiers. Snowboarders enjoy professional-level half-pipe, as the resort has hosted several USASA Alaska Snowboard Series amateur competitions

The after-ski ambience is great here, too, with a pool and fitness center plus the non-smoking Sitzmark bar and restaurant, featuring live music in the evenings. The Sitzmark is restricted to those ages 21 and older after 10:00 P.M. For family fun, check out the Glacier Tubing Park, with two tubing lanes and a lift. Reservations (907–754–2274) are a good idea, as the facility can accommodate only 40 tubers per session.

Hilltop Ski Area
7015 Abbott Road
(907) 346–1407
www.hilltopskiarea.org

With 80 percent of the terrain designated as "easiest," Hilltop is a convenient place to get comfortable with the slopes before tackling more challenging heights. The 30-acre facility includes a vertical rise of 294 feet and a slope distance of 2,090 feet. Operated by the non-profit Youth Exploring Adventure, Inc., Hilltop specializes in lessons, camps, and afterschool programs for area youth, but you'll find adults there as well. Snowboarders enjoy the "Mongoline," a permanent half-pipe for aerial stunts. Hilltop has a chair lift, a rope tow, and a platter lift. Adjacent to the ski area are Nordic ski trails and the Karl Eid Ski Jump Complex (907–346–2322).

Snowmobiling

Hatcher Pass, Eureka, the Iditarod Trail, Petersville, and portions of Chugach State Park are popular snowmobiling areas within day-trip distance of Anchorage. For a guided tour, head out into the backcountry with Alaska Snow Safaris (907–783–7669, 888–414–7669). Gear and equipment are provided. If you're going on your own, you can rent snowmobiles and trailers from Fast Cat

ℹ️ Alaskans refer to snowmobiles as "snow machines." Avid riders will want to check out GCI's Arctic Man, a highly competitive mountain race held in the Summit Lake area, off the Richardson Highway between Anchorage and Fairbanks. Held in early April each year, an estimated 10,000 riders and revelers attend.

Rentals and Repairs (907–336–7063, www .fastcatrentals.com). Twelve- and 24-hour rentals are available, as are lodging and tour packages. Ask about destination delivery.

Spectator Sports

Collegiate baseball, basketball, and hockey as well as minor league men's hockey— Anchorage has a nice array of spectator sports for a city its size.

In the summer the Anchorage Glacier Pilots and the Anchorage Bucs take on the competition at Mulcahy Stadium. Both teams are members of the Alaska Baseball League, which showcases collegiate players from around the country. Many of the players who spend a season with the Anchorage teams move on to major league play within a few years. Details on the season, including rosters and stats, may be found online at www .anchoragebucs.com and www.glacierpilots .com.

Mulcahy Stadium is just off A Street between 15th and 16th Avenues. In one of those only-in-Alaska stories, fans once had to vacate the stadium during a game when a Cessna 207 aircraft crash-landed just beyond the left-field fence.

In the winter, minor league hockey action takes center stage with the Alaska Aces, members of the East Coast Hockey League in affiliation with the NHL's St. Louis Blues. Since 1995 the Aces have been wowing their fans with top-shelf puck action at the Sullivan Arena. One of their stellar players, Scott Gomez, went on to play for the NHL, returning during a lockout year to play again for his

home team. For schedules, rosters, team stats, and other Aces information, visit the team's official Web site at www.alaskaaces .com.

The University of Alaska Anchorage (UAA) Seawolves compete in a variety of sports, including Division II men's and women's basketball, cross-country running, gymnastics, skiing, track and field, volleyball, and Division I ice hockey. Basketball and hockey tend to draw the biggest crowds. For details on UAA athletic events, visit www.goseawolves.com.

Swimming

As you might expect, indoor pools are the most popular places to swim in Anchorage, but in the summer you can also test the waters at select lakes throughout the Anchorage Bowl, provided you don't mind the water being a bit brisk.

Lap swim and workout times are available at Alaska Pacific University's Moseley Sports Center (907–245–7362), located on University Drive near the Bragaw Street intersection. In addition, community swim times are available at several Anchorage School District Pools, including Bartlett, Chugiak, Dimond, East, Service, and West High Schools. The pool at West High School also has a waterslide. Call the Swim Information Line at (907) 343–4402 for details on hours and admission fees.

For private indoor swimming, check out the YMCA and the Alaska Club, both featured in our Fitness section above. Memberships are required by both organizations. And don't forget about the H2Oasis Indoor Waterpark (907–522–4420, www.h2oasiswaterpark.com), where there's a wave pool, a children's lagoon, and all sorts of chutes and slides. The water park offers swim lessons and water aerobics, too. For a complete write-up, see this chapter's Kidstuff section.

Even though a city as far north as Anchorage might not seem like a swimming mecca, the city has played host to both the Western Zone Swimming Championship and the Speedo Junior Championship in recent years. If you're interested in competitive swimming,

i Alaskan lakes are prone to causing swimmers' itch, especially in mid- to late summer. This skin rash, caused by parasites that normally invade seabirds, develops within a few hours after leaving the water and can last for up to a week. To avoid it, swim in deeper water away from shore and towel off vigorously when you get out. If you develop a rash, treat it with baking soda baths and anti-itch creams.

the Anchorage Aquanauts Swim Club is a great place to get started.

The municipality of Anchorage maintains beaches at Jewel Lake (West 88th Avenue and Gloralee Street, off Jewel Lake Road) and Goose Lake (3220 East Northern Lights Boulevard, near UAA Drive) in the summer, with lifeguards on duty for supervised swimming during pre-designated hours. At Goose Lake's Paddleboat Café, you can pick up a snack and rent a paddleboat if you like. In Eagle River, there's unsupervised swimming at Mirror Lake (Mile 24 of the Glenn Highway) and Beach Lake, off South Birchwood Loop.

Wildlife Viewing

You'd be hard-pressed to find another city with the ample wildlife-viewing opportunities that Anchorage affords. Moose wander through residential neighborhoods and, on occasion, into downtown parking lots. They're especially prevalent during the winter. From the Ted Stevens International Airport, head north on Postmark Drive to Earthquake Park and Point Woronzof, where there's a good chance you'll see moose wandering not far from the north end of the airport runway. Specially designed chutes funnel the moose away from air traffic and out of harm's way. Point Woronzof is a great place to take in the view of Knik Arm and watch for eagles, too.

Another great place to see moose is Campbell Tract, a 730-acre park area that links Anchorage to the Chugach National Forest. You can access Campbell Tract by taking Campbell Airstrip Road, off the east end of Tudor Road, into Far North Bicentennial Park. From there you can hike in to get a close-up view of the park's wildlife. Other access points include Hilltop Ski Area on the south end of Campbell Tract, with access off the east end of Abbott Loop Road. Campbell Tract is also home to brown and black bears, coyotes, and lynx, but expect these to be much more elusive than the ubiquitous moose.

An estimated 300 black bears and 65 grizzly bears wander in and out of Anchorage, mostly from the Chugach Mountains, which cup around the east end of the municipality. Urban bears are problem bears, and despite such efforts as bear-resistant trash containers designed to curb bear-human interaction, the risk of mauling is always there. Your best bet for safe bear-watching is to sign on with one of the fly-out tours to Katmai National Park or Kodiak Island. Plan on dropping $400 to $500 per person for a day trip to Brooks Falls at Katmai National Park, where you're pretty much guaranteed to see bruins. Alaska Tours (907–277–3000, www.alaskatours.com) and See Alaska Tours (907–578–2707, www.alaska tours.net) offer full-day, fly-out bear-watching excursions.

Even if you're not interested in catching fish, Anchorage has a couple of great spots to watch salmon in their dramatic efforts to return to the places where they were hatched. Just north of downtown, A and C Streets converge into an access road for Ship Creek, which has salmon runs good enough to fish. Another fish-watching option is the Elmendorf State Hatchery, upstream from the downtown Ship Creek viewing area. Take Reeve Avenue north from East Fifth Avenue to the Post Road viewing area. The hatchery

i Wings over Alaska, a birding program sponsored by the Alaska Department of Fish and Game and Alaska Airlines, offers free certificates for identifying 50 to 275 species within the state. Get your free checklist at www.birding .alaska.gov.

ℹ The Eyes on Wildlife program, developed by the Alaska Department of Fish and Game in conjunction with the U.S. Forest Service, offers wildlife-viewing tips through brochures and Web sites. The program includes a wildlife checklist with benchmarks that allow participants to get achievement certificates for viewing live, undomesticated, and uncaged species. For more information, go to www.wildlife.alaska .gov and follow the wildlife-viewing links.

mingles warm water from the power plant at Elmendorf Air Force Base with creek water to create a year-round hatching facility for salmon and trout. King salmon return with amazing leaps up the fish ladder from mid-May into July, and there's a run of silvers from August through mid-September.

You also can see spawning salmon at Potter Marsh, a few miles south of Anchorage on the Seward Highway. Follow the wooden boardwalk through the marsh, stopping where it crosses Rabbit Creek, and you may see fish making their way upstream. Potter Marsh is also a popular spot for birders. From early spring through fall, you're likely to encounter canvasback ducks, Canada geese, and red-necked grebes, among other species. In the shorter summer season, you'll also see gulls, terns, and an occasional trumpeter swan.

Tours

If you're looking for a guided recreational experience, there are several tour companies that operate out of Anchorage, providing a wide range of options for seeing the country. For touring within the city, try the Anchorage City History Trolley Tours (907–276–5603), which offers an hour-long excursion for $10 a person. The trolley tours depart hourly between 9:00 A.M. and 6:00 P.M. during the summer season from 612 West Fourth Avenue, between F and G Streets. Another option is a carriage ride through downtown

Anchorage with The Horse-Drawn Carriage Company (907–688–6005). Rides start at $35 per couple for one-quarter hour. Hayrides and sleigh rides outside of town also are available.

Take off from the city on a flight-seeing adventure with Alaska Air Taxi (907–243–3944, 800–789–5232, www.alaskaairtaxi .com). Get up above it all in a DeHavilland Beaver or a Cessna 206 on one of a variety of packages, including a Knik Glacier and Wildlife Tour, a Blackstone Glacier Tour, a Mt. McKinley Tour, or one of several tours in conjunction with the Iditarod Sled Dog Race.

For backcountry adventures, you can head out with Alaska ATV Adventures (907–694–4294, www.alaskaatvadventures.com) or Alaska All-Terrain Tours (907–868–7669, 888–414–7669). These companies typically provide instruction and gear and will arrange transportation as needed for day trips both north and south of Anchorage. Alaska All-Terrain Tours also can arrange glacier jet boat tours, horseback riding, glacier dogsled tours, and flight-seeing expeditions. Another unique touring alternative is to go hiking with llamas. Leading Lady Llamas (907–258–2888) runs full- and half-day excursions on a variety of trails near Anchorage.

HIKING, CAMPING, AND FISHING

Hiking

Recently named one of the Top Trail Towns by the American Hiking Society, Anchorage has plenty to offer for both novice and expert hikers. Within the municipality, you'll find 300 miles of unpaved wilderness trails along with 120 miles of paved routes. Unless otherwise noted, trail mileage indicated here is one-way only.

Even though you'll be hiking close to town, many trails in the Anchorage area are real wilderness trails, so don't head out without a good supply of drinking water and snacks. Remember, too, that the weather can change quickly. Every year, it seems a hiker or two gets stranded on a trail close to one of

Flattop Mountain, on the east side of Anchorage, is a popular spot for day hikes. DEB VANASSE

the state's urban areas in conditions that quickly become life-threatening, especially with the risk of hypothermia.

One of the most scenic, accessible, and popular options in Anchorage is the Tony Knowles Coastal Trail. Named after an Anchorage mayor who went on to become governor, this 11-mile paved trail follows a coastal route from downtown past Westchester Lagoon and on to Kincaid Park, where it connects with the park's set of trails. On a clear day, views from the trail are nothing short of spectacular. You'll see the legendary Sleeping Lady Mountain, the Chugach Range, and the waters of Cook Inlet. Moves are under way to make the trail even longer, provided land-acquisition issues can be worked out.

For another nice walk right in the heart of Anchorage, try the Downtown Historical 10K Volkswalk. Pick up a map at the Historic City Hall, at Fourth Avenue and E Street, then follow the self-guided route past historical landmarks, with narrative provided on the map.

Ready access to the mountains is one of Anchorage's strong points, and you can't get much closer than Flattop Mountain, a popular day-hike adventure spot. The trail is only 3 miles long, but it rises to an elevation of 1,300 feet, so it's a nice challenge for hikers of all ability levels. From the top you'll enjoy great views of the city, the water, and the Alaska Range. Access to Flattop Mountain is from Upper Huffman Road to Glen Alps Road; follow the signs to Chugach State Park. Winter hikers be warned: Deadly avalanches have occurred here.

From the same Glen Alps trailhead, you can access other popular trails within Chugach State Park. For a short and easy hike, take the quarter-mile Anchorage Overlook Trail, a paved route that promises great views despite the minimal effort. More challenging is the 11-mile Powerline Trail to Indian, with an elevation gain of 1,300 feet and the promise of berry-picking opportunities toward the end of summer.

Another option is the 6-mile trek from Glen Alps to Williwaw Lakes, with nice views of Mt. Williwaw and nearby lakes. The Williwaw Valley also can be accessed via the Prospect Heights trailhead, which takes hikers 6.5 miles through some truly stunning wilderness to the largest of the chain of lakes. Plan on 8 to 12 hours for hiking the Williwaw, and don't be fooled by the proximity to town—this is a genuine wilderness hike. There are campsites throughout the valley, so if you want a more leisurely trip, plan an overnight outing.

From the Prospect Heights trailhead at the end of upper O'Malley Road, you can hike the 3-mile Near Point Trail, which goes past an old homesite in addition to offering views of the city, Cook Inlet, and the Alaska Range. The 5.2-mile Wolverine Peak Trail rises 3,380 feet from the Prospect Heights trailhead, with similar scenic views plus berry-picking opportunities toward the end of summer. You also can catch a glimpse of an old plane wreck at the trail's summit.

South of Anchorage you'll find several easy to moderately challenging trails accessible from the Seward Highway. Follow the 9.4-mile Turnagain Arm Trail from either the Potter trailhead at Mile 115 of the Seward Highway or the McHugh Creek trailhead at Mile 112 of the Seward Highway, and you'll be rewarded with great views of Turnagain Arm and wildflowers in season. From the McHugh Creek trailhead, you can hike less than a mile to the McHugh Scenic Overlook or follow the McHugh Lake Trail for 7 miles for nice views of McHugh and Rabbit Lakes as well as Suicide Peak.

Heading farther down the Seward Highway toward Girdwood, there are several trailheads near the tiny community of Indian. The Falls Creek Trail begins at Mile 105.6 of the Seward Highway and follows the creek for 1.5 miles, with an elevation increase of 1,450 feet, bringing hikers to a nice view of Suicide Peak. Another 1.5-mile trail with scenic views is the Bird Ridge Trail at Mile 102.2 of the Seward Highway. At Mile 103, the Indian Valley Trail heads up through a tundra-covered mountain pass for a 6-mile climb. If you're not inclined to hike uphill, the paved Indian to Bird Bike Path connects Indian, Bird, and the Bird Creek Campground, with views of Turnagain Arm along the way.

To the north the trails beginning at the Eagle River Nature Center are a great way to explore another section of Chugach State Park. For a quick hike, pick up the Rodak Nature Trail, which takes you down 0.75 of a mile to a salmon-spawning river and viewing area. The 3-mile Albert Loop Trail also offers river access from the same starting point. For an all-out adventure, you can hike the Historic Iditarod Trail, also known as the Crow Pass Trail. This 26-mile trek from Eagle River to Girdwood will take you past rivers, waterfalls, former mining sites, and glaciers. Public-use cabins are available along the trail, but be sure to reserve them well in advance; see our write-up on the Eagle River Nature Center in this chapter's Attractions section for details.

Other trails in the Eagle River area include the 0.75-mile River Trail at North Fork, with access at Mile 7.4 of Eagle River Road, and the 6-mile South Fork Valley Trail, accessed a short distance from Mile 7.5 of Hiland Road. For a multiday hike through the heart of Chugach State Park, take the Arctic to Indian Trail from Ski Bowl Road near the Alpenglow ski area south through the valley and up into Indian. A bit farther up the road, the 1-mile Thunderbird Falls Trail at Mile 25 of the Glenn Highway offers spectacular views of the falls and the canyon, while the 5-mile Peters Creek Trail off Malcolm Drive at Mile 21 also sports some great scenery.

Eklutna Lake offers some great options for hikers, too. This glittering lake, the largest in Chugach State Park, is only 35 miles from Anchorage, and it's the source of the city's drinking water. Take the exit at Mile 26 of the Glenn Highway to the campground, parking area, and trailhead. From there you can follow either the 3.2-mile Twin Peaks Trail or the 12.7-mile Eklutna Lakeside Trail. From the Lakeside Trail, you can access the 3.5-mile

Bold Ridge Trail and the 6.5-mile East Fork Trail. There also are two public-use cabins along the Lakeside Trail, one at Mile 3 and one at Mile 12. For information on reserving these cabins, contact the Anchorage Public Lands Information Center (907–269–8400) or check online at www.dnr.state.ak.us/parks/cabins/index.htm. Note that all-terrain vehicles are allowed on the Lakeside Trail Sunday through Wednesday.

Camping

You'll see plenty of RVs on Alaskan highways during the short summer season. Camping is a great way to get into the great outdoors and beat some of the expensive hotel rates in the city. For RV parking, you'll find everything from side-by-side parking to campgrounds where you can spread out and enjoy the scenery.

Anchorage RV Park
1200 North Muldoon Road
(907) 338–7275, (800) 400–7275
www.anchrvpark.com
Peace, quiet, trees, and flowers can be hard to come by in an urban campground, but you'll find them all at Anchorage RV Park, one of the premier camping spots in Anchorage. This 195-site RV park is surrounded by woods yet only a 10-minute drive from downtown. Enjoy long pull-throughs, laundry and shower facilities, wireless Internet and modem connections, and pay phones. A convenience store, gift shop, and barbeque pavilion are also on the grounds. Alaska Native–owned

i If you don't want to drive your RV to Alaska, consider renting one. Alaska Motorhome Rentals (907–258–7109, 800–254–9929) has lots of new, Class C motor homes for rent. Ask about their AAA and AARP discounts. One-way rentals are available, too. Great Alaskan Holidays (907–248–7777, 800–225–2752) offers friendly, year-round service, with a convenient location on the Old Seward Highway.

i As part of an ongoing effort to prevent vandalism at public schools during the summer months, the Anchorage School District permits camping with RVs on school grounds. For more information, contact the district at (907) 348–5170.

and –operated, Anchorage RV Park received the 2004 Governor's Award for ADA (Americans with Disabilities) design, and it is a pet-friendly facility. Rates range from $32 to $45 per night.

Centennial Camper Park
8300 Glenn Highway
(907) 343–6986, (907) 343–6992
www.muni.org/parks/camping.cfm
Operated by the municipality of Anchorage, Centennial Park has 100 campsites, with 6 of them set up for either drive-through or tent camping. The biggest draw for this park is convenience, as it's less than 15 minutes from downtown. Showers and firewood are available at an additional charge, while the use of the dump site is free for campers. Pets must be leashed or confined, and quiet hours are maintained after 10:00 P.M. The campground is open from mid-May through September.

Golden Nugget Camper Park
4100 DeBarr Road
(907) 333–5311, (800) 449–2012
Golden Nugget is one of those parking-lot-type campgrounds, but it's conveniently located near Russian Jack Springs Park in midtown Anchorage. They offer 215 sites, with full hookups and picnic tables at each. Free hot showers are a bonus, and there's a Laundromat plus fenced playground area. Camping spots are available for backpackers, too. Sites run from $20 to $30 per night. Unlike many other Alaskan campgrounds, the Golden Nugget is open year-round.

Fishing

For decent urban fishing, it's hard to beat Anchorage. Drive 30 to 60 minutes from town,

i Alaska has hundreds of wilderness cabins that may be reserved through state and federal agencies, including the Alaska Department of Natural Resources and the Bureau of Land Management. While each agency has its own system for reservations and guidelines for use, you can expect similar rugged digs at each. Access is typically by trail, boat, or small plane, and cabin users should be prepared for adverse conditions and weather delays.

and you'll find an even greater abundance of species in genuine wilderness settings.

Ship Creek is probably the best-known fishing hole right in town. Drive 10 minutes from the heart of downtown Anchorage to First Avenue and Loop Road, where there's parking on both sides of the creek. You can fish for salmon in the tidal portion of the waterway, just below the power plant. You won't have any illusions about being in the woods, but if you're fishing with the tide in some of the deeper holes near the road, there's a good chance you'll see some activity. Kings roll in during the late spring and stay till mid-summer, while silvers peak in late summer and continue into autumn. Don't forget about the extreme tidal activity in Knik Arm. Be careful around the mud, and be prepared for water that could rise up to 12 feet.

From high in the Chugach Mountains, Campbell Creek flows west and then south to empty into Turnagain Arm at a point south of the airport. The Campbell Creek Greenbelt, sporting several city parks, runs along most parts of the waterway. Above Dimond Boulevard, you can fish for silvers, rainbows, and Dolly Varden. Look for especially good silver fishing during the latter parts of August in the portion of the creek between Dimond Boulevard and C Street. The middle portion of the creek is stocked with rainbows early in the summer. Even though you're in the heart of the city, be on the lookout for bears.

Several Anchorage lakes are stocked with fish as well, with the fishing generally best in late spring and then again in late fall. For arctic char, rainbows, and landlocked salmon, try Jewel Lake, which offers good shore access and wheelchair facilities just off Dimond Boulevand, south of the airport. A bit more secluded but equally accessible is Campbell Point Lake near Kincaid Park, stocked with the same species as Jewel Lake. Closer to the airport, DeLong Lake sports the same fish. North of Anchorage, at Mile 23.6 of the Glenn Highway, Mirror Lake offers decent fishing for rainbows, char, and landlocked salmon. The best access is by small boat.

Also north of Anchorage is an area known as the Eklutna Tailrace. It's a spot where waters from the hydropower project are tunneled down from Eklutna Lake. Fishing can be a bit challenging here, but it is stocked with silvers and reds, and there is good road access with parking at Mile 4.1 of the Old Glenn Highway. South of Anchorage at Mile 101.2 of the Seward Highway, you'll find Bird Creek, one of the most popular salmon streams in the area. Look for chum and pink salmon during July, with heavy runs of silvers in the first part of August. Expect extreme tides and combat-style fishing when the runs are at their peak.

Farther down the road, about 45 minutes south of Anchorage, the Portage Area River Systems offer more secluded fishing opportunities for Dolly Varden and silvers. Twentymile River, running from Twentymile Glacier

i Many anglers practice catch-and-release techniques with slow-growing species like wild rainbow trout and northern pike. To follow this fish-conservation technique, use barbless hooks and strong line, and avoid playing the fish for too long. With the fish in the water, back the hook out without squeezing the fish or touching its gills and eyes. Point the fish upstream, swishing it gently back and forth until it swims away.

Wild Alaskan Salmon

You can't be in Alaska long without having a salmon encounter of one kind or another. Whether it's a tasty meal featuring a savory and healthful filet, a weekend spent casting from the shore of a pristine river, or a casual visit to the Ship Creek fish ladder just north of downtown Anchorage, you'll get to enjoy one of the finest fish you'll find anywhere.

Rich in omega 3 oils, the flavorful flesh of the salmon keeps growing in popularity. Try a taste test comparing farmed fish to wild Alaskan fare, and you'll come away singing the praises of our native species. Toss in the chance to catch your own, whether it's by trolling the ocean waters out of Valdez, Seward, or Kenai, or by combat fishing on the rivers and streams of the Kenai Peninsula, and the experience gets that much better.

If you're having a rough day, ponder the difficult life of the salmon and be assured things could be a lot worse. Hatched in freshwater streams, salmon face perils that include diving birds, predatory fish, extreme weather, and unpredictable river conditions. After a year or two in fresh water, the survivors head for the ocean, where many of them fall prey to larger fish, marine mammals, and com-

Silver salmon reach the end of their journey up the freshwater stream where they will spawn and die. DEB VANASSE

mercial fishing nets. The handful of young fish that manage to make their way back to freshwater must fight their way upstream to the place of their origin, where they are destined to spawn and die.

Though the uninitiated may think of salmon as one type of fish, there are actually five distinct species in Alaska. Best known for their size and their propensity to put up a good fight at the end of a line, Alaska's king salmon, also known as Chinooks, are typically the first to show up in significant numbers. The first kings arrive in May, with runs peaking in June and early July. In Southcentral Alaska, the earlier runs occur in drainages along the coast. Later runs in such places as the Kenai River may yield fish weighing more than 100 pounds, but these runs are rare. Chinooks make for good eating, with an oilier flesh that holds up well in cold-smoked strips.

Red salmon, or sockeyes, are coveted by Alaskans for bright, flavorful filets that are sure to please. They're a dramatic but difficult fish to catch, as they shun most lures and flies, but when they're hooked, they'll leap and dance with the best of them. Sockeyes, which average around six pounds, are the strongest swimmers of the five species. Significantly smaller than kings, sockeyes sport a metallic shimmer along their backs, with silver flanks and whitish bellies. After they spawn, the males turn bright red, with distorted heads and hooked jaws. Reds run almost concurrent with kings, though sometimes a bit later. In some of Alaska's larger, deeper lakes, you'll find landlocked sockeyes, also known as kokanee.

On the opposite end of the taste-test spectrum are pinks, or humpback salmon, which have a paler flesh that is most suitable for canning. Like their more flavorful cousins, male pinks turn especially ugly after spawning, with misshapen jaws and distorted backs that earn them the nickname "humpies." When they first come from salt water to fresh, humpies will put up a good fight, and their sheer numbers as they congregate in bays and river mouths are bound to impress. Their blue-green backs turn brown as they spawn, and their flesh turns soft. With a life span of only 18 months, pinks run in two separate genetic groups, so seasons in a given area will be for even- or odd-numbered years only. They generally return to freshwater in mid- to late summer, and spawn, sometimes in marginal conditions, in August and September.

Another lowly salmon species is the chum, or dog salmon. Like pinks, they're prolific, but they'll put up a bigger fight at the end of a line. Not nearly as tasty as reds but with a slightly firmer flesh than pinks, chums do get used as dog food among subsistence fishers and mushers, but they make for decent eating if you get to them early in their journey upriver. As they spawn, the males develop protruding teeth that also contribute to their association with dogs. You can distinguish chums from other salmon by the silver sheen on their bellies and the relatively narrow connection of the tail to the body. Chums run most of the summer, from early July through September, and later in some places.

Silvers, or coho salmon, are the last to run, arriving in mid-July and peaking about a month later. Though they average 6 to 9 pounds, it's not uncommon to

(cont'd)

(cont'd)

catch a silver that weighs 20 pounds or more. They easily can be mistaken for jack kings, smaller but sexually aggressive Chinooks. After spawning, cohos darken, and the heads of the males swell. Silvers make for good, all-purpose eating, though they're not as prized at the table as reds or kings. They make for great sportfishing, too, as they'll readily snap at a lure and put up a memorable fight. Before they spawn, silvers tend to gather in large groups in river mouths, bays, and sloughs, making them an easy target for anglers.

in the Chugach Mountains to Turnagain Arm, offers up red, chum, and silver salmon as well as Dolly Varden. Access is by boat launch. From Portage Lake, Portage Creek has all of the same species plus pink salmon. Clear sloughs and confluences throughout the system can be great spots to catch salmon and char, too.

KENAI PENINSULA

With its scenic rivers, mountain vistas, and bountiful forests, the Kenai is a favorite weekend getaway for city folks from Anchorage. And in the heart of the Peninsula, right along the Sterling Highway, you'll find some of the finest salmon fishing in the world.

Traffic from Anchorage funnels south on the Seward Highway across the 9-mile swath of land where the Kenai connects to the mainland. Alaskans complain about the crowded highways, especially on summer weekends, but by Lower 48 standards, there's not much cause to whine.

Once you get past the fishing hot spots near Cooper Landing, the crowds thin, and you'll find plenty of wild country to explore. Follow the Sterling Highway all the way to its end, or stick with the Seward Highway and end up in—where else?—Seward. Alaskans associate Seward with Prince William Sound, so we've covered it in that chapter, despite the fact that it's technically part of the Kenai landmass.

Soldotna and its sister city Kenai form the service hub of the Peninsula, with the small towns of Cooper Landing, Sterling, Kasilof, and Ninilchik rounding out the options for anglers, outdoor enthusiasts, and visitors who just want to get away to the woods. At the end of the road, there's the eclectic town of Homer, a vibrant community focused on fishing, outdoor activities, and the arts.

KENAI/SOLDOTNA

Soldotna is a young community, formed in the 1940s with homesteading offered to veterans returning from the war. Strategically located at the junction of the Sterling and Kenai Spur Highways, Soldotna now serves as the headquarters for the Kenai Peninsula Borough as well as for Peninsula branches of state offices.

Ten miles down the Kenai Spur Highway, the Kenai River empties into Cook Inlet at Kenai, the largest city on the Peninsula. The site was originally home to the Dena'ina Indians, and in 1791 the Russians established Fort St. Nicholas there. A few years later the Dena'ina defeated the 150 Russian settlers and reclaimed their community. The U.S. Army established Fort Kenai in 1869 in the aftermath of Seward's purchase of the Alaskan territory and the discovery of gold on the Russian River. More recently, natural gas and oil were discovered in the area, and there are now 15 drilling platforms off the coast in Cook Inlet.

Nearby Cooper Landing, with an estimated population of 500, was established as a miners' camp in the early 1900s. Tom and Frank Towle furthered development by building pioneer homes and offering guide services for moose, bear, and Dall sheep. In the 1930s, several fox farms added to the growth of the community.

Getting Here, Getting Around

Soldotna is 149 miles from Anchorage on the Sterling Highway, while Kenai is 159 miles from Alaska's biggest city. The highway is well-maintained, but it's only two lanes for much of the way, and traffic can be heavy during the summer when the fish are running. The Kenai Spur Highway connects Kenai and Soldotna. There's also commuter air service by small plane into the Kenai Municipal Airport.

However you arrive, a stop at one of the local visitor centers will help you get oriented. Check out the Soldotna Visitor Information Center (907–262–1337, www.soldotna chamber.com) at 44790 Sterling Highway, and the Kenai Visitor and Cultural Center (907–283–1991, www.visitkenai.com) at 11471 Kenai Spur Highway.

Accommodations

The summer season runs from May to September, peaking in July at the height of the salmon runs. Most accommodations are designed with anglers in mind, with fish-cleaning, packaging, and freezing facilities for guests to use. In general, you can expect clean, comfortable, and friendly facilities without a whole lot of frills.

Unless we say otherwise, you can assume that major credit cards are accepted, smoking is not allowed (except outdoors), there's no wheelchair access, and pets are not accommodated. Price codes indicate the average price for a double room, excluding taxes and gratuities, during the summer season. Rates will generally be lower in the winter.

Price Codes

$. . . . . Less than $100
$$ . . . . $100–$150
$$$ . . . . $151–$200
$$$$ . . . . More than $200

Kenai River

Alaskan Sourdough B&B $$
P.O. Box 812
Cooper Landing, AK 99575
(907) 595–1541
www.alaskansourdoughbb.com
Here's a fun combination: Eskimo and Cajun hospitality on the beautiful Kenai River. In addition to a clean, comfortable room with private bath, you'll get a hot, home-cooked breakfast every morning. Rooms come in a variety of bed configurations, with coffeemaker, microwave, minifridge, iron, ironing board, and free morning paper. Ready to relax after a full day of fishing? Fire up the sauna, or cook up a barbeque and have dinner at the picnic table. The Alaskan Sourdough is on the quiet side of the river, so you should get a good night's sleep. Despite all those jokes about wives and fishing, this B&B has found a unique way to marry the two, literally. They have an Eskimo wedding chapel in the heart of fishing country, where your host Willie Johnson can help you tie the knot or renew your vows. One guest room has wheelchair access.

Anglers Lodge $$$
36030 Stephans Drive, Sterling
(888) 262–1747
www.anglerslodge.com
Since 1987 this family-owned lodge has been providing full-service fishing packages with comfortable home-away-from-home accommodations on the banks of the world-famous Kenai River. Owner Roger Byerly is a patient, friendly, experienced fishing guide, while his wife Marlene serves up a big helping of Alaskan hospitality with her fresh-baked goodies and home-cooked meals. Rooms come with coffeemakers, mini-fridges, and use of the hot tub. The lodge offers a great wilderness setting next to a state park, but it's still on the road system and close to town. The room rate reflects the cost of accommodations only. Most guests at the Anglers Lodge book accommodations as part of a fishing package.

Frenchy's Fishing Cabins $$
Scout Lake Road, Sterling
(907) 344–4846, (800) 939–4846
www.adventurebnb.com
Anchorage B&B—owner Karen French offers cozy cabin getaways with Kenai River access. The fishing-themed rooms include kitchen privileges, private bath with shared shower, telephone, cable television, balcony, iron, ironing board, free morning paper, continental breakfast (or boxed lunch for your fishing trip), and discounts at local attractions. Frenchy is a longtime Alaskan, and she'll make sure you feel right at home.

Gwin's Lodge $$–$$$
Mile 52, 14865 Sterling Highway
Cooper Landing
(907) 595–1266
www.gwinslodge.com
For more than half a century, Gwin's Lodge has been hosting visitors to the salmon-rich confluence of the Kenai and Russian Rivers.

The original owners cut, hauled, and hand-peeled the logs to build this historic road-house, completing it in 1952. The Standard Log Cabins are a no-frills option with two full-size beds, private bath with shower, and a roll-away bed. Log Cabins with Kitchen and Loft add an extra bed plus kitchenette, while the Cottage House Units include a full kitchen, dining, and great room with satellite television and sleeping for five or six. The Standard and Deluxe Log Chalet Units are newer, with additional sleeping areas. Gwin's is almost like a little town, with a full-service restaurant and fishing-tackle shop on-site. They've also added wireless Internet access throughout the property. (Also see our write-up in the Restaurants section of this chapter.)

The Hutch Bed and Breakfast $
Mile 48.5 Sterling Highway, Cooper Landing
(907) 595–1270
www.arctic.net/~hutch
Pet rabbits provide the theme for the Hutch, a three-story cedar lodge with 12 guest rooms, each with private entrance, private bath, coffeemaker, and free continental breakfast. They have every size bed, from twin to king. The rooms are nothing fancy, but you'll enjoy the convenient and scenic location with picnic tables, a barbeque grill, and campfire pit. Take your continental breakfast of coffee, juices, hot chocolate, cider, cereals, muffins, breads, bagels and fruit on the outdoor decks, weather permitting. One room is wheelchair accessible.

Soldotna

Alaska Riverview Lodge $$–$$$
24771 Amber Drive
(907) 260–7477
www.alaskariverview.com
From the banks of the quiet Kasilof River, one of the Peninsula's hidden treasures, watch the eagles soar and the moose wading in the water. You can fish from the Riverview's private dock or just soak up the scenery and follow the river as it changes with the tides. Choose from cabin units, a fully-equipped two-bedroom suite, or the Honeymoon Suite/Cabin right on the riverbank. Rooms come with coffeemakers, microwaves, mini-fridges, and free continental breakfast. If you like, your friendly hosts will arrange for guided fishing in the area. Once you've caught your limit, you can make use of the Riverview's outdoor grill, freezer space, and fish-processing area with vacuum sealer. Wheelchair-accessible rooms are available, and pets are accepted on approval.

Aspen Hotel $$$
326 Binkley Court
(907) 260–7736
www.aspenhotelsak.com
The Aspen offers 63 rooms in the heart of Soldotna, including comfortable suites. All rooms include coffeemaker, refrigerator, microwave, iron, ironing board, hair dryer, telephone, and television with VCR. They also have an exercise room, a business center, a guest laundry room, and a conference room. A wheelchair-accessible suite is available.

Aurora Nights Bed and Breakfast $$
33215 Rensselaer Lane
(907) 262–2918
www.auroranightsbnb.com
If you're looking for privacy with a great location only 2 miles from several fishing hot spots, you'll enjoy Aurora Nights' guesthouse, complete with a stunning view of the Spur Mountains. On K-Beach Road between Soldotna and Kenai, the guesthouse sleeps six, but if you have a smaller group, you can rent just one room. Each bedroom has a queen-size and a twin bed, and there's a Jacuzzi tub in the bathroom as well as an outdoor hot tub on the lower deck. The guesthouse also includes a full-service kitchen, continental breakfast, laundry facilities, private deck, and use of the barbeque. Credit cards are accepted only through PayPal (www.paypal.com) online.

Escape for Two B&B Guesthouse $$$
49300 Charlie Brown Drive
(907) 262–1493
www.escapefortwo.com

Pamper yourself at this romantic getaway located 7 miles south of Soldotna on 40 acres with a private lake. Soak in the jetted tub for two, light the candles, turn on the music, and relax. From the rose petals on the bed to the luxury linens, attention to detail abounds. The guesthouse comes with coffeemaker, microwave, minifridge, and a hearty breakfast basket.

Gulls Landing Bed and Breakfast $$
485 Lingonberry Lane
(907) 262–6668
www.gullslanding.com
From a secluded bend in the Kenai River, Gulls Landing offers three comfortable guest rooms, one with private bath. Guests share a living room with river view as well as a fully equipped kitchen. Enjoy a hot breakfast in the riverfront sunroom, or if you're headed off for a full day of fishing, grab an early continental breakfast. Outside, you can relax on the landscaped lawn or soak up the view from multiple decks. Fish right from the dock, or have your guide pick you up there. Due to the proximity of the river, children younger than age 10 are not allowed. Pets are welcome, but they must stay in the garage. Gulls Landing is conveniently located next to Swiftwater Park, behind the Soldotna "Y."

Kenai River Retreat $$$
360 West Endicott Drive
(907) 262–1361, (800) 987–8201
www.kenairiverretreat.com
Who says you can't combine adventure with style? At the Kenai River Retreat, you'll enjoy first-class accommodations in a convenient yet secluded location next to a state recreation area, right on the Kenai River and just 1 mile from downtown Soldotna. Suites come with queen-size beds, full kitchens, irons, ironing boards, and leather furniture. Your friendly hosts will provide laundry facilities, fishing gear, mud boots, clam shovels, and a freezer for guests to use. You can even help yourself to fresh herbs from the greenhouse and grill your fish on your private deck. Enjoy

bank fishing and great hiking trails plus amazing views of the river, mountains, and wildlife.

Silvertip Lodge Guest Cabins $–$$
35930 Bowman Road
Mile 90.5 Sterling Highway
www.silvertiplodgeandcabins.com
Tucked away in a beautiful birch hollow 4 miles outside of Soldotna, Silvertip Lodge offers six cabins and three bed-and-breakfast rooms. The owners take a personal interest in making sure their guests have the quiet and relaxing stay that Alaskan visitors crave. Their cabins accommodate up to six people and come with full kitchens, including coffeemaker, microwave, minifridge, iron, ironing board, free morning paper, and continental breakfast. The bed-and-breakfast rooms, each of which has a television and VCR, are downstairs in an authentic log home. Anglers will appreciate the on-site fish-cleaning and freezing facilities.

Soldotna Inn $$
35041 Kenai Spur Highway
(907) 262–9169, (888) 262–9169
www.mykels.com
The Soldotna Inn has been providing quality lodging and fine dining since the early 1970s. Though the building is older, the inn is well-maintained and clean, with wi-fi Internet access throughout, a new continental breakfast area, and an expanded lobby. Each room features art by local Alaskans, and the furniture includes locally milled and manufactured pieces. The Alaskan flair and emphasis on customer service sets the Soldotna Inn apart from the usual chain hotel. They offer 18 rooms with microwaves, refrigerators, and coffeemakers. For great rates on long-term rentals, check out their fully furnished apartments, complete with living rooms and kitchens. Conveniently located in the heart of Soldotna, 0.75 mile from the Sterling Highway and a short walk from the Kenai River, the Soldotna Inn offers both smoking and nonsmoking rooms, and they accept pets in designated rooms.

Kenai

Daniels Lake Lodge $–$$
Mile 29.7 Kenai Spur Highway
P.O. Box 1444
Kenai, AK 99611
(907) 776–5578, (800) 774–5578
www.danielslakelodge.com
The log cabins and guest rooms at Daniels
Lake Lodge are spread across nine wooded
acres between Kenai and the Captain Cook
State Recreation Area. Watch for wildlife along
the scenic lakeshore, or get out on the water
by renting a rowboat, paddleboat, motorboat,
or canoe. There's great rainbow trout fishing,
and you can even take off in a floatplane right
from the dock. All cabins and guest rooms
come with full kitchen facilities and televisions.
Kitchens are stocked with the ingredients for a
self-serve breakfast, including homemade
bread, reindeer sausage, pancake mix, toaster
waffles, cereal, and even fresh duck eggs
when the ducks are cooperating. Laundry facilities, hot tub, telephone, and barbeque grills
also are available for guest use. Cabins sleep
four people, with a two-night-minimum stay.

Grouchy Old Woman Bed and Breakfast $
48570 North Earl Drive
(907) 776–8775
www.grouchyoldwoman.homestead.com
Who can resist a name like this? The grouchy
old woman herself runs this four-room bed-
and-breakfast, located 20 miles north of Kenai
on the peaceful shores of Daniels Lake. Three
rooms have queen-size beds and one has two
twins with a roll-away option. Expect a full
breakfast during your stay, with sourdough
pancakes, bacon, and fruit as one favorite.
Take a walk along the lake and onto the dock
to fully experience the peace and quiet here.
Two rooms offer wheelchair access, and pets
may be accepted on a case-by-case basis.

Kenai Landing Hotel $–$$
2101 Bowpicker Lane
(907) 335–2500
www.kenailanding.com
Ninety years of history make this restored

cannery a fun and unique overnight option on
the Kenai waterfront. In the historic Hen
House, you can get a private, newly remodeled guest room with shared bath and shower
facilities, queen-size bed, telephone, sink, and
television with DVD. Rooms at the richly decorated Machinist Bunkhouse offer the same
amenities with the option of two queen-size
or twin-size beds. Dating from 1922, the Fisherman's Cottages are perfect for families or
groups, with three bedrooms, a living room,
telephone, television, microwave, and refrigerator. Kenai Landing also offers scenic riverview rooms and suites with private baths. The
waterfront resort area also offers a full-service
restaurant, dock, and a warehouse market
with shops featuring local arts and crafts.

Restaurants

Though fish is the mainstay, you'll find a variety of menu items and dining options along
the Peninsula. These eateries will be busiest
in the summer, but you can assume they're
open year-round, seven days a week, unless
we say otherwise. You also can expect that
they'll take major credit cards. Reservations
are accepted but usually not necessary. We'll
note wheelchair access if it's available.

The price codes below include the average cost of a meal for two, excluding cocktails,
wine, appetizers, desserts, tax, and tips. Most
places that serve dinner have a license for
beer and wine, and many also serve cocktails.

Price Codes

$. . . . . Less than $15
$$ . . . . $15–$25
$$$ . . . . $26–$40
$$$$ . . . . More than $40

Kenai River

Gwin's Lodge $$$
Mile 52, 14865 Sterling Highway
Cooper Landing
(907) 595–1266
www.gwinslodge.com
Gwin's is a landmark stop along the Sterling
Highway, offering warm Alaskan atmosphere

and plenty of activity as great homemade food is dished out around the clock during the summer. Start your day with a hearty three-egg scramble, such as the Trapper Creek Alaskan smoked salmon and Monterey Jack cheese, or a Gwin's Breakfast Burrito with scrambled eggs, sausage, cheddar cheese, and onion wrapped up in a flour tortilla and served with a side of salsa. For lunch, choose a burger from Gwin's famous lineup or a homemade sandwich, such as the grilled halibut. Dinner favorites include grilled salmon (of course) and the Seafood Casserole, featuring shrimp, scallops, and crab in a cream white wine sauce with crumb topping. In addition to the tasty food, Gwin's has ample parking. (Also see our listing for Gwin's in the Accommodations section of this chapter.)

Soldotna

Froso's   **$$$**
35433 Kenai Spur Highway
(907) 262–5306
The Mediterranean facade may look a little out of place, but the food brings locals back again and again. They have a large selection of steak and seafood, including Stuffed Halibut ala Froso's and Milano Shrimp stuffed with crab meat, wrapped in bacon, and served with Froso's special cream sauce. They also offer pasta along with Mexican and Greek specialties, including their signature Souvlaki, featuring marinated cubes of sirloin seasoned, seared, and served with green pepper, onions, and mushrooms.

Mykel's Restaurant   **$$$$**
35041 Kenai Spur Highway
(907) 262–6736
www.mykels.com
Located in the Soldotna Inn (see our write-up in the Accommodations section of this chapter), Mykel's is a top dining choice for locals, featuring creative dishes with fresh ingredients, including local seafood. Try their Walnut Crusted Salmon with Raspberry Beurre Blanc, Prawns and Wild Mushroom Florentine, or Pepper Steak a la Jens, with twin tournedos of

filet mignon topped with Jens's "Almost Famous" pepper sauce. The friendly waitstaff will be happy to help you pair one of their fine wines with your dinner selection. The atmosphere is casual, and there's plenty of parking.

Kenai

Charlotte's Bakery, Café, and Espresso   **$$**
115 South Willow Street, Suite 102
(907) 283–2777
Charlotte's offers contemporary home-style cuisine for breakfast and lunch. For breakfast, try the Mediterranean Scramble, featuring Charlotte's potatoes surrounded by a deep dish omelet of spinach, tomatoes, feta, provolone, and a Kalamata olive garnish. Another breakfast favorite is Charlissa's Stuffed French Toast, made from Charlotte's honey-oat bread and topped with honey cream cheese. There's a great selection of salads for lunch, including the Gobbs of Cobb with bacon, blue cheese, hard-boiled egg, red onion, avocado, cubed smoked turkey, and tomato. You also can choose from a fun selection of sandwiches, such as the Hawaiian Wannabe Returns, with teriyaki chicken, ham, provolone, and grilled pineapple served with honey mustard on a warm croissant, or Terry & Jessica's Mushroom Swiss, featuring roast beef, Swiss cheese, and sautéed mushrooms on a grilled hoagie with roasted garlic aioli and au jus. Charlotte's is open Monday through Friday from 7:00 A.M. to 4:00 P.M.

Kenai's Old Town Village Restaurant   **$$**
1000 Mission Avenue, Suite 111
(907) 283–4515

i Looking for nightlife? Check out BJ's at 44695 Sterling Highway (907–262–1882), where Alaska's own Hobo Jim plays live folk music on select Friday and Saturday nights. Other popular spots include the Riverside House at 44611 Sterling Highway (907–262–0500) and Hooligan's at 44715 Sterling Highway (907–262–8346), featuring live music and pool.

A refurbished 1918 cannery building provides the ambience for this unique restaurant, where you can feast on Alaska seafood, steaks, and good old-fashioned home cooking. Beer, wine, and homemade root beer are available with your meal. Top it all off with Old Town Village's hand-dipped ice cream. Located 2 blocks from the visitor center, this eatery offers fabulous views of Cook Inlet, the Kenai River, and the mountains.

Shopping

You won't find any mega-malls in the small towns of the Kenai Peninsula, but Kenai and Soldotna have several grocery and retail options as well as specialty shops. If you're there on a Saturday, check out the farmers' market, held from mid-June to mid-September at the junction of the Kenai Spur Highway and Corral Avenue, where you'll find Alaska-grown produce, plants, and flowers and Alaskan-made gifts, arts, and crafts. Hours are from 10:00 A.M. to 2:00 P.M.

Soldotna

Birch Tree Gallery
P.O. Box 2589
Soldotna, AK 99669
(907) 262–4048
In a scenic wooded spot on the banks of the Kenai River, Birch Tree Gallery showcases the work of Kathleen Adell Logan, whose primary media is transparent watercolor, with flowers and Alaskan landscapes among her favorite subjects. The gallery also sells jewelry, hand-woven baskets, note cards, stained glass, and burl furniture. Hand-dyed silk scarves and ties, along with felted hats, are also featured. The gallery offers a full line of knitting supplies, including free knitting lessons and assistance. There's free gift wrapping and packaging for mailing, too.

Donna's Country and Victorian Gifts
Blacy Mall
(907) 262–9254
Fisherman's wife's revenge? Donna's specializes in it, offering an extensive selection of

beautiful items for your home, arranged room by room, from the cabin to the "red room" to the parlor and the closet. The Alaskana collection includes candles, cookie cutters, moose figurines, bear lamps, Eskimo dolls, and Glacier Ice Crystal Potpourri. In fact, a dozen different scents of Crystal Potpourri are made at Donna's. They also sell scented beads, candles, and lotions. They're open Monday through Saturday from 10:00 A.M. to 6:00 P.M.

Robin Place Fabrics
105 Robin Place
(907) 262–5438
Quilting is a favorite Alaskan pastime, and the Peninsula's "Must Stop for Quilters," Robin Place, features exquisite quilts, specialty fabrics, original wall hangings, and original Alaskan quilt patterns and kits. This cozy home-style shop hosts the Quilting on the Kenai summer quilt show on the third weekend in June.

Sweeney's Clothing
35081 Kenai Spur Highway
(907) 262–5916
Didn't pack quite what you need? Stop by Sweeney's, where you'll find a wide selection of brand-name outdoor clothing, including fleece wear, chest waders, rain gear, and knee boots. Levi's, Columbia, Sorel, Woolrich, and Wolverine are among the names you'll recognize on their racks. They run a big warehouse clearance sale all summer long, and they'll even ship your purchase for you.

Kenai

Fireweed Gifts
202 North Forest Drive
(907) 283–6107
www.fireweedgifts.com
Gifts, greenhouse, herb garden, espresso—you'll find it all at the Fireweed, located just north of the Kenai Visitor's Center. If you're looking for unique Alaskan gifts, check out their quilted wall hangings, spices, dips, soaps, candles, jewelry, pottery, ceramics, and wildflower seeds. They also sell music

boxes, wind chimes, fabric baskets, and decorative table accessories. Fresh plants and produce are available in season, and the gift shop is open year-round.

Kenai Fabric Center
115 North Willow
(907) 283–4595

Family owned and operated since 1970, the Kenai Fabric Center features more than 7,000 bolts of quilting cottons, including wildlife and nature prints, as well as a full selection of notions for quilting, sewing, knitting, and crochet. They have kits and pattern books along with sewing machines and sergers, and they also offer instructional classes. The store is open Monday through Saturday from 9:00 A.M. to 6:00 P.M. and Sunday from 1:00 to 4:00 P.M.

Warehouse Market at Kenai Landing
2101 Bowpicker Lane
(907) 335–2500
www.kenailanding.com

Wander the market and peruse 25 distinctive shops. For fine art, visit Art Works, the Jim Evenson Gallery, and Peninsula Art Guild Outlet. Carved gift items can be found at Alaska Decoy Company and Alaska Horn and Antler, featuring horn, antler, ivory, bone, and stone art. Fur slippers, gloves, and vintage clothing are for sale at Silver Fox Slippers, while Turtle Island Imports offers woolens, batik clothing, jewelry, and scarves. Raven's Trinket and Collectibles, The Cove Gallerie, and White Dove Paper and Design offer all sorts of gift and collectible items.

Attractions

While fishing is the big draw, it's not all the Kenai area has to offer. From history to native culture and wildlife, the area has great free and low-cost attractions to pique your interest.

Not all of these attractions are open in the winter, so be sure to note any seasonal restrictions in the write-ups. The price codes show what you'll generally pay for one adult admission. Children and seniors are eligible for discounts at many of these places, and some offer military discounts as well. If admission is free, there's no price code.

Price Codes

$	Less than $5.00
$$	$5.00–$10.00
$$$	$11.00–$15.00
$$$$	More than $15.00

Historic Kenai Landing
2101 Bowpicker Lane, Kenai
(907) 335–2500
www.kenailanding.com

Ninety years of history grace this unique waterfront cannery-turned-resort at the mouth of the Kenai River. A thriving arts and entertainment venue, Kenai Landing offers a full-service restaurant, lodging, waterfront promenade, theater, and indoor warehouse market with more than 25 specialty shops on 65 acres of prime waterfront. The landing also features a boat launch, dock facilities, custom fish processing, and a museum.

K'Beq $
Mile 52.6 Sterling Highway
Cooper Landing
(907) 283–3633

Just 5 miles south of Cooper Landing, directly across from the entrance to the Russian River Campground, you can journey back in time to learn the ways of the region's original Dena'ina Athabascan inhabitants. Interpretative walks hosted by tribal elders and youth feature archaeological sites, ancient artifacts, and traditional plants, highlighting the Dena'ina's respect for the good land of the Kenai. K'Beq also has a gift shop featuring traditional Dena'ina arts and crafts. Nominal parking and tour-pass fees apply. K'Beq (meaning "footprints") is open seasonally from Monday through Saturday, 10:00 A.M. to 6:00 P.M.

Kenai National Wildlife Refuge
Visitor Center
Ski Hill Road
P.O. Box 2139
Soldotna, AK 99669
(907) 262–7021
http://kenai.fws.gov
Plan your next outdoor adventure and learn about the wide range of habitats supported by the refuge at this full-service visitor center. Check out the wildlife displays, videos, and guided walks along the 0.75-mile Keen-Eye Nature Trail. They have complete information about camping, cabins, hiking, fishing, and wildlife viewing within the refuge. Summer hours are 8:00 A.M. to 4:30 P.M. on weekdays, and 9:00 A.M. to 6:00 P.M. on weekends.

Kenai Visitor and Cultural Center
11471 Kenai Spur Highway, Kenai
(907) 283–1991
www.visitkenai.com
This extensive visitor center includes exhibits featuring the history of Kenai, free interpretive programs, and an Alaska Native Arts Now museum-quality display of traditional and contemporary Native art. There's a gift shop on-site, too. There are no fees for the visitor center, but a $3.00 charge to view the Alaska Native art exhibits.

Soldotna Historical Society Museum
Centennial Park Road
P.O. Box 1986
Soldotna, AK 99669
(907) 262–3832
It might not seem old by other standards, but the founding settlers of Soldotna lived in rather primitive conditions when they arrived in 1947. The Historical Society Museum showcases a historic log village, including the last territorial school from 1958, where gas lanterns provided light in the cold, dark winters. Two of the "habitable dwellings" that entitled homesteaders to 80 acres of free land are on display as well. In Damon Hall, originally constructed for the Alaska Centennial, you'll find a large collection of wildlife mounts. The museum is open seasonally

from 10:00 A.M. to 4:00 P.M. Tuesday through Saturday and from noon to 4:00 P.M. on Sunday. You can drive here or follow a short woodland walking trail from the Soldotna Visitor Center.

Parks, Recreation, and Tours

More than two million acres of the Kenai Peninsula, from Cook Inlet to Kachemak Bay, are part of the Kenai National Wildlife Refuge. Over half of the refuge is designated wilderness, but the remainder is accessible for recreational use. Within the refuge are all the major habitats found in Alaska, home to brown and black bears, lynx, wolverines, mountain goats, eagles, moose, caribou, and a wide variety of shorebirds and fish. The refuge begins at Mile 55 of the Sterling Highway. Be sure to stop by the refuge visitor center in Soldotna to check out the wildlife displays, nature trail, and videos for an excellent orientation to the refuge and its habitats. Hunting and boating are permitted within the refuge, though motorized watercrafts are not allowed on the canoe-system lakes.

Soldotna boasts more river city parks than anywhere else in Alaska, with more than 3,700 feet of elevated boardwalk and 220 campsites among them. You can access the river at Centennial Park, Swiftwater Park, Soldotna Creek Park, and Rotary Park, with camping at Centennial and Soldotna Creek Parks. There are also five day-use parks with picnic tables and playground equipment. Minimal daily-use fees are charged at some of the river parks. Bring your binoculars, as there's a good chance of spotting bald eagles feeding on fish along the river.

In Kenai, you can relax at the Leif Hansen Memorial Park within the city limits or check out the view at Cunningham Park as you head out of town toward Soldotna. You can take a self-guided walking tour of Old Town Kenai, following maps available at the Kenai Visitor Center. Among the sites you'll see are a Russian Orthodox Church built in 1894, a cabin belonging to a homesteader with the colorful nickname of Moosemeat John, and Fort

Kenay, a replica of the original Russian Ortho-dox school built in 1900. For more history, head south on the Sterling Highway to the vil-lage of Ninilchik, where buildings from the 1800s include the first Russian school, the Ninilchik Village Cache, and the Village Store.

At the end of the Kenai Spur Highway, Captain Cook State Park offers spectacular views of the inlet and mountains. On clear days, you might even see Denali. Agate hunters and whale watchers especially enjoy the beach. Another great beach is at the base of the cliffs in Old Town Kenai, where you'll find nice sand, shells, and great mountain views. From the top of the bluffs, you might catch a glimpse of a beluga whale an hour or so before or after the high tide. Bring your binoculars and your tide table, as this is home to one of the fastest tides in the world.

The Bridge Access Road, about 6 miles west of Soldotna, is a great place to view Canada and snow geese feeding along the Kenai Flats. There's an outlook point with a telescope for checking out the geese and a variety of shorebirds. Another fun adventure is berry picking along Marathon Road, south of Kenai on the Spur Highway.

Want to see what goes on inside a fish-processing plant? Visit the BEACHM Fishery in Kasilof, 25 miles south of Soldotna. Your free tour will include a history of commercial fishing in the Kenai Peninsula. Call (907) 262–3233 to schedule a tour.

Alaska Birding Tours
P.O. Box 2465
Soldotna, AK 99669
(907) 262–5218, (800) 725–3327
www.alaskabirdingtours.com
The Kenai Peninsula isn't only about fish. Birders will marvel at the large variety of species here, including puffins, auklets, mur-relets, boreal chickadees, red-throated loons, spruce grouse, and three-toed woodpeckers. Alaska Birding Tours offers expeditions by powerboat, drift boat, hiking, and canoe. Choose from day-trip and inclusive package options in either fresh- or saltwater venues.

Send them your "must see" list, and they'll help you get it done.

Alaska C & C Stables
P.O. Box 2837
Soldotna, AK 99669
(907) 262–5401, (907) 398–4904
www.cowgalak.homestead.com
C & C Stables offers a nice variety of packages for exploring the Kenai wilderness on horse-back. Take a beach ride, where you'll see signs of the 1964 earthquake, eagles, local mammals, and shorebirds while you watch commercial fishermen pulling in their catch. Another fun option is the high-country moun-tain ride, with a campfire meal to top off your scenic trek. You also can try a two-and-a-half-hour fly-fishing expedition at a mountain lake, with glaciers and waterfalls along the way; a fishing guide plus float tubes, equipment, and lunch come with this all-day adventure. Other options include wilderness rides from Sol-dotna, pack trips, and family excursions. Lessons are available, and the ranch is open year-round. Children must be age seven or older to ride.

Alaska Rivers Company
Mile 50 Sterling Highway
Cooper Landing
(907) 595–1226, (888) 595–1226
www.alaskariverscompany.com
Whether you're looking for a scenic float, guided fishing, hiking, or cabin rentals, Alaska Rivers has it all. Try a three-hour float on the turquoise Kenai River, or a seven-hour rafting adventure through the Kenai Canyon rapids. They also will put together custom white-water packages on Class IV rapids. For anglers, there are half-day and full-day drifting packages, plus a fishing add-on for the Kenai Canyon trip. If you're a land-lubber, try a four-hour hike with your own naturalist guide. Water-based adventures include experienced guides, waterproof gear bags, life jackets, rain gear, and rubber boots. Be sure to ask about senior discounts, group rates, and half-price rates for children younger than age 12.

Great Alaska Adventure Lodge
33881 Sterling Highway, Sterling
(907) 262–4515, (800) 544–2261
www.kenaidaytours.com
From this three-star lodge on 25 acres at the confluence of the Kenai and Moose Rivers, you can set out on all sorts of wilderness adventures. Try fly-out bear viewing on a day trip, or stay overnight at the Lake Clark Bear Camp. Either way you'll get to see bears in their natural habitat as they feed, play, and fight. You also can use the lodge as a home base for fishing Kenai kings, reds, or silvers as well as trout or char. Overnight stays are not required, and you can opt for transportation direct from Anchorage if you like. For longer expeditions, the Kenai Wildlife Tent Lodge serves as a base camp to guided fishing, hiking, canoeing, and kayaking adventures. Safari Camp trips include camping in permanent adventure, wildlife, and kayak camps and explorations of the Kenai National Wildlife Refuge, Kenai Fjords National Park, and the Chugach National Forest.

Kenai Lake Sea Kayak Adventures
P.O. Box 801
Cooper Landing, AK 99572
(907) 595–3441, (907) 598–1102
www.kenailake.com
Paddle the headwaters of the world-famous Kenai River, keeping an eye out for mountain goats and Dall sheep on the slopes of the majestic Kenai Mountains. The three-hour kayaking excursion includes instruction, guided narration, snacks, and drinks. Kenai Lake Adventures offers single and double kayaks as well as kayaks sized for children, dry bags, life jackets, paddles, and rain gear. They also have mountain bike rentals, including repair kits and helmets, by the half or full day. Take a guided bike tour of the Crescent Lake area, or, for the ultimate adventure, land by seaplane on the lake and ride out on your mountain bike. They offer guided fishing on Crescent Lake, too.

North Peninsula Recreation Area
P.O. Box 7116
Nikiski, AK 99635
(907) 776–8472, (907) 776–8800
A full slate of year-round recreational activities awaits at this expansive facility at Mile 23.4 of the Kenai Spur Highway. There's a weather-protected outdoor rink for recreational skating and hockey, a multipurpose field for softball, baseball, and soccer, a picnic area, and nature/fitness trails. Inside, they have a recreational pool with waterslide, spa, and rain umbrella. The pool is surrounded by glass, so you can take in the scenery while you swim or relax in the spa. You also can reserve racquetball courts or work out in the exercise room.

Hiking and Camping

Through forests, over hills, along the beach, or among the mountains—you'll find great hiking and camping in the central Kenai Peninsula, with more than 200 miles of trails to enjoy. Within the Kenai National Wildlife Refuge, try the 5-mile (round-trip) Skilak Lookout Trail, where new growth following the 1996 Hidden Creek fire attracts moose, snowshoe rabbits, and hawks. At the trail's end, you can look back at Skilak Lake to see the cormorant and gull rookeries on the lake's islands. You also can pick up the Lookout Trail at Mile 5.4 of Skilak Lake Road. If you prefer a shorter hike, you'll find spectacular river and lake views along the 1.5-mile Hideout Trail, located at Mile 1.9 of Skilak Lake Road. Both hikes are moderate in difficulty.

The Kenai National Wildlife Refuge maintains several campgrounds along Skilak Lake

i There's even golfing on the Kenai Peninsula. Birch Ridge in Soldotna (907–262–5270, www.birchridgegolf.com) is a nine-hole course complete with Alaskan tundra and woods, with holes 4 and 5 overlooking Mt. Redoubt and Mt. Iliamna volcanoes. Golf/cottage packages are available. The Kenai Gold Course (907–283–7500) also offers good golfing at reasonable prices.

i An infestation of spruce beetles on the Kenai Peninsula has left dead standing trees that are ripe for forest fires. When building a campfire, try to use an existing campfire site or a fire pan, and keep water nearby in case flames spread. The Alaska Interagency Wildland Fire Management Plan does allow controlled burns for the natural cycling of ecosystem, but there are plenty of lightning-sparked blazes in Alaska, so the idea is to keep man-made fires to a minimum.

Road. The largest and most developed of these is the Hidden Lake Camground at Mile 3.6. There's a nice picnic area along the lake, with campfire programs on weekends throughout the summer. Smaller campgrounds with boat launches include the Upper Skilak at Mile 8.4 and the Lower Skilak at Mile 13.6. The Engineer Lake Campground at Mile 9.4 offers scenic canoeing.

Both the U.S. Fish and Wildlife Service and the Alaska State Park Service maintain rustic cabins that can be rented by the night. Some are remote, with no road access, and none have indoor plumbing. These cabins are quite popular, especially with locals, so it's a good idea to investigate your options well in advance of your trip. Contact the Kenai National Wildlife Refuge (907–262–7021, 877–285–5628, http://kenai.fws.gov/cabin.htm) or the State Park Service Kenai Area Office (907–262–5581, www.state.ak.us, click on Hot Topics, Online Services, State Park Cabins).

The Russian River Campground at Mile 52.6 of the Sterling Highway is a favorite when the red salmon are running, so be sure to get there early if you want a spot. There are 84 campsites, with water, toilets, tables, fire pits, and fish-cleaning stations within the campground. You'll also find phones and a dump station there. The campground is operated by Alaska Recreational Management (877–444–6777, www.reserveusa .com), with fees ranging from $13 to $20 for RV occupancy.

The city of Soldotna's Centennial Park Campground has 190 designated campsites, some with river frontage and several with wheelchair access. At the park booth, there are pay phones, ice, firewood, and newspapers. There's 95 feet of "fishwalk" for casting your line as well as two boat launches. It's a popular spot in the summer, but overflow parking is provided while you wait your turn for a site. The city's Swiftwater Park has 60 campsites in relative seclusion, with 1,200 feet of river boardwalk and an RV dump station. Day-use and overnight fees apply; call (907) 262–3151 or go to www.ci.soldotna .ak.us for more information.

Beluga Lookout Lodge and RV Park
929 Mission Avenue, Kenai
(907) 283–5999
www.belugalookout.com
Enjoy a unique camping experience with spectacular views of Cook Inlet, the Kenai River, and Mt. Redoubt. Beluga Lookout is located at the mouth of the Kenai River in historical Old Town Kenai. They offer view sites and pull-throughs, all with full hookups and cable television. They also have picnic tables, fire pits, Internet connections, and bike rentals. In addition to RV camping, Beluga Lookout rents rooms with kitchens by the day, the week, and the month.

Diamond M Ranch
P.O. Box 1776
Soldotna, AK 99669
(907) 283–9424
www.diamondmranch.com
With 80 acres to roam, the Diamond M features 50 amp full hookups with your choice of standard, super-size, or pull-through sites. If you're looking for activities, they have clam digs, tours, and Saturday-night socials. Walk to the Kenai River, hike or bike along the trails, or pick berries in season, all while enjoying stunning views of the Kenai River Flats and the Alaska Range. Leashed pets and well-behaved children are welcome. The Diamond M also rents modern cabins with kitchen and

bath, or you can opt to stay at their bed-and-breakfast, with hot tub, solarium, Alaskana collection, full breakfast featuring wild berry breads, and kitchen for guest use. Rates for RV sites are $28 to $35 per night.

Kenai Riverside Campground and RV Park
Mile 49.7 Sterling Highway
Cooper Landing
(907) 595–1406, (888) 536–2478
www.kenairiversidecampground.com

Camp along the Kenai River and fish right from the bank at Kenai Riverside Campground. They have 18 pull-through sites with 20/30 amp partial hookups as well as dry sites and tent camping. Since the campground is owned and operated by Alaska Wildland Adventures, you can stay on for guided rafting or fishing on the Kenai River if you like. Tent sites are $10 per night, dry sites are $15 per night, and partial hookups are $25 per night. Bed-and-breakfast rooms are available as well.

Klondike RV Park and Cabins
P.O. Box 1929
Soldotna, AK 99669
(907) 262–6035
www.klondikecabins.com

The Klondike features 27 full hookup RV sites, each 25 feet wide to accommodate slide-outs and tow vehicles. Standard sites have lawns, and premium sites have naturally wooded areas. 20/30/50 amp service is provided. Three authentic log cabins are also available for rent, 100 yards from the Kenai River. These handcrafted cabins are fully furnished and sleep four comfortably. RV rates are $30 to $35 per night.

Fishing

If there were an Alaskan thesaurus, Kenai would show up as a synonym for fishing. Alaskans who want hot salmon action with a rod and reel flock to the Peninsula every summer. If you don't like "combat fishing," standing shoulder to shoulder with hundreds of other anglers, you can opt for more exclusive fishing opportunities with drift boats and fly-out services.

The confluence of the Kenai and Russian Rivers offers the most productive red salmon fishing in the world; in fact, the crystal-clear Russian River is one of the few places where you can land a red with an artificial fly. The fish hole just downstream of the slow-moving waters is close to shore, making for excellent bank fishing. If you want a little more room to spread out, try the scenic waters upstream, near Russian River Falls. The Upper Russian River is closed to salmon fishing but offers great opportunities for rainbow trout in relative peace and quiet. In August and September, silver salmon show up in the same spots where you found reds earlier in the summer. You'll have the best luck with silvers using shiny lures and fly patterns.

The Russian and Kenai Rivers also offer trophy fishing for catch-and-release rainbow trout. On the Upper Kenai, only single-hook artificial lures are allowed. On the Russian, you're limited to flies only. If you really want a good shot at one of those trophy Dollies or rainbows, grab a drift-boat charter, putting in at either Mile 48 or Mile 54.8 of the Sterling Highway. You also have a good chance at salmon while drifting. Fly-out fishing for rainbows or grayling promises to be a more solitary pursuit.

During salmon season, sections of the banks along the Kenai River are periodically closed within 10 feet of either side of the waterline so that fish habitat may be preserved. Portions of the river are limited to drift fishing only, while other sections have

> **i** Snagging is illegal in all of Alaska's freshwater fisheries. In some areas, you may not remove a snagged fish from the water, even to snap a photo. If you accidentally snag a fish, land it quickly, use needle-nosed pliers to remove the hook, or cut the line if the hook cannot be readily removed. Point the fish upstream, cradling it until it resumes swimming on its own.

i It's hard to beat the fun and productive dip netting and gill netting for salmon out of the Kenai and Kasilof Rivers, but be warned that it's limited to residents only. Nonresidents cannot operate or even handle the gear when they're with resident dip or gill netters. Residents must have their permits and licenses with them at all times, and they must immediately record their catch and clip the tips of the tail fins.

limits on the motor horsepower used. For up-to-date information on regulations and restrictions, check with the Sport Fish Information Center (907–267–2218) or visit www.state.ak.us/adfg, click on Sport Fish, then select Southcentral Region.

King salmon season starts in mid-May and ends on July 31, with a limit of one fish per day. The season for reds (sockeye) begins in early June and ends in mid August, with a limit of three fish per day. Silver season starts in July and closes at the end of September, with a limit of two fish per day. Pinks can be caught only in even-numbered years, from mid-June to mid-August, with a limit of six fish per day.

Alaska Clearwater Sportfishing
P.O. Box 1181
Sterling, AK 99672
(907) 262–3797, (888) 662–3336
www.alaskaclearwater.com
Alaska Clearwater brings together experienced guides, quality equipment, and affordable pricing to offer dependable, professional guiding for red salmon, silvers, pinks, rainbows, and Dollies. Choose from guided drift-boat trips for rainbow trout on the Upper Kenai River, guided powerboat fishing for kings on the Lower Kenai, and guided drift-boat fishing for kings on the Kasilof River.

Alaska River Adventures
Mile 48 Sterling Highway
P.O. Box 725
Cooper Landing, AK 99572
(907) 595–2000, (888) 836–9027
www.alaskariveradventures.com
Guiding in the Peninsula since 1978, Alaska River Adventures offers both full- and half-day fishing along the Upper Kenai River, where you can expect plentiful salmon, rainbow trout, and Dolly Varden. Fly and spinning gear are provided. If you prefer, opt for a full day of fishing in relative peace and quiet on the Kasilof River, where you'll drift 5 miles above the ocean to catch salmon on the incoming tide. For fly fishing, you can try a full day of catch and release on a clear mountain stream, with salmon, rainbows, and Dollies the likely targets.

Alaska Troutfitters
P.O. Box 570
Cooper Landing, AK 99572
(907) 595–1212
http://aktroutfitters.com
Close to all the action at Mile 48.2 of the Sterling Highway, Alaska Troutfitters has a fly-fishing school, guided trout and salmon fishing, tackle store with rentals, and rooms with a view. They cater to all ability levels, from beginners to advanced, offering drift fishing on the Upper Kenai, fly fishing on the lower river, and three- or five-day fly-fishing schools

i If you get to see one of the Peninsula's big moose, keep your distance: There are more fatal moose encounters than fatal bear attacks in Alaska. To warn other drivers of moose on the road, Alaskan drivers flash their headlights. You need to be equally wary if you're on foot, as a moose's kick has 1,000 pounds of force behind it. Stay at least 75 feet away from moose in the wild, and don't get between a cow and her calves.

on either the Kenai River or Quartz Creek. For the nonanglers in your group, they have access to flight seeing, glacier tours, hiking, horseback riding, and rafting.

Alaska Wildland Adventures
Mile 50.1 Sterling Highway, Cooper Landing
(907) 595–1279, (800) 478–4100
www.alaskarivertrips.com
One of the first companies to snag lucrative permits for floating the Kenai River, Alaska Wildland Adventures has been providing professional guides and top-notch gear to area anglers since 1977. Their full-day packages include approximately eight hours of fishing, top-quality tackle, waders, gear, and a generous lunch. Opt for either the Willie Predator Powerboats or Mackenzie-type drift boats, both of which seat four anglers. Fish the Lower Kenai River for king or silver salmon, or the Kasilof River for kings. On the Upper Kenai River, you can partake of great fly fishing for Dollies, rainbows, and salmon, peaking in August and September. You can fish comfortably from the boat or wade from the bank for salmon. Alaska Wildland also has a Resurrection Bay silver salmon package. Guides are U.S. Coast Guard licensed with CPR and first-aid training.

Angle 45 Adventures
Mile 8.1 Hope Highway, Hope
(907) 782–3175
www.angle45.com
A bit off the beaten path to Kenai, you'll find Angle 45 Adventures in the small but scenic waterfront town of Hope. Forty-five-degree angles offer the least resistance and the most pleasure in working the currents of the river, and that's the goal of this family-owned guiding service. Permitted through the Chugach National Forest and the state of Alaska, they can take you drift-boat fishing on the Upper Kenai, the Kasilof, or the Middle Kenai Rivers. Top-quality rods and tackle plus a selection of waders are provided. If you'd just as soon sightsee as fish, try the two-hour float on the Upper Kenai River or

on Granite Creek. Angle 45 also will create custom packages and multiday adventures, including fly-out fishing, wildlife and glacial tours, private hiking, and white-water rafting. They have two four-season cabins available for rent as well.

Kenai Fishing Academy
Kenai Peninsula College
34820 College Drive, Soldotna
(907) 262–0300
Where was this class when we were in college? After 20 hours in the classroom learning fishing techniques from the experts, you'll head out to the fabulous fishing holes of the Kenai Peninsula with some of the region's top guides to practice what you've learned. Despite the bountiful supply of fish in the area, there are anglers who get skunked year after year, and the mission of the academy is to make sure they have a fighting chance. Choose from Hard Tackle and Fly Fishing packages, both of which include 20 hours of classroom/hands-on instruction, five nights of lodging, meals, tackle, and transportation to fishing destinations. You won't earn college credit, but you'll come away with a new understanding of Alaska's most-sought-after sport fish and how to catch and process them.

Silent Run Drift Boat Guide Service
1803 Roosevelt Drive, Anchorage
(907) 562–5455
www.silentrunak.com
To keep your fishing experience personal and allow for instruction of novice anglers, Silent Run takes out no more than two people on any given trip. Choose from full- or half-day drift or walk-in fishing. In addition to the usual drift and walk-in fishing for trout and salmon, they have a guide permit for some of the small but productive streams in the Chugach National Forest. All trout are catch and release only. Your knowledgeable guide is first-aid and CPR certified, licensed, and insured. Snacks, soda, bottled water, coffee, tackle, and life jackets are included.

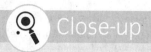

Kenai Combat Fishing

It might not be exactly what you had in mind when you dreamed of salmon fishing in the Alaskan wilderness, but the popular and productive Russian and Kenai Rivers offer a unique angling experience nonetheless. At the peak of the season, the confluence of these scenic rivers resembles a jam-packed urban intersection with rods and waders in place of honking cars. When the salmon are running thick, upwards of 1,000 anglers may be fishing at the same time.

What makes this fishery so hot? For one thing, more freshwater king salmon are caught in the Kenai River than anywhere else in Alaska, with the average season yielding 17,500 kings. The Kenai River produces not only quantity but also quality, having given up the world-record rod-and-reel king, a whopping 97-pounder, back in 1985. You can see the big lunker on display at the Soldotna Visitor Center. The average annual return of red salmon on the Kenai River is an incredible one million fish, with the season peaking the last two weeks in July. The silver run, peaking in mid-August, produces a harvest of some 41,000 salmon. Factor in two big runs of Russian River reds, one at the end of June and one in mid-July, and you have a recipe for quite a bit of excitement.

So don't let a little competition scare you off. Pack some patience along with your fishing gear and look on your fishing adventure as a chance to rub shoulders, literally, with fellow enthusiasts from all over the world. Join the crowds that line the banks for about a half-mile beginning just south of Cooper Landing and wait for a spot to open up. Don't elbow your way in, and remember not to walk in right behind someone who's casting. Eyes have been lost that way; you'll see anglers wearing protective eye gear for that very reason.

Once you've snagged your spot, try to cast in unison with others around you. When you have that fish on the line, yell "Fish On" and land it quickly. Playing the fish only adds to the chaos, increasing the chances you'll tangle with another line, and your fellow anglers won't be happy about having to stop fishing while you have all the fun. A stout, medium-weight rod and 20-pound test line will help you haul your fish in with minimal disruption. Remember to bring a spare—rods break all too often when those feisty 10-pound reds get to fighting, with the strong currents of the Russian or Kenai River adding to their power.

If you snag a salmon, break the line rather than trying to pull it upstream tail first. Once you've caught your limit, step aside and let the next angler in. Hopefully someone will repay the favor when you're waiting for your turn. It's a simple application of the Golden Rule that makes combat fishing fun and productive despite the crowds.

HOMER

Ask Alaskans where in the state they'd most like to live, and a good number of them will name Homer, an end-of-the-road seaside town with gorgeous scenery, easy access to outdoor fun, a healthy emphasis on the arts, and a warm sense of community. Visitors name Homer as one of the top Alaskan destinations for friendliness, hospitality, and beauty.

Approaching Homer by road, you'll be struck by breathtaking views of Kachemak Bay and the Kenai Mountains as you mount Baycrest Hill. Ahead lies great fishing, bear viewing, kayaking, birding, shopping, galleries, and dining with a fun and funky flair. The town stretches out into the ocean via the 4.5-mile Homer Spit, a strip of sand and gravel lined with shops, restaurants, campgrounds, and charter outfits. From nearly everywhere in town, you'll enjoy magnificent views of glacial mountains, distant volcanoes, and the sparkling waters of Kachemak Bay. Beachcombing and clamming are favorite seaside activities. The surrounding wilderness is home to wolves, bears, moose, and hundreds of thousands of shorebirds.

There's evidence that the Spit and the rest of the lower Peninsula have been inhabited off and on for thousands of years, first by Pacific Eskimos and later, in the 18th century, by Russian explorers. As the Americans entered the picture, coal was discovered in the region, and Homer became a hub for transporting the fuel. The first village, located at the tip of the Spit, was abandoned in 1902 for a more sheltered location a bit farther inland. Settlers spread into the hills around Homer as the road system drew fishing and transportation activity from landlocked Seldovia and Halibut Cove.

Today, with a population of more than 4,000, Homer is the hub of the lower Kenai Peninsula, with a hospital, two newspapers, commercial and public radio stations, a branch of the University of Alaska campus, numerous sport- and commercial-fishing fleets, and an award-winning educational system. The climate is temperate, with an average summer temperature of 57 degrees Fahrenheit and an average winter temperature of 23 degrees Fahrenheit.

Getting There, Getting Around

Homer is a scenic four-and-a-half-hour drive from Anchorage, though on weekends traffic is heavy and you should plan more time for traveling the mostly two-lane road. ERA Aviation offers scheduled small-plane service from Anchorage. Once you're in Homer, you can rent a car or take a taxi to get around town. There are also a number of bike trails for cycling enthusiasts. The Alaska Marine Highway system (907–235–8449, 800–642–006, www.ferryalaska.com) offers regular service to Seldovia and beyond, including vehicle transportation if you like.

Accommodations

Aside from high-end luxury hotels, you'll discover just about every kind of accommodation imaginable in Homer, from all-inclusive wilderness lodges to primitive yurts for camping. As in most of the region, reservations are definitely a good idea in the summer season, which begins in mid-May and ends in early September.

You can assume major credit cards are accepted and that rooms are available year-round unless we tell you differently. For the most part, facilities are nonsmoking only, with no pets allowed, but we'll note any deviations to those policies. Wheelchair access is noted wherever it applies. Many accommodations include fish-cleaning, packaging, and freezing facilities for guest use. Price codes indicate the average cost for a double room, excluding taxes and gratuity.

Price Codes

$ . . . . Less than $125
$$ . . . . $125–$175
$$$ . . . . $176–$225
$$$$ . . . . More than $225

Among the unique accommodations available through Alaska Adventure Cabins is the fully restored Double Eagle, *with three decks and full galley.* DEB VANASSE

A Memorable Experience
Bed and Breakfast $$
P.O. Box 940
Homer, AK 99630
(907) 235–7374, (800) 720–9275, ext. 7374
www.amemorableexperience.com
Enjoy a parklike setting overlooking Homer, with spectacular views of Kachemak Bay and the glacial mountains beyond. You'll find incredible birding and hiking right outside the front door and all the comforts of home inside. The burgundy and green Alaskan-themed rooms have private baths and king-size beds, private decks, and a private entrance. In the common area, there's satellite television, a kitchenette, and freezer space for storing fish. Larger parties can opt for a separate cottage that sleeps five and has a full kitchen. Room rates include a continental breakfast featuring fresh coffee, fruit, homemade granola, and pastries. In addition,

there's a $5.00 food voucher for each guest to sample the tasty fare at the Fresh Sourdough Express, owned and operated by your hosts (see the Restaurants section below). Pets are accepted on approval, and rooms are wheelchair accessible. Group, weekly, and off-season rates are available, too.

Alaska Adventure Cabins $$$$
2525 Sterling Highway
(907) 223–6681
www.alaskaadventurecabins.com
Some of the most unusual accommodations you'll find in Alaska, or just about anywhere for that matter, are offered by Alaska Adventure Cabins. Check out the Moose Caboose, a genuine Alaska Railroad car lovingly converted into a two-story cabin with terrific views and a spacious deck, or the *Double Eagle,* a gleaming 75-foot ship with three decks, full galley, two bedrooms, and two and

a half baths. Cabin options include the Dove-tail Log and the Canyon Creek. All properties offer splendid views of the water and mountains from a convenient location just off the Sterling Highway. Alaska Adventure hosts corporate events as well as individual travelers.

Alaska Center for Creative Renewal   **$$$$**
P.O. Box 6448
Halibut Cove, AK 99603
(907) 296–2283
www.centerforcreativerenewal.com
If you're really looking to get away from it all, check out this top-notch wilderness lodge nestled in the heart of Halibut Cove, a short ferry ride across Kachemak Bay from Homer. Run by Jan Thurston, one of 15 professional artists exhibiting work at the local gallery, the lodge hosts workshops and retreats, but most of their guests are independent travelers looking for a place to get away from it all. Rates include three meals per day, with an emphasis on fresh fish and oysters from local fisheries along with produce from their scenic gardens. The lodge provides kayaking and hiking opportunities, and massage is also available. The center places a special focus on their environmental practices and has garnered awards for its unique architecture.

Alaska's Sadie Cove
Wilderness Lodge   **$$$$**
P.O. Box 2265
Homer, AK 99603
(907) 235–2350
www.sadiecove.com
Wild Alaskan beauty by the sea is yours at Sadie Cove, 10 miles by boat from Homer, nestled on a remote fjord within Kachemak Bay State Park. Keith Iverson was able to acquire this property in the 1970s, before the park was formed, and he is dedicated to providing a nonintrusive, ecofriendly, genuine wilderness experience that is one of the top ecodestinations in the country. The all-inclusive rate includes lodging in one of five handcrafted guest cabins, all meals, and the use of kayaks, fishing gear, lodge, sauna and plunge pool,

and private hiking trails. The Iversons provide a noncommercial atmosphere of casual elegance, maintaining a rustic wilderness feel while offering such amenities as wireless Internet and cellular telephone access. Their attentive all-Alaskan staff serves up gourmet seafood meals and, if you like, they'll guide you on local trails to see wildlife, ancient petroglyphs, and neighboring Native villages. It's their hope that you will be able to escape the stresses of modern life and come away with a new appreciation for the wonders of the wilderness and the fun of meeting new friends.

Bay View Inn   **$**
2851 Sterling Highway
(907) 235–8485
www.bayviewalaska.com
Guests rave about the spectacular views from every room, looking out over the big blue of Kachemak Bay. All rooms come with firm beds, telephone, television with HBO, outside entrances, and an Adirondack chair for soaking up the magnificent view. Options include kitchenettes, a suite with fireplace, and a honeymoon cottage. The decor is nothing fancy, but the rooms are clean and comfortable. Rounding out the hospitality are a free continental breakfast, an espresso bar, use of picnic tables, and recommendations on local tours and activities.

Beach House Bed & Breakfast   **$$**
P.O. Box 48
Homer, AK 99603
(907) 235–3232
www.alaskabeachhouse.com
Offering quiet deluxe accommodations with fabulous views of beautiful Kachemak Bay, the Beach House has four rooms with king-size and twin beds. Guests also enjoy a 32-foot waterfront deck and hot tub perched on the bluff. Rooms come with coffeemakers, microwaves, minifridges, free continental breakfast with homemade breads and muffins, and airport transportation. In the Galley House, you can enjoy complimentary homemade cookies, tea, and coffee while

relaxing in viewing chairs that overlook the bay. Local smoked salmon, cold drinks, and snacks are available for purchase. Open since 1999, the Beach House is convenient to both the town and the Spit.

Best Western Bidarka Inn $$
575 Sterling Highway
(907) 235–8148, (866) 685–5000
www.bestwesternbidarkainn.com
With a convenient location just off the Sterling Highway, the Best Western Bidarka has a wide range of amenities, including free parking, high-speed Internet, tour desk, reservations services, coin-operated laundry, barber/beauty shop, courtesy van, and game room. Grab a meal at the Glacier View Restaurant (open seasonally) or a drink in the Otter Room Sports Bar with open fireplace. To take care of your catch, there's a fish-packing and -cleaning station plus freezing station. The Bidarka has 74 clean, comfortable rooms, each with television, alarm clock radio, coffeemaker, hair dryer, iron and iron board, and telephone with dataport. Children age 17 and younger stay free with an adult. Smoking rooms and rooms with wheelchair access are available.

Chocolate Drop Inn $$–$$$
P.O. Box 70
Homer, AK 99603
(907) 235–3668, (800) 530–6015
www.chocolatedropinn.com
The professional innkeepers at the Chocolate Drop, named after a candy-shaped mountain peak across the bay, having been providing comfortable accommodations for visitors to Homer since 1993. Their 8,000-square-foot log inn features five guest rooms plus a family suite, each with private entrance and private bath, queen-size beds, telephones, and televisions. Guests can enjoy the outdoor hot tub, the recreation room with video library and games, the sauna, and the fisherman's freezers. Hot breakfasts are standard fare here, featuring fresh seafood, reindeer sausage, and other local treats. Rooms come in a variety of configurations and rates, from

two-person Halibut Haven to the Forget-Me-Not Suite that sleeps six. From throughout the inn, catch views of Kachemak Bay, the Kenai Mountains, and four glaciers.

Driftwood Inn $–$$
135 West Bunnell Avenue
(907) 235–8019, (800) 478–8019
www.thedriftwoodinn.com
If you're looking for a variety of reasonably priced options, the Driftwood Inn is a great place to start. Fifth- and sixth-generation Homer residents operate the Driftwood Lodge, the Driftwood Inn, and the Kachemak Cottage. Room rates include wireless Internet access, guest laundry, fish-cleaning area, and freezer. Common areas include a great room with stone fireplace, kitchen with microwave, and picnic area with barbeque and shellfish cooker. At the Driftwood Lodge, you'll find deluxe rooms overlooking the beach and the bay, with king-size beds, private baths, soaking tubs, in-room televisions, and free local phone calls. The Driftwood Inn offers 21 economy rooms, some with shared baths. Groups of up to eight will enjoy the seaside setting of the Kachemak Cottage. Pets are allowed in select rooms.

Homer Inn & Spa $$
895 Ocean Drive
(907) 235–2501, (800) 294–7823
www.alaskawaterfront.com
Enjoy the beauty of Kachemak Bay from a minisuite with ocean-view windows, king-size bed, private bath, keyed entrance, and optional gourmet breakfast. Guests appreciate the Homer Inn's spectacular beachfront view with glacial mountain backdrop and convenient location between the downtown arts district and the harbor. There's plenty of beach strolling to be done, and an ample menu of on-site spa packages if you're more inclined to just relax. The inn features custom hand-lain wood and stone mosaic floors; sculptured walls with paintings by local artists; in-room dining area with wineglasses, bottle opener, and scented candles; kitch-

enettes with minifridge, microwave, and coffeemaker; television/VCR; and CD player with music by local Alaskan artists. Guests share the inn's Jacuzzi hot tub, barbeque deck and outdoor seating, log swing, and herb gardens with colorful flowers and fountain. If you're inclined toward adventure, take a run in the two-man kayak, borrow a kite and see where it flies, or pack a beach picnic with the supplies provided by your hosts. The inn can accommodate parties of up to 14 people.

Island Watch B&B and
Vacation Rentals $$
4241 Claudia Street
(907) 235–2263
www.islandwatch.net
On the private landscaped grounds of Island Watch, you can choose from a collection of comfortable cabins and guest rooms with views of Kachemak Bay and the mountains beyond. There's the handcrafted Log Cabin with adjoining Sea Star Room, the secluded Garden Cabin with queen-size bed and full kitchen, and the charming Eagle Room and Suite in the fanciful main house. Rooms and cabins come with coffeemakers, microwaves, minifridges, private baths, telephones, iron and ironing boards, free morning papers, and your choice of continental or full breakfasts. They have maps of hiking trails and other great local information to share, along with a horseshoe pit and a swing for relaxing. Island Watch has wheelchair-accessible facilities, and they accept pets in one room. To accommodate large groups, check out their guest cottage at www.homerguestcottage.com.

Land's End Resort $$–$$$
4786 Homer Spit Road
(907) 235–0400
www.endofthespit.com
Providing food and lodging since 1958, Land's End Resort is a Homer icon. In the old days, when you could only get to the small boat harbor during high tide, fisherman gathered at Land's End to swap stories. Perched on the end of the Spit, the resort has retained its nau-

tical flavor and friendly Alaskan ways while adding creature comforts. Featuring custom-built furniture and museum-quality exhibits, there are 94 rooms, some with stunning views of the mountains and the ocean. Guests enjoy the oceanfront hot tub, indoor pool, exercise room, and complete menu of spa services along with access to miles of beachfront for strolling and beachcombing. Loft rooms and suites can accommodate families. Be sure to check out their getaway specials, including the Flyaway and Raven's Nest Spa packages. Three rooms have wheelchair access, and there's fine dining in the Chart Room Restaurant.

Silver King Lodge $$$$
73590 Beach Access Road, Anchor Point
(907) 235–6089, (907) 235–5262
You'd be hard-pressed to find a more charming spot to stay than the Silver King Lodge. Stepping inside the 1,300-square-foot private cabin is like going back a few decades to a more charming era when vacations were truly laid-back affairs. Cast a line right out the back door into the Anchor River, then cook up your catch in the fully stocked lodge-style kitchen. They'll even make arrangements for a cook to come in if you're feeling lazy. The table's set for dinner when you arrive. Between the private master bedroom and the bunk-style guest room, you can pack in quite a few people—seven, to be exact. Enjoy the live jukebox, play board games, read something out of the Alaska collection, or just marvel at all the fun stuff tucked in every corner of this eclectic getaway, a sort of mix of Alaska provincial and Lenox china. Out back you'll find a gas grill, fire pit, deck, and picnic tables to enjoy. Ocean access is just down the road, or drive 20 minutes south to Homer. The Silver King Lodge is one of several unique properties run by Alaska Adventure Cabins.

Tutka Bay Wilderness Lodge $$$$
Halibut Cove
(907) 235–3905, (800) 606–3909
www.tutkabaylodge.com
Here's a great wilderness option across the

bay from Homer, about 9 miles by boat. The lodge is actually a cluster of buildings, boardwalks, decks, and dock on a private cove next to Kachemak Bay State Park. You'll enjoy uncluttered views of the forest, mountains, and ocean from the shores of a pristine fjord that plays home to sea otters, sea lions, porpoise, seals, whales, and seabirds. There are an assortment of cabins and suites to choose from, and meals are included with your stay. All rooms have coffeemakers, minifridges, and hair dryers. Enjoy wildlife viewing, dock fishing, rowboating, clamming, birding, hiking, and guided nature walking. When you're all tuckered out, relax in the wood-fired sauna or soak in the jetted hot tub in the open-air gazebo. Special-interest activities can be arranged, including guided sea kayaking, fly-out brown bear viewing, and salmon or halibut fishing. Known for quality service, Tutka Bay consistently gets rave reviews from guests. Even the meals are special, as the lodge hosts celebrity chefs and food writers and reprints recipes in national magazines.

Restaurants

For a town its size, Homer has a great reputation for dining of all types. Restaurants on the Spit are open mostly during the summer tourist and fishing season, but you'll find the others open year-round. Major credit cards are accepted unless we note otherwise. We'll let you know if there's no wheelchair access or if they're closed one or more days each week. Price codes indicate the average cost of a dinner for two, excluding drinks, appetizers, tax, and gratuity.

Price Codes

$. . . . . Less than $15
$$ . . . . $16–$25
$$$ . . . . $26–$40
$$$$ . . . . More than $40

Boardwalk Fish and Chips $$
4287 Homer Spit Road
(907) 235–7749
Since 1982 the folks at the Boardwalk have

been serving up their famous fresh halibut fish and chips, homemade chowder, and draft beer. There's an outdoor deck for taking in all the action along the Spit, with views of the mountains and the ocean. If seafood isn't your thing, try the teriyaki or Cajun chicken salads, a charbroiled burger, or the Alaskan reindeer bratwurst. The New England clam chowder is popular, too, along with the bread bowls and ice-cream shakes. Parking can be tight on the Spit, so make the Boardwalk a stop on your foot-bound sightseeing tour of the oceanfront. Open seasonally for lunch and dinner.

Café Cups $$$$
162 Pioneer Avenue
(907) 235–8330
www.cafecupshomer.com
A favorite with locals, Café Cups serves up eclectic meals that are as artful as its decor, which features mosaics of cups and glasses, iron sculptures, and works by local artists adorning the walls and tables. The ever-changing menu features fine local seafood, steaks, salads made with locally grown greens, burgers, and daily specials. Try the charbroiled fresh salmon and halibut topped with a fruit pico de gallo or charbroiled filet mignon with Gorgonzola whiskey cream. Dave's Fettuccini with clams, shrimp, and scallops in a raspberry-chipotle alfredo sauce is another favorite. Their fresh halibut tacos are fabulous, too. Homer Brewing Company's draft beer and a selection of fine wines complement the tasty food. Conveniently located across from the public library, Café Cups has ample parking and is open for lunch and dinner every day except Sunday.

Chart Room Restaurant $$$$
Land's End Resort
4786 Homer Spit Road
(907) 235–0400
www.endofthespit.com
Fine dining with a spectacular view is the trademark of the Chart Room, perched at the very end of Homer Spit. Floor-to-ceiling win-

dows offer breathtaking views of wildlife, glaciers, and waterfront activities from tables
decked with huge ship's wheels and wood
carvings. In typical Alaskan style, everyone's
comfortable, from those dressed to the nines
to those in flannel shirts. There's a well-
rounded menu featuring halibut, salmon,
clams, oysters, rockfish, scallops, prime rib,
and steaks. Try the Halibut Iliamna, a fresh
filet baked with a topping of crab, artichokes,
cream, and Parmesan. The Chart Room has a
full bar and ample parking, and they're open
365 days a year for breakfast, lunch, and dinner. When you've had all you can eat, check
out the spa facilities upstairs.

Cosmic Kitchen $
510 East Pioneer Avenue
(907) 235–6355
Every day the folks at the Cosmic Kitchen
cook up fresh salsas, grill marinated chicken
and steak, and offer up a homemade soup
plus daily specials. Their rice, beans, sauces,
and most soups are vegetarian. For breakfast, try the Cosmic Frittata, an open-faced
cheddar/jack omelet with your choice of two
toppings: fajita veggies, avocado, bacon,
ham, sausage, chorizo, soy sausage, hash
browns, and sour cream. Later in the day, you
can order off their Mexican menu, including
the Fajita Fish Burrito or the Big Bang Burrito
with steak, chicken, and rice. There's also a
nice selection of burgers, including buffalo
and salmon, and sandwiches, such as the
Chicken Tikka with Chutney and the Gryo.
Salad choices include the Cosmic Caesar with
blackened halibut and the Tostada Salad with
Beef and Beans. The Cosmic Kitchen serves
beer and wine, and takeout and catering are
available. Reservations are not required, and
there's ample parking.

Don Jose's $$
127 West Pioneer Avenue
(907) 279–5111
The Ramos family opened their first restaurant in Homer in 1982, and they've now
expanded to three locations around the

state. Start out with complimentary chips,
then check out one of Carmen's specials for
lunch, such as the halibut or shrimp tacos, or
the Vegetarian Chimi Dinner, an oven-
roasted flour tortilla filled with sautéed zuc-
chini, cauliflower, bell peppers, green
onions, and carrots. If you're really hungry,
try the Macho Combos, such as Don Jose's
chili relleno stuffed with beef and cheese,
tamale, and chicken flauta served with rice
and beans. Gourmet specialties included the
Camarones Rellenos with prawns and Dungeness crab and the Scallops Mazatlan,
sautéed with tomatoes, fresh onions, and
peppers. In addition to their extensive Mexican menu, Don Jose's serves pizza, calzones,
and American fare.

Eric's Bayside BBQ $
4025 Homer Spit Road
(907) 235–9197
For casual dining on the boardwalk, Eric's Bay-
side offers takeout, boardwalk seating, and
limited local delivery. Try one of Eric's BBQ
sandwiches featuring oven slow-baked beef,
chicken, or pork, or a bread bowl brimming
with clam chowder. Specials include the Two
for Tuesday pork sandwich meal, featuring
two pork sandwiches, chips, and soda. On
Saturday, Eric's has pork ribs (while they last)
slow-cooked, grilled, and basted with homemade barbeque sauce, then served up with
fresh-baked corn bread and beans. Eric's is
open only during the summer season, and
parking along the Spit can be a challenge, so
be prepared to walk a bit.

Fat Olives $$
276 Ohlson Lane
(907) 235–8488
A local favorite for pizzas and other Italian
fare, Fat Olives offers casual dining and takeout. Check out their House Calzone, with
pesto, mushrooms, spinach, artichoke hearts,
ricotta, smoked Gouda, and mozzarella, or
one of 19 classic Neapolitan pizza options.
Want more choices? How about 15 specialty
meat pizzas, including pesto-smoked king

salmon or thai chicken? For veggie lovers, they have 11 pizza options, including Olive's Special, with olive oil garlic base, roma tomatoes, pineapple, cream cheese, olive tapenade, fresh jalapeños, and mozzarella.

Fresh Sourdough Express $$$
1316 Ocean Drive
(907) 235–7571
www.freshsourdoughexpress.com
From its humble beginnings in 1972 as a bread-wagon-on-wheels that limped in off the Alaska Highway, the Fresh Sourdough Express has grown into a full-service bakery and cafe. Grains for organic breads are ground daily, and all baked goods are baked fresh daily. Fresh Sourdough Express serves organic coffee, ice tea, and their own organic Ah!laska cocoa and chocolate syrup. All salad dressings and sauces are homemade, as is their trademark salsa. For breakfast, try the Saint Augustine, a mountain of Alaskan-grown potatoes and sautéed veggies topped with cheese and salsa. For lunch, there are soups, salads, burgers (free range buffalo), sandwiches, and savory filled croissants. On the dinner menu, sample the Grilled Alaskan Wild Salmon with cranberry peppercorn glaze or the All-Natural New York Strip Steak smothered with roasted-onion marmalade.

The Homestead Restaurant $$$
Mile 8.2 East End Road
(907) 235–8723
www.homesteadrestaurant.com
Established in 1961, the award-winning Homestead Restaurant is famous for its fabulous seafood. Specials include Thursday's World Tour, when the chefs display their creativity with regional appetizers and entrees, and the Friday and Saturday Prime Rib Nights. The Homestead also offers a full selection of wines and classic cocktails, with Dinner at the Vineyard options throughout the year featuring five-course meals with paired wines. They're open Wednesday through Saturday at 5:00 P.M., and reservations are a great idea.

Nightlife

Sure, it's a small town, but there are quite a few friendly nightspots in Homer, which is also known as "a quaint drinking village with a fishing problem." Homer also has some great local bands and, on occasion, a few headliners from Outside.

Duggan's Waterfront Pub
120 West Bunnel Street
(907) 235–9949
Duggan's is one of those places where you can make a friend just about as soon as you walk through the door. The place likes to mix it up with nightly entertainment, including Thursday's Untamed Karaoke and live rock and roll on Friday and Saturday nights, with both local bands and headliners. Duggan's makes some of the best margaritas in town and features a full bar menu with all sorts of seafood and chips, burgers, sandwiches, steaks, and barbequed ribs. The kitchen's open till midnight, so it's a great place for a late-night snack.

The Salty Dawg
Homer Spit Road
P.O. Box 2581
Homer, AK 99603
(907) 235–6718
It's definitely a Homer landmark, so when you're down on the Spit, be sure to stop by this famous bar tucked inside three interconnected cabins and lighthouse tower. The tower once held water, and the bar itself is the result of the splicing together of a former schoolhouse, an early post office, and the headquarters of the Cook Inlet Coal Fields

i Homer Brewing Company produces popular local brews, including Broken Birch Bitter, Old Inlet Pale, Red Knot Scottish, China Poot Porter, and Oddessy Oatmeal Stout. Be sure to sample some while you're on the Peninsula, because distribution is limited and only draft beer is sold.

Company, all dating from early in the 1900s. The quarters are cramped and the ceilings are low, but the place is full of charm.

Shopping

Like everything else in Homer, the shopping here is fun and eclectic. You'll find everything from art galleries to coffee roasters to outdoor-gear specialists, plus a whole lot of practical shopping spots. There's a lot of multitasking in a small town like Homer, so you'll find that some of these shops also offer overnight lodging. Stores with obvious tourist appeal tend to have shortened hours in the winter.

Art Galleries and Shops

Art Shop Gallery
202 West Pioneer Avenue
(907) 235–7076, (800) 478–7076
www.artshopgallery.com
Scenically situated in downtown Homer, the Art Shop Gallery has a large selection of Alaskan arts and crafts, from the ubiquitous moose and bear to more original items, such as walrus whisker earrings and seal gut baskets. They have a large inventory of handmade Alaskan Christmas ornaments, ivory and bone carvings, qiviut products made of musk ox yarn from Sheep Mountain Creations, and tiles from Brecht Studios. Among the Alaskan artists featured are perennial favorites Fred Machetanz, Rie Munoz, Jon Van Zyle, Byron Birdsall, and Barbara Lavallee. Enjoy a complimentary cup of tea or coffee while you browse. They're open daily in the summer, with shortened hours on Sunday and in the winter.

Picture Alaska Art Gallery
448 East Pioneer Avenue
(907) 235–2300, (800) 770–2300
www.picturealaska.com
Another diverse gallery in the Pioneer Avenue arts district, Picture Alaska features original paintings, fine art prints, jewelry, mixed-media sculpture, pottery, wildlife photos, and vintage Alaskan photography. They also have a nice selection of Alaskan Native arts and crafts. Upstairs you'll find fashion art, including accessories, sportswear, dress wear, and fine lingerie. The gallery is open year-round, with extended hours in the summer.

Sea Lion Fine Art Gallery
Homer Spit Road
P.O. Box 2095
Homer, AK 99603
(907) 235–3400, (907) 235–8767
www.sealiongallery.com
Of the many shops along Homer Spit, the Sea Lion is notable for its emphasis on fine art. Started in 1993 by local artists Gary and Terri Lyon, the gallery features the work of notables Byron Birdsall, Barbara Lavallee, and Nancy Yaki. The collection of Alaskan Native art includes baleen and grass baskets; walrus ivory and whalebone carvings; and multimedia and antique pieces. If you're worn out from all that shopping, they have two efficiency suites upstairs that can be rented by the night, both with beautiful views of the ocean. Like pretty much everything else on the Spit, the Sea Lion is closed in the winter.

Outdoor Wear and Sporting Goods

Eagle Enterprises
2355 Kachemak Drive
(907) 235–7908
Whether it's for commercial or recreational use, this retail store has what you need to stay safe and warm in the great outdoors. You'll find life jackets, rain gear, survival kits, flares, flashlights, and camping gear. The friendly, well-trained staff will help with questions on maintenance and repair of life-saving equipment. They offer propane tank inspection, hydro testing, inflatable sport boat repair, and scuba tank refills, too.

Kachemak Gear Shed
3625 East End Road
(907) 235–8612
The Gear Shed is the kind of full-service outfitter that Alaskans depend on. For the kitchen, they stock canning and cooking supplies, including smokers. In the clothing department, there's practical Alaskan footwear, including

hip waders and chest waders, along with the usual selection of brand-name outdoor wear. Knives? They have a full selection plus sharpeners. And you can browse a full selection of sportfishing equipment, from tackle to downriggers to licenses to coolers for shipping your fish home. For help with big toys, the Gear Shed carries boat trailer parts, four-wheelers, outboards, and generators, too.

Main Street Mercantile
104 East Pioneer Avenue
(907) 235–9102

Main Street Mercantile is a 21st-century version of an old-time general store, tucked inside a charming historic building near downtown Homer. They carry brand-name outdoor gear, camping supplies, cast-iron cookware, and old-fashioned kitchen tools, along with Nikon-brand camera supplies. Be sure to check out their line of Nomar polar fleece and travel bags, made right in Homer.

Souvenir and Specialty Shops

Alaska Wild Berry Products
528 East Pioneer Avenue
(907) 562–8858
www.alaskawildberryproducts.com

If you love chocolate, you won't want to miss all the goodies at this Homer store. In addition to their signature chocolate-covered berries and chocolates with berry filling, there are all kinds of Alaskan-crafted chocolates, truffles, and candies, plus a whole bunch of other themed food items, including Raven's Brew Coffee, salmon and seafood, and Alaskan teas. Check out the gift baskets for indulging the folks back home.

Coal Point Seafood Company
4306 Homer Spit Road
(907) 235–3877, (800) 325–3877
www.welovefish.com

Located right on the docks of Homer Harbor, Coal Point buys direct from fishermen who pride themselves in keeping their catch fresh. They offer custom flash freezing and vacuum packing for anglers, but you can fake it by

bringing home some of Coal Point's fresh and smoked halibut, salmon, cod, crab, shrimp, prawns, or scallops. They also have fun seafood gift packs for your friends back home, along with an assortment of nonedible gift items. If you work up an appetite while shopping, there's an oyster bar where you can sample their wares.

Funky Planet
158 Pioneer Avenue, #B
(907) 235–3274
www.funky-planet.com

Lotions, knickknacks, decorative masks, wall art, sarongs, mermaid mobiles—you name it, and there's a good chance you'll find it at Funky Planet, provided it's something fun and artsy. They stock imported women's clothing in sizes from juniors to plus, and in styles from contemporary to (what else?) funky. To complete your outfit, choose from their selection of purses and scarves, along with custom jewelry, including earrings, bracelets, bone and antler rings, and necklaces. The friendly folks at Funky Planet keep the store open Tuesday through Saturday, and they offer shipping services for your convenience.

Homer's Gold Mine Gifts
3695 Lake Street
(907) 235–6886
www.alaska.net/~homergm/

Whether it's souvenir clothing, canned salmon, homemade fudge, or fireweed honey that strikes your fancy, you'll find it at Gold Mine Gifts. In addition to the usual T-shirts and sweatshirts, they offer denim shirts and heavier coats, along with locally made fleece items and handmade layettes for the wee ones. You'll find a large selection of gemstone jewelry, including hematite, jade, rose quartz, garnet, lapis, tiger eye, and obsidian, as well as handcrafted ivory pieces. Another specialty is their in-store line of gold nugget jewelry, from rings to watches to pendants and money clips. If you're more into fun than fancy, check out their fish spinner and fish fly earrings. In the fine art department, you'll find oil originals, prints, and sculptures by well-known Alaskan artists as well as hand-carved moose antlers. When you're done shopping, treat yourself to a drink at the Espresso Bar, or indulge in fudge made right in the store. Nonshoppers can take in an Alaska sportfishing video and sample the hand-dipped Alaska Supreme ice cream. You can even "chat" with a life-size re-creation of Homer Pennock, for whom the town was named.

Old Inlet Bookshop
3487 Main Street
(907) 235–7984
www.oldinletbookshop.com
Browsing in Homer's Old Inlet Bookshop is a bit like perusing the attic of a friendly but oh-so-literary grandmother. The place is stacked from floor to ceiling with both old and new books in the ambience of a log cabin with hardwood floors. But don't be fooled: This is a serious booklovers' paradise, owned by third-generation booksellers and carrying more than 20,000 titles. They specialize in rare, used, and out-of-print books as well as Alaskana, with plenty of mainstream titles, too. Attached to the original cabin, estimated to be more than100 years old, is the Mermaid Café and B & B.

Attractions

If you can pull yourself away from the gorgeous scenery for an hour or two, Homer has some great low-cost attractions that will help you get acquainted with the area, and all of them are easy on the pocketbook.

Price Codes

$	Less than $5.00
$$	$5.00–$15.00
$$$	$16.00–$30.00
$$$$	More than $30.00

Alaska Islands and Ocean Visitor Center
95 Sterling Highway
(907) 235–6961
This joint venture of the Alaska Maritime National Wildlife Refuge and the Kachemak Bay Research Reserve is a must-see spot for learning about the natural history of the area. There are great exhibits highlighting the world's largest seabird refuge and exploring the dynamic estuary environment. Discover how dories and bidarkas (Eskimo kayaks) have transported voyagers across the waters of the bay, learn how the first peoples of the region survived, and review the effects of newcomers and war on the refuge area. A favorite exhibit is seabird theater, where you can see, hear, and even smell a simulated nesting colony. After taking in the stunning interactive exhibits and well-stocked bookstore, stretch your legs on the Beluga Slough interpretive trail to Bishop's Beach Park. Open daily from 9:00 A.M. to 6:00 P.M. during the summer and Tuesday through Saturday from 10:00 A.M. to 5:00 P.M. in the winter, the center has a limited number of strollers and wheelchairs for visitors to use at no charge, and all exhibits may be accessed by wheelchair. There's ample parking for RVs, but overnight parking is not allowed. Admission is free.

Homer Chamber of Commerce Visitor Information Center
201 Sterling Highway
(907) 235–7740
www.homeralaska.org
The chamber of commerce operates a full-service visitor center with information, maps, and brochures to orient you to the area. It's worth a stop just to see the gorgeous mosaic in the floor. The chamber publishes a great full-color brochure that you can pick up there or have mailed to you. Of course, there's no charge for their services.

Pratt Museum $$
3779 Bartlett Street
(907) 235–8635
www.prattmuseum.org
For a great introduction to the region and its natural history, check out the Pratt Museum. You'll find videos, photo essays, and remote video technology to give you an in-depth look

at contemporary and historic Kachemak Bay. The exhibit Bears, Beetles, and Darkened Waters explores the effects of climate change and development on local habitat and wildlife. Also on display are more than 75 species of wildlife, including an aquarium with sea stars, octopus, and flounder as well as intertidal specimens. Adjacent to the museum is the Harrington Cabin, which houses exhibits on homesteading in the area. In the summer, enjoy more than 150 species of flowers and plants along the garden path, as well as a self-guided ecology trail. The only natural history museum on the Peninsula, the Pratt attracts 30,000-plus visitors a year. It's open daily from 10:00 A.M. to 6:00 P.M. in the summer, with shortened hours and Sunday closures in the winter.

The Arts

If you love the arts, Homer is the place to be. The gorgeous scenery is complemented by high-quality art at nearly every turn, from top-notch galleries and studios to a variety of dance, theatrical, and musical events. In fact, Homer was selected as one of 100 best small towns for the arts in the country. If you're lucky enough to be in town at the beginning of the month, be sure to set aside time to participate in the First Friday Art Walk, where you'll have opportunities to meet artists and chat about their work. Local writers' groups and writing workshops round out the arts scene. The library even keeps the unpublished works of local authors available for public reading in their special "top drawer" collection.

Bunnell Street Gallery
106 West Bunnell Street
(907) 235–2662
www.bunnellstreetgallery.org

i The Homer Public Library offers free Internet access on a sign-in basis. The facilities are well-used in the summer, so plan to wait a bit for your turn.

This nonprofit gallery features monthly solo shows of Alaskan artists and also plays host to juried exhibits, readings, concerts, workshops, artists in the schools, and other special events. Located in the historic Old Inlet Trading Post along the shore of Bishop's Beach, the gallery displays paintings, photography, ceramics, fiber pieces, sculpture, and contemporary Alaskan art. They're open from 10:00 A.M. to 6:00 P.M. Monday through Saturday and from noon till 4:00 P.M. on Sunday. In the winter the gallery is closed on Sunday and Monday.

Kachemak Bay Writers' Conference
533 East Pioneer Avenue
(907) 235–7743
http://writersconference.homer.alaska.edu
Sponsored by the Kachemak Bay campus of the Kenai Peninsula College, a branch of the University of Alaska, this annual conference is quickly gaining fame and attracting writers from all genres. Recently, the conference featured a former U.S. Poet Laureate plus a faculty of 20 writers who presented workshops, readings, and panel discussions. Fiction, poetry, nonfiction, and the business of writing are among the topics of the conference.

Kenai Peninsula Orchestra
315 West Pioneer Avenue
(907) 235–4899
www.homeronline.addr.com/kpo/
These volunteer musicians from Homer, Kenai, Soldotna, and Seward have one thing in common: They love music, so they collaborate to offer a full season of musical entertainment for residents of the Peninsula. The orchestra gets a big boost every year by hosting the Summer String Festival, in which the DeVere Quartet from Syracuse, New York, plays with the local group and conducts workshops. Throughout the years, the orchestra has hosted world-class guest artists, including the Boston Pops Jazz ensemble and Broadway vocalists. They sponsor multiple events throughout the year, including a family concert, a winter recital series, and a community Messiah sing.

i For more fine art, take the ferry *Danny J* across the bay to Halibut Cove, where you can stroll along the boardwalk to Experience Gallery and the studio of Diana Tillion, who has drawn for decades with octopus ink.

Pier One Theatre
P.O. Box 894
Homer, AK 99603
(907) 235–7333
www.pieronetheatre.org
For top-notch community theater, it would be hard to beat the shows put on at Pier One. They run a full schedule from June through August, and they're often sold out. There's a nice range of productions, from comedic to literary, along with theatrical camps for young people. Pier One is splendidly located at the beginning of the Spit, with plenty of parking. You'll generally find shows at 7:30 P.M. on Thursday and Sunday and at 8:15 P.M. on Friday and Saturday. Be sure to call ahead for reservations.

Parks, Recreation, and Tours

If Homer is an artist's paradise, it's equally heavenly for outdoor enthusiasts. You'll find ample opportunities to explore and recreate in the great outdoors in and around Homer. Within the city limits, there are several parks waiting to be enjoyed. The Karen Hornaday Memorial Park and campground hosts summertime Concerts on the Lawn featuring local talent and sponsored by the local public radio station. There's also occasional live music at a park with an unusual name, the WKFL (Wisdom, Knowledge, Faith, and Love). Bishop's Beach Park at the end of Bunnell Street is a great place to view wildlife and enjoy the ocean view, and Ben Walters Park, behind McDonald's on Lake Street, offers a boardwalk for crossing the marsh and a gazebo with barbeque facilities.

The Carl E. Wynn Nature Center (907–235–6667, www.akcoastalstudies.org), a nonprofit organization dedicated to promoting responsible interaction with the coastal and marine ecosystems of Kachemak Bay, is a great place to start. Take a guided walk on the system of nature trails for a nominal use fee, or treat yourself to the full-day Low Tide Tour and Coastal Forest Hike across Kachemak Bay. You'll see rich tidal pools, a seabird rookery, live tanks at the Peterson Bay Field Station, and many of the animals that live in the tidal zone. In conjunction with the tour, you can add overnight yurt camping or a half-day of guided kayaking.

A short jaunt across the water will take you to Kachemak Bay State Park and Wilderness Park, the state's first state park. There you'll find ample opportunities for boating, hiking, kayaking, camping, sportfishing, and mountains sports on 400,000 acres. Harbor seals, sea otters, porpoise, whales, black bears, puffins, mountain goats, wolves, and bald eagles are among the abundant wildlife in the park. Favorite spots include Halibut Cove Lagoon, Leisure Lake, China Poot Bay, Grewingk Glacier, and Humpy Creek.

If you'll be visiting Kachemak Park, be sure to leave a travel plan with friends or family, or use the Trail Registers, as weather can be unpredictable and the bay can be rough at times. The tides in Kachemak Bay are the second strongest in the world due to strong currents and rapids formed by narrow passages, so take no chances. Pick up a tide book at any of a number of local sporting goods stores to carry with you, and secure your boat if you plan to leave it unattended. Riptides and shallows can make access to Halibut Cove Lagoon hazardous at times, so the lagoon is best accessed only with shallow draft boats during high tide. Even if you leave a travel plan for your adventures in the park, you should be ready and able to handle emergency situations on your own.

Hikers can trek more than 85 miles of trails within Kachemak Park, and camping is permitted in many locations. Rustic cabins may be rented by reservation only. Contact the Division of Parks and Outdoor Recreation in Soldotna (907–262–5581) or visit www.alaskastateparks.com for more information or to reserve a cabin. Campfires are allowed on nonvegetated beaches or gravel bars only, or within metal rings in one of the park's developed campsites. Hang food away from camp and use bear-proof containers. Land vehicles, including bicycles, are not permitted in the park, but powerboats may be used in salt water and on designated lakes. Mooring buoys and the Halibut Cove Lagoon Dock are available for public use.

Bicycling enthusiasts will find great spots to ride, including a couple of trails on either side of Kachemak Park across the bay. East Hill and West Hill Roads offer great hill climbing; for flatter terrain, peddle from Diamond Ridge Road to the end of Skyline Drive. You also can ride the paved trail along the Spit. For a more challenging trek, take the switchback at the end of East End Road down the beach to the village of Kachemak Selo and head from there onto the Fox River flats. On the other end of town, take the four-wheeler trail above the Russian village of Nikolaevsk.

To really experience the ocean, hop in a kayak and paddle at eye-level with the sea lions and sea otters out in the bay. Remember the tides are strong and the weather can be unpredictable, so those new to the sport are advised to stay along the sheltered coves on the south side of the bay. Water taxis will transport you across to those safer waters, and some of them have kayaks available for rent. If you're a first-timer, be sure to head out with a guide or an experienced companion as well as the proper safety equipment. If you're among the experienced, you can take off from Homer Harbor in the early evening, after the breeze dies down, for Peterson Bay and Gull Island.

Birders have a heyday in Homer, with up to 241 species spotted in the area. In early May, you can see hundreds of thousands of shorebirds as they're passing through, with the Annual Shorebird Festival featuring more than 50 events to celebrate the grand migration. Take a water taxi or tour boat to Gull Island in the summer, and you'll be treated to the sight of hundreds of seabirds nesting on rock outcroppings. Even the Christmas bird count yields quite a few species. Check the Bird Alert Info Line (907–235–7337) for current information on what's been spotted. For a checklist of Kachemak birds and where to find them, visit www.birdinghomeralaska.org.

Clamming is another fun activity in Homer. Grab your fishing license, tide table, rubber boots, gloves, and a shovel, and head to the beach at low tide, preferably at the minus tide. The best clamming is at—where else?—Clam Gulch, about 20 miles north of Ninilchik. Wherever you see a dimple in the sand, dig beside it and reach for the clam, quickly but with care, remembering that they're called razor clams for a reason. July and August are the best months for clamming, with a limit of 60 allowed. You also can dig for steamers, cockles, and mussels on beaches near Homer, but the technique is different. Paralytic Shellfish Poison (PSP) alerts are rare in Kachemak Bay, but check with the Department of Fish and Game (907–235–6930, 907–235–8191) to be certain it's safe to eat your catch.

Homer's also a great jumping-off point for bear-watching excursions to Katmai National Monument. Travel by boat or bush plane from early June to late September to see bears feasting on wild salmon and berries. Some tour operators offer viewing from elevated platforms while others take you right into bear habitat. Both day trips and longer excursions are available.

Alaska Kayak School
P.O. Box 3547
Homer, AK 99603
(907) 235–2090
www.alaskakayakschool.com
Whether you're a novice or an experienced paddler, the Alaska Kayak School will help you get the most out of your water-based adventures. They offer instruction for sea, surf, flatwater, and white-water kayaking and canoeing as well as winter paddling, pool courses, and Eskimo Rolling. Alaska Kayak School's guided trips emphasize personal

instruction. Advanced and experienced paddlers may rent kayaks and gear or apply for longer exploratory expeditions. Instructors are members of the British Canoe Union and American Canoe Association.

Bay Excursions
P.O. Box 3312
Homer, AK 99603
(907) 235–7525
www.bayexcursions.com
Lifelong Alaskan Karl Stoltzfus has been running boats on Kachemak Bay since 1970, and he's happy to match his schedule to yours for birding or wildlife tours. In addition, he provides regular water-taxi service to cabins and trailheads at Kachemak Bay State Park. The boat has outside seating for 6 and inside seating for 12. Bay Excursions also offers kayak and cabin rentals.

Hallo Bay Bear Camp
P.O. Box 2904
Homer, AK 99603
(907) 235–2237
www.hallobay.com
Established in 1994, Hallo Bay Wilderness gives visitors a chance to see bears in their natural habitat, without viewing platforms or man-made trails. Guest groups are kept small to minimize impact on the bears, and nothing is done to discourage the natural curiosity of the animals. Translation: The bears will come into camp with you, but thanks to the well-trained staff, the bears at Hallo Bay Bear Camp have earned a reputation for behaving themselves. Opt for either five-hour ($425) or eight-hour ($550) fly-out trips from Homer, or try a two- to seven-day Nature and Wildlife Tour. Hallo Bay also offers photography workshops and tours for all levels, from beginner to advanced.

Rainbow Tours
P.O. Box 1526
Homer, AK 99603
(907) 235–7272
www.rainbowtours.net

Shuttle to Seldovia? Full-day whale-watching cruise? Half-day halibut fishing charter? Rainbow has it all. The shuttle to Seldovia leaves daily at 9:00 A.M., returning at 5:00 P.M. The cost is $35 round-trip, with reduced rates for seniors and children. Kayaks and bikes can ride along for an extra charge. The folks at Rainbow Tours will be happy to book accommodations if you want to spend the night. If you're more interested in whales than in the picturesque seaside town of Seldovia, stay on the boat and cruise to the entrance to Cook Inlet in hopes of spotting humpback, orca, finback, minke, and gray whales. You also have a good chance of seeing Stellar sea lions, sea otters, porpoise, puffins, cormorants, and auklets. For those who want to fish but don't have all day, hop aboard the *MV Sizzler* or the *MV Jackpot* for a taste of sportfishing Homer style.

True North Kayak Adventures
P.O. Box 2319
Homer, AK 99603
(907) 235–0708
www.truenorthkayak.com
Since 1993, True North has been offering guided kayaking trips that include water-taxi service, equipment, and instruction. Head out to the protected waters of Yukon Island for a half-day or full-day expedition, or take a three-quarter's-day excursion to Elephant Rock. With any luck you'll get a close-up look at seals, puffins, eagles, sea otters, or even whales while enjoying the gorgeous scenery and unspoiled coastline. If you have more time, try a two- to six-day jaunt to Eldred Passage, with meals, gear, and yurt or cabin rental included. No experience is necessary, though paddlers with previous experience can rent kayaks and head out on their own.

i Take a historic walking tour of Homer and check out some of the oldest buildings in the area. You can pick up more information at the Pratt Museum or the Homer Chamber of Commerce Visitor Center.

Hiking and Camping

Homer's spectacular oceanfront setting makes for great hiking opportunities. If you're looking for a short and easy hike, try the Pratt Museum Trail (0.75-mile long) behind the Pratt Museum. It's a self-guided forest trail with markers and occasional outdoor art exhibits; if you're lucky, you might spot a moose. Another easy walk is the Beluga Slough Trail, with six-tenths of a mile of gravel and boardwalk beginning at the Alaska Islands and Ocean Visitor Center and winding through woods and marshes to an overlook of Beluga Slough, where you'll see lots of waterfowl and shorebirds during the migratory seasons.

For hikes that are longer but not too challenging, check out the Homer Spit Trail, a paved path that begins at the base of Homer Spit Road and goes for 3.2 miles to Fishing Hole, or for 4 miles if you go all the way to the harbor. You'll see shorebirds and waterfowl in the spring and fall, while sea otters gather with the shifting ice in the winter. In addition, the Carl E. Wynn Nature Center Trails offer both guided and self-guided hikes along trails of various lengths. The center's paths follow a migratory corridor for black bear and moose, and you'll trek through great bird habitat as well. The user fee supports the nature center and its programs. In the winter, trails are open for snowshoeing.

If you'd like a longer hike, try the 6.7-mile Homestead Trail. Park at the trail head on Roger's Loop (off the Sterling Highway) and follow the trail up a south-facing slope to the Reuben Call Memorial, which overlooks Kachemak Bay. If you take the trail in June or July, a showy display of wildflowers awaits. As you make your way to Bridge Creek, you'll see an abundance of bushes, shrubs, and flowers before you reach a meadow dotted with alder and spruce. The trail ends at a parking area near Bridge Creek Reservoir.

You also can walk the beach near Homer, hiking 7.5 miles from Bishop's Beach to Diamond Creek Trail, or 15 miles to Anchor Point. Be careful, though. There's no defined trail, and when you walk the beach, you run the risk of being cut off by incoming tides. The hike is best at low tide, when you can hope to see eagles, otters, whales, sea ducks, and tide pools. Pick up a tide book at a local sporting goods store or at the Chamber of Commerce Visitor Center. If you pick up marine life from the tidal pools, remember to handle it with care and return it gently to its habitat.

The Spit used to be something of a camping free-for-all during the summer, but now things are a bit more upscale, with tent camping restricted to one of the private or city-run campgrounds on the seaward side of Spit Road or at Mariner Park near the beginning of the Spit. Another option for tent camping is above town at Karen Hornaday Park, where you can explore the woods and enjoy great views of the bay. You'll find RV parking at private campgrounds along the Spit, and the city maintains two dump stations, one near the Fishing Hole and one by the post office.

Alaska Angler RV Resort and Cabins
P.O. Box 39388
Ninilchik, AK 99639
(800) 347–4114
www.afishunt.com

The picturesque village of Ninilchik, just a little closer to Homer than to Kenai, makes a great jumping-off point for all your fishing fun. They have on-site charters for fishing for halibut out of Deep Creek and king salmon in the Kasilof River. You can walk to local beaches for clamming or to local rivers for salmon fishing, too. The Alaska Angler has 50 amp full hookups, cable television, laundry, showers, fish-processing facilities, propane, wi-fi Internet, and modem ports. In addition to standard and super-size sites, they have four fully furnished cabins available for rent. RV rates range from $26 to $35 per night.

Heritage RV Park
3350 Homer Spit Road
(907) 226–4500, (800) 380–7787
www.alaskaheritagervpark.com

Park right next to the ocean and take in the action at the Fishing Hole at this Good Sam Park. Included with all sites is 20/30/50 amp power, telephone with voice mail/modem, septic/water hookups, and satellite television. They offer extrawide RV sites with room for boats and other toys, as well as shower, restroom, and laundry facilities. At the Espresso Café, they serve up breakfast items with a great ocean view and free wireless Internet. Enjoy the private half-mile beach with campfire pit and picnic tables, and a great location next to the Homer Spit bike path and walking trail. At the gift shop, you'll find all sorts of Alaskana, including baleen and ivory carvings, gold nuggets, Alaska Native baskets and beadwork, and berry edibles. Rates range from $60 to $70 per night.

Village Barabara
42745 Sterling Highway
(907) 235–6404
www.villagebarabara.com
This spacious campground sits high on a bluff 2 miles north of Homer. Check out the view in all directions, from peninsula lakes to the volcanoes across Cook Inlet to breathtaking Kachemak Bay. Besides the RV park, there's a convenience store, a gift shop, pay phones, a gas station, a restaurant, an ATM, satellite television, laundry, showers, Internet access line, a tour-booking service, and rental cabins. The employees are longtime Homer residents who are happy to help with directions and tips on the area. Barabara, by the way, is a term of Russian origin for the sod dwellings used by the first peoples of Alaska. Prices range from $25.00 to $29.50 per night.

Fishing

If you can't find fish in Homer, you aren't trying very hard. From barn-door halibut to feisty king salmon and Dolly Varden, there's plenty of action to be had. The town earned its reputation as the "Halibut Capital of the World" due to the abundant catches and trophy-size flat fish brought in by sport anglers every season. When the halibut action heats up in the

i What are all those gorgeous peaks you see across the bay from Homer? Four of them are active volcanoes of the "Rim of Fire": Mt. Douglas, Mount St. Augustine, Mt. Illiamna, and Mt. Redoubt. The acronym DAIR will help you remember which is which, from south to north. Augustine and Redoubt both have erupted within the last few decades.

spring, king salmon fishing isn't far behind. You'll get good trolling action starting in May off Deep Creek, Anchor Point, and Ninilchik. Freshwater fishing for kings begins on the Saturday of Memorial Day weekend, with runs of silvers, reds, and pinks cycling through streams on both sides of the bay throughout the summer.

You can charter out for halibut and salmon from late spring to early fall, or try your luck surf-casting, fly fishing, jigging, or drifting on local beaches and rivers. Look for Dollies at the tip of the Spit and into the inlet, with shore-cast spinners and spoons getting the best results. Take a skiff into the waters east of the harbor entrance for silvers, or try fishing off the rocks at high tide. Across the Kachemak Bay, you'll find good angling at China Poot Bay, Seldovia Bay, Halibut Cove Lagoon, and Turka Bay.

North of Homer at Mile 134 of the Sterling Highway, the Ninilchik River is a hot spot for kings, silvers, Dolly Varden, and steelhead, but you'll encounter a lot of people traffic there, too. Deep Creek, just south of Ninilchik, is another popular spot for river fishing. You also can fish the Anchor River, about 20 miles north of Homer, for Dollies, silvers, steelheads, and rainbows. Be sure to check regulations with the Alaska Department of Fish and Game (907–235–6930, 907–235–8191) before you plan your fishing trip, as there are a variety of different opening days and limits for the various species.

A favorite hot spot in Homer is The Fishing Hole, a man-made lagoon stocked with

ℹ️ Across the bay from Homer, you can visit the charming seaside town of Seldovia by riding the Alaska Ferry, taking a bush plane, or hiring a water taxi or charter boat. Seldovia has a visitor center and museum with walking maps of the village and surrounding beaches. See www.seldovia.com for details.

silver and king salmon that return every year. Look for kings from mid-May through the first part of June, with silvers returning from July into September. It's shoulder to shoulder around the hole, but it's fun to watch as even youngsters pull in big fish when the action heats up.

Out on the open water, the daily halibut limit is two per person, with the fish typically averaging 20 to 30 pounds each, though it's not uncommon to wrestle in barn door flat fish weighing in at more than 100 pounds. King salmon fishing is best from May to the middle of June, while the silver run peaks during the first three weeks in August. Bait, tackle, cleaning, and filleting are typically included with your charter. Flash freezing, vacuum packing, and shipping are available locally.

Full-day charters leave early in the morning from Homer Harbor. Pack a tote with rain gear, your fishing license, a camera, a lunch (many restaurants and hotels sell box lunches), and motion sickness pills, just in case. Wear layered clothes and waterproof, nonslip shoes. Don't be surprised when your boat journeys a couple of hours only to pull up next to several others; captains communicate by radio to let each other know where the fish are.

If you're going to do any serious fishing, don't forget about Homer's Halibut Derby, which runs from the first of May to the middle of September. There's a cash jackpot for the largest fish of the season along with tagged fish prizes, catch-and-release prizes, and monthly cash prizes for the five biggest fish. They're still talking about the poor schmuck who landed a 407-pound halibut a few years ago but failed to buy a derby ticket.

Daniel's Personalized Guide Service
P.O. Box 918
Homer, AK 99603
(907) 235–3843, (800) 230–3843
www.homerfishing.com
Captain Daniel Donich develops and teaches innovative techniques for controlled-depth fishing, and he has acquired a reputation for excellence in angling the waters of Kachemak Bay. On any given trip, you can fish for a variety of species, from salmon of all types to halibut, steelhead, and Dolly Varden. You'll get the added treat of checking out the Dungeness and Tanner crabs he pulls up from traps. Bait, tackle, and fish cleaning are included with your charter, and if you'd like to end your day with a cookout on the beach, they can arrange that, too. Too tired to go home after all that fun? You can rent the Captain's three-bedroom guesthouse with hot tub, washer/dryer, and full kitchen.

North Country Charters
P.O. Box 889
Homer, AK 99603
(907) 235–7620, (800) 770–7620
www.northcountrycharters.com
This is Homer's oldest charter fishing operation, still run by its original owners, Sean and Gerri Martin, along with their sons. They have a nice fleet of twin-engine diesel boats, including the *Irish*, the *Pacific Sun*, the *Coastal Predator*, and the *Obsession*, each with a captain who takes pride in his boat and its catch. Whether you're a beginner or a veteran angler, they'll tailor the trip to your needs. Charter out for salmon or halibut, or try a combination of the two. They also offer long-range trips that take anglers along the coastline of Kachemak Bay and into the entrance of Lower Cook Inlet to the shallow waters along Shuyak Island. Most of these are three-day trips, and they include the use of tournament-quality tackle and all meals.

Bear Facts

Most Alaskans and Alaskan visitors would love to see a bear, as long as it's on their own terms. With an estimated 35,000 brown bears and 100,000 black bears sharing the state with approximately 600,000 people, the odds of encountering a bear would seem high, but in fact bears tend to keep to themselves, so most of us have never seen one at close range. Still, close encounters of the bear kind do occur, and those that end badly provide ample fodder for newspapers, books, and movies.

Assuming you'd rather make your claim to fame without finding yourself at the wrong end of a bear attack, your best defense is a good understanding of these powerful animals. Start by being able to distinguish between black and brown bears. It's not just a matter of color—there are black brown bears and brown black bears. Black bears are smaller than brown bears, with sloped as opposed to dish-shaped heads, no shoulder hump, and short, curved claws for climbing trees.

Black bears tend to retreat from danger, so if one charges, assume its intent is predatory and fight back. A brown bear is more likely to stand its ground, and your best bet is to treat it much as you would a threatening dog. Talk to it in a low, firm voice, and do your best to show that you're not afraid. If the bear is not heading toward you, try slowly backing away, but never run. Bears may look big and clumsy, but they can travel at speeds of 35 mph, so there's no outrunning them.

If a brown bear charges, stand firm unless the bear makes physical contact. Most charges will stop short of injury. Only if the bear makes contact should you "play dead," falling to the ground on your stomach, protecting your neck and face, and staying as still as possible. If the bear continues to be aggressive, assume the attack is predatory and fight back. Likewise, fight any bear that comes into your tent.

Pepper spray can be an effective deterrent at close ranges, but make sure you don't use it in a way that disables you instead of the bear. Always spray downwind and never in confined spaces. And pepper spray can't be taken on commercial flights, so visitors should plan on buying it and leaving it here.

The best bear strategy is to avoid coming nose to nose with these big animals. Bears are at the top of the food chain and aren't necessarily on the lookout for you, so be aware of your surroundings and do your best not to surprise a bear. When you're in the woods, make noise and travel in a group, shoulder-to-shoulder, if possible. Stay out of thick brush and away from carcasses, flocks of scavengers, or gulls feeding on fish. Try to walk with the wind so that bears will smell you before they see you.

Keep your campsites clean, with dishes washed and food cached aboveground or in bear-proof containers. Don't have smelly foods like bacon or smoked fish at your camp, and do your best to keep food smells off your clothing. Savvy campers sometimes cook on the trail so they're not sleeping in an area with lingering food smells. Burn whatever garbage you can and pack out the rest. Burying garbage is pointless, as bears can easily sniff it out and dig it up.

If a bear approaches while you're fishing, stop and gather your belongings. Be ready to throw your fish into the current, away from the bear, if you have to. If you have a fish on the line, cut the line before getting into a confrontation with the bear. Remember that it's illegal to feed bears (or any large mammals, for that matter), and if bears learn they can get fish simply by approaching a fisherman, there's a good chance they'll turn into nuisance bears.

Silver Fox Charters
P.O. Box 402
Homer, AK 99603
(907) 235–8792, (800) 478–8792
www.silverfoxcharters.com
Silver Fox is one of the largest charter outfits in Homer, and they've been in business since 1974. If you have your sights set on a big barn-door halibut, the odds are good with Silver Fox, as they have a reputation among charter services for bringing in the most fish weighing more than 100 pounds. In addition to halibut, they do salmon and ling cod charters. They run one 56-foot boat and five 30-foot boats, all with twin diesel engines, modern navigational equipment, heated cabins, and restrooms. Boats typically go out for about 10 hours, with one-and-a-half to two hours running time each way. Expect to catch at least two fish on your average day, with about 30 pounds of fillets to show for your fun. The larger boat sleeps 12 for long-range trophy trips, and they offer a new 12,000-square-foot log lodge for overnight stays. Military discounts are available.

PRINCE WILLIAM SOUND

On the north end of the Gulf of Alaska, east of the Kenai Peninsula, you'll find Prince William Sound, a 70-mile stretch of ocean jutted with fjords and peppered with islands. It's tough to play favorites in a state with as much scenic beauty as Alaska, but the Sound stands out with its vistas of soaring mountains and endless miles of forests stretching down to the ocean. Unlike the Kenai with its frenzied fishing activity and the Mat-Su Valley with its steady stream of commuters, peace and solitude prevail in this most remote of the Southcentral's getaways.

Most of the Sound is inaccessible by road, which makes the on-road harbor towns of Whittier, Seward, and Valdez all the more special. The scenery is spectacular and the marine wildlife plentiful. Cruise ships dock in Whittier and Seward, letting loose swarms of tourists, but Valdez is mostly an Alaskan's paradise, as is Cordova, which is accessible only by air and water.

Columbia Glacier, the world's fastest-moving glacier, is a popular attraction in the Sound. You can take a cruise from Valdez to get a close look at the calving ice as the glacier recedes at speeds of up to 115 feet a day. And if you love water sports or fishing, Prince William Sound is a great place to do both.

PORTAGE/WHITTIER

Just about an hour's drive from Anchorage, you can get a taste of Prince William Sound's spectacular scenery and glacial activity with a stop at Portage, in the heart of the Chugach National Forest. Portage isn't really a town and it's not on the ocean, but it's a popular destination for visitors who want to get up-close and personal with Portage Glacier, accessed by boat from Portage Lake.

At Whittier, you can take in all sorts of waterfront activity during the summer season. And it's a fun spot to visit because the town itself and the way you get there are unique. The U.S. Army made Whittier a "secret" deepwater port and petroleum delivery center during World War II. Originally, it was accessible only by water or by rail from Portage; the railroad was completed in 1943. Today it's a charming seaside community with road access, a great day trip from Anchorage.

Getting Here, Getting Around

These days you reach Whittier via the 2.5-mile Anton Anderson Memorial Tunnel, the longest vehicle tunnel in North America. There's only one lane, and the railroad still uses the tunnel, but that adds to the novelty. Vehicles gather in a staging area, traveling to Whittier on the hour and back on the half-hour, subject to rail delays. A toll is charged on the way to Whittier but not on the way back. For up-to-date schedules and toll information, contact the Alaska Department of Transportation (907–566–2244, 877–611–2586, www.dot.state.ak.us).

There's also ferry service between Whittier, Valdez, and Cordova via the Alaska Marine Highway (907–272–7116, 800–642–0066, www.dot.state.ak.us) and rail service to Whittier on the Alaska Railroad (907–265–2494, 800–544–0552, www.alaskarailroad.com).

No matter how you get to Whittier, you'll love the spectacular scenery along the waterfront. It's a unique little town. At first the only

i If you're catching the ferry or a cruise in Whittier, give yourself plenty of time to get through the tunnel, as delays are not uncommon.

place to live in Whittier was the now-abandoned Buckner Building, once one of the largest buildings in Alaska. Today the 14-story Begich Towers and the Whittier Manor provide condominium housing for the town's 290 residents.

For a small town, Whittier's got a good deal going on, at least in the summer. In June, there's an annual Walk to Whittier, when for one day the tunnel is open to pedestrian traffic. There's a big Fourth of July celebration plus a summerlong Halibut Derby, not to mention silver salmon fishing in the early fall. Watch out for winter, though. With a mean snowfall of 260 inches, the place gets pretty well buried.

Accommodations

There is nowhere to overnight in the little town of Portage, but Whittier has a handful of fun options for overnight guests. Unless otherwise stated, you can assume that major credit cards are accepted and that the accommodations are available year-round. Expect no smoking, no pets, and no wheelchair access unless we say otherwise. Price ranges below indicate the average cost of a room for two adults during the peak season.

Price Codes

$................ Less than $100
$$ .... $100–$150
$$$ .... $151–$200
$$$$ .... More than $200

June's B&B Condo Suites $$–$$$$
P.O. Box 715
Whittier, AK 99693
(888) 472–2396
www.breadnbuttercharter.com

Here's your chance to mingle with the locals in one of the residential complexes for Whittier residents. Located in the historic Begich Towers, these condo units include private baths, full kitchenettes, telephones, cable televisions with VCRs, and continental breakfast. You'll find a variety of bed sizes, including futons and sleeper sofas for large groups, in June's one- and two-bedroom units. Larger units offer an ocean view. Breakfast, delivered in a basket, includes fruit, cereal, toast, bagels, juice, coffee, and tea. On the first floor of the Towers, there's a post office, store, beauty shop, and non-denominational church. Rooms are wheelchair accessible, and there are designated smoking areas. After a good night's rest, you can head out on a sightseeing or fishing charter captained by June's husband Ken.

The Inn at Whittier $$$$
Harbor Loop Road
P.O. Box 609
Whittier, AK 99693
(907) 472–7000
www.innatwhittier.com

This four-story, timber-framed inn with its 70-foot lighthouse tower is a focal point of the Whittier harbor. From the grand fireplace in the lobby to the restaurant with sweeping views of the harbor, there are plenty of spaces to relax and enjoy the quiet ambience of the waterfront. Down-filled pillows and comforters as well as crisp bed linens mean guests sleep in comfort here. Choose from Mountain View or Ocean View Rooms, each with television and dataport telephone. For a more luxurious experience, try a Junior Suite with ocean view, king-size bed, deluxe bath, Jacuzzi tub, soft terry robes, and sitting area; or indulge in a Townhouse Suite, a two-story retreat with all the features of the Junior Suite plus ocean and mountain views, plasma television, and a fireplace on each floor. The inn offers packages for meetings, retreats, weddings, or just plain old getaways.

Restaurants

Unless you get out on the water or hike into the hills, there's not a whole lot to do once you get to Whittier except take in a meal at one of the seaside eateries. Along the waterfront triangle, you'll find a variety of seasonal cafes, most featuring seafood and outdoor seating. Unless otherwise stated, these restaurants are open daily in the summer season and accept major credit cards. No need to worry about reservations. There's wheelchair access for the outdoor tables, but don't assume it's available inside unless we say so.

Price Codes

$	Less than $15
$$	$15–$25
$$$	$26–$40
$$$$	More than $40

Café Orca and Gallery $$$
Lot 9 Business Harbor Triangle, Whittier
(907) 472-2549

Here's a great place to enjoy distinctive cuisine while taking in the million-dollar view. With its cozy seaside-cottage atmosphere, the Orca caters to an eclectic group of travelers, including outdoor enthusiasts, Europeans, and families on day trips from Anchorage. Popular menu items include the fresh, wild, grilled halibut and salmon; the Euro Sandwich with Brie, roasted garlic mayo, and tomato; and the Glacier Burger with bacon and blue cheese. All seafood is grilled, not deep-fried, and they bake most of their own pastries. The Orca offers up espresso and pastries for breakfast as well as a full lunch and dinner menu. There's counter and take-out service only, with great seating on the sunny deck overlooking the ocean. No reservations are necessary, and there's ample parking out front. The restaurant is wheelchair accessible, and it's open only during the summer season.

Varly's Swiftwater Seafood $$
Business Harbor Triangle, Whittier
(907) 472-2550

For hand-battered seafood in a waterfront setting, Varly's is the place. Fries come with the deep-fried shrimp, fish, and halibut, and for landlubbers the menu includes cheeseburgers, chicken sandwiches, and chicken strips. If deep-fried food isn't your thing, try the Peel & Eat Shrimp, the crab cakes, or homemade clam and seafood chowders. Varly's also serves homemade desserts. On Friday and Saturday nights, check out their Smoked

Prime Rib Dinner with red potatoes, corn on the cob, coleslaw, and a roll with butter. Wine and beer, including specialty and import lagers, are available. The cafe is open seasonally for lunch and dinner.

Attractions

Throughout the Prince William Sound, you'll find most attractions offer insight into the biggest attraction of all, the great outdoors. Expect limited hours in the off-season and a fair number of tourists during the summer.

Price Codes

$	Less than $5.00
$$	$5.00–$15.00
$$$	$16.00–$30.00
$$$$	More than $30.00

Alaska Wildlife Conservation Center $
Mile 79 Seward Highway, Portage Glacier
(907) 783-2025
www.alaskawildlife.org

A popular, affordable stop for both independent travelers and tour buses headed to Portage, the Alaska Wildlife Conservation Center offers an opportunity to see that elusive moose or bear in outdoor settings resembling their natural habitats. And it's not just big game that you'll see—dozens of other species benefit from this nonprofit effort to rehabilitate injured or orphaned animals while educating visitors in the 140-acre wildlife park. Admission fees are quite reasonable, and proceeds go toward supporting the continued efforts on behalf of the animals. Open daily throughout the year, from 8:00 A.M. to 8:00 P.M. during the summer season, from 10:00 A.M. to 6:00 P.M. from April to mid-May, and from 10:00 A.M. to 5:00 P.M. September through March.

> **i** For shopping in Whittier, check out the Triangle near the harbor. You'll find fresh fudge at Sound Ideas Gallery and Gifts, local carvings at Log Cabin Gifts, and fresh fish at Fee's Custom Seafoods.

Begich, Boggs Visitor Center
Portage Valley Road, Portage
(907) 783–2326
This impressive visitor center, operated by the U.S. Forest Service, is definitely worth a stop. A walk through the exhibits mirrors a walk through Portage Valley and down to the Sound. Listen to calls of area wildlife, including cranes, wolves, fox, raven, and ptarmigan, or check out the narratives told by the human inhabitants of Prince William Sound. Kids, as well as the young at heart, will love the spotting scopes that let them see like a bee, and an otter, and a deer. There's even a black cushioned ice worm replica that's large enough to straddle, if you're so inclined. Admission is free, and the center is open daily in the summer, weekends only during the off-season.

Parks, Recreation, and Tours

The tiny town of Whittier is surrounded by the majestic Chugach National Forest, the second-largest national forest in the country. For information on the trails and recreation within Chugach National Forest, visit the forest service yurt at the West Boat Launch Ramp, or the Begich, Boggs Visitor Center (see the Attractions section above). If you'd like guided recreation, there are several tour companies to assist you during the summer season.

Grayline of Alaska
745 West Fourth Avenue, Anchorage
(907) 277–5581, (800) 544–2206
www.graylinealaska.com
Grayline offers all sorts of water-related tour and charter options in Portage and Whittier, including one-hour cruises for $29 that will take you in for a close-up look at Portage Glacier and its dramatic calving ice. Cruises leave from Portage Lake and are narrated by the U.S. Forest Service.

Major Marine Tours
411 West Fourth Avenue, Anchorage
(907) 274–7300, (888) 764–7300
www.majormarine.com
If you'd like a longer glacier cruise including an all-you-can-eat meal, depart from Whittier with Major Marine Tours. A Chugach National Forest interpreter will point out highlights on the five-hour cruise of Blackstone Bay, where you'll see 1,700-foot active glaciers, icebergs, and spectacular glacial terrain from multiple viewing decks. They'll even shut off the engines so you can hear the impressive cracking and calving of the ice.

Phillips Cruises Tours
519 Fourth Avenue, Anchorage
(907) 276–8023, (800) 544–0529
www.26glaciers.com
More of a landlubber? Check out the 26-Glacier Cruise with Phillips Cruises and Tours. They guarantee no seasickness in their high-speed catamaran, the *Klondike Express*. The boat features wide aisles, inside seating, large picture windows, a full-service saloon, and a snack bar. Learn about the history and the wildlife of the area as you take in the scenery along College Fjord and in Barry Arm.

StarBound Alaskan Adventures
1241 West 27th Avenue, Anchorage
(866) 764–7354
http://starboundalaskanadventures.com
If you're feeling really adventurous, try exploring the Sound aboard your own personal watercraft. StarBound will set you up with a dry suit, a personal watercraft, and a guide. At $500 per day, it's not cheap, but they offer substantial discounts for groups.

Fishing

In Prince William Sound, you can enjoy world-class fishing while feasting your eyes on some of the most beautiful views in the state. Because of the limited road access to most parts of the Sound, you'll need to charter out by boat or floatplane to reach many of the hot spots. Expect to pay between $150 and $250 per angler for your charter, depending on the type and length of the trip.

In Whittier, you'll find good salmon fishing in bays and near the mouths of streams, with lots of pinks in July and silvers in August. Early in the summer, you can troll for a hatchery run of kings along the head of Passage Canal, and later in the season you'll find reds and chums around Esther Island. For shore fishing right in Whittier, wait until the September silver run. You may find some halibut in the waters close to shore, but the bottom drops fast and deep, so your best bet is to charter out.

Alaska Good Time Charters
P.O. Box 876257
Wasilla, AK 99687
(907) 373–7447
www.alaskagoodtimecharters.com
Spend three to six days sailing the pristine waters of the Sound aboard this outfit's 50-foot yacht, and you're bound to come home with some great fishing stories. Halibut, lingcod, rockfish, and salmon sharks are among the saltwater species you can pursue, and you also can fish for salmon in either salt or freshwater. The charters aren't cheap, but meals, lodging, tackle, bait, ice, and fish cleaning are included. Owner/captain David Pinquoch has decades of fishing experience in Alaska and can provide combination fishing/sightseeing or fishing/hunting packages, too.

Sea Mist Charters
P.O. Box 682
Whittier, AK 99693
(907) 472–2459
www.pwsoundcharters.com
Specializing in bottom fishing for halibut, rockfish, and lingcod, Sea Mist will take you out for 10 hours on the *M.V. Gold Runner,* their 28-foot Bayliner with heated cabin and marine head. All gear, tackle, and bait are provided, and the first mate will clean, filet, and bag your catch. Check in for your excursion at Quigley's Ice Cream Parlor on the waterfront in Whittier. Reservations are recommended.

Hiking and Camping

Once you've had your fill of water-based fun in Portage and Whittier, head for the hills around Whittier on either the Horsetail Falls Trail, a 1-mile trail with views of the town and

the canal, or the 2-mile Portage Pass Trail, which ends at Divide Lake and offers glacier views along the way. Access the Horsetail Falls Trail from Salmon Run Road, just past the Buckner Building. Access to the Portage Pass Trail begins at the forest service access road near the tunnel.

For overnight stays, try the campground near the parking area off Whittier Street or the overnight parking area at the Whittier end of the tunnel. Note, though, that there are no services at either location. For a more complete camping experience, there's the scenic Williwaw Campground at Mile 4.3 of the Whittier Access Road. Maintained by the U.S. Forest Service, Williwaw has 60 campsites with access to toilets, Dumpsters, water, fire pits, and picnic tables. Campfire programs and self-guided nature trails will enhance your stay. At Mile 1.7 of the access road, there's Portage Valley RV Park (907–783–3111), a private facility designed to accommodate those larger rigs.

SEWARD

Seward is a quintessential Alaskan seaside town, not too trendy, not too big, but rich in history and spirited in its sense of community. It was a lot sleepier until the cruise ships swapped it into their itineraries in place of Valdez. Now there's plenty of activity, especially in the summer, and the locals have been scrambling to pull together a nice variety of services and activities to accommodate visitors. It's a place with plenty of character, from the softball field with harbor views to the

i Two big annual events in Seward are the Fourth of July Mount Marathon Race and the Silver Salmon Derby in August. Since 1915, hardy runners have been dashing up the 3,022-foot peak of Mt. Marathon and back, posting record times of less than 45 minutes. The fishing derby offers prizes for the heaviest salmon plus purses of up to $50,000 for catching specially tagged fish.

combination diner-lodging-bike-rental-business in an old Alaska railroad car to the big tree downtown yard festooned with dozens of large, bright fishing buoys.

In 1791, Russian explorer Alexander Baranof took shelter from a storm in a bay he later named Resurrection after the Sunday of his misadventure. The town of Seward was established on that ice-free bay in 1903 to serve as an ocean terminus and supply center for the railroad. In 1910 the town became the starting point for the famed Iditarod Trail. The trail served as a mail route to Nome until 1924; much later, the Anchorage to Nome portion of the Iditarod Trail began playing host to one of the most famed dogsled races in the world. Like Whittier, Seward's port was an important staging area during World War II.

Seward is on the Kenai Peninsula, but it's a great jumping-off point for Prince William Sound, so that's the association most Alaskans make. From Seward, boats head out in two directions, some for fishing and recreation in the Sound, and some to tour the bays and coves of the Kenai Fjords National Park.

Getting Here, Getting Around

Driving to Seward on the scenic 127-mile Seward Highway (Route 9) is a real treat; with its soaring mountains and rushing streams, the U.S. Department of Transportation has designated the route a National Scenic Byway. You also can reach Seward via the Alaska Railroad, by small plane from Anchorage, and by the Alaska ferry MV Tustumena, which links Seward to Kodiak and Valdez.

Gather up visitor information by stopping at the Seward Chamber of Commerce Visitor Center at Mile 2 of the Seward Highway (907–224–8051, www.sewardak.org). It's open daily in the summer from 8:00 A.M. to 6:00 P.M. Another great resource is the Kenai Fjords National Park Visitor Center (907–224–3175) in the Small Boat Harbor; the street address is 1212 Fourth Avenue. You'll find a wealth of information there, including slide shows, interpretive programs, and a bookstore.

Accommodations

You'll find a nice variety of accommodations in Seward, from cabins along the water to stateside hotel chains near the harbor to a historic downtown hotel. It's a small town with a high volume of seasonal tourist traffic, so make your reservations well in advance. These establishments are open year-round unless we state otherwise, and they accept major credit cards. We'll make specific mention of any that allow pets or smoking, along with any that have wheelchair access. Price ranges below indicate the average cost of a room for two adults during the peak season.

Price Codes

$	Less than $100
$$	$100–$150
$$$	$151–$200
$$$$	More than $200

Alaska's Third Avenue Lodging $$–$$$
309 Third Avenue
(907) 224–3635, (877) 239–3637
www.seward-alaska.com/cabin
Here's another one of those eclectic Alaskan options for travelers. Choose from one of three private cabins on Lowell Point, 3 miles south of Seward, or opt for your own apartment with private entrance right in town. The modern apartments with huge windows include full kitchens and private baths along with a variety of bed sizes and configurations. Many offer views of the bay. Located 1 block from downtown and 2 blocks from Resurrection Bay, the apartments are within walking distance to shopping, restaurants, the Seward Museum, and the Alaska SeaLife Center. The cottage-style cabins are 1 block from the bay and equipped with VCRs, phones, baths, and kitchenettes.

The Beach House $$
P.O. Box 2525
Seward, AK 99664
(907) 244–7000
www.beachhousealaska.com

Enjoy a private, home-style beach experience at one of two guesthouses at Lowell Point on Resurrection Bay. Each two-bedroom house has queen-size beds, a queen-size sofa bed, bath, and fully-furnished kitchen, so they're perfect for families or small groups. There's also an overflow cabin that sleeps three. The two-story cottages are just what you'd expect of beachfront hideaways, with weathered siding, comfortable quilt-topped beds, and lots of windows for soaking up the view. Beach access is across the street, where you might spot a bald eagle soaring or a salmon jumping in the bay. Take off out back, and you can hike up to Caines Head or out to Tonsina Point.

Box Canyon Cabins $$
31515 Lois Way
(907) 224–5046
www.boxcanyoncabin.com
Tucked away in the woods off Mile 3.5 of the Seward Highway, Box Canyon offers comfortable, handcrafted log cabins in a secluded forest setting complete with its own pond. Choose from two one-bedroom and four two-bedroom cabins, with twin-, full-, and queen-size beds. Vaulted ceilings and hardwood floors add charm to the newer cabins, or you can opt for a cozy 16-foot-by-18-foot "historic" unit. All include full kitchens, private baths, and phones. You'll feel right at home with a barbeque area, picnic area, satellite TV, wi-fi zone, Laundromat, games, books, and magazines for guests to enjoy.

Breeze Inn $$–$$$
P.O. Box 2147
Seward, AK 99664
(907) 224–5238, (888) 224–5237
www.breezeinn.com
Most of the 108 rooms at this modern motel and annex offer views of Resurrection Bay and/or Mt. Marathon. Centrally located and within walking distance to galleries, boat charters, and shopping in the harbor area, the Breeze Inn also offers courtesy shuttles to the railroad depot, the cruise ship dock, and the Alaska SeaLife Center. There's an on-site restaurant featuring steaks and

Alaskan seafood, a motel gift shop, and complimentary coffee in the lobby. All rooms have cable TVs with HBO, coffeemakers, alarm clocks, telephones with free local calling, and private baths. Smoking and wheelchair-accessible rooms are available on request. If you'd like a little pampering, choose one of the Jacuzzi suites.

Camelot Cottages $–$$
Mile 1.4 Salmon Creek Road
(907) 224–3039, (800) 739–3039
www.camelotcottages.com
For a bit of privacy away from the busloads of tourists, check out these charming, self-contained cottages just 10 minutes from downtown Seward. Tucked away in a natural woodland setting with gardens complementing the native foliage, you'll enjoy peace and quiet without sacrificing comfort. All cottages have private baths and kitchens with coffeemakers, microwaves, and minifridges. Gourmet coffee, tea, cocoa, oatmeal, dishes, and linens are provided. Guests also may use the on-site hot tub, laundry facilities, barbecue grills, and fish freezers. Your hosts will even share herbs from the gardens to go with your fresh-grilled fish. They also assist guests with reservations and recommendations for activities, as well as providing lists of recommended clothing and gear for all types of outdoor fun.

Holiday Inn Express Seward Harbor Hotel $$$$
1412 Fourth Avenue
(907) 224–2550, (800) 465–4329
www.hieseward.com

i Retired or active military? Check out the Seward Resort, offering motel rooms, town houses, a log cabin, and yurts as well as RV and tent camping. Laundry facilities, mountain bikes, fishing gear, and snow machines also are available for guest use. For more information, call (907) 224–2659, (800) 770–1858, or visit www.seward resort.com.

Enjoy all the modern conveniences, including wireless Internet access, from a fabulous setting overlooking Seward's small boat harbor. Many of the 82 rooms have Resurrection Bay or Mt. Marathon views, and some have private balconies. A picturesque boardwalk leads from the hotel to the dock and retail shops. Choose between a king-size bed or two queen-size beds in tastefully decorated rooms that include coffeemakers, hair dryers, irons, ironing boards, and telephones with free local calling. There's an on-site swimming pool, whirlpool, guest laundry, and business center. Start your day with the free continental breakfast, featuring the hotel chain's signature "Express Start" cinnamon rolls. Smoking rooms and wheelchair-accessible facilities are available.

Miller's Landing $$–$$$
13880 Beach Drive, Lowell Point
(907) 224–5739, (866) 541–5739
www.millerslandingak.com

You'll find a little bit of everything at Miller's Landing, from tent camping among hundred-year-old spruce trees to RV parking on the scenic oceanfront to full accommodation cabins with such seaworthy names as the Admiral's Cottage. They also have economy rooms and "camping cabins." Miller's Landing offers a full Prince William Sound experience, with bald eagles soaring overhead, sea otters playing in the surf, and Stellar sea lions floating in the water. Accommodations lean toward the rustic, but there's wireless Internet available, and the full-service cabins have full kitchens and baths. There's great hiking nearby, and Miller's offers scheduled water-taxi service around Resurrection Bay and Aialik Bay, including

You can rent one of 17 remote cabins through the Seward Ranger District (907–224–3374, 877–444–6777, or www.fs.fed.us/r10/chugach). Cabins have an oil stove or woodstove, bunks, and outhouse facilities. Drinking water is not provided, and some require fly-in access.

Northwestern Fjord. In fact, you can take advantage of all sorts of ocean-based opportunities at Miller's, including kayak rentals, tours, and lessons; motorboat rentals; and beach or charter boat fishing. Miller's Landing is pet friendly, and they offer early-bird discounts for reservations made before April 1.

Renfro's Lakeside Retreat $$
27121 Seward Highway
(907) 288–5059, (877) 288–5059
www.seward-alaska.com/renfros

If you're looking for an Alaskan-style getaway, Renfro's offers 30 acres of recreation and relaxation along the shores of Kenai Lake. Nestled in the Chugach Mountains, this picturesque retreat includes five lakefront cabins and four with lake access; rates vary by size and location of the unit. Each features a loft, bath with on-demand hot water heater, kitchen with stove and refrigerator, and private porch. Every log cabin has a queen-size bed in addition to various configurations for additional sleeping. Guests have access to on-site telephone, iron/ironing board, paddleboats, playground, and laundry facilities. Porta-cribs at this family-friendly retreat are available on request. Limited housekeeping is provided, with fresh towels, trash pickup, and coffee basket refills daily. The Renfros keep their Newfoundland and Pomeranian indoors, and they allow guests to bring their pets as well. Ten RV sites also are available.

Seward Windsong Lodge $$$$
Mile 3.7 Seward Highway
(907) 224–7116, (888) 959–9590
www.sewardwindsong.com

If you're looking for an Alaskan-lodge experience on the Sound, the Seward Windsong fits the bill. From the log and wood exterior to the Alaskan-themed rooms to the off-the-beaten-path location, this Alaska Heritage Tours property offers comfort and style with a wilderness touch. Mountain peaks and the nearby Resurrection River form the backdrop for 108 guest rooms, a lounge, on-site restaurants with a large selection of microbrews on tap, and meeting facilities. Each room has a private exterior entrance and features full bath, coffeemaker, TV/VCR with free movies, telephone with dataport, and hair dryer. For family accommodations, check out the deluxe suites with kitchenettes and Jacuzzi tubs. Children younger than age 11 stay free. The lodge offers complimentary shuttle service to local activities, with a full tour desk to help you plan your adventures. Wheelchair access is available.

Van Gilder Hotel $$
308 Adams Street
(907) 224–3079, (800) 204–6835
www.vangilderhotel.com
There's lots of character at the Van Gilder, a Seward landmark that was built in 1916 and joined the National Register of Historical Places in 1980. Step into turn-of-the-century charm with brass beds, period antiques, an Alaskana book collection, and historic photo displays. Along with the nostalgia, you'll enjoy such modern conveniences as private baths, cable TVs, and in-room telephones. Considered one of the finest buildings in Alaska when it was first constructed, the white and maroon stucco-fronted hotel has hosted scruffy miners, upscale law-firm employees, and even President Harding's territorial executives. Located 2 blocks from the Alaska Sea-Life Center and the Seward Museum, the hotel is convenient to downtown restaurants and shopping. Choose from View Suites, View Rooms, Standard Rooms, and Pension Rooms. The hotel is open year-round.

Restaurants

Given the growing numbers of hungry tourists in the summer, there aren't a whole lot of restaurants in Seward, but you'll still find some nice options. These eateries accept major credit cards and reservations unless otherwise stated, and you can assume daily, year-round service. We'll make a special note if the facility is wheelchair accessible. Price categories reflect the average cost of dinner for two, excluding drinks, tip, and dessert.

Price Codes

$.	Less than $15
$$	$15–$25
$$$	$26–$40
$$$$	More than $40

Apollo Restaurant $$$
229 Fourth Avenue
(907) 224–3092
For Greek and Italian cuisine plus Alaskan seafood and charbroiled steaks, check out the Apollo Restaurant in downtown Seward. They offer fine dining in an eclectic atmosphere, featuring homemade pizza and their own custom-smoked salmon. They'll even cook up the fresh fish you haul in from your day out on the ocean. Specialties include Halibut Calabreze, Halibut and Salmon Monte Mio, Athenian Chicken, Italian Scampi, gyros, and Musaka. Enjoy a full selection of beer, wine, and specialty desserts with your meal. There's good parking out front, and the restaurant is wheelchair accessible. The folks at the Apollo are used to people calling from all over saying how much they enjoyed their meal and requesting recipes.

Chinooks Waterfront $$$$
1404 Fourth Avenue
(907) 224–2207
www.chinookswaterfront.com
At the north end of the small boat harbor, Chinooks offers fine dining with a superb view. Specializing in fresh seafood, pasta, and steaks, Chinooks also has a full wine list and a brewpub featuring Alaskan ales. Try their Seafood Sauté, a blend of Alaskan crab, mussels, salmon, halibut, and prawns in a sauce of white wine, garlic, and butter, served with vegetables over a bed of steaming rice. Another favorite is the Pepper-Seared Salmon, a fresh filet coated with cracked pepper and topped with a homemade dill sauce. Chinooks is open from 11:30 A.M. to 10:00 P.M. seven days a week during the summer season. They offer wheelchair access and have their own parking lot.

Exit Glacier Salmon Bake Restaurant $$
¼ Mile Exit Glacier Road
(907) 224–4752
www.sewardalaskacabins.com
Here's a restaurant and pub that doesn't take itself too seriously, advertising "cheap beer and lousy food." In actuality, the Salmon Bake is a fun Alaskan-style establishment complete with wood timbers and a stone fireplace in a quiet forest setting. On the menu you'll find fresh Alaskan salmon, red snapper, and halibut along with burgers and steaks. On tap, they have a large selection of Alaskan microbrews, including Alaskan Amber, Moose's Tooth, and Glacier Brewhouse Blonde. There's also a nice selection of wines. The Salmon Bake is open only in the evenings, daily during the summer and on weekends during the winter. The restaurant is wheelchair accessible, and reservations are not accepted.

Le Barn Appetit $$$
11786 Old Exit Glacier Road
(907) 224–8706
Boasting its own Belgian chef, this inn, eatery, and health food store offers full breakfast, lunch, and dinner menus. For breakfast, try eggs your way, served with homemade bread and jams; a three-egg build-your-own omelet; or specialties including eggs Benedict, Crème Beef, crepes, and Belgian waffles. The lunch menu features a variety of soups and sandwiches as well as pizzas and salads. For dinner, choose from traditional entrees such as smoked or steamed fish, barbequed ribs, or chicken cordon bleu, or sample their cultural entrees, including Mexican, Italian, and Asian dishes. Dessert choices include Belgian chocolate eclairs, crème custard, Franchi Pan, or Belgium apple pie. Alcohol is not served, but you can enjoy a variety of espresso beverages with your meal, including rich Belgian hot cocoa. This is a family-style eatery that also offers sleeping accommodations in rooms with such names as the Passion Pit and the Adorable Tree House, which is actually built around a tree. For advance reservations, payment is required.

Shopping

There aren't any big malls or department stores in this little seaside town, but you'll find some fun gift shops and galleries for browsing and buying. Most of these are within walking distance of the small boat harbor or the historic downtown district.

Bardarson Studio
1317 Fourth Avenue
(800) 354–0141
www.seward.net/bardarson
Follow the waterfront boardwalk to Bardarson's, where you'll find a gallery filled with Alaskan art, posters, reproductions, and handcrafted gift items. The studio showcases the colorful Northwest art of Seward watercolorist Dot Bardarson along with other limited-edition work by artists from around the state. When you tire of shopping, relax on their sunny deck and enjoy the flowers, music, and seaside view.

Brown and Hawkins
209 Fourth Avenue
(907) 224–3011
www.sweetdarlings.com
Brown and Hawkins has been outfitting Alaskans since 1900; in fact, they claim to be the oldest family-owned retail establishment in the state. Choose from a large selection of brand-name outdoor clothing, or browse the huge selection of Alaskan-made gifts and souvenirs, including ivory, jade, and gold keepsakes. While you're there, check out the old bank vault and turn-of-the-century cash register, and sample some of the fresh fudge, bark, brittle, and saltwater taffy being made on-site. There's even an old-fashioned soda fountain featuring real Italian gelato and other treats.

Juneau Goldnugget and Diamond
232 Fourth Avenue
(907) 224–8800
For handcrafted jewelry, this is the place, specializing in Alaskan gold nugget jewelry and fine 14 karat gold jewelry. They're a great source for Alaskan sea life and wildlife charms

in both 14 karat gold and sterling silver. You'll also find precious stones, both loose and set, including blue topaz, tanzanite, and amethyst.

Peak Anteak
Mile 35.8 Seward Highway, Moose Pass
(907) 288–5644
Although teak is not a wood usually associated with Alaska, the folks at Peak Anteak craft it into unique furniture that's popular with locals and visitors alike. Located just south of the junction of the Sterling and Seward Highways, this charming shop makes a fun stop on the way to or from Seward. In addition to the old-growth teak furniture made from wood that's between 50 and 1,000 years old, check out their collection of wearable art, ethnic blankets, handwoven baskets, handblown glass, elegant jewelry, and silk accessories. They're open daily from 8:00 A.M. to 9:00 P.M. in the summer, with abbreviated hours in the off-season. Worldwide shipping is available, and there's ample parking for cars and RVs.

Attractions

The waterfront and all of its adjunct activities are the primary attraction in Seward, as they are throughout the Prince William Sound. Still, there are a couple of great places to get your bearings and learn more about the history and natural wonders of the land and water around Seward.

Price Codes

$. . . . . Less than $5.00
$$ . . . . $5.00–$15.00
$$$ . . . . $16.00–$30.00
$$$$ . . . . More than $30.00

Alaska SeaLife Center   **$$**
301 Railway Avenue
(907) 224–6300, (800) 224–2525
www.alaskasealife.org
SeaWorld it's not, but the Alaska SeaLife Center fulfills an important role in research, education, and wildlife rehabilitation. Open since 1998, the center is a popular stop for both tour groups and independent travelers. You'll see Stellar sea lions, harbor seals, octopus, and seabirds in naturalistic settings, along with the standard fish behind glass. Youngsters, and the young at heart, enjoy the touch tanks, where they gently can fondle sea urchins, star fish, and the like. Live cam footage from a Stellar sea lion rookery 35 miles from Seward lets you get a look at the daily activities of these large mammals, including the birthing of pups in the spring. The center is wheelchair accessible. Ask at the ticketing desk about daily feedings, lectures, tours, and special presentations.

The Seward Museum   **$**
336 Third Avenue
(907) 224–3902
Operated by the Resurrection Bay Historical Society, this small museum provides a glimpse into Seward's past, dating from 1793, when the Russians operated a shipyard on the bay. Highlights include an exhibit on artist Rockwell Kent, who wintered on Fox Island in 1918, as well as a collection of native baskets. You'll also discover Seward's ongoing role in transportation, from the early days of the Iditarod Trail to the establishment in 1903 of a railroad terminus. There's a popular exhibit on the 1964 earthquake, a 9.2 shaker that set fire to oil storage tanks along Resurrection Bay and killed 12 people in Seward. The museum is open daily from 9:00 A.M. to 5:00 P.M. in the summer. Catch slide shows on the Iditarod Trail or the history of Seward on Monday, Wednesday, or Friday at 7:00 P.M.

Parks, Recreation, and Tours

Surrounded by the majestic Chugach National Forest and the Kenai Fjords National Park, Seward offers a stunning array of recreational opportunities on both land and sea. The 607,000-acre Kenai Fjords National Park was formed by retreating glaciers of the spectacular Harding Ice Field, accessible by a 7-mile uphill climb from the foot of Exit Glacier or by charter plane from Seward. Check with Bear Lake Air and Guide Service (907–224–5985) or ERA

ℹ️ Take a walking tour of nine Registered National Historic Landmarks, including the Diversion Tunnel and St. Peter's Episcopal Church. Pick up maps at the Van Gilder Hotel at 308 Adams Street.

Helicopters (907–224–8012, 800–843–1947) for flight-seeing options.

A visit to Exit Glacier is a popular park attraction. Stop at the Exit Glacier Nature Center at the end of Exit Glacier Road, off Mile 3.7 of the Seward Highway, and from the parking lot you can walk a half-mile to the glacier. The first quarter-mile of the path is paved. Pay attention to the warning signs when you reach the glacier, as the ice is notoriously dangerous and unpredictable. Ranger-guided hikes are an option in the summer.

The best way to see the park's ample marine life, including sea otters, porpoises, sea lions, whales, and harbor seals, is by charter or tour boat. Check with Kenai Fjord Tours (907–224–8068, 888–478–3346, www.kenai fjords.com) for cruises of three to five hours that feature wildlife and glacier viewing. Land/cruise packages are also available. Major Marine Tours (907–224–8030, 800–764–7300, www.majormarine.com) offers half-day and full-day cruises with heated cabin seating, buffet-style meals, and narration by a Kenai Fjords National Park ranger. Birders will enjoy cruising to the Chiswell Islands, sporting prime habitat for some of the park's 100,000 nesting birds.

Three public-use cabins are available within the park for summer use by reservation only. These are remote cabins with limited access. Check with the Alaska Public Lands Information Center (907–271–2737) for information and reservations. Limited beach camping is also available, but boaters should be aware that much of the coastline is owned by Native corporations, and campers must have permits. To check on Native holdings and to acquire permits, call (907) 284–2212.

For a glimpse into the recent past enhanced by the natural beauty of the oceanfront, check out the abandoned World War II fort at Caines Head State Recreation Area. To get to the site, you'll have to travel by boat or hike four hours from Tonsina Point at low tide; because of the tides, you'll have to stay 12 hours if you walk in. You'll find campsites and latrines at Tonsina Creek, about halfway to Caines Head. Be sure to take a flashlight so you can explore the underground passages and rooms at the abandoned fort. For more information, contact the Kenai Peninsula state parks office at (907) 262–5581.

If off-shore exploration sounds like fun, try kayaking or sailing in Resurrection Bay. A recent issue of *Sail* magazine named Seward one of the top ten places to sail, thanks to its daily 15- to 20-knot winds. Check with the folks at Sailing, Inc. (907–224–3160, www .sailinginc.com) or Alaska Sailing Tours (907–299–7245, www.alaskasailingtours .com) for details on their sailboat charters. On calmer days you can rent a kayak or, if you're a novice, join a guided kayak tour of the bay. Try Kayak Adventures Worldwide (907–224–3690, www.kayakak.com), Liquid Adventures (907–224–9225, 888–325–2925, www.liquid-adventures.com), or the activities staff at Miller's Landing (see Accommodations, above) for a variety of floating options.

To get up close and personal with the landscape, try a two-hour horseback ride with Brady's Trail Rides (907–224–7863, www .sewardhorses.com). You'll travel beside the river to the bay, through parts of old-town Seward that were destroyed by the 1964 earthquake, often spotting bald eagles overhead. For a real Alaskan adventure, you can travel the country by dogsled, even in the summer. The folks at Iditaride Sled Dog Tours (800–478–3139, www.iditaride.com) will harness up your wheeled sled for a 2-mile ride and tour of the kennels with an Iditarod racer. If you're looking for a taste of winter in July, Godwin Glacier Dog Sled Tours (907–224–8239, 888–989–8239, www.alaskadogsled .com) will transport you by helicopter onto Godwin Glacier, where a dog team waits to

For more information about recreational activities in the Seward area, check out the Seward Chamber of Commerce Web site at www.seward.net/chamber, the Kenai Fjords National Park Web site at www.np.gov/kefj, and the Chugach National Forest Web site at www.fs.fed.us/r10/chugach.

pull your sled across the ice. There are no minimum fitness requirements, and the adventure is wheelchair friendly. Godwin's also offers cross-country ski tours and glacier walks along with custom helicopter flightseeing packages.

Hiking and Camping

You'll find plenty of hiking opportunities in the Seward area. Under the jurisdiction of the Chugach National Forest, there's the Resurrection River Trail, accessed from Mile 8 of the Exit Glacier Road. Follow the trail for 6 miles to a forest service cabin. The Lost Lake/Primrose Trail is a steep but scenic 15-mile trek beginning at Mile 5 of the Seward Highway and ending at Mile 17. For a shorter hike, try the Grayling Lake Trail, covering 2 miles and beginning at Mile 13.2 of the Seward Highway. Other forest service trails include the 7.5-mile (one-way) Ptarmigan Creek Trail, the 23-mile Johnson Pass Trail, and the 3.3-mile Carter Lake Trail. For maps and information, stop by the Seward Ranger District office at 334 Fourth Avenue (907–224–3374).

If you're looking for a challenge, you can check out the Mount Marathon Trail, which rises 3,022 feet from the trailhead off Lowell Canyon Road. Or you can hike the Iditarod National Historic Trail, beginning at the Founders' Monument on Ballaine Boulevard and picking up again 2 miles down Nash Road and again at Bear Lake. Once you leave the confines of town, this historic trail becomes rugged, and you should be prepared to cross some streams. For lighter fare, check out the

Two Lakes Trail, accessed from behind the Alaska Vocational Technical Center.

Within the Chugach National Forest, there are several campsites near Seward. At Mile 17 of the Seward Highway, you'll find the Primrose Campground, with 10 sites. The Ptarmigan Creek Campground at Mile 23 is a great place to see red salmon in season. There's also the Trail River Campground at Mile 24 of the Seward Highway, offering 63 sites and berry picking later in the summer.

Bear Creek RV Park
33508 Lincoln Street
(907) 224–5725, (877) 924–5725
www.bearcreekrv.com
Within walking distance of the rushing waters of Bear Creek, this family-owned RV park offers a full range of services in a picturesque Alaskan setting. They have both full and partial hookups, private restrooms and showers, cable TV, a dump station, pay phone, and Laundromat. Retail services include a convenience store, video rentals, and a liquor store. Relax and swap fishing stories at Lyn-Dav's Water Hole, a bar with a big-screen TV. Lynn and Dave also will book your tours and fishing trips, including van service to activities arranged through them. There's even a mechanic just around the corner.

Stoney Creek RV Park
13760 Leslie Place
(907) 224–4760
www.stoneycreekrvpark.com
Six miles north of Seward, flanked by majestic mountains, you'll find this comfortable RV park along Stoney Creek. Their 30-foot sites can handle even big rigs. All campsites come with power, water, and satellite TV hookups. Many sites have sewer and phone jacks as well. Fire pits are available along the creek. You'll have your choice of 81 sites on 15 acres. They also offer laundry and shower facilities, phone and Internet services, a hospitality room, courtesy shuttle service to Seward, and even doggy day care.

Fishing

For road-accessible freshwater fishing along the Seward Highway, try for Dolly Varden in Salmon Creek (Mile 5.9), Grouse Lake (Mile 7.4), Golden Fin Lake (Mile 11.3), and Trail River (Mile 24.1). You'll also find grayling at (where else?) Grayling Lake (Mile 13.2), as well as rainbow trout at Vagt Lake (Mile 25.2) and Carter Lake (Mile 33.1).

From either Whittier or Seward, you can access great ocean fishing at Knight Island Passage and Montague Strait. Surf casters may see some action at Knight Island, but the folks in boats catch most of the fish. Halibut in the passage are plentiful but not huge, and salmon run there seasonally. Feeder streams offer up trout and char.

Montague Strait and Montague Island are farther out and more susceptible to bad weather than Knight Island, but some of the best bottom fishing in Alaska is found there, and it's a regular salmon highway in season. Much of Alaska's trophy halibut catch comes from Montague, and there are abundant rockfish and lingcod as well. In the island streams, you may find some Dolly Varden and cutthroat trout, but not many salmon. Your best bet if you're land-bound is to surf cast for salmon at the mouths of the streams, or to have a charter plane drop you off on the beach so you can fish the productive Nellie Martin-Patton River system. Montague can be reached from Valdez, but it's a longer haul than from Seward or Whittier.

Aurora Charters
P.O. Box 241
Seward, AK 99664
(907) 224-7230
www.auroracharters.com
The folks at Aurora own four of their own vessels and partner up with eight others to give you a wide range of options for your sportfishing charter. Choose from half-day, full-day, and combo packages for rockfish, salmon, and halibut. If you have nonanglers in your group, Aurora offers a combo fishing and sightseeing charter to keep everyone happy.

Aurora also offers special off-season and active-military rates

The Fish House
P.O. Box 1209
Seward, AK 99664
(907) 224-7108
www.thefishhouse.net
Believe it or not, this family-owned and -operated charter business (since 1973) runs 60 Coast Guard–licensed boats, with either full-day or half-day trips for salmon or halibut. Combo and custom packages also are available. Beginners are welcome, and there's sure to be great wildlife viewing along with the hot fishing action. If you like, you can make your reservations online.

VALDEZ

Whittier might have been the U.S Army's secret during World War II, but Valdez has become something of an in-house secret for Alaskans. Abandoned by cruise ships a few years ago and left for residents and independent travelers to enjoy at their leisure, it's a friendly little town with stunning mountain and ocean vistas and a wealth of outdoor activities. Alaskans from the state's land-locked interior think nothing of driving eight hours each way to spend the weekend in Valdez—that's how lovely it is.

It's not as if the rest of the world has never heard of Valdez. The famous 1964 earthquake wiped out a big chunk of the original town, and what survived was moved a few years later. Then there was the infamous *Exxon Valdez* oil spill in 1989, when a tanker named *Valdez* ran aground as it was leaving the port of Valdez, causing an oil spill that took millions of dollars to clean up. But many visitors don't get to Alaska's "Little Switzerland" because it's a good day's drive each way, off the Denali Park–Anchorage–Kenai Peninsula loop.

What they're missing is a resilient little town of about 4,000 residents that plays host to both industry and nature. Down past Allison Point, Alyeska Pipeline Service Company operates the terminal facility for the Alaska Pipeline (closed to the public), with nine million barrels of storage and 400 tankers docking there each year. Spill prevention is now a top priority for the company, for while Alyeska rules the economic front, it's the wildlife and scenic beauty that are the real calling cards of Valdez. You'll know you're headed somewhere special as you drive in on the Richardson Highway, flanked on both sides by rugged peaks, roaring waterfalls, rushing creeks, and glacial ice dotting the mountaintops like icing. Pull into town, and the harbor stretches out before you, promising all sorts of water-related fun, from glacier cruises to deep-sea fishing to paddling among the sea otters and eagles.

Tucked at the end of a stunning fjord, where the purple peaks of the Chugach Mountains meet the ocean, Valdez was first established as an entry point to the Klondike during the 1898 Gold Rush. The treacherous Valdez Trail was eventually abandoned in favor of a route through Thompson Pass, a sled and wagon road that brought a new wave of development to Alaska's interior. Copper followed gold, but even after that boom ended, Valdez hung on as the most northerly ice-free port in the hemisphere, a perfect place to drop off cargo bound for the state's vast landlocked regions.

Getting Here, Getting Around

If you're heading to Valdez from Anchorage, you'll take the Glenn Highway east to Glennallen, then head south on the Richardson Highway. Expect a travel time of about six hours. From Fairbanks, it's a straight shot on the Richardson Highway, more or less following the route of the old wagon road, about an eight-hour drive. Those big poles along the highway as you go through Thompson Pass? Those are so you can find the road in the winter, when an average of 27 feet of snow blankets the area around Valdez.

There's also small-plane service from Anchorage on Era Aviation, or you can take the state ferry from Cordova, Whittier, or Seward. Reservations are a must for the ferry, especially during the summer months; call the Alaska Marine Highway at (907) 835–4436 for more information.

Once you get to Valdez, you won't have any trouble finding your way around. It's a planned community, more or less, thanks to the big shaker back in 1964 that led the Army Corps of Engineer to decide that the whole town needed to be rebuilt on firmer ground. There's a little business district leading to and stretching along the waterfront and a parklike residential area nestled up against the mountains. You can walk to most attractions, restaurants, and shopping, but there's also taxi service if you need it.

Accommodations

Valdez offers a little bit of everything as far as accommodations go, from hotels to bed-and-breakfasts, many located in the downtown area and along the waterfront, within walking distance of just about everything. The only thing lacking is the abundance of private cabin rentals available on the other side of the Sound.

Price ranges below indicate the average cost of a room for two adults during the peak season. Major credit cards are accepted at all the establishments shown here. Assume no smoking, no wheelchair access, and no pets unless we tell you otherwise.

Price Codes

$. . . . . Less than $100
$$ . . . . $100–$150
$$$ . . . . $151–$200
$$$$ . . . . More than $200

Aspen Hotel $$$
100 Meals Avenue
(907) 835–4445, (800) 478–4445
www.aspenhotelsak.com
Part of the Alaskan-based Aspen Hotel chain, this is the largest and most modern-looking option for overnight stays in Valdez. Choose from spa, family, and extended-stay suites. All 102 spacious rooms have coffeemakers,

microwaves, refrigerators, TVs with VCRs, irons and ironing boards, hair dryers, and telephones with speaker features and data-ports. Guests can relax in the pool with adjoining spa, work out in the exercise room, and keep up with their obligations at the hotel's business center. The complimentary continental breakfasts feature Belgian waffles, and there's wireless Internet access through-out the hotel. Guest laundry facilities are avail-able, and you can earn Alaska Airlines frequent flier miles with your stay.

Best Western Valdez Harbor Inn $$
100 Fidalgo Drive
(907) 835–3434, (888) 222–3440
www.valdezharborinn.com
Located right on the harbor, this newer hotel, built in 2002, features 88 comfortable rooms and an on-site restaurant, Alaska's Bistro, that's a favorite with locals. From the tiled floor of the post-and-beam lobby to the large bistro windows that look out over the water, this modern facility is designed to fit in with the stunning landscape. Choose from king-size, queen-size, and double beds in rooms that have microwaves, refrigerators, and cable TVs with DVD players. Business rooms also have recliners, desks, and Internet access. Many units in the two-story, wood-sided hotel offer views of the boat harbor, the mountains, or the small but vibrant down-town area. The Harbor Inn has workout and laundry facilities for guest use. Smoking rooms are available, and two rooms offer wheelchair access.

Downtown B&B Inn $
113 Galena Drive
(907) 835–2791, (800) 478–2791
www.alaskaone.com/downinn
There's nothing fancy here, but you'll find clean, reasonably priced rooms at the well-situated Downtown B&B Inn. It's a large build-ing with a chalet-style exterior housing 31 rooms, and the accommodations are more like those of a small motel than a typical Alaskan B&B. Hosts Glen and Sharron Mills

are longtime Alaskans who can give all kinds of advice about what to do and see in Valdez. Rooms include private baths, telephones, and cable televisions. There's a free continental breakfast in the motel-style dining room, fea-turing fresh fruit and juices, doughnuts, rolls, breads, assorted cereals, yogurt, hot choco-late, coffee, and tea. Guests can help them-selves to hot beverages anytime. Some rooms have minifridges, microwaves, and balconies. The inn is centrally located, 1 block from the small boat harbor and within walking distance to shopping, restaurants, the town's museum, and the ferry. Some rooms offer wheelchair access, and pets are welcome.

Keystone Hotel $
117 Hazelet Street
(907) 835–3851, (888) 835–0665
www.keystonehotel.com
Housed in the sort of metal-sided building that Alaskans associate with the pipeline era, the Keystone offers 100 rooms with single, double, and king-size beds. It's a sort of plain-Jane, seasonal hotel that serves a complimen-tary continental breakfast of freshly baked rolls, muffins, and pastries along with juices, coffee, and tea. Each room has a private bath, color TV, and telephone. A laundry facility is available to guests. The hotel is within walking distance of the museum, the port of Valdez, the ferry terminal, fishing, shopping, and restaurants. Ask about their discounts for sen-ior citizens, military, Alaskan residents, and government employees. Guests may bring one dog, as long as it weighs less than 60 pounds. Four rooms are wheelchair accessi-ble, and there are smoking rooms as well.

The Lake House $$
Mile 6 Richardson Highway
(907) 835–4752
www.geocities.com/lakehousevaldez
Surrounded by the towering peaks of the Chugach Mountains, the Lake House gives you a chance to stay beyond the downtown area with only a 10 minute drive from Valdez. This large home sits on four acres overlooking Robe

Lake, with several decks and balconies for wildlife viewing. Guests enjoy a bit of quiet, home-style privacy in the common areas, including a reading room, covered picnic areas, and a TV room with a large-screen television. There are six rooms with king- and queen-size beds; all have private baths. Feel free to prepare your dinner on the gas grills and indulge in yard games or the outdoor hot tub while taking in the grand view. You'll find a complimentary bottle of Lake House wine in your room at check-in, and you can help yourself to coffee and tea whenever you like. The complimentary breakfast includes juices, coffee, tea, muffins, bagels, fresh fruit, and six selections of cereal. There are cats on the premises.

**Mountainside Gardens
Bed and Breakfast** $$
1130 Ptarmigan Place
(907) 835–3868
www.mountaingardensbb.com
If you're looking for accommodations with a little more character than the downtown Valdez hotel/motel scene, Mountainside Gardens offers just what you're after. Nestled at the foot of the mountains, yet walking distance to town and the bay, this bed-and-breakfast is surrounded by beautiful gardens. Victorian-style rooms feature queen-size quilt-covered beds and antiques. Each room has a coffeemaker, microwave, minifridge, private bath, telephone, cable television, iron, and ironing board. At breakfast, you'll enjoy fruits, breads, yogurt, juices, cereals, coffee, and tea. Snacks are provided in the evening. Pets are accepted on a case-by-case basis.

Totem Inn Hotel and Suites $$
144 East Egan Drive
(907) 835–4443, (888) 808–4431
www.toteminn.com
Family-owned and -operated since 1973, this is a genuine Alaskan hotel with an emphasis on customer service. Two 15-foot totem poles and a massive stone fireplace grace the lobby, in the company of full-size mounts of brown bear, Dall sheep, and a wolf. You'll find a variety of options among the 70 guest rooms. The hotel's Alaskan Suites offer private master bedrooms with washer/dryer, luxury linens, and television; in the living room, there's another television with DVD player. The suites also come with full kitchens, large corner windows, and free DSL Internet access. The Alaskan Cottages feature private porches, full kitchens, queen-size beds plus pull-out couches, and televisions with DVD players. Standard Deluxe rooms have queen-size beds, private baths, televisions with DVD players, coffeemakers, and minifridges. There's an on-site laundry, and the Totem Inn Restaurant is a local favorite for burgers, steaks, and seafood. Smoking rooms and wheelchair-accessible rooms are available, and pets are allowed in select rooms.

Wild Roses by the Sea B&B Retreat $$
629 Fiddlehead Lane
(907) 835–2930
www.alaskabytheseab&b.com
Offering casual elegance with contemporary Asian-Western ambience, Wild Roses by the Sea combines spectacular views with real Alaskan-style hospitality. Choose from the Canyon Suite overlooking Mineral Creek Canyon or the Sea View Room with views of the ocean and mountains. The Oceanview Guesthouse, with separate entry and full kitchen, offers even more privacy. Located 1.5 miles from Valdez on a wooded bluff overlooking Anderson Glacier and Valdez Bay, this is a great jumping-off point for enjoying the great outdoors. It's a five-minute walk to the creek and 1 mile to the ocean. Rooms come with private baths, cable televisions, jetted tubs, irons, and ironing boards. You'll be greeted with a dish of almonds and fruit upon check-in, and hot beverages are available all daylong in the dining room. For breakfast, there's fresh-baked pastry, fresh-baked bread, a platter of fresh-sliced fruit, juice, coffee, and a hot menu item. If you're lucky, you'll get to sample their ginger Belgian waffles made with 1899 sourdough starter and topped with vanilla yogurt, sliced bananas, and peaches.

Restaurants

There may not be a lot of restaurants to choose from, but you can't beat the fresh seafood and views that you'll find at most of these eateries. We'll let you know if reservations are needed or if the establishment is open only during the summer season. Assume no smoking and no wheelchair access unless we tell you otherwise. Price codes indicate the average cost of a dinner for two, excluding drinks, tip, appetizers, and dessert.

Price Codes

$	Less than $15
$$	$15–$25
$$$	$26–$40
$$$$	More than $40

Alaska's Bistro $$$$
100 Fidalgo Drive
(907) 835–5688
Take in spectacular ocean and mountain views while enjoying fine Mediterranean and American cuisine at Alaska's Bistro. They offer fine dining Alaskan-style, with white tablecloths and a selection of 265 wines contributing to the ambience. Among the favorites that have been on the menu since 1972 are Crab-Stuffed Halibut as well as Shrimp and Scallops in Saffron Cream Sauce. Pepe's World Famous Seafood Paella features fresh shrimp, local fish, peppers, and saffron rice cooked slowly and traditionally in a large, flat pan; order in advance, as preparation takes 40 minutes, and bring a friend, as there's a two-person minimum for paella. The bistro is open for breakfast, lunch, and dinner, and reservations are always appreciated; sometimes, they're a must. Parking is ample, and the restaurant is wheelchair accessible.

Alaska Halibut House $$
208 Meals Avenue
(907) 835–2788
There's nothing fancy here, but for a quick breakfast or lunch, there's a nice selection of omelets, seafood, and sandwiches. Try the halibut basket, featuring four pieces of local Alaskan halibut, hand-dipped and deep-fried to perfection. There's also a Catch of the Day, a Combo Basket with prawns and halibut, and Alaska Salmon Wedges, with local boneless salmon breaded and deep-fried, in season. Scallops and clam strips round out the seafood options. For lunch, they offer a variety of burgers, including the Gold Digger, with a double patty, bacon, cheese, onion rings, and barbeque sauce. For healthier fare, sample the fresh salad bar.

Bad Ass Coffee $
205 North Harbor Drive
(907) 835–2340
Here's a place that will remind you of that house you shared with your friends in college, only better, because there's a bountiful supply of brownies and bars, espresso, and sandwiches you can order before retreating upstairs to enjoy the guitar, xylophone, comfy couches, television, stereo, and killer view of the harbor. There's even a large deck and barbeque grill up top. In short, this is a great place for the young and the young at heart to feel at home on the edge of Prince William Sound. Internet access is free with a purchase, but there's a 10-minute limit if others are waiting. You also can buy a box lunch to take on your next outdoor adventure.

Mike's Palace Ristorante $$$
201 North Harbor Drive
(907) 835–2365
A longtime local favorite, Mike's Palace Ristorante is one of those quintessential Alaskan establishments that serves up a little bit of everything. They have fresh Alaskan peel-your-own shrimp, fresh Copper River red salmon, fresh seafood fettuccine, and fresh king crab—all when they're in season, of course. For ethnic fare, there's a large selection of Italian entrees with veal and chicken, as well as a full menu of authentic pastas and pizzas. If Mexican food is more to your liking, sample the South-of-the-Border lunch and dinner specials, including Aca-

pulco Shrimp and the Cinco-Cinco nacho platter. There's also a selection of light meals for smaller appetites. The atmosphere is a little of this and that, but it's close to the waterfront and there's a good crowd of locals to testify to the quality of the food.

Shopping

Valdez is hardly a shopping mecca, but you should be able to find what you need, plus a few things you don't, including souvenirs and Alaskan gifts.

Harbor Landing General Store
Kobuk and Meals
P.O. Box 872
Valdez, AK 99686
(907) 835-2331
Harbor Landing is the largest gift store in Valdez, featuring a big selection of Alaskan gifts, souvenirs, post cards, and shirts. For edible remembrances, they carry smoked salmon and Alaska Wildberry candies, jams, and teas. In the jewelry department you'll find jade, ivory, hematite, and gold nugget treasures. When you've worn yourself out from all that shopping, you can treat yourself at the espresso bar. Packing and mailing services are available.

Valdez Prospector
141 Galena Street
(907) 835-3858
If you want to shop where the locals do, the Prospector is the place, offering a modern version of the old-fashioned outfitters store. Packed into their large retail space, you'll find complete selections of everything you need for your outdoor adventures: fishing tackle, camping gear, name-brand clothing, and sporting goods of all kinds. The Prospector is open seven days a week, and there's ample parking out front.

Attractions

For a small town, Valdez offers a nice variety of attractions focused mainly on the history and scenic beauty of the region. Thanks in part to the revenues generated by the pipeline terminus and port, admission to most attractions is either free, as indicated by the lack of price code in the write-up, or a reasonable cost.

Price Codes

$. . . . . Less than $5.00
$$ . . . . $5.00–$15.00
$$$ . . . . $16.00–$30.00
$$$$ . . . . More than $30.00

Alaska Cultural Center $
300 Valdez Airport Road
(907) 834-1690
Prince William Sound Community College houses the small, eclectic Alaska Cultural Center, home of the Maxine and Jesse Whitney Museum. During 50 years of travel throughout Alaska, the Whitneys assembled the largest private collection of Alaskan Native art and artifacts in the world. Maxine Whitney's accounts of her Alaskan adventures along with her collections of ivory, fur clothing, beadwork, Eskimo dolls, masks, tools, and artifacts give visitors a glimpse of life from a not-so-distant era in the state's history. You'll also see trophy-class mounts of Alaskan mammals and full-size Eskimo kayaks and umiaks.

Bridal Falls
Mile 13.8 Richardson Highway
This spectacular waterfall in Keystone Canyon is a popular photo stop as you drive into Valdez, along with Horsetail Falls at Mile 12.8. There's interesting information on the Gold Rush on the interpretive plaque at the turnout. The trailhead for Valdez Goat Trail, a restored section of the military pack train trail that offered an alternate route to the dangerous gold rush trail over glacial ice, is located here, too. The trail is 2 miles long, with a scenic overlook about a quarter-mile up.

Crooked Creek Salmon Spawning
Viewing Area
Mile 0.9 Richardson Highway
The short drive from town to this small U.S. Forest Service information station is well

worth making during July and August when the salmon are running. The poignant drama of salmon returning from the ocean, driven by an urge to spawn in the freshwater streams where they were born, plays out before your eyes. In season the stream is choked with these migrating fish in their final stages of life, their shapes deformed and colors distorted by their re-entry into freshwater. You'll see them hovering in schools, resting in eddies as they gather strength for the next leg of their journey upstream. If the prevailing odors of death and decay are too much, you can watch the underwater action from the live cam inside the Forest Service station. Across the highway at Duck Flats, you can watch nesting birds in the summer and migratory waterfowl in the spring and fall.

Remembering Old Valdez Exhibit $
436 South Hazelet Street
(907) 835–5407
The 1964 Good Friday earthquake, registering at 9.2 on the Richter scale and centered in Prince William Sound, destroyed the waterfront and killed 33 residents of Valdez. After the quake, the town was moved to a safer location 4 miles west of its original site. In a massive project that tapped the memories of those who lived in Old Valdez, a detailed, three-dimensional replica of the old town was built in a warehouse near the new waterfront, on a scale of 1 inch to 20 feet. You can walk between sections of the model while you listen with headsets to narration that goes building by building through the town as it was in 1963. Admission to the Valdez Museum includes admission to the Remembering Old Valdez exhibit. After you've caught a glimpse of how life once was in Old Valdez, you can drive out to the old town site and marvel at how quickly and completely a town can rise and fall.

Valdez Museum $
217 Egan Drive
(907) 835–2764
www.valdezmuseum.org

With a nice variety of colorful exhibits, the Valdez Museum is a great place to get a feel for the roller-coaster history of this picturesque town. From the huge Hinchenbrook Lighthouse lens to the Pinson Bar restoration from the Gold Rush era, there are all sorts of life-sized exhibits that bring you back to the excitement of years gone by. You'll find out about such adventurers as Lillian Moore, one of 20 women who traveled the Valdez Trail to the Klondike, and Capt. W. R. Abercrombie, who led a relief expedition to stranded miners. Your walk through the history of Valdez includes sections on the area's original inhabitants, the Ahtna-Athabaskan Indians and the Chugach Eskimos, an interactive display on the construction of the Alaska Pipeline, and an overview of the Exxon Valdez oil spill. The museum is open year-round, with extended hours in the summer. Admission to the museum also covers admission to the Remembering Old Valdez Exhibit a few blocks down the road.

Worthington Glacier
Mile 28.7 Richardson Highway
This access point, maintained by the state park service, offers a great roadside opportunity to get up close and personal with the massive Worthington Glacier, a National Natural Landmark. You can view the glacier from the comfort of the paved parking area or climb the paved path, complete with interpretive plaques and benches, to get a closer look. The more rugged Ridge Trail also provides access to the glacier, but beware of falling ice, and remember that glacier walking should be attempted only by those with experience dealing with the hazardous ice and hidden crevasses.

Parks, Recreation, and Tours

Valdez is an adventurer's paradise, surrounded by accessible wilderness on both land and sea. Since most of the terrain goes up, recreation on dry ground primarily involves your own two feet, while watercraft opportunities include kayaking, rafting river rapids through the Keystone Canyon, and cruising Prince William Sound for a close-up look at Columbia Glacier.

Anadyr Adventures
225 North Harbor Drive
(907) 835–2814, (800) 865–2925
www.anadyradventures.com

For all sorts of adventures in and around Valdez, the friendly, knowledgeable folks at Anadyr are ready to help. From short kayaking tours for beginners to more extensive day trips that include hiking, wildlife viewing, beachcombing, kayak fishing, or single-person sailing, you'll find all sorts of great options with the oldest sea-kayaking business in Valdez. Their emphasis is on personal, intimate outdoor experiences at such destinations as Gold Creek, Shroup Glacier, and Columbia Glacier. All sorts of longer packages are available, too, including wilderness kayak camping, yacht-based tours, and lodge-based ecotours. They do their best to accommodate walk-ins, but advance reservations are recommended, especially in the peak of the season. Shoulder-season adventures in May and September, weather permitting, can be a lot of fun if you're not put off by the cool temperatures. Even if you're not heading out on the water, Anadyr's waterfront office is a fun stop, with an art gallery featuring Alaskan-made pottery and prints as well as an on-site masseuse.

Glacier Wildlife Cruises
P.O. Box 1832
Valdez, AK 99686
(907) 835–5141

Captain Fred Rodolf takes you on a narrated tour to Columbia Glacier aboard the yacht *Lu-Lu Belle*. As you travel across Prince William Sound, you'll get a maritime view of fishing boats, the port of Valdez, the fjords of the Chugach National Forest, and, of course, the rapidly retreating Columbia Glacier. On a good day you'll see all sorts of wildlife, including whales, sea lions, otters, porpoise, and bald eagles, from the comfort of the *Lu-Lu*

Belle's teak and mahogany cabin, complete with snack bar.

H2O Guides Alaska Glacier Tours
100 North Harbor Drive
(907) 835–8418, (800) 578–4354
www.h2oguides.com

Stop by the H2O office and gift shop, located in the Best Western Harbor Inn, to book one of a variety of tours, including visits to nearby Worthington Glacier. You can choose from a one-hour interpretive Glacier Face Discovery Walk to full-day guided ice-climbing adventures. They also offer custom guided photography expeditions, as well as fishing, rafting, mountaineering, and flight-seeing adventures.

Keystone Raft and Kayak Adventures
P.O. Box 1486
Valdez, AK 99686
(907) 835–4638
www.alaska/whitewater.com

If you're looking for a heart-thumping water-based adventure, check out these river-rafting options. You can float the Lowe River through the Keystone Canyon, snagging a close-up view of Bridal Veil Falls, or try a half-day white-water run on the Class IV rapids of the Tsaina River through both the upper and lower canyons. Another popular option is a six-hour run on the Class III and IV rapids of the Tonsina River, which includes a lunch stop and some time for rest and relaxation. Guides and equipment are provided, depending on the package.

Pangaea Adventures
101 North Harbor Drive
(907) 835–8442
www.alaskasummer.com

Sea kayaking, backpacking, and multisport trips are among the specialties of this well-established outdoor adventure company. With an average guide ratio of one guide for every four guests, Pangaea strives for a personal, informative wilderness experience. They offer day tours for the novice as well as longer kayak camping options for the more

Each June, Valdez hosts the Last Frontier Theater Conference, where drama critics, playwrights, and theater lovers gather to talk shop and discover new talent. Pulitzer Prize–winner Edward Albee founded the conference, which has been an annual event since 1993.

rugged adventurer. Beyond the sea, choose from glacial hikes, river rafting, and mountain-backpacking packages. Experienced paddlers can rent kayaks by the day, and water-taxi service can be arranged for custom expeditions. Pangaea teams up with Stan Stephens Cruises to offer kayaking near the Columbia Glacier.

Stan Stephens Glacier and Wildlife Cruises
P.O. Box 1297
Valdez, AK 99686
(907) 835–4731, (866) 867–1297
In business since 1971, Stan Stephens is pretty much a household name in Alaska. Owners of the only Valdez-based cruise company operated by Alaskans, the Stephens family and their crew bring a personal touch to sightseeing on the Sound. Choose from 7-, 9-, and 10.5-hour family-friendly tours on a variety of comfortable boats. Along the way you'll learn about the human and natural history of Prince William Sound, with lots of chances to spot wildlife, including sea lions, sea otters, whales, porpoise, eagles, and puffins. All cruises make a stop at the dramatic Columbia Glacier, and all include a meal. Free shuttle service is provided between local RV parks and the harbor.

Hiking and Camping

On a sunny day in Valdez, there's nothing finer than getting out on one of the many local trails. Stop by the visitor information center and pick up the Valdez Trail Series brochures. There's a separate flyer for each trail, including a map, trail description, estimated hiking time, difficulty rating, distance, and safety advisories. All

the brochures warn of sudden weather changes, and most warn of bears in the area, so take proper precautions.

For a short, easy walk, take the 0.75-mile Dock Point Trail, which begins just past the gate off Kobuk Drive, across from the boat ramp. The circular trail winds up a hill, then down to a meadow with viewing platforms that overlook Valdez Bay. Another fairly easy and rewarding hike is up the 1.75-mile Mineral Creek Trail. Flanked by mountains with cascading waterfalls, you'll trek up the hill until you reach the W.L. Smith Stamp Mill, dating from 1913. The 3.8-mile Solomon Gulch Trail begins at Allison Point on Dayville Road and climbs a steep hill before dropping into the gulch, which in 1915 was the site of an aerial tram used to transport copper.

Bear Paw R.V. Park
(907) 835–2530
www.bearpawrvpark.com
If you don't mind forsaking the forest for convenience, Bear Paw has a great location, right on Harbor Drive, so you can walk to just about everything. They offer both full and partial hookups, private showers and bath stalls, a dump station, and a coin-operated laundry with ironing facilities. They also have a select number of "adult only" sites on the waterfront, with guest lounge, cable TV, and cable modem. Up Porcupine Hill, there's tent camping for adults as well. Bear Paw has a nice gift shop, and they'll help you book tours and even meet you at the ferry if you have reservations.

Captain Jim's Campgrounds
P.O. Box 1369
Valdez, AK 99686
(907) 835–2282
www.valdezcampgrounds.com
Captain Jim's operates both the Allison Point and Valdez Glacier facilities for the city. At oceanside Allison Point, a favorite salmon fishing spot at the end of Dayville Road, you'll find 70 campsites with public telephones and handicap access. The Valdez Glacier Campground

on Airport Road offers 101 private campsites with fire rings, picnic tables, and free dump station. There's also a covered picnic area, drinking water, toilets, and room for 17 pull-throughs, all in a wooded spot with a natural waterfall.

Eagle's Rest RV Park
(907) 835–2373, (800) 553–7275
www.eaglesrestrv.com

Eagle's Rest is right in the middle of Valdez, and while the immediate scenery will be the pavement beneath you and your neighbor's RV next door, the whole town is surrounded by a panorama of mountains and water, so you'll still know you're in Alaska. They have 20-, 30-, and 50-amp plug-ins, unmetered hot showers, telephone and cable television hookups, a dump station, and a Laundromat. On-site, you'll also find an ATM machine, an e-mail station, a fish-cleaning table, and a walk-in freezer for stashing your catch. They offer full ticketing to tours and attractions, and there's gas and propane right next door.

Fishing

Fishing fanatics flock to Valdez every summer seeking all species of salmon, char, and halibut. The cold, gray-green waters of Valdez Arm are chock-full of pink and silver salmon at the peak of their runs. Valdez hosts three salmon derbies each season, with the Silver Salmon Derby in August offering a total of more than $65,000 in cash and prizes. Believe it or not, the silvers run so thick that the occasional fish has been known to jump into a boat or onto a dock. The Solomon Gulch Hatchery along the bay is responsible for a good part of the exciting silver run, which normally peaks during the second and third weeks of August.

Boaters trolling with down-riggers often catch their limit of six fish, but you don't have to charter out to get in on the action—there's good fishing for pinks and silvers along beaches, docks, and creek mouths during July and August. If you're hoping for a lunker halibut, sign on with one of the charter boats

and fish the deep waters of Valdez Arm out to Hinchinbrook. The halibut derby runs most of the summer, with the lucky winner taking home $15,000 and a brand-new pickup truck.

Northern Comfort Charters and Tours
P.O. Box 1684
Valdez, AK 99686
(907) 835–3070
www.northerncomfortcharters.com

From late April through September, Capt. Steve Pyle and his crew will take you out on one of their three twin-diesel-powered boats with comfortable cabins, toilets, and all-around fishing decks. They also have a fast six-pac boat and a 42-foot vessel for overnight and extended charters. Halibut is the target of choice, but lingcod, rockfish, and an occasional salmon may add to the action. Beginning in late July, you can charter out specifically for silver salmon, with a limit of six per day.

Orion Charters
P.O. Box 3577
Valdez, AK 99686
(907) 835–8610
www.orioncharters.com

Try fishing Orion's new six-person boat, which is powered by twin-engine diesels and has a cruise speed of 35 knots. It's equipped with a heated cabin and a large, stable fishing platform for maximum productivity on your 12-hour jaunt. During the last 10 years, Orion reports that 90 percent of their clients have caught two or more halibut per day, with an average size of 45 to 50 pounds for the keepers. They also offer salmon shark fishing, with a similar 90 percent success rate over the last six years. The average salmon shark caught is between 7 and 8 feet long and weighs in at about 300 pounds.

i The nightlife in Valdez still has a rugged pipeline flavor, with places such as the Club Bar and the Pipeline Club offering pool, horseshoes, shuffleboard, and dancing.

CORDOVA

The landlocked town of Cordova is the most isolated community on the Prince William Sound, a fact that contributes to a good deal of its charm. Formerly a shipping port for copper ore from the interior's Kennecott mines, Cordova is now sustained by commercial fishing for salmon, cod, crab, and shrimp as well as by tourists, primarily those looking for fishing, bird-watching, and other outdoor adventures. As fishing prices have dropped in recent years, the town has become quieter and more laid-back, but what it lacks in excitement, it makes up for in friendliness and quaint seaside appeal.

Getting Here, Getting Around

You can't drive to Cordova, but you can arrive by jet from Anchorage, Juneau, or Seattle. There are also ferry connections with Whittier, Seward, and Valdez. Once you're there, you can drive the 48-mile Copper River Highway to access fishing and enjoy the scenery, but you'll have to turn around and head back where the road dead-ends just past the famed Million-Dollar Bridge. If you don't bring your own car on the ferry, there's taxi service and car rental available locally.

Accommodations

In keeping with its small-town flavor, most of the accommodations in Cordova are at bed-and-breakfasts, small inns, or cabins. If you're coming to fish, you may find combination packages that offer overnight stays along with charter services.

The U.S. Forest Service has several public-use cabins available for rent in Cordova's Cop-

per River Delta. Cabins are comfortable but rustic, with no running water and outhouse facilities in lieu of indoor plumbing. Check with the Chugach Ranger District Office (907–424–7661, www.fs.fed.us/r10/chugach/cordova/index.html) for details and availability.

For the listings below, assume there's no smoking, no wheelchair access, and no pets allowed unless we tell you otherwise. Major credit cards are generally accepted; we'll let you know if there's an exception. The peak season in Cordova is when the silver salmon are running in August and September, so make sure to reserve well in advance if you're looking at that time frame. Price ranges below indicate the average cost of a room for two adults during the peak season.

Price Codes

$ . . . . Less than $100
$$ . . . . $100–$150
$$$ . . . . $151–$200
$$$$ . . . . More than $200

Cordova Rose Lodge $–$$
P.O. Box 1494
Cordova, AK 99574
(907) 424–7673
www.cordovarose.com
Located on the shores of Prince William Sound and only 5 blocks from town, the Cordova Rose offers stunning views of the water and the mountains. Choose from 13 rooms and 2 private cabins in a variety of configurations. Full hot breakfasts and optional evening meals are part of the hands-on hospitality, which also includes assistance with all sorts of adventure and tour planning. Guests share the television lounge, library, sitting room, and dining room. Pets are allowed on a case-by-case basis.

Eyak River Hideaway $$
P.O. Box 2573
Cordova, AK 99574
(907) 424–3922
www.eyakriverhideaway.com
This comfortable getaway is right on the

ℹ️ If you're looking to eat out while in Cordova, try the grilled steaks and seafood at the Powder House Restaurant on Eyak Lake (907–424–3529) or the home-cooked meals at Cordova Rose Lodge (907–424–7673, see listing under the Accommodations section).

Annual events in Cordova include the Ice Worm Festival in early February, the Copper River Delta Shorebird Festival in early May, and the Wild Salmon Festival in June, featuring a marathon and a bake-off.

shores of the Eyak River, which offers some of the best salmon fishing in town. The hosts make a point of providing great service to their guests, whether they're avid anglers or folks who just come to get away from it all. They offer a house unit that sleeps six and an apartment that sleeps five. A continental breakfast including juice and muffins is provided, and the refrigerator is stocked with eggs, breakfast meats, and milk for those who prefer a hot breakfast. The units have full kitchens with coffeemakers, microwaves, and full-size refrigerators, private baths, telephones, and cable televisions. Outside there's access to a riverfront deck, outdoor grill, and fish-processing facilities, including chest freezers. Credit cards are not accepted, and there's a family dog on-site.

Seaview Condo   **$$**
109 Council Avenue
(907) 424–5269
Enjoy a breathtaking view of the harbor, bay, and islands from the privacy of your own condo unit conveniently located in downtown Cordova. The unit sleeps six and comes complete with coffeemaker, microwave, minifridge, and free continental breakfast. There's also a private phone line and cable television, with Internet access available for a fee. The owners live in the same building and can provide local information as needed. There's a covered outdoor deck for smokers, and some pets are allowed on approval.

Attractions and Recreation

Most of what you'll find to do in and around Cordova will be in the great outdoors, but you can also check out the Cordova Museum (907–424–6665, www.cordovamuseum.org) to get a look at the history of the region,

including interpretive and cultural displays as well as original pieces by famed Alaskan artist Sydney Laurence. The museum is open from 10:00 A.M. to 6:00 P.M. Monday through Saturday during the summer season, and there's a nominal admission fee.

For scenic drives on Cordova's limited road system, head out Power Creek Road, which follows the shore of Lake Eyak, or drive the Copper River Highway to the Million Dollar Bridge. Along the way you'll have a good chance of seeing trumpeter swans, as more than 7 percent of the world's population breeds in the Copper River Basin. Just before the bridge, you can see the 350-foot actively calving face of Childs Glacier. As always, exercise caution in the vicinity of calving ice; in this particular area, ice chunks the size of cars have fallen into the water, causing potentially hazardous waves.

Built in 1910 at a cost of $1.4 million dollars, the Million Dollar Bridge spanned the Copper River until it collapsed during the 1964 earthquake. It was repaired and reopened in 2004, but the road still goes only 10 miles farther than the bridge. Plans for a highway connecting Cordova with the Richardson Highway via the town of Chitina have never materialized, though they are still under discussion.

You also can drive out Whitshed Road to Hartney Bay or Alaganik Slough to view some of the delta's plentiful supply of shorebirds. Birders have spotted more than 31 different species among the five million shorebirds passing through on their spring migration routes.

For rafting or kayaking adventures, try Alaska River Rafters (907–424–7238, 800–776–1864, www.alaskarafters.com) or Orca Adventure Lodge (907–424–7249, 866–424–6722, www.orcaadventurelodge .com; see the listing in the Fishing section below).

Hiking and Camping

The U.S. Forest Service maintains 25 miles of trails within the Chugach National Forest

Close-up

Valdez Oil Spill

For those of us who were around in the 1980s, Valdez is almost synonymous with oil spill. All eyes were riveted on the waters of Valdez Arm after the *Exxon Valdez* ploughed into Bligh Reef on March 24, 1989, spilling an estimated 11 million gallons of crude oil. A massive clean-up effort involving 10,000 workers, 1,000 boats, and $2.1 billion dollars followed.

Why did a tanker with an experienced crew run aground? The National Transportation Safety Board investigation concluded that a number of factors contributed to the accident, including a lack of effective escort services, an ineffective traffic system in the Sound, the failure of Exxon to provide a sufficiently supervised and rested crew, and the failure of the ship's captain to provide proper navigation watch. In a jury trial, Capt. Joseph Hazelwood was found not guilty of operating a vessel under influence of alcohol, but he was fined $50,000 and sentenced to 1,000 hours of community service for the misdemeanor of negligent discharge of oil.

Thanks to the clean-up efforts and subsequent winter storms that gave the beaches a natural scrubbing, you won't find any obvious reminders of the spill when you visit Valdez today. But much has changed as a result of the accident. For one thing, spill prevention has become the number one priority for the folks at Alyeska Pipeline Service Company. Tankers now have dike-lined enclosures with a capacity 15 percent greater than the tankers themselves. Three tugs follow every large tanker, with two tugs shuttling each smaller one. And two barges stand ready in the port with spill-response equipment. An act of Congress has prohibited the *Exxon Valdez*, now refurbished and renamed, from ever again entering Prince William Sound.

Along the 1,300 miles of impacted shoreline, it is estimated that 250,000 seabirds, 2,800 sea otters, 300 harbor seals, 250 bald eagles, and perhaps 22 orca whales died as a result of the spill. In addition, countless salmon and herring eggs were impacted. In the years following the incident, scientists have noted declines in the

surrounding Cordova. Try the 2.4-mile Crater Lake Trail, accessed at 1.8-mile Power Creek Road. You'll get to enjoy great views and a mountain lake stocked with rainbow trout. A little farther down Power Creek Road, you can access the 4.2-mile Power Creek Trail, with scenery that includes glaciers, waterfalls, and views of the valley. Other popular hikes include the 0.8-mile Haystack Trail at Mile 19.1 of the Copper River Highway and the 3.5-mile Heney Ridge Trail at Mile 5.1 of Whitshed Road.

If you're looking to camp, there's the Odiak Camper Park on Whitshed Road, with 24 RV spaces, and a small campground with five sites at Mile 48 Copper River Highway.

Fishing

In addition to the commercial fishing activity in Cordova, there's great sportfishing along the Eyak River/Lake and Alaganik River/Slough systems. You can access the glacial waters of the Eyak River by trail, with reds striking on bright lures in late June and early July. Silvers

pink salmon population as well as increased mortality rates among ducks and sea otters, perhaps as a result of ingesting contaminated invertebrates. Mussel beds in particular may take decades to recover.

The pristine beauty of Prince William Sound has been fully recovered following the 1989 oil spill, thanks to the efforts of thousands of clean-up workers and the natural scrubbing effects of wind and water. AMANDA BAUER

run in abundance in the late summer and early fall, and they're not so finicky about lures. Salmon fishing is not allowed in Eyak Lake, but you can try for Dolly Varden and cut-throat trout at the lake outlet. Dolly Varden are also plentiful at Power Creek, with road access heading north from Cordova. Be warned, though: Bears love this spot.

Follow Cordova's Copper River Highway to the boat launch at Mile 17 for access to the Alaganik River system. The best fishing for red and silver salmon is at the slough near the boat launch. You can also find cut-throat and Dolly Varden at McKinley Lake early in the season.

Alaskan Wilderness Outfitting Company
P.O. Box 1516
Cordova, AK 99574
(907) 424–5552
www.alaskawilderness.com
Family owned and operated since 1982, Alaskan Wilderness Outfitting offers a full range of options for game fishing in the abun-

i A shoppers' paradise it's not, but you will find two supermarkets, a bookstore, a general store, and a couple of outfitters as well as liquor stores and espresso shops in Cordova.

dant waters around Cordova. Fly fishing, spin casting, bottom fishing—they do it all with a reputation for excellence that brings clients back year after year. Select from their full-service lodge packages, their do-it-yourself outpost cabin packages, or their combination packages. If packages aren't your thing, they can design a custom trip just for you. Photography, flight seeing, clamming, hiking, and kayaking can be arranged, too.

Orca Adventure Lodge
P.O. Box 2105
Cordova, AK 99574
(866) 424–ORCA
www.orcaadventurelodge.com
One of the best known fishing services in the Sound, Orca offers all sorts of water-based adventures from their base lodge in a restored cannery 2 miles north of Cordova. Try their well-priced skiff fishing for salmon and smaller halibut in Orca Inlet, or wait till fall and try skiff fishing for silvers along the road system. Orca also runs a high-speed riverboat offering both spin and fly casting. Saltwater expeditions target salmon, halibut, and rockfish, or opt for a fly-out fishing adventure on a remote lake or river. Orca provides licensed guides, full fish-processing facilities, fish shipping, a well-stocked guide and tackle room, fly-tying and fly-fishing instruction, and a junior angler program. Nonanglers in your group can opt for brown bear photography, rafting, or kayaking adventures.

THE MATANUSKA-SUSITNA VALLEY

Less than one hour north of Anchorage, the Matanuska-Susitna (Mat-Su) Valley has become a favorite place to live and play. Surrounded by mountains and water, Anchorage has nowhere to grow except north, and that's where the Valley comes in. Housing is more affordable there, with plenty of acreage, woods, water, and mountain views to enjoy. A growing number of people do the daily commute of 45 minutes to an hour each way in order to work in Anchorage and come home to quality of life in the Valley. Visitors find lodging is more affordable in the Valley, too, and there's great access to all the outdoor fun that draws so many people to Alaska in the first place.

The sister communities of Palmer and Wasilla are the heart of the Mat-Su Valley. Palmer, with a population of approximately 3,000, has a friendly farm-town feel, while Wasilla, registering 5,000 plus inhabitants, is more suburban. The Matanuska-Susitna Borough adds another 27,000 residents who use the two towns as service centers. Both communities have growing residential areas with plenty of new construction, though Wasilla has the edge in terms of retail shops and services. North of Wasilla, the smaller communities of Big Lake, Willow, and Talkeetna

provide additional gateways into the Alaskan wilderness. Big Lake is a resort community just west of Mile 52 of the Parks Highway. There you'll find a big blue lake with 67 miles of wooded lakeshore dotted with lodges and restaurants.

Farther up the Parks Highway, the tiny town of Willow is most notable for on-and-off-again efforts to move the state capital there, partway between Anchorage and Fairbanks. At Willow, you can access the beautiful recreational area at Hatcher Pass via the gravel Fishhook-Willow Road that connects with the Wasilla-Fishhook Road along the east end of Wasilla. Finally, at Mile 98.7 of the Parks Highway, you can turn off to explore the whimsical town of Talkeetna, a frequent tour-bus stop and jumping-off point for adventurers planning to scale Denali, the highest peak in North America.

Be sure to plan a stop at the Mat-Su Visitor Center, near the junction of the Parks and Glenn Highways, to pick up free brochures and visit with the staff about what to see and where to stay in the Valley. The visitor center also has a gift shop.

GETTING HERE, GETTING AROUND

Since this is primarily a commuter area, the best way to get around is by car. From Anchorage, head north on the Glenn Highway (Route 1), and you should reach the Palmer-Wasilla Highway within 45 minutes to an hour, depending on traffic. Be advised that this stretch of roadway has the highest rate of traffic fatalities in the state, primarily due to the sheer numbers of commuters that travel it daily. The now infamous "bridges to nowhere" funding for a bridge over Knik Arm would provide another

i For a little town, Talkeetna has a lot going on. There's an annual Moose Dropping Festival during the second weekend in July, and come winter there's the Talkeetna Winterfest, featuring the rollicking fun of the Wilderness Women Contest and Bachelor Auction. For more information on the Wilderness Women Contest, see the complete write-up in the Annual Events and Festivals section of the Anchorage chapter.

route from the Valley to Anchorage, but with a price tag of some $600 million, it's a long ways from becoming a reality. Ferry service from Anchorage to Knik-Goose Bay Road may provide a short-term fix to the traffic problem.

From the Palmer-Wasilla Highway, you can head west and north toward the Parks Highway (Route 3), which continues on to Denali National Park and Fairbanks, or you can continue east and north on the Glenn Highway toward Glennallen. The stretch of the Glenn Highway from Anchorage to the Eureka Roadhouse is designated as a scenic byway, passing between the Talkeetna Mountains and the Chugach Mountains, with access to the Matanuska and Knik Rivers Scenic Overlook at Mile 49.9, the King Mountain State Recreation Site at Mile 76, the Matanuska Glacier State Recreation Area at Mile 101, and the Eureka Summit Area trailhead at Mile 132.5.

In the summer the Alaska Railroad also offers daily service connecting Wasilla and Talkeetna with Anchorage, Denali National Park, and Fairbanks. Once you're in the Valley, you can get around by ATV, sled dog, or horseback, if any of those strike your fancy. Check out the details in the Parks, Recreation, and Tours section below.

HISTORY

The Dena'ina Indians inhabited the rich and scenic land of the Matanuska-Susitna Valley for centuries. With the development of small-scale mining in Hatcher Pass, the Valley became an access route to the thriving seaport of Knik. Once a port was established in Anchorage, Knik was all but abandoned, but the Alaska Railroad brought the Valley to life in 1916 as it pushed through from Anchorage to Fairbanks.

In 1935, Franklin Roosevelt's Federal Emergency Relief Administration established the Matanuska Valley Colony at Palmer with the goal of relocating Depression-struck farm families to develop the agricultural potential of the Valley. Two hundred and three families from the northern counties of Minnesota,

Michigan, and Wisconsin were sent to the Mat-Su Valley, where they set about growing vegetables with the help of Alaska's legendary "midnight sun." Though some of the farms failed, many of the colonists stayed, and today the Mat-Su Valley still supplies fresh produce to Anchorage residents during the summer.

ACCOMMODATIONS

As noted above, one of the advantages to staying in the Valley instead of in the city is that room rates are noticeably cheaper. In addition, you're a lot more likely to find peace and quiet, mountain views, access to trails, and even lakeside docks as part of your package. There are more bed-and-breakfasts than full-size hotels in the Valley, reflecting the small-town feel of things here.

Price codes indicate the cost of a room for two during the peak season, generally May through mid-September. You can assume that major credit cards are accepted and that the establishment is open year-round unless we note otherwise. Count on bringing the kids but not the pets unless the listing says differently. While hotels and motels generally have rooms with wheelchair access and rooms for smokers, we'll make a special note if these are available at B&Bs, hostels, guesthouses, and inns.

Price Codes

$. . . . . Less than $100
$$ . . . . $100–$150
$$$ . . . . $151–$200
$$$$ . . . . More than $200

Hotels, Motels, and Lodges

Agate Inn $$–$$$
4725 Begich Circle, Wasilla
(907) 373–2290
www.agateinn.com
Located on 16 acres off the Palmer-Wasilla Highway, the Agate Inn has 15 rooms in a variety of settings, including the Agate Guest House and Aurora King Suite, the Knik Building,

the Agate Suites and Guest Laundry, and the Susitna Cottage. Beds come in a variety of configurations as well, from twin all the way through king-size mattresses. Rooms come with coffeemakers, microwaves, minifridges, irons and ironing boards, voice mail, and satellite televisions. A free continental breakfast is offered each morning, and there's a whirlpool available for guest use. The staff at this country-style inn likes to make sure each guest feels at home. A resident reindeer provides a unique Alaskan touch. All rooms are nonsmoking, and there are two rooms with wheelchair access.

Colony Inn $
325 East Elmwood Avenue, Palmer
(907) 745–3330

This former teachers' dormitory for the Depression-era Matanuska Colony has been restored into lodging with 12 unique rooms. Ten rooms have whirlpool tubs, while the others have showers only. Enjoy a great view of the mountains or chat with other guests in the great room, complete with bay window and fireplace. Registration is at the Valley Hotel on South Alaska Street. Ask about special rates for groups and seniors. All rooms are nonsmoking.

Gold Miners Hotel $
918 South Colony Way, Palmer
(907) 745–6160
www.goldminers.com

One of the best deals in the Valley, this hotel in the center of historic Palmer features deluxe rooms with mountain views and a sun terrace with barbeque grills. All rooms include minifridges, and kitchenettes are available in select rooms. There's cable television with HBO and free local calls as well. This hotel is especially well-suited for large parties, as the rooms sleep up to six people.

Grandview Inn and Suites $$$
2900 East Parks Highway, Wasilla
(907) 352–1700
www.grandviewak.com

One of the newer options in the Valley, the Grandview is decorated in soothing shades of green, maroon, and beige, blending a country-inn flavor with hotel-style amenities. Most of the 139 rooms have queen-size beds, with king-size beds in the Jacuzzi rooms. Rooms come with refrigerators, microwaves, hair dryers, irons, ironing boards, and coffeemakers. Guests have access to laundry facilities and high-speed Internet as well. There are great mountain views from the back, and don't miss the massive wildlife carving over the stone fireplace in the downstairs lobby. This is one of the few Valley hotels with an indoor pool and spa. A free continental breakfast is served seasonally.

Lake Lucille Inn $$$
Mile 43.5 Parks Highway
1300 West Lake Lucille Drive, Wasilla
(907) 352–0149
www.bestwestern.com/lakelucilleinn

This Best Western hotel overlooks the lake, with spectacular mountain vistas beyond. Rooms come with coffeemakers, irons and ironing boards, free morning papers, and free continental breakfasts. There's good food and a relaxing bar on the premises in the form of the Shoreline Restaurant and the Lakeview Lounge. The 54 rooms include standards with queen-size beds and suites with king-size beds. A sauna, a Jacuzzi, and an exercise room are available for guest use, and there's wireless Internet throughout the hotel. Rooms are nonsmoking only, and pets are allowed. One suite has wheelchair access.

Mat-Su Resort $
1850 Bogard Road, Wasilla
(907) 376–3228

Twelve acres of Lake Wasilla waterfront provide the backdrop for this log-style hotel that originally opened back in the 1950s. From this lakeside setting, you can rent paddleboats and rowboats, swim, snowmobile, or cross-country ski, depending on the season.

Volleyball and horseshoe pits are nearby, plus they have covered picnic areas for guest use. Most of the 12 rooms have color cable televisions, kitchenettes, and telephones. There are also three cabins available. Rates include all taxes, and all rooms are nonsmoking. The on-site restaurant and bar are favorite local hangouts.

Motherlode Lodge $$
Mile 14 Palmer-Fishhook Road, Hatcher Pass
(907) 746–1464
www.motherlodelodge.com
This historic lodge nestled in the heart of the Hatcher Pass recreational area offers old-time hospitality and ambience. Everything about the lodge feels uniquely Alaskan, from the wilderness setting to the weathered exterior to the down-home comfort inside. There are no in-room telephones or televisions, but plenty of books and games plus a pool table will help you wind down. From the front door you have access to 300,000 acres of wilderness crisscrossed with hiking, skiing and snowmachine trails. The lodge's 12 rooms have queen-size and twin beds, with cozy bedding and great views. Guests enjoy a free continental breakfast plus use of a wood-burning sauna. There's Sno-Cat access to the powdered peaks in the winter. The dining room opens by reservation only—you can call ahead for a meal prepared by the lodge's gourmet chef, a graduate of the Culinary Institute of America. The entire lodge can be

rented for weddings and other private functions. The facility is nonsmoking, and they do allow mature and social dogs. Despite the totally private feel to the place, it's only a short drive from Palmer.

Valley Hotel $
606 South Alaska Street, Palmer
(907) 745–3330
This affordable historic hotel first opened its doors in 1948, advertising 42 rooms and 42 baths to attract miners, farmers, and other guests. Owned and operated by longtime Alaskans, the hotel features comfortable accommodations and personal service. Rooms have twin and queen-size beds. Within the hotel are a restaurant and coffee shop, the Caboose Lounge, and the Iron Horse Liquor Store. The downtown location makes it an easy walk to local services. Wheelchair access is available on the first floor only.

Bed-and-Breakfasts/ Cottages and Cabins

Alaska Birch Cottages $$
2361 North Cotswold Circle, Palmer
(907) 745–0558
www.alaskabirchcottages.com
Nestled among birch and spruce trees on a quiet cul-de-sac between Palmer and Wasilla, these newer cottages are exceptional in design and ambience. They offer four one-bedroom cottages and two two-bedroom units with twin and king-size beds. Attention to detail abounds, from the furnished kitchen, gas fireplace, Jacuzzi tub with massaging double showerheads, vaulted ceiling, and half bath upstairs. Breakfast fixings, including homemade whole wheat rolls and free-range eggs, are left in the kitchen for your first night's stay. Every cottage has a fireplace, futon for extra guests, coin-operated washer and dryer, television, telephone, and screened-in porch. Irons and ironing boards are available on request. The owners will happily store your luggage if you're heading out on a short-term expedition. All of the cottages are nonsmoking.

i None of the local hotels offer shuttle service from the Anchorage airport, but Airport-Valley Shuttle (907–373–4359) does—five times daily, with extra shuttles on weekends. Valley drop-off and pickup points are the Lake Lucille Inn, the Grandview Inn, and the Trunk Road Park and Ride. At the Anchorage Airport, the shuttle stops at the bus loading area outside door number one in the baggage claim area. Forty-eight-hour advance reservations are required.

Alaska Creekside Cabins $$
P.O. Box 4356
Palmer, AK 99645
(907) 746–7632
www.alaskacreeksidecabins.com
With seven waterfront cabins on Wasilla and Cottonwood Creeks, Alaska Creekside offers salmon viewing right from your deck. One of the locations sports a great mountain view as well. Each cabin has one queen-size bed and three twin beds, so families and groups of four to six people are easily accommodated. Coffeemakers, microwaves, irons, ironing boards, complimentary coffee, stereos, telephones, cable televisions, gas fireplaces, jetted tubs, full-sized kitchens, and private decks come standard in each of these newer cabins. There's also a fire pit, and RV parking is available at each site. The cabins are nonsmoking only, and small kenneled dogs are accepted at one of the units.

Alaska Garden Gate Bed and Breakfast $
950 South Trunk Road, Palmer
(907) 746–2333
www.gardengatebnb.com
Tucked away on 10 acres near the Glenn and Parks Highways junction, Alaska Garden Gate offers rooms and guest apartments with Jacuzzis, fireplaces, and private entrances. Generous hot breakfasts are served between 7:00 and 10:00 A.M. each morning, featuring such Alaskan favorites as apple sourdough pancakes and caribou sausage. In the Forest Haven guest apartment, you'll enjoy fabulous views of Pioneer Peak and the Chugach Range while surrounded with north woods decor, while the Midnight Sun Gardens apartment opens onto a patio of brilliant flowers. Cool blues and mountain views are featured in the Forget Me Not Room, with roses as the theme in the Arctic Rose Room. The Blossoms and Berries Room features mountain views and botanical information on some of Alaska's splendid plants. All rooms come with coffeemakers, microwaves, minifridges, private baths, telephones, balconies, irons, and ironing boards. Horseshoe and tennis courts are available for guest use, and there's access to

miles of hiking and ski trails. All rooms are nonsmoking, two offer wheelchair access, and two are designated as pet friendly. Ask about AAA, AARP, and military discounts.

Alaska Gold Rush Inn and Cabins $$
7850 Lucky Shot Lane, Palmer
(907) 745–5312
www.alaskagoldrush.com
These six Alaskan-themed vacation cabins located near Hatcher Pass are convenient to both Palmer and Wasilla. The cabins are equipped with lots of extras, including coffeemakers, microwaves, minifridges, private baths, telephones, cable televisions, irons, ironing boards, and videos. An evening snack is offered at check-in, with a hearty continental breakfast served in the morning. As a special Alaskan touch, gold-panning supplies are available for guest use. The emphasis here is on service and a personal touch. All rooms are nonsmoking.

Alaska's Harvest Bed and Breakfast $
2252 Love Drive, Palmer
(907) 745–4263, (877) 745–4263
www.alaskasharvest.com
On 15 acres of secluded forest 2 miles from Palmer, this spacious B&B features Alaskan decor with amazing mountain views. Choose from the Bear's Den, the Reindeer Room, the Creekside Room, the Gold Mine Room, and the Pioneer Suite. Rooms come with coffeemakers, microwaves, minifridges, private baths, telephones, cable televisions, balconies, irons, and ironing boards. Kitchenettes are stocked with a variety of snacks, teas, and breakfast supplies, including muffins, cereals, pastries, yogurt, fresh fruits, coffee, tea, and milk. Enjoy peace and quiet in a country-style setting where sheep, alpacas, and miniature goats roam the pastures. All rooms are nonsmoking.

Alaska's Lake Lucille B&B $
235 West Lakeview Avenue, Wasilla
(907) 357–0353
www.alaskaslakelucillebnb.com

Located on the shores of Lake Lucille, this bed-and-breakfast offers more than 1,600 square feet of space for private guest use, including two standard rooms and two suites. The decor includes Alaskan art and rustic pine beds, all queen-size. Rooms come with coffeemakers, microwaves, minifridges, private baths, telephones, cable televisions, jetted tubs, irons, and ironing boards. In addition to home-style breakfasts, guests are offered afternoon coffee, cakes, and pies. All rooms are nonsmoking. Crafting and quilting retreats are among their specialties.

Alaska's Snowed Inn
Bed and Breakfast $
495 South Begich Drive, Wasilla
(907) 376–7495, (866) 799–5169
www.snowedinn-ak.com

Decorated with antiques, this two-room B&B offers a private guest entrance plus access to an inviting common area with dining facilities. The Alaska Suite features a northern theme, while the Lighthouse Suite offers a nautical theme. Situated on two quiet country acres, the inn serves a hearty breakfast as well as providing complimentary tea, juice, soda, bottled water, hot chocolate, hot cider, and coffee. Rooms come with private baths, telephones, cable televisions, balconies, irons, and ironing boards. Both rooms are non-smoking.

Country Pleasures
Bed and Breakfast $$–$$$
720 Tammy Lane, Meadow Lakes
(907) 376–9030, (866) 376–9030
www.countrypleasuresbedandbreakfast.com

Follow a beautifully landscaped trail from this two-suite B&B down to Zak Lake, where you can soak up the peace and quiet just minutes from downtown Wasilla. Each suite has its own private entrance and bath, while the Lighthouse Suite, which sleeps four, has a fireplace, whirlpool tub, fully furnished gourmet kitchen, large balcony, and hardwood floors. There's a gazebo along the lakeside trail and also one near the suites that has a gas grill, smoker barbeque, and gas fireplace. Break-

fasts include specialty homemade breads, and the owners promise that no one will leave hungry. Check out the on-site gift shop featuring handmade linens, quilts, and other items. Pets are accepted in the Alaska Suite only.

Dragonfly Gardens
Bed and Breakfast $$
1501 North Shoreline Drive, Wasilla
(907) 357–8498, (877) 357–8498
www.dragonflygardensbnb.com

Offering a quiet studio apartment on the shores on Cottonwood Lake, this B&B includes gardens, a private deck and private balcony, and dock access. The studio sleeps four, with a private bedroom and queen-size sleeper sofa, and the kitchen is stocked with a variety of breakfast items. Decorated with local art and capturing great views of the mountains, the lake, and the private gardens, this is a private, peaceful getaway. Telephone, cable television, wireless Internet, and a fire pit are included with the apartment. Pets are allowed, and there are border collies and a cat on the grounds.

Finger Lake B&B $
2700 Green Forest Drive, Palmer
(907) 745–4540, (888) 263–0768
www.fingerlakebnb.com

Enjoy a beautiful lakeside setting and relaxed atmosphere at this comfortable bed-and-breakfast located midway between Palmer and Wasilla. Located at the east end of a lake that's large enough for landing floatplanes, the B&B offers a large deck for guest use. There's even a resident ivory carver who is happy to talk about his craft and display his custom jewelry. Choose from either the Iris Room or the Alaska Room; both offer private baths, cable televisions, whirlpool tubs, and a free full breakfast, cooked to order. There is a small dog on the premises.

Moose Wallow Bed & Breakfast $$
13388 East Moose Wallow Avenue, Palmer
(907) 745–7777
www.moosewallow.com

Besides the fun name, this B&B offers three fully furnished cabins, all handcrafted from logs on the property. Located on 80 acres at the foot of the Talkeetna Mountains, Moose Wallow offers access to miles of groomed trails for both summer and winter use. In addition to the clean, cozy cabins in a peaceful setting, guests enjoy a full breakfast with foods such as omelets, pancakes, biscuits and gravy, blueberry muffins, and homemade bread. Fresh cookies and cinnamon rolls are provided at snack time. Cabins are equipped with coffeemakers, microwaves, private baths, telephones, TV/VCRs, irons, and ironing boards. Full breakfasts are for the first three days of your stay; thereafter, the breakfasts are continental. There's a gift shop, hair salon, and coffee shop on-site. Both owners are assistant hunting guides, and Bonnie makes museum-quality antler bowls. Pets are allowed, and the cabins offer wheelchair access.

Pioneer View Bed and Breakfast　　$
P.O. Box 3820
Palmer, AK 99645
(907) 745–2505
www.youralaskavacation.com
Four rooms are available in this comfortable family home, where you'll enjoy a great view of Pioneer Peak and access to several hiking trails. Located 5 miles south of Palmer on the Old Glenn Highway, Pioneer View includes a free continental breakfast and discounts on ATV tours to Knik Glacier. Breakfasts include Alaskan specialties such as Breakfast Burritos with reindeer sausage or breakfast meats such as bear, caribou, or moose along with the more traditional eggs, fried potatoes, bagels, and cereal. There's a barbeque in the yard for guest use, and fresh raspberries to be picked in season.

Rose Ridge Bed and Breakfast　　$–$$
8614 East Highlander Circle, Palmer
(907) 745–8604, (877) 827–7673
www.roseridgebnb.com
Located near scenic Hatcher Pass just a few

miles from Palmer, Rose Ridge offers two spacious rooms plus a vacation chalet. From the chalet, you'll enjoy views of Pioneer Peak and Knik Glacier. Rooms come with coffeemakers, private baths, TV/VCRs, and Internet modem connections. On the 15-acre premises, guests can make use of the fire pit and picnic area. Guests may choose from full or continental breakfasts that include Alaskan-themed items such as blueberry pancakes, reindeer sausage, homemade jams, and birch syrup. Rooms are nonsmoking only, and there's a $5.00 extra charge for children ages 5 to 12.

RESTAURANTS

Though the Valley's population can't support the variety in eateries that Anchorage does, you still can find a place to suit just about every taste and budget. True, some of these establishments are in strip malls, but once you get inside, you'll be impressed with how the owners have transformed the decor into something truly pleasing. Many of the finer establishments boast killer views that will leave you lingering at your table long after the plates have been cleared. For whatever reason, animal mounts on the wall seem to be the dominant decorating theme at many of the more casual spots.

Unless otherwise noted, you may assume that these places are open year-round, seven days a week. Credit cards and reservations are accepted but not necessary unless otherwise noted, and the restaurants are wheelchair accessible.

The price codes indicate the average cost of a meal for two, excluding cocktails, wine, appetizers, desserts, tax, and tips. Most establishments that serve dinner have a license for beer and wine, and many also serve cocktails.

Price Codes

$	Less than $30
$$	$30–$39
$$$	$40–$50
$$$$	More than $50

Chepos $

731 West Parks Highway, Wasilla
(907) 373–5656

With a nice Southwestern decor including murals of Mexican scenes and a big wrought-iron chandelier, this family-owned restaurant has an extensive menu that's sure to please. The clientele ranges from teens to families to professionals and tourists. Choose from a huge list of Mexican dinner combinations, or order from a large selection of a la carte items. Among the favorites are Camerones Rancheros, a shrimp dish with traditional ranchero sauce, and the Polla Fundido, a deep-fried flour tortilla stuffed with seasoned chicken and melted cheese, served with pico de gallo salsa. They also have a nice selection of margaritas and occasional mariachi music. Don't be put off by the strip mall location—the good food and atmosphere have kept locals coming back since they first opened in 1986.

Colony Kitchen/The Noisy Goose $

Mile 40.5 Glenn Highway, Palmer
(907) 746–4600

A perennial local favorite for home-style cooking served in one of those places where the customers are friends and the staff actually has fun most of the time, the Noisy Goose caters to locals year-round, with a hearty crop of tourists mixed in during the summer. Owners Bill and Glenda Hafus began with the Frontier Café in downtown Palmer, then opened the Colony Kitchen across from the fairgrounds a few years later. Eventually the place came to be called the Noisy Goose, in part a tribute to the good-natured conversation that makes the place feel so comfortable. Check out the narrative that comes with the menu for a fun look at the evolution of this popular cafe, including the unsolved mystery of the stolen toilet. Among their specialties are homemade pies, eggs Benedict, homemade meatloaf, and prime rib on Sunday. You can call ahead for large groups, but they don't typically take reservations. The Noisy Goose is open for breakfast, lunch, and dinner.

Evangelo's Restaurant $$$$

Mile 40 Parks Highway, Wasilla
(907) 376–1212

Spacious, open, and elegant, Evangelo's offers a nice selection of mostly Italian fare coupled with excellent service. Decorated in rich hues of maroon and green, Evangelo's also is graced with a fireplace and great mountains views from the tables in the back. For starters, try the Deep-Fried Ravioli or the shrimp. Regular diners like Evangelo's Special Pizza with sausage, Canadian bacon, pepperoni, hamburger, mushrooms, and olives. Other favorites include the Halibut Olympia and the Prime Rib Sandwich. Private, curtained seating for parties of up to 25 is available upstairs, and there are banquet rooms downstairs. Open for lunch and dinner, Evangelo's has a full beer and wine menu plus ample parking.

Glacier Canyon Grill $$$

2900 East Parks Highway, Wasilla
(907) 352–1720
www.grandviewak.com

Located downstairs at the Grandview Inn, the Glacier Canyon Grill features windows overlooking the lake, a stone fireplace, and a trophy-room motif, with animal mounts from both Alaska and Africa. Open primarily for dinner, the grill's menu includes such favorites as halibut with lemon-caper sauce, the 16-ounce Glacier Canyon ribeye steak, and the King Crab and Shrimp Pot with Nantua lobster sauce served over pasta. This newer restaurant is not large, but there's ample parking and a full bar.

Great Bear Brewing Company $$

238 North Boundary Street, Wasilla
(907) 373–4782

This restaurant and adjoining bar appeal to a far-ranging crowd, from after-church Sunday diners to a younger crowd mixing it up nights at the bar. The atmosphere in the strip-mall location is nothing fancy, but from the natural wood bar at one end of the establishment you can catch a glimpse of the brewing vats. In addition to the full bar and microbrews made on-site, Great Bear Brewing serves its own root beer made with 100 percent pure Alaskan birch syrup. Open for lunch and dinner, the menu includes favorites such as the Lazy Mountain Burger with pepper jack cheese mixed in with the beef, and the April Burger, topped with wood-smoked bacon, cheese, and April's barbeque sauce. Great Bear Brewing is open daily from 11:00 A.M. until midnight. They don't take reservations, but they appreciate "fair warning" for large parties. The whole place, bar included, is nonsmoking until 9:00 P.M.

Mat-Su Resort $
1850 East Bogard Road, Wasilla
(907) 376-3228
Locals flock to the Mat-Su Resort, offering casual dining on the shores of Wasilla Lake. Open since the 1950s for lunch and dinner, the restaurant specializes in steaks and seafood. Menu favorites include the Mat-Su Steak Sandwich with Black Angus steak served on garlic toast, the halibut fish and chips, and the Seafood Alfredo. The log building makes for a cozy atmosphere, and in the summer you can enjoy outdoor dining on the large deck overlooking the lake. After you've finished your meal, take a spin around the lake in one of the paddleboats available for rent.

Settlers Bay Lodge $$$
Mile 8 Knik-Goose Bay Road, Wasilla
(907) 376-5466
With its vaulted ceilings, accent lighting, exhibition kitchen, and huge windows capturing a spectacular mountain view, Settlers Bay is undeniably one of the most romantic dinner spots in the Valley. It's also one of the newer restaurants, having opened in 2004 adjacent to the golf course in the burgeoning residential development at Settlers Bay. Touting "casual dining at its finest," the menu features creative specials including duck, oysters, and clams. During the summer, Settlers Bay Lodge uses locally grown

Mat-Su produce in all their menu items. Try the Mushroom Crusted Halibut served over fresh spinach in a cream reduction and topped with frizzled potatoes, or the grilled ribeye served with cremini mushrooms and topped with tobacco onions and compound butter. The restaurant and adjoining bar, both completely nonsmoking, are open from Wednesday through Sunday, with abbreviated Sunday hours in the winter.

Tokyo Restaurant $$
735 West Parks Highway, Wasilla
(907) 357-8888
Don't be fooled by the strip-mall location—this restaurant opens up with a vaulted ceiling and tons of wood accents that manage to skillfully blend Asian and Alaskan influences with a pleasing ambience. Serving Japanese and Chinese cuisine as well as sushi, the restaurant's menu is varied enough to draw tour-bus crowds on their way from Anchorage to Denali and points beyond. Open for lunch and dinner since 2000, the Tokyo Restaurant offers beer, wine, and sake. Menu favorites include chicken teriyaki, Mongolian beef, and shrimp tempura. The restaurant occasionally has a no-check policy, so be sure to bring cash or a credit card.

NIGHTLIFE

Though it's not a place people would flock to for the exciting nightlife, the Valley takes care of its own with a good selection of local hangouts ranging from classy joints with killer views to stereotypical hole-in-the-wall bars. Several places have live music on weekends, and most are open till 1:00 or 2:00 A.M., with the occasional almost-all-nighter.

Remember that if your blood alcohol level is .08 percent or higher, you're risking a DUI conviction in the state of Alaska. As in most states, this is a serious offense, resulting in confiscation of your license at the time of your arrest followed by a minimum of three days in jail, a $1,500 fine, and a three-month license suspension if you're convicted.

i The Valley's population expanded by 18 percent between 2000 and 2004, making the Mat-Su Borough the third-largest population center in Alaska after Anchorage and Fairbanks. With the influx, the area is becoming decidedly more sophisticated, with two theater companies, an Arts Council, and galleries that sell as much contemporary art as typical Alaskan fare.

Arctic Circle Club
2750 Palmer-Wasilla Highway, Wasilla
(907) 357–6888

With a sports theme and a facility that's refreshingly clean right down to the bathrooms, this newer bar, also known as ACC or Flatley's, is a popular local hangout. Owner Jim Flatley is a friendly guy with diverse interests that include car racing and Robert Service poetry. As Klondike Jim, Flatley has done Robert Service shows all over the world. Occasionally he does a show at the bar in two 45-minute sets with a local band to open. Seating is limited and tickets sell out fast, so it's best to let the bartender know you'd like to get in on a show, and they'll call you when the next one is scheduled. The ACC is expanding out back to include a horseshoe pit and golfing green. Flatley also contends that his is the only authentic Irish bar in the Valley.

Fish Heads
3250 East Palmer-Wasilla Highway, Wasilla
(907) 357–6600

Head around to the back of the bowling alley to find this Valley hot spot for the younger crowd. It doesn't look like much from the outside, but inside there's plenty of action all the way till 5:00 A.M. A local favorite, Fish Heads has a DJ and dancing.

Grandview Inn and Bar
2900 East Parks Highway, Wasilla
(907) 352–1720
www.grandviewak.com

Another hotel, bar, and restaurant combination, the Grandview is new and upscale. It's smaller and darker than some of the other hotel bars, but the atmosphere is warm and appealing. The Grandview used to draw primarily a younger crowd, but now the clientele is mixed. There's live music on the weekends, complemented by Candlelight Jazz in the adjacent dining room. The bar is nonsmoking, and they offer a great bar menu, including a generous nacho plate and such specialties as stuffed mushrooms and Lamb Lollipops.

Great Bear Brewing Company
238 North Boundary Street, Wasilla
(907) 373–4782

This smaller bar draws a crowd with its own microbrews and live music on weekends. In addition to the house beers, the bar menu includes five premium whiskeys. The weekly roundup of bar-time fun includes Dart Night, a pasta bar, Open Mic, and a Showcase Night. Located in a strip mall, the bar opens into a small restaurant, so you can order up a meal as well. There's no dance floor, and the bar is nonsmoking until 9:00 P.M. (Also see our write-up in the Restaurants section of this chapter.)

Lakeview Lounge
Lake Lucille Inn
1300 West Lake Lucille Drive
Wasilla
(907) 373–1776

With a big vaulted ceiling and killer view of the lake and the mountains, you'd expect the bar here to be jam-packed, but it's actually rather quiet except when there are special events going on, like car races on the frozen lake in the winter. Most of the clientele are tourists, with some locals in the mix. There's a small stage set up for occasional live entertainment. Go through the restaurant and around the back to get to the bar.

Motherlode Lodge
Mile 14 Palmer-Fishhook Road, Hatcher Pass
(907) 745–6171

Even though it's not technically a nighttime

affair, the Jazz Club from 3:00 to 6:00 P.M. on the last Sunday of each month definitely counts as quality entertainment in the Valley. Flanked by mountains, this historic lodge makes a great backdrop for these informal, eclectic jam sessions. If you want to make an evening of it, there's food in the bar and you can rent one of the lodge's 12 rooms for the night. There is a cover charge for the show. For more information, see our listing under Accommodations in this chapter.

Mug Shot Saloon
251 West Parks Highway, Wasilla
(907) 376–1617
This is one of those dark, semirustic bars that you find sprinkled across Alaska, a place where regulars love to hang out even in the middle of the day. The walls are hung with caricatures of patrons and friends, and out

back there's a large deck and horseshoe pit. With 13 TVs and NFL Sunday ticket, it's the place to be during football season. Rumor has it that they pour a generous drink.

Schwabenhof
Mile 6.5 Palmer-Wasilla Highway
Wasilla
(907) 357–2739
This impressive octagonal log built perched on a hill is one of the classier hangouts in the Valley. Expect a nice view and quiet atmosphere, with no pool tables, pinball machines, or blaring TVs.

Settlers Bay Lodge
Mile 8 Knik-Goose Bay Road
Wasilla
(907) 376–5466
One of the prettiest bars in town, Settlers Bay draws lots of locals, especially residents of the Settlers Bay residential development who are looking for a night out close to home. They have more than 70 wines plus a signature martini list. Even without the occasional live music, this is a great place to bring a date. Golfers from the adjacent course stop by to celebrate their wins, though the indulgent King Louis XIII bourbon at $85 a shot is no longer available.

ATTRACTIONS

As in much of Alaska, animals and history are the primary themes of Valley attractions. From dog kennels, reindeer farms, and museums, there's something for everyone to see and remember. Price codes indicate the cost of admission for one adult. Attractions that don't charge admission have no price code assigned to them.

Price Codes

$	Less than $5.00
$$	$5.00–$10.00
$$$	$11.00–$15.00
$$$$	More than $15.00

Shopping Tips

Most folks head to Anchorage to do their serious shopping, but the Valley also has such big box stores as Gottschalks, Sears, Fred Meyer, and Wal-Mart. For specialty shops, check out the gold jewelry at Double J Mining in the Hunter Plaza in Wasilla (907–376–1000) and the kitchenware at All I Saw Cookware in downtown Wasilla (907–376–3177, 866–376–3177, www.allisawcookware.com). And don't miss the Palmer Open Air Market (907–761–3500, www.palmerchamber.org), featuring locally grown produce, arts and crafts, and live entertainment, every Friday from May through August. You'll find it in downtown Palmer, across from the visitor center. There's also a farmers' market every Wednesday at the Old Wasilla Town Site.

Palmer

Colony House Museum $
316 East Elmwood Avenue
(907) 745–3703

Guided tours of this original Colony Farm House are given by descendants of some of the first colonists who were transplanted in the Valley as part of the New Deal agricultural effort. It's far from an extensive museum, but the history of the place is unique, and it's fun to see the Sears and Roebuck furnishings that outfitted the home back in the Depression era. The museum is closed on Sunday and in the winter.

Musk Ox Farm $$
Mile 50 Glenn Highway
(907) 745–4151
www.muskoxfarm.org

In the 1800s, musk ox disappeared from Alaska, but in 1954, Palmer's Musk Ox Farm began a domestication project to bring them back. This is a great chance to see these prehistoric-looking animals up close, to learn about their history, and to find out about the use of qiviut, the exceptionally soft wool of the musk ox. This private nonprofit organization also includes an interpretive museum, a gift shop, and a picnic area. The farm is open daily from May to September.

Reindeer Farm $$
Mile 11.5 Old Glenn Highway
(907) 745–4000
www.reindeerfarm.com

At the foot of Bodenburg Butte, this original Colony farm has been transformed into a place where visitors can walk among reindeer, petting and feeding them. The farm also does rehabilitation for elk, moose, and deer. The Chugach Mountains, with the Valley's signature Pioneer Peak, make a great backdrop for spending time with these very Alaskan mammals. The farm is open daily from the beginning of May through the middle of September.

Wasilla

Dorothy Page Museum $
323 North Main Street
(907) 373–9071
www.cityofwasilla.com/museum

This small log museum served as a community hall when it was built in 1931. Restored in 1967 as part of the Alaska Centennial events, it now houses history and art exhibits and provides a setting for classes and lectures. Eight additional historic structures are preserved on the adjacent lots, all part of the original town site. A farmers' market and picnic area also are found on the museum grounds. The museum is open Tuesday through Saturday from April to September.

Dream a Dream Dog Farm $$$$
Mile 64.5 Parks Highway, Houston
(907) 495–1198
www.vernhalter.com

Veteran Iditarod musher and Yukon Quest champion Vern Halter opens his kennels to the public from June 1 to September 1. The dog-farm tour includes a 45-minute video

---

Annual Events

Annual events and festivals in Anchorage are just a short drive away, but Palmer and Wasilla also host events of their own. The Iditarod Days Festival in Wasilla runs for 10 days from late February into early March, culminating with the start of the world-renowned sled-dog race. In Palmer, catch the Colony Days celebration during the second weekend in June, the 11-day Alaska State Fair ending on Labor Day each year (see the complete write-up in the Annual Events and Festivals section of the Anchorage chapter), and the Colony Christmas Celebration on the second Friday and Saturday in December.

The Iditarod headquarters on Knik-Goose Bay Road is a great place to learn about the Last Great Race.
DEB VANASSE

presentation, a guided walking tour of the kennel, and an opportunity to get up close and personal with the pups, dogs, and mushers. Sled-dog rides are available at an extra charge, and winter tours may be scheduled by appointment. The Dog Farm is open Tuesday through Sunday. Children younger than age six are admitted free of charge.

Happy Trails Kennels $$$$
Mile 4.5 West Lakes Boulevard, Big Lake
(907) 892–7899
www.buserdog.com
Four-time Iditarod champion and Leonard Seppala Humanitarian Award winner Martin Buser is at Happy Trails on most days to meet and greet visitors after they've viewed a multimedia tour complete with Iditarod Trail footage. In addition to watching demonstrations of the art of sled-dog mushing, visitors get to meet and handle pups that will eventually train for some of the world's most

arduous races. The admission fee includes a free dog bootie and a Martin Buser trading card. The kennels are open from mid-April through mid-October.

Iditarod Trail Sled Dog Race Headquarters
Mile 2.2 Knik Goose Bay Road
(907) 376–5155, (800) 545–6874
www.iditarod.com
Trophies and photos are among the race memorabilia on display at the Iditarod Trail Headquarters Museum. Thanks to the wonders of taxidermy, you can even see Leonard Seppala's lead dog Togo, who took his team 340 miles through a Norton Sound blizzard to deliver diphtheria serum to Nome. You'll also see Andy, Rick Swenson's lead dog that took his team to four of his five Iditarod wins. You also can watch video footage of past races and visit the extensive gift shop. Admission to the museum is free, with sled-dog (cart) rides available in the summer, weather permitting,

for an additional charge. The race headquarters is open daily from mid-May through mid-September and Monday through Friday during the winter.

Museum of Alaska Transportation and Industry $$
3800 West Neuser Drive
(907) 376–1211

Given the vast expanse to be traveled in our state, it's no wonder that transportation is a vital part of its history. This museum preserves, exhibits, restores, and interprets artifacts connected with industry and transportation in the 49th state. You'll see the Bush Pilot Hall of Fame, restored vehicles, a gold mining exhibit, and lots of engines. On the 20-acre museum grounds, you'll find aircraft, trains, snow machines, cars, boats, and tractors. Located three-quarters of a mile off the Parks Highway at Mile 47, the museum is open year-round.

Northern Trappers Fur Industry Museum
5401 East Mayflower Lane
(907) 376–5873
www.fortgreen.com

Trapping is not always in vogue, but it does form an important part of Alaska's history. Tucked inside the Fort Green Gift Shop, the Northern Trappers Museum displays artifacts from the past two centuries, including art, posters, calendars, and antique traps. Located 3.2 miles toward Palmer on the Palmer-Wasilla Highway, the shop also features eight big-game mounts.

PARKS, RECREATION, AND TOURS

In the Valley you'll find a great selection of parks, some operated by the borough and some operated by the state. The 101-acre Matanuska River Park at Mile 17 of the Old Glenn Highway was developed on land that came from one of the original Valley pioneers. Running along the length of the river's braided channel, the park offers camping, picnicking, and five short hiking trails. The Sherrod Little

League Baseball complex is part of the park, as are two small ponds.

South of Wasilla at Mile 2.4 of Knik-Goose Bay Road, Lake Lucille Park includes four short trails, soccer fields, 64 campsites, volleyball and horseshoe courts, a picnic area, and firewood. This 80-acre park includes frontage on Lake Lucille, which at 362 acres is one of the largest lakes in the Valley. Only nonmotorized activities are allowed on the lake, which is stocked with rainbow trout and fingerling silvers.

Hatcher Pass is a favorite place to get out and enjoy hiking, sightseeing, kayaking, and winter sports. The Hatcher Pass Management Area, accessible from either the Wasilla-Fishhook Road out of Wasilla or from the Fishhook-Willow Road out of Willow, is large enough to provide great wilderness experiences without venturing too far from town.

Avalanche Safety

Hatcher Pass is a known avalanche area. Snowmachiners should travel steep slopes in groups of no more than four people, riding up one at a time while the others watch. Everyone should wear an avalanche beacon and pack a shovel and probe. Try to stick with windward slopes that fan out at the bottom, avoiding steep-sided waterways, gullies, and slopes with cliffs below. Stop periodically to take off your helmet and get a feel for the snow. Watch for signs of recent avalanches, including wind-loaded snow, recent rain, shooting cracks, hollow-sounding or "whumping" snow, and any signs of rapid warming conditions. High-markers should start on the side of the slope and turn back toward the edge rather than toward the middle.

Marmots are among the wildlife you'll see at Hatcher Pass. DEB VANASSE

Hatcher Pass Road is gravel, and it can be narrow and steep in spots. The Fishhook-Willow section of the road is closed during the winter.

Trail options for hikers and mountain bikers include everything from day hikes to week-long expeditions including glacier crossings. Kayaking the Class V white water of the Little Susitna River presents a challenge best left to well-seasoned boaters. Winter sports opportunities abound, with good snow cover generally arriving by mid-October and staying until the end of April. Alpine skiers, telemark skiers, Nordic skiers, snowboarders, and snowmachiners all make good use of Hatcher Pass. Trails on the west side of the pass are especially popular with snowmachiners, while Nordic skiers concentrate in the area of Independence Mine. Downhill skiers and snowboarders congregate at Government Peak and the Mile 16 Trail.

Independence Mine, a former hard rock gold mine now turned state historical park, is

a worthy attraction within the state recreational area. You can take a self-guided tour through the mine camp, beginning at the Mine Manager's House, where you'll find interpretive displays on gold mining and the natural history of the area. Guided tours will bring you inside some of the other buildings, or you can try your luck at finding some of the glittering rock—just bring your own pan and shovel.

Several state recreation sites provide additional opportunities to access the great outdoors from within the Mat-Su Valley. Rocky Lake, Big Lake, Finger Lake, King Mountain, and the Matanuska Glacier State Recreation Sites all have camping and picnic areas, while Kepler-Bradley Lakes and Summit Lake offer trail access.

For biking trails close to town, try the 3-mile Parks Highway bike path from Lucas Road to the railroad overpass in Wasilla, the 5-mile Palmer-Wasilla Highway bike path from

Wasilla Lake to Schelin Spur Road, the 3-mile Old Glenn Highway Gravel Trail from Plumley Road to the Mantanuska River Bridge, and the 1.5-mile Old Glenn Highway path that heads south from Ye Old River Road.

If you're looking for other fun ways to get out into the backcountry, various recreation and tour businesses in the Valley have plenty to offer. For guided and unguided horse trail riding, check out Alaska Riding Adventures (907–745–8768). They offer year-round riding by the hour, as well as overnight rides and pack trips. Located eight minutes from Palmer off Fishhook Road, Alaska Riding Adventures also operates Hatcher Pass Frontier Retreat, with ATV, snowmachine, and cabin rentals. Kim's Scenic Tours (907–745–4000) also offers guided horseback riding by the hour, with views of the Matanuska Valley, Knik Glacier, the Matanuska and Knik Rivers, historic Colony farms, and the famed Sleeping Lady Mountain. Children younger than age eight may do corral rides only.

What better way to see Iditarod country than by sled dog? At Plettner Kennels. (907–892–6944, www.plettner-kennels.com), you'll take a kennel tour with Lynda Plettner, an 11-time Iditarod finisher, then try a sled ride that gives you a hands-on experience with the dogs. No snow necessary for this tour—the dogs train with wheeled carts in the summer.

If you're looking for motorized adventure, Guardian Alaska Adventure Tours (907–232–6773, www.youralaskavacation.com) offers year-round guided ATV (all-terrrain vehicle) tours. No riding experience is necessary,

You can tour the historic sites of downtown Palmer by picking up a map at the Palmer Visitors Center. Another self-tour option features farms of the valley, including an Agricultural Experiment Station, a wilderness nursery, dairy farms, a reindeer farm, and a llama farm. Get your guide to this unique driving tour at the Palmer Visitors Center.

and reservations are recommended. For personalized custom tours using more ordinary transportation, Mat-Su Tours (907–373–5820, 866–383–5820) will take you to such attractions as the Musk Ox Farm, the Reindeer Farm, Wolf Country USA, Independence Mine, the Iditarod Headquarters, the Matanuska Glacier, Eklutna village, and even up to Talkeetna. Tours are offered year-round, with specials for Fur Rondy and the Iditarod. Check out their Aurora Viewing Trips in the winter, too.

FISHING

The Mat-Su Valley offers some of the most popular and productive fishing spots in South-central Alaska. The Susitna River drainage is the big player here, with salmon, grayling, and trout circulating through its clear-water tributaries. We'll focus primarily on road-accessible fishing here, but keep in mind that you can charter out by boat or floatplane if you're craving a more remote experience.

The Little Susitna River, or the Little Su as locals call it, is a great place to check out what Valley fishing is all about. Take either the Parks Highway to Houston or the Knik-Goose Bay Road from Wasilla to Burma Road to fish for all species of salmon. The upper and middle parts of the river yield the best take for shore-bound anglers, with boaters fishing the tides downstream. Silvers run here in exceptionally large numbers, and with a little luck you may catch kings in the 50- to 70-pound range. Pinks and chums also are abundant, making for a lot of angling excitement except during hot or rainy spells, when the waters turn muddy.

Willow Creek is another popular stream with road access. You can fish from shore after parking at the town of Willow or along Hatcher Pass Road. Salmon run in the Willow throughout the summer, with a lot of the fishing attention going toward kings that generally weigh between 15 and 30 pounds. You'll have a lot of company if you fish near the road, but if you hike into the upper and middle parts of the river, you'll lose the crowds and have a chance at trout and grayling as well.

North of Willow you can access the lower end of Sheep Creek from a Parks Highway bridge. Sheep Creek is another great place to fish from shore for all four species of salmon, with kings being the big draw. Some years the chums run quite well, too. Like many of the Susitna tributaries, Sheep Creek can be high and muddy during hot or rainy spells.

A little farther up the highway, you can access Montana Creek, which tends to run clear most of the time. You'll find good fishing at the mouth of the creek, within walking distance of the state campground. Look for decent-size kings early in the summer, with silvers, pinks, chums, and rainbows in the late summer to early fall.

If you have access to boats, especially those with jet units, or if you want to charter out, you'll find Alexander Creek, accessible from Deshka Landing, a productive spot for all types of salmon, particularly silvers, along with Dolly Varden and grayling. Alexander Lake also offers some great Northern Pike fishing, with a few fish weighing in at more than 30 pounds. The Deshka River is another popular spot that's accessible by boat or floatplane. King salmon run in numbers upward of 30,000 most years. Other species of salmon are also present, along with rainbows, grayling, and northern pike.

For lake fishing, try Nancy Lakes, off Mile 67.3 of the Parks Highway. You'll find a series of lakes and ponds stocked with Dolly Varden, rainbow trout, and, in some lakes, salmon. The Kepler/Bradley Lake area is another popular spot, accessed at Mile 36.4 of the Glenn Highway. Each of the nine landlocked lakes is stocked with three species of sportfish. The best lake fishing is in the fall and the spring. Ice fishing is productive, too.

HIKING AND CAMPING

The Mat-Su Valley offers some great opportunities for accessible hikes that will get you out into the wilderness and, in many cases, up to

where you can get a good look around. For an easy to moderate 3.1-mile hike, you can access the Plumley-Maud Trail at either the end of Maud Road or at the corner of Plumley and Caudill Roads. This trail, originally used for logging, can be wet in spots, and you may find yourself sharing space with mountain bikers and ATV riders.

West Butte Trail offers a moderate to difficult 1.5-mile hike to the top of Bodenburg Butte, where you'll be rewarded with striking views of Knik Glacier, Pioneer Peak, and the Knik River Valley. Pick up the trail by taking the Old Glenn Highway 5.5 miles from Palmer, turning right onto Bodenburg Loop and then left onto Mothershead Circle to the trailhead parking area. This is a well-kept trail, 2- to 6-feet wide, but be warned that the last half mile is steep.

Follow the 2-mile Lazy Mountain Trail to the top of the mountain, and you'll be treated to a sweeping view of most of the Valley. Since about a fourth of the trail is quite steep, you should plan on four hours or so for the round-trip. Pick up the trail at the Lazy Mountain Recreation Area parking lot, which you'll find by accessing the Old Glenn Highway at Mile 42 of the Glenn Highway, driving through Palmer and across the Matanuska River Bridge. Take a left onto Clark-Wolverine Road, a right onto Huntley Road, and go east to Mountain Trail Circle, where you'll find the parking area.

The Lazy Mountain Trail intersects with the 6-mile Matanuska Peak Trail, which starts off Smith Road past the Clark-Wolverine Road intersection. An hour to an hour and a half down the trail, you'll reach the tree line, where you'll have a great view of Matanuska Peak and the McRoberts Creek drainage. Within another one and a half to two hours, you should reach the base of the summit ridge, at an elevation of 3,800 feet.

For a variety of trail options, you can't beat the Crevasse Moraine Trail System, with 13 contiguous loops in lengths from 0.4 mile to 2.2 kilometers. At Mile 1.98 of the Palmer-Wasilla Highway, take Loma Prieta Drive to the end, where you'll find the trailhead access road. Trails are wide and well-marked; note that the do not enter signs apply to skiers, not hikers. From Loop 7, you can pick up a 2-mile trail that connects with the Long Lake Trail, part of the Kepler-Bradley Lakes State Recreation Area.

Hatcher Pass Recreation Area offers great hiking as well. A couple of favorites are the Gold Mint Trail, with the trailhead across from the Motherlode Lodge, and the Reed Lakes Trail, off the end of Archangel Road.

For camping you can opt for one of the borough or state parks, or go with a private campground. The Mat-Su Borough's Lake Lucille Park and Matanuska River Park both offer tent and RV camping for a fee. Picnic tables, grills, trash barrels, water, and restrooms are provided. The River Park also has coin-operated showers. For more information on these parks, see this chapter's section on Parks, Recreation, and Tours.

State park camping can be found at Big Lake North, with 60 sites, and at Big Lake South, with 20 sites. Picnic sites, drinking water, and toilets are all available at these parks, which are located on Big Lake Road. There's also camping at the Finger Lake State Recreation Site, located at Mile 0.7 Bogard Road in Palmer. You'll find toilets, drinking water, and trails at Finger Lake.

Alaskan Trails RV and Camper Park
Mile 48.2 Parks Highway, Wasilla
(907) 376–5504

This is a big campground, with 125 full hookup sites (20/30/50 amp), plus 54 pull-through sites and 28 smaller sites. Sites with hookups are $20 per night, while sites with no hookups are $10 per night. Laundry and shower facilities are included, and there is a dump station. Internet access is available in the coffee shop. Ask about their discount for members of the military and the Good Sam club. There is an extra charge for pets.

Big Bear RV Park
Mile 37 Parks Highway, Wasilla
(907) 745–7445
Choose from full hookups at $25.00 per day, electric only at $22.50 per day, tent sites for $14.00 per day, or cabins for $45.00 per day. Showers and dump stations are included in the prices, or the use of them may be purchased separately. A gift shop and laundry facilities are also available.

The Homestead RV Park
Mile 36.2 Glenn Highway, Palmer
(907) 745–6005
www.homesteadrvpark.com
Square dancing every Thursday night sets this RV park apart from the rest. Other special touches are wi-fi, modem, and mobile service, as well as restrooms with nonmetered showers. They also have the usual hookups, dump station, and laundry. The Homestead has 70-foot pull-throughs plus tent sites. There's a pavilion on-site, and hiking trails and fishing are available nearby.

DENALI NATIONAL PARK AND PRESERVE

Six million miles of wilderness—that's what this place is all about. Toss in North America's highest mountain, an abundance of wildlife, and a road-accessible location between Anchorage and Fairbanks, and you have a major visitor attraction. Arriving at the park entrance, you may suffer a twinge of disappointment—where you'd been hoping to see grazing caribou, meandering moose, and howling wolves, you're greeted instead by herds of an all-too-common variety: people. Denali plays host to about 360,000 visitors each year. But thanks to the efforts of the National Park Service and a slew of local vendors, you'll find a nice variety of options for getting past the crowds and into the wilderness you came to enjoy.

The mountain, whether you call it Denali or McKinley (to find out about the controversy over its name, see this chapter's Close-up,) or the Native name The Great One, is the crown jewel of the magnificent 600-mile Alaska Range, which cuts an arc across the center of the state. Several hundred million years ago, a collision of tectonic plates pushed the seafloor over the emerging continent, and the Alaska Range was born. If you ventured to the top of Denali, you'd find hunks of granite thrust through what was once ocean sediment. The mountain is huge, and it's still growing, though at the very slow rate of one millimeter per year. For a bit more action, there's the 1,300-mile Denali Fault, a source of frequent earthquakes—so don't be surprised if you feel a shaker while you're at the park.

We enjoy this wilderness today thanks to the foresight of naturalist Charles Sheldon, who visited the area between 1906 and 1908 with Harry Karstens, who later led the first ascent of the mountain. In 1917, Mt. McKinley National Park was formed, with Karstens as its superintendent. In 1976 the park was named an International Biosphere Reserve for research involving subarctic ecosystems. It became Denali National Park and Preserve in 1980, when Congress tripled its size. Six million acres, by the way, is larger than the state of Massachusetts.

While the park's big draw is the chance to see large mammals such as caribou, moose, bears (both grizzly and black), Dall sheep, and the occasional wolf in their natural habitat, the area's thriving ecosystem supports a dazzling array of flora and fauna that's no less fascinating for its size. Watch for smaller mammals such as lemmings, voles, shrews, beavers, porcupines, pikas, ground squirrels, marmots, marten, lynx, wolverines, weasels, and fox. Bring your binoculars and a good camera for memorable wildlife viewing.

Several glaciers adorn the mountain. You can get a close-up view of 35-foot-long Muldrow Glacier, which stretches to within half a mile of the shuttle-bus portion of the park road. Below the timberline at 2,700 feet, you'll discover taiga, a type of northern evergreen forest. Above, there's both wet and dry tundra. More than 650 vegetative species manage to adapt to these unique land types in which all but a thin layer of topsoil remains frozen year-round.

i When viewing wildlife or taking photographs, pay attention to separation distances recommended by park rangers. You should venture no closer than 50 feet from a bear, and that's only if you're right beside a vehicle. Distances of 75 to 900 feet are recommended for other animals. You won't get a photo of that elusive wolf: A 1-mile separation must be maintained.

GETTING HERE, GETTING AROUND

You can get to Denali by road or by train. Via the George Parks Highway (Highway 3), Denali is 237 miles north of Anchorage. Actually, it's the Glenn Highway (Highway 1), a paved four-lane, that heads north from Anchorage, but at Mile 35, just before Palmer and Wasilla, the Glenn Highway cuts east and the Parks Highway begins. The Parks is a paved two-lane road that's relatively easy to drive, even in the heights of the Alaska Range, but be prepared to encounter snow and ice at the higher elevations beginning in mid-September and continuing through early May. Milepost addresses for Denali businesses on the Parks Highway are measured from Anchorage.

Even though it's a main thoroughfare for access to the park, there's a 95-mile stretch of the Parks Highway between Trapper Creek and Cantwell with few services. Don't head north out of Trapper Creek if you're low on gas. Keep an eye out for moose and for the mountain. On clear days, you can catch nice roadside glimpses of The Great One as you wind your way north.

The **Alaska Railroad** (907–265–2494, 800–544–0552, www.alaskarailroad.com) runs daily passenger service to the park from both Anchorage and Fairbanks in the summer. Winter service is limited. It's about a seven-and-a-half-hour trip from Anchorage as compared to about a five-hour drive (depending on summer road construction), but the scenery can be spectacular and you'll enjoy the personal narratives provided by Alaskan guides, many of them well-trained local high school students, who travel with each passenger car. Flag service in the vicinity of the park adds to the novelty of the railroad experience. The railroad offers packaged tours in conjunction with its regularly scheduled service.

For an alternate rail experience, Princess Tours operates the Midnight Sun Express, also connecting Denali with Anchorage and Fairbanks. This upgraded service includes "ultra-dome" railcars with glass ceilings and fresh food prepared onboard. Tour packages include accommodations at one of the Princess Lodges near Denali National Park, and you don't have to be a cruise passenger to sign up for one of the land tour packages. For more information, call **Princess Tours** at (800) 426–0500 or visit www.princesslodges.com.

You also can reach Denali by bus, or with bus/rail packages. In addition to scheduled services, there are a variety of tour packages to choose from. Try **Grayline of Alaska** (800–478–6388, www.graylineofalaska.com) for coach tour options. **Alaska/Yukon Trails** (800–770–7275, www.alaskashuttle.com) runs smaller buses of the airport-shuttle variety between a number of Alaskan destinations, including Anchorage, Denali National Park, and Fairbanks.

Getting around within the park is a bit complicated. Private vehicles are not allowed past Mile 15 of the park road. Visitors must pay an entrance fee of $10 per person or $20 per family and hop on one of the Park Service shuttle buses, aka the Visitor Transportation System (VTS), to travel deeper into the park. You can opt for round-trips of 5 to 13 hours. Starting at Mile 20 of the park road, visitors can get on and off the shuttle buses to do some exploring and/or day hiking. Just be aware that you may need to wait an hour or more for another bus to pick you up when you're ready to return.

Regardless of your destination, you can't just hop on a VTS bus—you'll need reservations. The reservation system, which has been known to change from year to year, allows 65 percent of shuttle bus tickets to be reserved by fax, mail, or online beginning on December 1 of the prior year. Phone reservations can be made beginning February 15. The remaining seats become available for reservation two days in advance by phone, fax, or in person. Same-day reservations must be made in person. For complete information, including fares and tour options, contact **Denali Park Reservations,** a joint-venture concessionaire run by Doyon, an Alaskan Native corporation, and Aramark (907–272–7275, 800–622–7275, www.reservedenali.com).

The purpose of the Visitor Transportation System is to preserve the expansive wilderness within the park. Bus drivers point out wildlife and stop for photo opportunities. Shuttle buses run seasonally, from mid-May to mid-September. In the latter part of September, weather permitting, winners of a Park Service lottery may drive their private vehicles down the normally restricted length of the park road.

ATTRACTIONS

You'll want to start your visit by getting oriented at the Denali National Park and Preserve Visitor Center, a splendid facility that opened in the summer of 2005. You'll find the center 1.5 miles inside the park. Open daily from 9:00 A.M. to 9:00 P.M. during the late May to mid-September season, the visitor center offers slide shows, interpretive programs, and displays, plus general park information. There's even a food court. A short walk away is the park's bookstore, a large, bright facility packed with books on all sorts of topics pertaining to the park and the natural history of the area.

Another component of the visitor complex is the Murie Science and Learning Center, located at Mile 2 of the park road. Open from 8:30 A.M. to 4:30 P.M. during the summer, the Murie Center serves as the winter visitor center from 10:00 A.M. to 4:00 P.M. during those chilly months. Even in the summer, you take in a free Sled Dog Demonstration, including a tour of the park kennels. Buses leave from the visitor center approximately one-half hour before each demonstration.

The former visitor center at Mile 0.5 of the park road has been converted into the

Wilderness Access Center. That's where you'll make reservations for camping as well as for the shuttles and tours that take you into the park (see the Getting Here, Getting Around section above). The Eielson Visitor Center at Mile 66 of the park road reopens in 2008 with a brand-new 8,500-square-foot facility.

RECREATION AND TOURS

Organized tours are a great way to see Denali. The park's concessionaire offers two tour options daily, in season. For an emphasis on the cultural history of the park, take the four- to five-hour Denali Natural History Tour, which covers the first 17 miles of the park road. Along the way you'll stop for several programs describing local Native culture and the pioneer history of the area. The popular Tundra Wilderness Tour takes you all the way to Mile 62 of the park road, weather permitting. A certified resource interpreter will narrate your trip, and a box lunch is included. For more information, contact **Denali Park Reservations** (907–272–7275, 800–622–7275, www.reservedenali.com), the same folks who operate the shuttle buses.

If you want to go farther and deeper into the park, you'll need to sign up for a Kantishna tour. The tiny town of Kantishna, population 135, predates the park by 32 years. After no small amount of controversy, private vendors with ties to the original Kantishna claims were allowed to bring visitors down the full 91 miles of the park road. On the **Denali Backcountry Adventure Tour** (800–841–0692, www.denalitravel.com), you'll leave early in the morning in the company of a trained naturalist/driver, making several stops before you reach the end of the road and lunch at the Denali Backcountry Lodge in Kantishna. After lunch you can try gold panning or take a nature walk before heading back to the park entrance.

Outdoor enthusiasts will find plenty of other ways to explore the park. Short hiking trails near the entrance to the park, ranging in length from 0.4 to 2.4 miles, can be traversed

i Summer weather at the park can be cool, wet, and windy. Be prepared for temperatures between 35 and 75 degrees Fahrenheit. Gloves or mittens, a hat, rain gear, and sturdy shoes are recommended. Winter temperatures can reach 50 below, and that's not considering wind chill.

independently or with a ranger on scheduled hikes. Rangers lead visitors on 30- to 90-minute exploratory walks each day, including the Horseshoe Lake and Mount Healy Walks. For a more in-depth ranger-led adventure, sign up in advance for a Discovery Hike, with hiking times of two to five hours plus bus travel of two to eight hours, depending on the destination. The cost of a Discovery Hike is $23.75, which includes the bus ticket.

Special camper buses, with reserved seating through the same system as the shuttle buses, transport independent trekkers to their starting-off points. Cyclists may travel all 91 miles of the often dry and dusty park road, but off-road biking is prohibited.

If you're planning more than a day trip, bring your tent and obtain a backcountry permit. Permits may not be reserved in advance. To get a permit, you must visit the Backcountry Information Center (BIC) at the Riley Creek Entrance Area, taking about an hour to plan your itinerary, watch a backcountry video, listen to safety information, mark your route, and purchase your camper bus ticket. A quota system is used to make sure you have a genuine wilderness experience. Virtually all of the off-road area is "trailless wilderness." Pets and firearms are not allowed in the backcountry, and bear-resistant food containers, available at the BIC, must be used. Garbage must be packed out.

If you want to get up close and personal with the mountain and the wilderness, check out area vendors offering wild rides of all types. For flight seeing, try **Kantishna Air Taxi,** exclusive concessionaire for charters within

i Plastic portable containers called Bear-Resistant Food Containers (BRFCs) are part of the park's "bear/human conflict management" program. Backcountry travelers are required to use BRFCs to store food, garbage, and scented items. BRFCs are available free of charge in both three- and five-pound sizes, but they must be returned within 48 hours after a trip.

the park (907–683–1223, www.katair.com). **Talkeetna Air Taxi** departs Talkeetna and lands Cessna and DeHavilland aircraft right on the slopes of Denali (907–733–2218, 800–533–2219, www.talkeetnaair.com). Fully narrated helicopter tours are offered by **Era Helicopter Flightseeing** (907–683–2574, 800–843–1947, www.flightseeingtours.com), located at Mile 238 Parks Highway.

For a rugged ground experience in the wilderness surrounding Denali, try some four-wheeling with **Denali Jeep Backcountry Safari.** The adventure begins near the park entrance, where you'll meet your guide and your Jeep. From there you'll head north to the Stampede Road, an old gold-mining trail filled with the bumps and dips that four-wheeling drivers love. Via two-way radio, your guide will point out the sights and narrate the history as you bounce along. You won't be in the park proper, but there's a good chance you'll see some wildlife anyhow. Contact **Alaska Travel Adventures** (907–561–6777, 800–791–2673, www.bestofalaska.com) for more information.

Then there's the wet and wild wilderness experience. Several companies offer rides in the Class I through IV rapids of the Nenana River near the park. Choose between paddle rafts, which you help steer, and oar rafts, where the guide does the steering and you hang on for the ride. Either way, it's bound to be exciting. Dry suits are provided, but bring warm clothes to wear underneath. Choose between two-, four-, six-, and eight-hour trips. Reservations are recommended but not required. Try **Denali Raft Adventures** (907–683–2234, 888–683–2234, www.denaliraft .com), **Nenana Raft Adventures** (907–683–RAFT, 800–789–RAFT, www.raftdenali .com), or **Denali Outdoor Center** (907–683–1925, 888–303–1925, www.denali outdoorcenter.com), which also rents inflatable kayaks and mountain bikes.

Unless you're a true die-hard fisherman, you can leave your pole at home, as the silt surging through most of Denali's rivers is not fish friendly. If you're really determined, you can try for grayling in a small number of mountain streams or for lake trout in Wonder Lake, a 2.6-mile watershed near the end of the park road. No license is required for fishing within the park boundaries.

For the hardy and experienced, there's mountaineering. To learn more about climbing requirements, glacier hazards, high-altitude medical problems, search and rescue, and self-sufficiency, consult the Park Service's Mountaineering Booklet. For a copy of the booklet as well as detailed information on hiking, backpacking, wildlife viewing, photography, and winter activities, visit the park's Web site at www.nsp.gov/dena.

Winter brings new options for exploring the park. The flood of tourists diminishes to a trickle, and the shuttle buses take the winter off. Strap on your cross-country skis and head down the park road, or set off on a backcountry ski adventure. You can try telemark skiing and snowboarding as well, but expect long climbs to get to the action, and be aware of avalanche hazards. Call the **Park Headquarters** (907–683–2294) or check online (www.nps.gov/dena) for up-to-date weather and backcountry conditions. The friendly folks at the Park Headquarters also can tell you the dates for the annual Winterfest Celebration, featuring three days of skiing, skijoring, stargazing, and winter ecology programs. When snow cover is sufficient, the park superintendent may open the 1980 additions to the preserve (but not the original park) to snowmobile travel.

In the winter you can even traverse Denali the way park rangers do, by dog team. A limited number of park concessionaires offer mushing excursions. **Denali West Lodge** can take you to within 10 miles of the Wickersham Wall, the highest vertical rise in the world (907–674–3112, 888–607–5566, www.denaliwest.com). **EarthSong Lodge and Denali Dogsled Expeditions** offers a variety of dogsled adventures from lodge-based to weeklong expeditions in Denali National Park. (See the EarthSong Lodge listing in our Accommodations section below; 907–683–2863, www.earthsonglodge.com.)

ACCOMMODATIONS

Wilderness is the byword at Denali, and there was a time when most of the places to stay near the park could be described only as rustic. Options have expanded over the years, and now visitors can enjoy the full gamut from rustic tent camping to full-service lodges and hotels perched on the edge of the wilderness. Be prepared for a bit of sticker shock, though. Don't expect a full range of amenities because you're paying a lot for your room. Prices have more to do with the short visitor season (the end of May to the beginning of September) and the isolated setting than with elegant rooms and plush amenities. If you're traveling on the cheap, be warned that lower-end cabins may not have the luxury of indoor plumbing. Even more expensive digs may lack in-room phones and televisions, the big draw being the wildlife, the scenery, and the park itself.

Lodge is a ubiquitous term used to describe all sorts of Alaskan accommodations, or sometimes even establishments that offer no lodging at all, such as bars or restaurants. If they're operated by big companies, such as Princess or Aramark, the Denali Park concessionaire, expect large hotels designed to blend with their wilderness setting, typically featuring big timbers, decks, and windows to capture the view. Smaller lodges offer a more intimate experience, more like bed-and-breakfasts in their ambience, and a range of amenities from simple to relatively plush. Likewise, resorts up here are not the full-featured luxury hideaways you'd find in more southern climes. Expect hotel-class services and not a whole lot more at most Alaskan resorts.

i There's not a lot of shopping at Denali, but you'll find gift shops in the major hotels, and the bookstore inside the park is definitely worth a stop. Stock up on groceries before you go, as you'll find only convenience stores between Talkeetna and Nenana.

Along the same lines, you'll find few genuine bed-and-breakfast inns here; most bed-and-breakfasts will be ordinary homes with a few rooms open to guests during the summer season. What you'll lose in ambience you'll gain in great Alaskan hospitality and a chance to visit with your hosts about what it's really like to live in our great state. And if you opt for a cabin hoping for some privacy in the woods, be sure to get some particulars on how the cabins are situated. Some of those closest to the park are packed in like cordwood.

The larger lodges and hotels, most operated by the park concessionaires and tour companies, are clustered along the highway near the park entrance, along with a few smaller operations. There you'll be shoulder-to-shoulder with the vast majority of the park's visitors, so if you're looking for peace and quiet, you might want to venture farther out. Ten miles north of the park, in the vicinity of Healy (population 889), you'll find a nice selection of cabins and bed-and-breakfast establishments that offer some distance from the hordes of people closer to the park. If you're driving to Denali from Anchorage, you can do as the mountaineering folk do and take the easy 19-mile detour off the highway to the charming town of Talkeetna (population 868), but you'll have to head out early for the park, which is another 122 miles to the north.

Even with the expanded number of places to stay near Denali, there are still a huge number of visitors to be accommodated, so advance reservations are a good idea. For a quicker response, use the phone instead of e-mail during the peak of the season. Better yet, make your reservations before the summer season begins. Some establishments have different phone numbers during the off-season, so you may want to check online before calling.

Unless otherwise stated, you may assume that the places listed here are not open during the winter, and, remember, at Denali, winter begins in September and ends in May. Most establishments only allow smoking outside, but we'll note those that offer smoking rooms.

Many smaller facilities do not offer wheelchair access, so we'll comment on those that do. The same goes for pets—assume no pets allowed unless noted differently.

We'll list toll-free numbers when available, local phone numbers, and price range symbols for all accommodations. Price codes show the average cost per night for a standard room for two adults. Codes do not include the borough bed tax of 7 percent. Major credit cards are accepted unless otherwise stated.

Price Codes

$. . . . . Less than $100
$$ . . . . $100–$150
$$$ . . . . $151–$200
$$$$ . . . . More than $200

Hotels and Motels

Backwoods Lodge $$
Mile 133.8 Denali Highway
(907) 768–2231
www.backwoodslodge.com
Get away from the crowds at this small lodge on 12 wooded acres. You'll find it near the intersection of the Parks Highway (Route 1) and the Denali Highway (Route 8), 27 miles from the park entrance. Backwoods is the northernmost lodge offering a view of Denali, weather permitting. Open year-round, the lodge offers rooms with queen-size or twin beds, coffeemakers, microwaves, and minifridges. Built in the 1990s, the single-story, cedar-sided lodge offers clean, comfortable rooms. You can walk trails on the property, barbeque on the covered deck, or put your feet up and enjoy the quiet. Long-time employees attend to guests' comfort and special needs. Small pets are allowed, with restrictions. Coffee, tea, and hot chocolate plus microwave popcorn are complimentary, and they keep a stock of steaks (for barbequing), microwave potatoes, vegetables, and desserts on hand in case their guests want to cook some of their own meals. There are two cafes nearby, one of which is within walking distance.

Camp Denali and North Face Lodge $$$$
P.O. Box 67, Denali National Park
Denali, AK 99755
(907) 683–2290
www.campdenali.com

If you want to stay inside the park without a tent or an RV, you'll have to head for one of the few wilderness lodges near Kantishna. They're not cheap, and they're not luxurious, but the experience they offer is unique. Under long-standing family ownership since 1952 and granted unique historic operator status by the National Park Service, Camp Denali and North Face Lodge specialize in learning adventures for active travelers. At Camp Denali, you may opt for one of the 17 rustic guest cabins, and in this case, rustic means no running water. Each cabin has its own hand-built outhouse, and there's a common bathhouse with showers and flush toilets. North Face Lodge offers 15 small guest rooms, each with private bath, renovated from a five-acre homesite claim staked by Park Superintendent Grant Pearson in 1957. The adventure begins with the Camp Denali/North Face Lodge visitor bus transporting guests from the park entrance to the end-of-the-road accommodations past Wonder Lake in the company of a naturalist-guide. Once you arrive at your destination, you can plan independent treks using Camp Denali's resource center, bikes, and canoes, or you can join one of the camp's special emphasis programs on such topics as wildflowers, the aurora borealis, and Native culture. Meals are included, and there's a minimum three-night stay. Credit cards are not accepted.

Denali Bluffs Hotel $$$$
Mile 238.4 Parks Highway
(907) 683–7000, (800) 276–7234
www.denalinationalpark.com

One of four hotels operated by Aramark, the park concessionaire, in conjunction with Doyon, an Alaskan Native Corporation, the Denali Bluffs includes several modern buildings in a village-type arrangement near the park entrance. The landscaped facilities fea-

ture sitting rooms and a stone fireplace in the lobby for lounging after a full day of sightseeing in the park. Many of the 112 rooms have private balconies with views of the Alaska Range. Each room is decorated in Alaskan theme and includes two double beds, satellite TV, coffeemaker, minifridge, and private bath. Special facilities include an on-site gift shop and wheelchair-accessible rooms. A full range of activities can be booked at the tour desk, and the Mountaineer Pub and Grille offers a full-service menu (see the listing in the Restaurants section below). This is a pet-friendly (with deposit) hotel.

Denali Lakeview Inn $$
Mile 1.2 Otto Lake Road
(907) 683–4035
www.denalilakeviewinn.com

All rooms here look out over a stunning view of Otto Lake and the mountains beyond. Follow Otto Lake Road off Mile 247 of the Parks Highway, 10 miles north of the park entrance, and you'll discover this modern lodge-type inn perched beside the water. Huge windows in the great room frame picture-perfect vistas. Within walking distance you'll find a restaurant, a nine-hole golf course, walking trails, covered wagon rides, ATV rentals, and canoe and paddleboat rentals. Sporting such fun names as Purple Caribou, Blue Moose, and Northern Sky, the inn's ample rooms are decorated by theme and feature cushion-top mattresses, coffeemakers, microwaves, minifridges, and deck access. Half of the rooms have jetted tubs, and there are wheelchair-friendly facilities as well. All rooms have satellite televisions and telephones. In-room continental breakfast is included with the room rate. Some rooms have interconnecting doors to accommodate larger groups.

Denali Park Hotel $$
Mile 247 Parks Highway
(907) 683–1800, (866) 683–1800
www.denaliparkhotel.com

Surprisingly nice for the price, the Denali Park

Hotel offers comfortable, accessible (including wheelchair-accessible) rooms in the heart of the Denali wilderness area. It's nothing fancy and it's located along the highway, but the facility is one story, so you don't have to worry about noise from upstairs. Each room comes equipped with coffeemaker, microwave, and minifridge, and pets are welcome with a pet deposit. Just 10 miles north of the park entrance, the hotel is well-situated for excursions into Denali. As a bonus, the hotel has three vintage railroad cars on-site. Circa 1943, these troop-carrying cars house the lobby, restaurant, and hotel offices, but they're also available for guests to take a quick look and snap a photo or two.

Denali Princess Wilderness Lodge $$$$
Mile 238.5 Parks Highway
(907) 683–2282, (800) 426–0500
www.princesslodges.com

Though the lodge caters to tour groups, approximately half the guests at Denali Princess are independent travelers. Located 1 mile north of the park entrance, the hotel overlooks a spectacular vista of the Nenana River and the Alaska Range; you can take in the view while soaking in one of the hotel's outdoor hot tubs or relaxing on the deck. Patterned after the great National Park Lodges, the Denali Princess features a massive 50-foot mural of the mountain, grand staircases, and a 65-foot river-rock fireplace. You'll have plenty of dining options with the hotel's many eateries, including the Base Camp Lounge, The River Run Deli and Espresso, the Lynx Creek Pizza, and the elegant Summit restaurant. You can pick up souvenirs at one of the Courtyard Shops or take in the Music of Denali Dinner Theatre. Meeting rooms and exercise equipment also are available, and there's an Internet cafe and kiosk. You can even check out a climbing demonstration. Room choices include standard, riverfront, deluxe, or suites. With the Princess connection, you'll be able to sign up for a variety of tours from the hotel desk, and free transfers are available from the Denali Train Depot and the park's visitor center. Rooms are wheelchair accessible.

Grande Denali Lodge $$$$
Mile 238.2 Parks Highway
(907) 683–5100, (800) 276–7234
www.denalinationalpark.com

From a peaceful mountain setting just north of the park entrance, the Grande Denali offers 154 ample rooms plus six cabins that accommodate five guests each. In the guest rooms, you'll find two queen-size beds, telephone with dataport, television, hair dryer, private bath, coffeemaker, and air-conditioning (once in a while you'll need it, even up here in the mountains). The log cabins offer similar features, but there's one queen-size bed, a double sofa sleeper, and a twin sofa sleeper, plus a microwave and private deck. There's daily shuttle service to and from the train depot, visitor center, and other nearby facilities. On-site you'll also find a gift shop, self-service laundry, and tour desk. Enjoy fine dining at the hotel's Alpenglow Restaurant (see listing the Restaurants section below). The Grande Denali is pet friendly with a deposit and wheelchair accessible.

Bed-and-Breakfasts

Denali Dome Home
Bed and Breakfast $$$
137 Healy Spur Road
(907) 683–1239, (800) 683–1239
www.denalidomehome.com

Guests at this 7,200-square-foot home on five private acres just 12 miles north of the park entrance are treated to Alaskan-style comfort and privacy. Hosts Terry and Ann Miller opened for business in 1990, and they love to share stories of their Alaskan adventures while cooking made-to-order breakfasts of eggs, sausages, pancakes, or French toast. Fresh fruit, cereals, special breads, and muffins are offered as well. In addition to cooking a great breakfast, Terry knows road conditions, fixes tires, and offers his take on the best shopping, restaurants, and trails in the area. Each of the seven rooms has either a queen- or king-size bed, and some also have twin beds. Private baths, minifridges, telephones, and jetted tubs are standard. Guests may use business facilities in the office. For more relaxing fare, enjoy the Alaskan library, the cozy fireplaces, and splendid views of the northern lights, darkness and solar activity permitting. Parts of the home are wheelchair accessible. Two resident Scotties plus the Miller children will help you feel at home.

**Denali Touch of Wilderness
B&B Inn** $$$
Mile 2.9 Stampede Road, Healy
(907) 683–2459, (800) 683–2459
www.touchofwildernessbb.com
Nestled in the woods along what was the original Stampede Trail, this nine-room B&B offers fabulous views of the Alaska Range. Guests enjoy relaxing by the fire or in the outdoor hot tub. The home-style inn features your choice of continental or hearty breakfasts, including dishes such as French toast and reindeer sausage or crepes with hollandaise sauce and bacon. All rooms have private baths, telephones, and hair dryers; most have either a country or Victorian theme, with quilts and soft colors. Satellite TV and computer access are available in the common areas, along with a selection of books, movies, and games. Guests also share a kitchenette with refrigerator, microwave, coffeemaker, and sink. One room is wheelchair accessible. The inn is open year-round and hosts retreats in the off-season, including a two-day spa package for Valentine's Day.

Cabins and Hostels

Denali's Crow's Nest Log Cabins $$$
Mile 238.5 Parks Highway
(907) 683–2723, (888) 917–8130
www.denalicrowsnest.com
Every room boasts a lovely view at this locally owned and operated establishment situated as close as you can get to the park entrance—about 1 mile north. With 39 rooms, they're small enough to give personal attention to their guests, offering hotel com-

forts with an Alaskan flair. The cabins aren't plush (no in-room phones or TVs) and they're right next to each other, but from the vantage point on Sugarloaf Mountain, you'll enjoy great views of Horseshoe Lake and the Nenana River. There's an outdoor hot tub for guests, and the Overlook Bar and Grill offers a cozy gathering spot with 76 varieties of beer and a full menu, including box lunches. Courtesy shuttles run to the park and railroad depot, and tour bookings are available.

Denali Mountain Morning Hostel $
Mile 224.5 Parks Highway
(907) 683–7503
www.hostelalaska.com
If you're just looking for a place to lay your head while visiting the big park, Denali Mountain Morning Hostel offers a great budget alternative. Unlike some of the "strip mall" cabin complexes, Denali Mountain's facilities are grouped in a cozy cluster beside Carlo Creek, 13 miles south of the park entrance, with a stunning mountain backdrop. The hostel features single or double bunks with access to a fully equipped kitchen and hot shower, or guests may opt for private rooms and cabins, including a creekside cabin that sleeps eight. Your enthusiastic hosts offer free shuttle service to the park four times daily as well as backpacking gear rental and sales. There's also a tour desk, Internet access, lounge, and store, plus three restaurants nearby.

The EarthSong Lodge $$–$$$
P.O. Box 89, Healy, AK 99743
(907) 683–2863
www.earthsonglodge.com
Seventeen miles north of the crowded Denali

i Study up on the many wonders of Denali before you arrive. The Alaska Natural History Association features a large assortment of books, DVDs, and maps that will add to the fun of your grand adventure. Check them out at www.alaskanha.org.

National Park hotels, this hand-built lodge featured in *National Geographic* and *Conde Nast Traveler* boasts 12 unique, charming cabins offering privacy and sweeping views of the mountains. Hosts Jon and Karin Nierenberg are dogsled concessionaires for the park, so kennel tours and dogsled rides (for a fee) are among the special amenities here. Cabin sizes range from the standard, sleeping two in a double bed, to two-bedroom cabins that accommodate families. All have private baths, hair dryers, fans, coffeemakers, and wireless Internet access. Enjoy breakfast and dinner as well as an espresso bar at Henry's coffeehouse, where you can also take in a slide show presented by the staff naturalist most evenings. Packaged lunches may be ordered for takeout.

McKinley Creekside Cabins $$
Mile 224 Parks Highway
(907) 683–2277, (888) 533–6254
www.mckinleycabins.com
On beautiful Carlo Creek beneath the breathtaking Alaska Range, McKinley Creekside Cabins are a world apart from the busy park entrance area. Thirteen miles south of the park, guests enjoy local color with the adjunct McKinley Creekside Café, a popular eatery (see the Restaurants section below). You'll find affordable cabins with a relaxed and friendly atmosphere where guests are treated like friends. Thirty units with full- and queen-size beds are available, all with coffeemakers, minifridges, linens, and private baths; some have microwaves. There's a northwoods feel to the cabins, and most of the beds feature handmade log posts crafted by one of the locals. There's no in-room phone or TV, but you can

i For a real learning experience, check out the small group classes, field seminars, and research internships offered by the Denali Institute. The schedule is updated each December for the following summer. Call (888) 688–1269 or e-mail courses@denaliinstitute.org for more information.

get your entertainment the old-fashioned way by meeting fellow travelers around the creekside campfire pit, the outdoor grill, or the horseshoe pit. There's a family suite cabin, and children will love the playground. One cabin offers wheelchair access.

Motel Nord Haven $$
Mile 249.5 Parks Highway, Healy
(907) 683–4500, (800) 683–4501
www.motelnordhaven.com
Just off the Parks Highway in Healy, you'll find a comfortable, affordable option in the Motel Nord Haven. In business since 1994, the motel has 28 rooms, all with queen-size beds. With your room, you'll get a free morning paper plus continental breakfast in the summer season. There are four kitchenettes set up for microwave cooking. Ironing boards, irons, roll-aways, and cribs are available at no extra charge. They have a nice collection of Alaskan art on display, and they offer meeting rooms with catering as well. Two rooms have wheelchair access. The motel is open year-round, and a knowledgeable local resident is always on-site to assist with your phone inquiries.

Campgrounds and RV Parks

Denali Grizzly Bear Cabins and Campground
Mile 231 Parks Highway
(907) 683–2696, (866) 583–2696
A dizzying array of options awaits the weary traveler here, from tent cabins with no linens, no heat, no water, and no electricity to modern cabins with linens, heat, electricity, running water, and private riverfront decks. Basic campsites and RV hookups are available, too. Owned and operated by an Alaskan pioneer family, the Denali Grizzly Bear is 6 miles south of the park entrance, just off the highway. Each cabin is unique, with older buildings reassembled on-site and newer dwellings built with milled logs and tongue-and-groove walls. You can drive to each of the cabins, but you must walk in from nearby parking areas to the riverside tent sites. There's a tour desk to assist with activities, but no shuttle service

is provided to the park. Rates range from $19 for a campsite to $188 for a cabin with full kitchen and bath set up to sleep six.

Denali National Park Campgrounds
(907) 272–7275
www.reservedenali.com

Within the park itself, the Denali National Park concessionaire, Aramark, operates 5 campgrounds. Riley Creek, right at the park entrance, offers 146 sites for RVs and tents and is open year-round. All other campgrounds are open only during the summer season, with Wonder Lake (for tents only) opening later than the rest due to the higher altitude. Savage River has 33 sites for RVs and tents, with 3 sites for large groups. At Sanctuary River, only tents are allowed, while the Teklanika River Campground is for hard-sided campers only.

Campground use may be restricted or closed in response to wildlife activity. In 2001, for instance, the Igloo Campground was closed due to wolf activity, but it may be returned to normal use when the wolves move on. Check on-line for up-to-date information on such closures.

Like most everything within the park, the reservations system for campgrounds is a bit complicated and subject to change. Generally, you can make reservations online or by fax beginning December 1 of the year prior to your stay. Faxed requests must be received at least two days prior to travel, and mail-in requests must be received at least 30 days in advance. Keep in mind that Denali National Park is one of the premier Alaskan vacation destinations, so the sooner you make your reservations, the better. Check online for current fees, restrictions, and cancellation policies. If you're tent camping beyond Riley Creek, remember to reserve a spot on the shuttle or camper bus as well. Note that there is a maximum total stay of 14 nights per year within the park's established campgrounds.

Fees range from $12 and up for walk-in camping to $19 and up for RV facilities. The cheaper options have pit toilets. There are no RV hookups at park campgrounds. As an added plus to camping in the park, you can opt to attend free ranger-led campground programs, informal 30- to 45-minute presentations on a wide range of topics. Schedules are posted on bulletin boards throughout the park.

Denali RV Park and Motel
Mile 245.1 Parks Highway
(907) 683–1500, (800) 478–1501
www.denalirvparkcom

Ninety full and partial RV hookups are available here, ranging in price from $18 to $28. There's also a dump station and 30-amp electrical plugins, and there's even seven-channel cable TV at most sites. Bathrooms and showers are private; showers cost $2.00 for five minutes. The campground/motel complex features laundry facilities, pay phones, a gift shop (with free coffee), and an outdoor cooking area. You'll find the campground 8 miles north of the park entrance. Enjoy hiking trails and terrific views of the Alaska Range. If you get tired of camping out, you can opt for one of the 14 motel rooms starting at $79 per night. Reservations are recommended.

RESTAURANTS

Given the park's remote location and distance from major urban areas, there's a surprising array, if not a huge number, of choices when it comes to dining. In addition to the restaurants, bars, and grilles housed in the area's major hotels, you'll find fun local spots offering everything from trendy cuisine to no-frills steak and potatoes, though there's not much ethnic cuisine available.

Given the limited numbers, we've left the restaurants uncategorized here. If you're trying to maximize your daylight time in the park, or if you're taking one of those long shuttle-bus rides, you might want to pick up a box lunch, offered at most of Denali's casual dining establishments.

For the most part, reservations aren't needed at these eateries, but you can assume they will take them unless otherwise noted. Most facilities offer some wheelchair access, so we'll note only those that do not. Major credit cards are accepted almost everywhere, so bring your plastic. Many of these restaurants, particularly the ones associated with hotels, are only open seasonally, from the end of May to the beginning of September, or thereabouts. We'll note those that are open year-round.

The price codes show what you can expect to pay for dinner for two, not including appetizers, cocktails, dessert, and tips.

Price Codes

$. . . . . Less than $30
$$ . . . . $30–$45
$$$ . . . . $46–$60
$$$$ . . . . More than $60

Alpenglow Restaurant $$$$
Grande Denali Lodge
Mile 238.2 Parks Highway
(907) 683–5100, (800) 276–7234

Offering fine dining with a mountain view, this Alaskan steak house serves up regional favorites along with chef-inspired creations. Featuring Hurst Ranch organic beef, the Alpenglow also promotes sustainable cuisine by using organically grown vegetables from a supplier in Alaska's fertile Matanuska-Susitna Valley. Baked French Onion Soup, Prime Rib of Beef, a 24-ounce porterhouse steak, and filet mignon are among the favorites on the menu. For a side dish, try the Chugiak Grains, a custom blend of rices and other whole grains. There's a full bar along with a generous selection of wines and desserts. Open seasonally for breakfast, lunch, and dinner.

Black Diamond Resort Company $$$
Otto Lake Road, Mile 247 Parks Highway
(907) 683–4653

For fresh Italian and American food, this is a great Denali-area find. Ask the friendly, accommodating waitstaff to seat you at one of the restaurant's big windows so you can take in the panoramic mountain view while you enjoy specialties such as Fresh Grilled Alaskan Salmon and Herb-Crusted Prime Rib. All entrees come with a choice of Caesar salad, mixed green salad, or homemade soup. Sides include risotto, seasonal vegetables, grilled vegetable skewers, and Yukon Gold baked potatoes with all the fixings. Beer and wine are available with your meal. Nestled beside a small lake, the restaurant is off the beaten path, but it's worth the trip. Open year-round.

Courtyard Café $
McKinley Chalet
Mile 238 Parks Highway
(907) 683–8200, (800) 276–7234

If you're looking for a simple, hearty meal close to the park, this is the place. You'll know you've found it when you see the glass-cased, floor-to-ceiling rotisserie oven. The cafe has a casual feel, with both indoor and (on those warmer days) outdoor seating. There's a big breakfast buffet daily, featuring fruits, cold cereals, and pastries, plus a full lineup of eggs and meats. At lunch, try their homemade soups and generous sandwiches, or sample the salad bar. Carving stations with slabs of meat are set up for both lunch and dinner. One of a couple of restaurants claiming Denali's best burgers, the Courtyard is open all day long, serving dinner as well.

McKinley Creekside Café $$
McKinley Creekside Cabins
Mile 224 Parks Highway
(907) 683–2277, (888) 533–6254

Here's a chance to mingle with Denali locals hanging out on the creekside deck and basking in the long rays of the summer sun. The Creekside, as locals call it, is an A-frame cafe popular for its breathtaking views and tasty Alaskan fare. Two enterprising women opened with a tiny eatery and a few cabins back in 1997, and their business has been growing by leaps and bounds ever since. Try the Alaskan Baked Salmon with apples, brown sugar, and almonds; Alaskan Baked Halibut smothered in a creamy sauce of artichoke hearts, spinach, and Parmesan cheese; the Coconut Salmon and Chips; or Holly's Homemade Chili and Cornbread. The Creekside is open seasonally for breakfast, lunch, and dinner. Beer and wine are available. You'll find the cafe 13 miles south of the park entrance, and there's a gravel parking lot in front. While reservations are not required, they appreciate advance notice for large groups.

Mountaineer Pub and Grille $$$
Denali Bluffs Hotel
Mile 238.4 Parks Highway
(907) 683–7000, (800) 276–7234

If you're looking for fun, casual dining, the Mountaineer Pub and Grille offers Alaskan-brewed beers and microbrews along with a full menu for breakfast, lunch, and dinner. There's something for everyone on the eclectic menu, from such comfort foods as Baked Macaroni and Cheese to their popular Caesar salad and Alaskan Salmon Chowder, served in a fresh bread bowl. There's a wide assortment of burgers, including the salmon burger, and sandwiches, too. The Wild Turkey Wrap is a popular choice. You'll find the Alaskan-themed restaurant inside the Denali Bluffs Hotel.

Nenana View Bar and Grille $$$$
McKinley Chalet Resort
Mile 238 Parks Highway
(907) 683–8200, (800) 276–7234

Fireside dining with stunning river views, along with a diverse menu, create the draw at the Nenana View Bar and Grille, located within Aramark's McKinley Chalet Resort. Fresh from the huge wood-fired oven, enjoy such specialty pizzas as the Solstice, with sun-dried tomatoes, spinach, onion, and goat cheese, or the Grande Alaskan, with smoked salmon, carmelized onions, mushrooms, roasted red peppers, and provolone. Lamb shanks, Caribou Tenderloin, and Kodiak Diver Scallops seared with spinach, fennel, and saffron are popular entrees. This place offers the largest wine selection between Anchorage and Fairbanks, pouring some 80 wines by the glass. The Nenana View Bar, with log decor and a river

view, sports a menu of appetizers and entrees. For those who burned a whole bunch of calories hiking around the park, the bar hosts a late-night "Hungry Hour" featuring complimentary snacks and half-price menu items.

Rabideau's Clear Sky Lodge $$$
Mile 280 Parks Highway
(907) 582–2251

For hearty, traditional fare in a big-woods setting, you can't beat Rabideau's. The restaurant is rustic but clean, with a log bar and animal hides on the walls. It's a great place to mingle with the locals, including servicemen from nearby Clear, and enjoy a steak or burger. Their claim to fame is steak, with the 12-ounce New York steak and steak sandwiches as popular fare. Open since 1961, Rabideau's is a real sourdough establishment. They serve lunch and dinner, and they're open year-round. There's a full bar and ample parking, but the restaurant is not wheelchair accessible. Reservations are accepted only for parties of eight or more.

Rose's Café $
Mile 249.5 Parks Highway, Healy
(907) 683–7673

Here's a clean, family-oriented cafe that serves traditional roadside fare for tourists, locals, and workers in the area. Large windows, front and back, showcase mountain views. Forget your diet and indulge in cafe favorites, such as the Crispy Chicken Burger with Ham and Cheese, the Bacon Burger with Fries, the Denali omelet, or the Plate-Size Pancakes. Still hungry? There's always the one-pound Grizzly Burger with ham, egg, Swiss, and American cheese. The cafe also features

i It might be hard to imagine, but 70 million years ago, dinosaurs roamed the area that is now Denali National Park. In 2006, a unique three-toed print was discovered at the park. Scientists speculate that the creature resembled an ostrich, but had teeth, a tail, and arms instead of wings.

The Great One

It's a big mountain, so it's no surprise that it comes with big controversies, big dreams, and big risks.

The controversies begin with the simple matter of its name. In 1896, prospector William Dickey made a political statement in favor of the gold standard by naming the mountain after Presidential nominee William McKinley of Ohio. But Alaskans refer to the mountain as Denali, one of its traditional Athabascan names, commonly translated as "the great one" but more accurately meaning "the high one." Proponents of the traditional moniker point out that President McKinley never visited the state and had little to do with it during his short and rather undistinguished term as president. Moreover, they say, naming a geographic feature after a person is not in keeping with Alaska Native traditions.

In 1975, Gov. Jay Hammond, with the support of the Alaska Legislature and the Alaska Board of Geographic Names, appealed to the U.S Board of Geographic Names for an official name change. But the Ohio congressional delegation fought back with what has become an annual stall tactic: introducing federal legislation to attach the name McKinley permanently to the mountain. So far, the ploy has worked. The U.S. Board of Names has a long-standing policy of not considering changes while legislation is pending, and legislation on this matter seems to be perpetually pending. The only concession to the state's request has been an official change in the name of the park from Mount McKinley National Park to Denali National Park and Preserve.

Then there's the controversy over who was first to scale the mountain. There's no disputing the claims of the Stuck expedition, which included Alaska Native Walter Harper, to the first ascent of the true summit, the higher south peak. Stuck, by the way, insisted on calling the mountain Denali, out of respect for the Native people whom he served as Episcopal archdeacon of the Yukon. However, two parties made earlier claims to reaching the top. The 1910 Sourdough Expedition planted a spruce pole at the top of the north peak but provided no evidence of mounting the south peak. Even earlier, in 1906, Dr. Frederick Cook claimed his expedition reached the summit, but the photograph he offered as evidence proved to be of a lesser peak. The debate over the validity of Cook's ascent continues to rage.

Most visitors are content with just seeing the 20,320-foot peak. Or maybe it's 20,306 feet, according to a survey done in 1989—that's another controversy. But the dream eludes many. Depending on who you talk to, there's a 20 to 40 percent chance of actually seeing the mountain on any given day. It's tall enough to make its own weather, and that means lots of clouds. The lucky ones are treated to a magnificent sight. The south slope rises 17,000 feet in just 12 miles, making for a spectacular vista.

If you really want to see the mountain, you can try scaling it yourself. It's no small feat, fraught with risks, but enough quasi-amateurs have tried that it's earned the dubious distinction of "the midlife crisis mountain." In no uncertain terms, the Park Service warns that ascents should not be attempted by the unprepared, the uninitiated, or the inexperienced.

Would-be climbers must register at the Talkeetna Ranger Station 60 days in advance of their trek, pay the requisite fees, and attend to the rules, regulations, and advice of those who know what they're in for. Though there are some 30 routes up the mountain, the West Buttress route (also known as "The Butt") is by far the most popular. Climbers fly in by ski plane from Talkeetna to the base camp at 7,200 feet and then work their way up the slope in an average of 17 days. During the short climbing season from May through July, the route is not exactly a wilderness journey, as several hundred climbers follow the same route up and back.

Though the climb is not technically difficult, the hazards are many. Bad weather often strikes without warning, spinning off a semipermanent low pressure area near the Aleutian Islands. Strong storms also can move in from the Gulf of Alaska, bringing hurricane-force winds and swirling snow. Even when the skies are clear, winds at the summit may exceed 100 mph—strong enough to toss unsuspecting climbers down the mountain. Winter climbing? Don't even think about it. Even the most experienced have disappeared or been found flash-frozen from wind chills so cold that they're off the charts.

Rescue operations are perilous for everyone. Climbers are warned to be self-sufficient and not depend on others to bail them out of dangerous situations. Solo climbers are particularly at risk, given the deadly crevasses that crisscross the glaciers. Crevasses may be either faintly visible or not visible at all, and the strength of snow bridges may not be easily discernible. For a well-roped climber in a group, these hazards are merely frightening; for the solo climber, they may end up providing a final resting place.

Proper gear is essential. Climbers need double boots with vapor barriers (Alaskans call the military variety "bunny boots"), worn with several pairs of socks. To avoid trench foot, which can be as debilitating as frostbite, feet must be kept dry at night. Sleeping bags must be large enough to accommodate extra layers of clothes, inner boots, and a water bottle. Each person in the party needs a pair of snowshoes or skis to help "float" hidden crevasses. Snow shovels, snow saws, expedition-quality tents, rope, ice axes, crampons, snow and ice anchors, eye protection, medical kits, sleds, stoves, radio—the list of necessities is long and crucial. In addition, you'll need three weeks' worth of food that will provide 4,000 to 5,000 calories per person per day and at least four liters of fluid per person per day.

At Latitude 60, the barometric pressure is lower than in more southerly climes, so Denali is more like a peak of 23,000 feet in terms of its physiological effects on climbers. Acute mountain sickness and its deadly counterparts, high altitude cerebral edema and high altitude pulmonary edema, are among the hazards to be reckoned with. Frostbite, diarrhea, and dehydration threaten climbers as well. Mountaineers on Denali also have died of carbon monoxide poisoning, the result of poorly vented ice-glazed igloos and snow caves.

With the lack of oxygen at high altitudes, climbers can become their own worst enemies as mental function is impaired. Bradford Washburn, pioneer of the mountain's West Buttress route, ran his stranded party through a series of mathematics problems at 18,200 feet and found it took them twice as long to answer as it did at the 7,000-foot base camp. In other words, their mental function was decreased by 50 percent. Experienced climbers admit that impaired judgment and apathy can set in along with irritability and phobias, leading to them potentially risking both life and limb.

(cont'd)

(cont'd)

Every summer, reports of accidents and fatalities at Denali are common fare in Alaskan newspapers. Most of these, according to the Denali Park Rangers, could have been prevented by better planning and judgment, including preparation for worst-case weather scenarios. The Great One is nothing to fool around with.

homemade pies, cakes, and desserts. Sack lunches are available for takeout. Rose's is open year-round, seven days a week, serving breakfast, lunch, and dinner. There's plenty of parking, even for big RVs. You'll find the cafe about 12 miles north of the park entrance, next to the Motel Nord Haven in Healy.

Summit Dining Room $$$
Denali Princess Wilderness Lodge
Mile 238.5 Parks Highway
(907) 683–2282, (800) 426–0500
Overlooking the Nenana River Canyon near the entrance to Denali National Park, the Summit Dining Room offers a fine-dining experience complete with live music and, yes, real linens. Tables on three levels offer unobstructed views from a huge wall of windows. The menu features Alaskan cuisine with an emphasis on Northwest specialties and wines. Favorites include Tenderloin Medallions sautéed in ginger soy sauce and served with toasted garlic Parmesan baguette slices, and the Alaskan King Crab, featuring a full pound of king crab legs split, steamed, and served with drawn butter and lemon. Despite its distance from major urban areas, the restaurant makes a point to serve only the freshest produce. Open seasonally for breakfast, lunch, and dinner, there's a full bar and ample parking. Tourists and locals alike enjoy the casual elegance of the Summit Dining Room.

NIGHTLIFE

With Alaska's long summer days, there's not a whole lot of night, or nightlife, at Denali

National Park, but locals and visitors alike enjoy relaxing at local bars and swapping tales of their adventures. In addition to the hotel bars, try the Overlook, with great views of the Nenana River and Horseshoe Lake. They offer courtesy transportation anywhere in the Denali park area (907–683–2723). Another local favorite is the bar at the Cantwell Lodge, a roadhouse dating from the 1930s that features blue jeans and T-shirt hospitality (907–786–2300, 800–768–5522).

For more structured entertainment, you can take in a show at one of the park hotels. To find out what it's like to scale North America's highest peak, check out the Climb Denali Show ($19) at the Grande Denali Lodge. An experienced mountaineer demonstrates techniques, recounts his adventures, and provides a virtual climbing experience in a dazzling multimedia presentation. For more information, contact the folks at the Peak Experience Theatre (907–683–8500, 866–683–8500, www.denalialaska.com).

You can enjoy song, dance, and stories while feasting on a family-style meal served by one of the actors at the Denali Dinner Theatre, located in the Denali Princess Wilderness Lodge. Nightly shows at 5:30 and 8:30 P.M. feature tales of the pioneers who first conquered the mountain.

For more classical entertainment, there's the nightly 35-minute photo-symphony show *Denali: Song of the Land* at the Mt. Foraker Room at the McKinley Princess Hotel. Here's your chance to catch the northern lights, filmed for summer viewers, along with spectacular photo views of Denali's wildlife and scenery.

RELOCATION

Adventure and opportunity bring people to Alaska. Those who stay just for the money are among the most miserable, while those with an affinity for the place are among the happiest.

Billed as the land of opportunity, Alaska has drawn seekers of fortune since the Klondike Gold Rush of 1898. Construction of the oil pipeline in the 1970s brought another wave of workers who put up with remote job sites and rugged living conditions in exchange for cash. Even today you'll find opportunities in Alaska that are hard to find elsewhere. Young workers can rise quickly to positions of authority, and paychecks in many sectors of the economy reflect healthy wages.

Since the late 1980s, Anchorage has experienced steady economic growth. Anchorage still serves as a major administrative and supply center for oil and gas development. Expansion of the port of Anchorage is under way in anticipation of a $20 billion natural gas pipeline project that has been discussed for several years. After a disastrous plunge in oil prices in the mid-1980s, the state has paid close attention to economic diversification, so subsequent dips in oil prices have not had nearly the same impact. One in 10 Anchorage jobs is related to air travel, with top-of-the-world cargo flights increasing at rates topping 5 percent each year. Tourism is increasing at about the same rate. The oil industry, while still a major player in the state's economy, employs only about 1 percent of the workers in Anchorage, albeit at wages that are twice the city's average.

Unemployment rates in Anchorage typically run around 5 percent. Keep in mind that though wages may be good, the cost of living is also high, with expenses in all categories except utilities running higher than the national average. Thankfully, tax rates are low.

There is no state income tax, and no sales tax is collected in Anchorage. Specialty taxes include an 8 percent bed tax, aircraft tax, rental car tax, fuel tax, tobacco tax, and alcohol tax. Property tax rates run from 10 to 14 mills. Overall, the cost of living is roughly comparable to that of Seattle. It's important to remember, though, that when you relocate to Anchorage, you're a long way from wherever you began, and getting back even for an occasional visit can be expensive.

Alaska is no longer a place where men far outnumber women. In Anchorage, the demographics are nearly even, with a population that's 48.7 percent female and 51.3 percent male. One out of 11 Anchorage residents was born in a country other than the United States, and one in seven speaks a second language at home. Nearly 10 percent of the city's residents consist of military personnel and their families. The average age of Anchorage residents is 32.4, and the number of those older than age 65 is expected to climb to 11 percent by 2020.

REAL ESTATE

Only decades ago, newcomers to Alaska were able to pick up prime parcels of land as 40-acre homesteads. A few of the big homesteads remain as private property, but most have long since been subdivided to provide smaller building lots throughout Anchorage and the rest of Southcentral Alaska.

With more than 586,000 square miles of land, Alaska is almost one-fifth the size of the continental United States. When Alaska achieved statehood in 1959, the federal government allowed the state to select 104 million acres from what was essentially all federal land. By 1967 the state had identified 26 mil-

Close-up

Anchorage and the Military

A glance at the globe shows why the Anchorage area is home to two strategic military posts, Fort Richardson and Elmendorf Air Force Base. Over-the-pole air routes to Europe and Asia make Alaska the perfect quick-response site for action on a variety of fronts.

Located on 13,000 acres just north of downtown Anchorage, with additional access from the Glenn Highway, Elmendorf is the largest Air Force base in the state. The base is home to the 3rd Wing of the Pacific Air Forces, the Eleventh Air Force, and the Alaskan NORAD Region. It also serves as headquarters for the Alaskan Command.

The original Elmendorf Field, named after a key Army Air Force commander who was killed while testing an experimental aircraft in 1933, was part of Fort Richardson, but in 1948 it was reconfigured into an Air Force base. During the Cold War era, the base's NORAD headquarters monitored communications and radar systems in Alaska, including the White Alice radar sites that can still be seen in remote areas throughout the state.

Under the motto "Top Cover for America," the base saw its peak activity during the 1950s, when nearly 200 fighter aircraft were positioned at either Elmendorf or Ladd Field in Fairbanks. Today the four groups of Elmendorf's 3rd Wing support five squadrons that provide primary air defense for the North Pacific. In addition, the base hosts visiting squadrons from around the world during the Air Force's large-scale Cope Thunder exercises.

East of Elmendorf is Fort Richardson, with access from the Glenn Highway. This 25,000-acre army post is bordered by the waters of the Knik Arm to the north and by Chugach State Park to the south and east. Fort Richardson is the headquarters for the United State Army, Alaska (USARAK), with a capacity of 2,175 soldiers, the primary unit being the 1st Battalion (Airborne) of the 501st Infantry.

Fort Richardson, like the Richardson Highway to the east, was named for Brig. Gen. Wilds P. Richardson, who commanded troops along the Yukon River and supervised construction of many of the roads, bridges, and railroads that aided in settlement of the region. Established during the early years of World War II, the post was moved to its present location in the 1950s. After overseeing operation of three off-post Nike-Hercules Missile sites and serving as headquarters for the 172nd Infantry, Fort Richardson now concentrates on providing a deployable combat force in support of the 172nd, which was recently moved to Fort Wainwright in Fairbanks.

lion acres, but land claims were frozen as Native groups asserted their rights to various parcels. With the discovery of oil at Prudhoe Bay the following year, there was a fury of interest in settling the Native lands issue so that development could be pursued. Native corporations were formed and authorized to select 44 million acres in federal lands in Alaska under the Alaska Native Claims Settlement Act (ANCSA). Individuals hold title to

The entrance to Elmendorf Air Force Base is located on Government Hill, just north of downtown Anchorage. DEB VANASSE

On post, soldiers and their families enjoy access to medical and dental facilities, a theater, a commissary, golf and ski courses, cross-country trails, two elementary schools, libraries, and a craft shop. The post is unique in its commitment to wildlife conservation, with fox, bear, eagles, and moose among the populations found there.

Military personnel from both Fort Richardson and Elmendorf were instrumental in providing emergency services to the Anchorage area in the aftermath of the 1964 Good Friday Earthquake. Soldiers, Air Force personnel, and Department of Defense civilian employees also play a vital role in the economy of Anchorage, thanks to cost-of-living and housing allowances that make this "international" tour a popular choice for servicemen and women. While many of them arrive as transients, a good number sign on for extra rotations and even return after retirement to become permanent residents of the community.

much of this land, with the corporations retaining the rest.

Pressure from conservation groups to protect the remaining federal lands in Alaska led to the signing of the Alaska National Interest Lands Conservation Act (ANILCA) in 1980. This measure protected more than 100 million acres from development and expanded the national park system in Alaska by more than 43 million acres. The net result is that there's

i One benefit of using an Alaskan-based mortgage lender is that Alaska has a no-prepayment penalty law that applies to in-state financing. Out-of-state lenders may charge a prepayment penalty if you sell your house within a certain number of years. You also must use an Alaskan-based lender if you want to take advantage of any of the Alaska Housing Finance Corporation subsidies, such as the first-time homebuyer or five-star energy programs.

not a huge amount of land left for private development.

The state does occasionally release state land into private hands through a bidding process known as the Alaska State Land Offering program, administered by the Department of Natural Resources (DNR). On an as-available basis, the state puts together land-disposal packages and opens a period for sealed bids. Applicants must have a minimum of one year of Alaskan residency in order to bid for most parcels, but anyone can make purchases over the counter for the parcels that are not taken by bidding. For more information on this program, visit the land-sale page at www.dnr.state .ak.us. A Remote Recreational Cabin Sites Staking Program is also administered by the DNR.

The Alaska Housing Finance Corporation offers reduced interest rates on purchases by first-time homebuyers as well as on purchases of energy efficient homes rated through their five-star program. For more information on purchasing with the help of one of these programs, contact any Alaskan-based mortgage lender.

Property values throughout Southcentral Alaska have been on the rise in recent years, with Anchorage showing the greatest spike in prices. The average cost of a single family home on the Kenai Peninsula hovered between $150,000 and $160,000 in 2005, while the average home price in the Matanuska Valley pushed above $200,000 the same year. In Anchorage, the average sales price of a single family home edged above $315,000 in 2006.

Anchorage

Anchorage is running out of land. With Cook Inlet on one side and mountains on the others, areas for development in Anchorage are few and far between. New construction within the city is tapering off as builders and prospective buyers look north to Eagle River and beyond to the Matanuska Valley where land is more plentiful. South of Anchorage, prices in Girdwood are skyrocketing as well, as the town anchored by the Alyeska Ski Resort has become a trendy residential area that, with its towering mountains, also has little room for growth.

Land prices within Anchorage reflect the shortage of space. Lots in the upscale Hillside area run from $200,000 up, while lots in popular downtown neighborhoods such as Government Hill, South Addition, Turnagain, Huntington Park, and Geneva Woods may top $150,000. In fact, buyers are scooping up older homes in these original townsite areas and are either tearing them down to rebuild or embarking on massive renovation products that promise to keep these neighborhoods among the most sought after in town. South Anchorage, with its relatively new construction, is another popular location with buyers, but Midtown neighborhoods are starting to come into their own, too. Even rougher neighborhoods such as Mountain View are benefiting from revitalization efforts, including a new mall with entrances off Mountain View Drive.

Residential architecture throughout Anchorage, especially in newer homes, reflects the need to build on small, narrow lots. Builders such as the popular Spinell Homes favor designs stacking a portion of the house over the garage, the latter being considered by many to be an Alaskan necessity, though that has diminished a bit with the popularity of auto-start technology. Another interesting aspect of residential real estate in Anchorage is the mix of neighborhoods. Due to some irregular zoning practices from decades past, you'll find mobile home courts interspersed with residential neighborhoods in some of the older sections of town.

Coldwell Banker Fortune Properties
2525 C Street, Suite 100
(907) 562–7653, (800) 982–5205
www.wesellalaska.com
With an upscale office in a prime midtown location, Coldwell Banker Fortune maintains a commitment to customer service and cutting-edge technology. Their service guarantees both buyers and sellers a commitment to delivering professional assistance in all aspects of real estate transactions. With more than 30 Realtors in their Anchorage location and 5 in Eagle River, Coldwell Banker Fortune represents several builders and offers concierge services to their clients as well.

Prudential Jack White Real Estate
3801 Centerpoint Drive #400
(907) 563–5500, (800) 770–2001
www.jackwhite.com
With more than 300 Realtors in five offices throughout Anchorage, Eagle River, Girdwood, and the Mat-Su Valley, Prudential Jack White is one of the largest brokerages in town. This is a full-service agency, with services including residential sales and leasing, corporate and residential relocation, commercial sales and leasing, mortgage loan affiliates, property management, and property maintenance.

RE/MAX of Anchorage
110 West 38th Avenue, Suite 100
(907) 276–2761
http://remax-anchorage-alaska.com
A major player in the Anchorage real estate market since 1981, RE/MAX of Anchorage has 85 sales associates. True to the RE/MAX tradition of attracting some of the top-producing Realtors in their market, the Anchorage office boasts a higher number of experienced

i Especially when purchasing raw land, be sure to ask about access to the property. Some lower-priced parcels may lack road access. Even if there's a plat map showing roads to a property, not all of those roads may have been developed.

licensees, more Certified Residential Specialists, more Certified Relocation Professionals, and more Accredited Buyer Representatives than any other brokerage in the area.

Kenai Peninsula

Realtor Glenda Feeken of RE/MAX of the Peninsula reports that buyers can get more for their money on the Kenai Peninsula than in any other part of Southcentral Alaska. Second-home sales are strong, especially as prices continue to rise north of Anchorage. Riverfront homes can still be had for $500,000 and up, while riverfront lots may run up to $200,000 per acre. Feeken notes that deals can still be had on raw land with no view or waterfront.

After several years of relatively flat growth, the Homer real estate market is booming, according to broker Sharon Minsch of Alaska Real Estate in Homer. View properties are at a premium, and high-end condo projects are selling in the $500,000 range. Older homes in neighborhoods close to town put most services within walking distance, while on the outskirts of town there are several new subdivisions in the works. The trade-off for out-of-town living is dealing with septic systems and, in some cases, hauled water.

Alaska Real Estate in Homer
5260 Kachemak Drive, Homer
(907) 235–4090
www.realestateinhomer.com
Broker Sharon Minsch has been helping buyers relocate to Homer since 1984, so she knows what is needed for a smooth transition to your new home. She pays close attention to detail and is quick to respond to inquiries by phone or e-mail. Mail-outs of current listings, computer data, and even travel information are among the many services she provides in addition to all the usual sales and listing management.

Freedom Realty
502 Lake Street, Suite 2
Kenai
(907) 263–1690
www.freedomrealty.com

i If you're purchasing where city water and sewer services are not available, be sure to research well and septic issues. Well water in some parts of Alaska may contain arsenic or nitrates, which can be filtered through reverse osmosis systems. Septic system tests, though not required for most types of financing, can alert you to potentially expensive system repairs or replacements needed.

With offices in both Kenai and Soldotna, Freedom Realty has more than 15 licensees with experience in single-family, multifamily, lots and acreage, and commercial sales. They also represent the builders of the Mountain Rose retirement community project.

RE/MAX of Homer
412 East Pioneer Avenue, Suite 100
Homer
(907) 235–7733
The only franchised real estate brokerage on the Lower Peninsula, RE/MAX of Homer maintains a full staff of seasoned professionals to assist with residential and investment sales and purchases. Located in the center of the Homer business district, this RE/MAX office has maintained a strong community presence and a commitment to service since 1984.

RE/MAX of the Peninsula
100 Trading Bay Drive, Suite 6
Kenai
(907) 283–5888
Serving the central and upper Kenai Peninsula, RE/MAX provides full real estate services in Cooper Landing, Soldotna, Kasilof, Clam Gulch, Ridgeway, Kenai and North Kenai, and Sterling. You can expect assistance with buying and selling, relocation, commercial real estate, and raw land sales.

Matanuska-Susitna Valley

As buying a home in Anchorage becomes less and less affordable, growth is spilling out into the Mat-Su Valley, where a relative abundance of land not only keeps costs down but also affords buyers the kind of wooded acreage that most Alaskans covet. The Valley is a doable commute for servicepersons at both Elmendorf Air Force Base and Fort Richardson, making it a popular choice for military families. According to Realtor Kelly Fisher of Coldwell Banker Fortune Properties, appreciation in the Valley is strong, with a surge of residential construction keeping the market competitive for sellers of older homes. Among the popular subdivisions in the area are Serendipity Hills northwest of Wasilla, Equestrian Acres west of Palmer, and Settlers Bay on the Knik-Goose Bay Road. Buyers in the Valley should consult their real estate professionals about issues such as well/septic systems, restrictive covenants, and areas that are best for resale.

Coldwell Banker Fortune Properties
851 East Westpoint Drive, Suite 101
Wasilla
(907) 373–7653
The Wasilla branch of Coldwell Banker Fortune Properties is a full-service real estate brokerage with 20 sales associates to assist buyers and sellers with purchases in the Valley. They are fast becoming local leaders in electronic marketing, offering ready access to virtual tours and other media-based services. As relocation specialists for Cendant and USAA, Coldwell Banker deals with a large number of military buyers. Their concierge program offers clients access to preferred vendors for a variety of services.

RE/MAX of Wasilla
3161 East Palmer-Wasilla Highway
Suite 1, Wasilla
(907) 376–4515
Providing brokerage services in the Valley since 1983, RE/MAX of Wasilla has consistently been the leading office in sales, listings, and service. With a staff of more than 20 full-time professionals, RE/MAX offers a complete array of residential services. They also represent close to a dozen area builders.

ⓘ Perhaps due to our remote location, Alaskans tend to be on the cutting edge of technology in many realms, including real estate. Your Alaskan real estate professional can do an electronic search of all listings that meet your criteria and forward the results to you by e-mail. The search also can be set up to automatically notify you of new listings as they come on the market.

Valdez

Valdez has a small but steady market, with a limited number of residential developments in the core area and on the outskirts of town.

Sound Realty
Harbor Court Building
P.O. Box 1628
Valdez, AK 99686
(907) 835–5818
www.soundrealty.com
For assistance with rentals, land sales, commercial properties, and residential sales, Sound Realty is the point of contact in Valdez. Popular neighborhoods include Blueberry Hill, Alpine Woods Estate, Cottonwood Subdivision, and Robe River Subdivision. Visit their Web site for information on schools and neighborhoods as well as local listings.

EDUCATION

Despite the challenges of serving a huge geographic area and low population density, Alaska has a reputation for innovative, high-quality educational programs in its public school systems. As a result of the Molly Hootch court decision in the mid-1970s, the state is obligated to provide local schools even in remote areas as long as a minimum number of students are in attendance. Most students in Southcentral Alaska attend rather traditional schools, but there also are a handful of remote and nontraditional schools, including the innovative programs and services offered by the Chugach School District.

All public post-secondary institutions in Alaska are affiliated with the University of Alaska statewide system, which dates from 1916, when the Territorial Legislature created the Alaska Agricultural College and School of Mines. Today the university has campuses in Anchorage, Fairbanks, and Juneau as well as several satellite campuses at what were formerly part of the Alaska Community College system, which was restructured due to budget cuts in the late 1980s. Kenai Peninsula College, Matanuska-Susitna College, and Prince William Sound Community College are now affiliated with the University of Alaska Anchorage (UAA). In addition, UAA offers educational programs at Fort Richardson and Elmendorf Air Force Base.

Higher Education

Alaska Pacific University
4101 University Drive, Anchorage
(907) 564–8248, (800) 252–7528
www.alaskapacific.edu
Alaska Pacific University (APU) is an independent private university with an emphasis on liberal arts and pre-professional programs. Founded in 1959 as Alaska Methodist University, the university was reorganized and renamed Alaska Pacific University in 1977. Today the 200-acre campus serves more than 650 students per semester with a variety of four-year degree programs. With a student-teacher ratio of 12 to 1, students can expect a higher level of individual attention than they might get at a larger university. APU is fully accredited by the Northwest Association of Schools and Colleges.

Alaska Vocational Technical Center
809 Second Avenue, Seward
(907) 224–4141, (800) 478–5389
http://avtec.labor.state.ak.us/
Sanctioned by the Alaska Department of Labor and Workforce Development, the Alaska Vocational Technical Center (AVTEC) offers vocational and technical training in a variety of program areas, including automotive technology, business technology, culinary

arts, diesel and heavy equipment training, facility maintenance, industrial electricity, information technology, pipe welding, power plant operation, Web development technology, and welding technology. AVTEC's primary mission is to provide vocational education for Alaskan residents. Nonresidents may attend on a space-available basis, but the tuition is double what residents pay. Dormitories and apartments for students and their families are available.

Kenai Peninsula College
34820 College Drive, Soldotna
(907) 262–0330, (877) 262–0330
www.kpc.alaska.edu

Under the auspices of the University of Alaska Anchorage, Kenai Peninsula College (KPC) operates campuses in Soldotna, Homer, and Seward. In addition to offering two-year Associate of Arts and Associate of Science degrees in a number of fields, including Nursing, Paramedical Technology, Business, and Digital Arts, KPC also provides access to UAA distance delivery courses in several four-year degree programs, including Elementary Education, Psychology, Anthropology, and Fine Arts. Certificate programs in a number of vocational areas are available as well. The college offers a full range of student services, including academic advising, financial assistance, career counseling, and tutoring. Serving nearly 2,000 students at its various locations, KPC emphasizes small class sizes and personal attention.

The Kenai River Campus in Soldotna enjoys a prime riverfront location on nearly 300 acres, with classrooms, laboratories, vocational and computer facilities, a library and media center, an art gallery, a cafe, a career center, and a learning center for student use. At Homer's Kachemak Bay Campus, facilities include classrooms, a learning center, a science lab, student commons, a bookstore, and a library. The Resurrection Bay Extension Site in Seward uses high school classrooms for delivery of general education and personal enrichment courses. The Kenai

Peninsula College also offers on-site instruction in Anchorage through its Mining and Petroleum Training Service (MAPTS) program.

Matanuska-Susitna College
P.O. Box 2889
Palmer, AK 99645
(907) 745–9774
www.matsu.alaska.edu

Originally part of the statewide community college system, Matanuska-Susitna (Mat-Su) College is now affiliated with the University of Alaska Anchorage, serving approximately 1,650 students each semester. The campus has a 102,676-square-foot facility on the trunk road between Palmer and Wasilla, where the college offers courses leading to both Associate of Arts and Associate of Applied Science degrees. Vocational certificate programs in drafting, computer systems, refrigeration and heating, and information technology are also available.

Prince William Sound Community College
P.O. Box 97
Valdez, AK 99686
(907) 834–1600
www.pwscc.edu

Serving a geographic area of more than 44,000 square miles, this off-shoot of the University of Alaska Statewide system maintains a campus in Valdez with extensions in Cordova and Copper Basin. Baccalaureate programs in Human Services and Science and Technology are provided in conjunction with the University of Alaska Anchorage, with associate degree options in Disability Services, Industrial Technology, and Computer Information Systems as well as two-year general Associate of Arts and Theater programs. Each summer the college hosts the popular Last Frontier Theatre Conference. With the pipeline terminus right in Valdez, the community college also offers training and certificates in Industrial Technology, Oil Spill Response, Safety Management, and Electrical Power Generation.

University of Alaska Anchorage
3211 Providence Drive, Anchorage
(907) 786–1800
www.uaa.alaska.edu
As the parent school to all public post-secondary options in Southcentral Alaska, the University of Alaska Anchorage (UAA) serves more than 20,000 students every year. Vocational certificate, associate, baccalaureate, and masters degree programs are offered in more than 120 areas of study. The Anchorage campus has a student health center, learning resource center, library, and a variety of student services programs. The Seawolves athletic programs include a whole host of Division I and Division II competitive sports options. The university also hosts eight research institutes and centers. UAA and its affiliated campuses are accredited through the Northwest Association of Schools and Colleges.

Public Schools

Anchorage School District
P.O. Box 196614
Anchorage, AK 99519-6614
(907) 742–4312
www.asdk12.org
Anchorage has the largest school district in the state and the 86th largest in the country, with approximately 50,000 students attending district schools. There are 59 elementary schools, 9 middle schools, and 7 high schools. In addition, there is 1 middle/high school combination, 1 K–12 school, and 11 specialized programs and schools, including the King Career Center. Student test scores reflect performances that are higher than both national and state averages, and parent surveys show a high level of overall satisfaction with the district's programs and teachers.

The Anchorage School District also includes five charter schools. The Winterberry Charter School for kindergarten through grade six emphasizes creativity, the arts, and the imagination, with use of the Waldorf methods. Rigorous academic performance is the standard at the K–6 Aquarian Charter

i Cold and snow are expected here, so elementary students go out for daily recess as long as the ambient temperature or wind chill is higher than 10 degrees below zero. Our schools close less often for weather than in many other places around the country. Information about emergency closures is broadcast over local television and radio stations, but you also can sign up for e-mail notification by going to www.asdk12.org.

School. The Eagle Academy also emphasizes achievement of performance standards, while the K–12 Frontier Family Partnership facilitates homeschooling through individual learning plans. At Highland Tech High School, the focus is on entrepreneurship and a digital learning environment. For more information on any of the district's alternative options, contact the Charter School liaison at (907) 868–3103.

The district's student population represents a rich diversity of cultures, with 42 percent of the school population coming from ethnic minority groups. In addition, 93 different languages are spoken among various students in the Anchorage Schools. In addition to offering a strong curriculum in the core areas of math, science, language arts, social studies, physical education, and health, programs throughout the district emphasize both music and art.

Chugach School District
9312 Vanguard Drive, Suite 100
Anchorage
(907) 522–7400
www.chugachschools.com
Though the district office is in Anchorage, the Chugach School District's 214 students live throughout sometimes isolated parts of Southcentral Alaska. Though it has only 30 staff members, the district has won the prestigious Malcolm Baldrige Quality Award. Approximately half of the student population represents ethnic minorities, particularly Alaskan Natives. Schools at Whittier, Chenega

i Though most of the regional boarding schools for Alaska Native students were closed years ago, Mount Edgecombe in Sitka still attracts Alaska Native students from across the state.

Bay, and Tatitlek make up the physical facilities of the district, and a homeschool program is an integral part of the efforts.

From preschool through high school, Chugach students engage in life-based learning, with instruction in the workplace, the home, the community, and the schools. A standards-based system is used instead of traditional Carnegie Units and grades. Each student works from an Individual Learning Plan. Through the support of the Gates Foundation, the Chugach model of nontraditional learning and assessment has been shared with a dozen districts in Alaska and the Lower 48.

Kenai Peninsula Borough School District
148 North Binkley Street, Soldotna
(907) 714–8888
www.kpbsd.k12.ak.us
Despite the challenges of serving an area larger than the state of West Virginia, with 44 school sites in 21 communities, the Kenai Peninsula Schools have a great deal to show for their efforts. A high percentage of their teachers have achieved Highly Qualified status, and 76 percent of the district's high school graduates go on to some kind of post-secondary training or education.

Serving more than 9,000 students is a staff of approximately 1,200, making the district the largest employer on the Peninsula. Nearly half of the faculty and staff have been with the district for 10 years or more. The district has 14 elementary schools, 4 middle schools, 8 high schools, and 18 small schools that serve multiple grade levels, including 4 in communities so remote that they are accessible only by air or water, and another that can be accessed only on foot or by all-terrain vehicle. In additional to traditional programs, the district also offers alternative and charter school options in select communities.

Matanuska-Susitna Borough School District
501 North Gulkana Street, Palmer
(907) 746–9255
www.matsuk12.us
Serving the Valley's growing population of families and young learners, the Mat-Su School District includes 8 high schools, 5 middle schools, and 20 elementary schools. They also have a correspondence program, a K–12 school, an extended learning program, and two charter schools.

In addition to schools in the larger towns of Palmer and Wasilla, the district includes smaller schools in Houston, Talkeetna, and Trapper Creek. Through the district's open-enrollment program, parents may apply for boundary exemptions for their children provided the schools they request are not above their student capacity.

Valdez City School District
1112 West Klutina Street, Valdez
(907) 835–4357
www.valdezcityschools.org
With more than 50 percent of its funding from local appropriations, the Valdez City Schools has a strong base of community support for its K–12 system, which serves approximately 850 students. Approximately 60 certified staff members facilitate the district's commitment to a favorable student-teacher ratio of 14 to 1. In addition to Hutchens Elementary School, Gilson Junior High School, and Valdez High School, a new middle school is being opened. Valdez High School was the first secondary school in the state to receive the National Department of Education's Excellence in Education Award, and they offer a dual-enrollment program with Prince William Sound Community College. A full slate of extracurricular activities is provided as well.

Private Schools
Anchorage Christian Schools
6401 East Northern Lights Boulevard
Anchorage
(907) 337–9575
www.acsedu.org

i In remote parts of the state, the Bureau of Indian Affairs used to operate elementary schools. These federal schools have been incorporated into regional school districts. Because villages and towns in remote areas have no tax base, the state supports these schools now.

Founded in 1972 by Dr. Jerry Prevo, well-known pastor of the Anchorage Baptist Temple, the Anchorage Christian Schools complex has grown into one of the largest religious school sites in the state. Committed to the spiritual, mental, physical, social, cultural, and vocational aspects of its students, the Anchorage Christian Schools system offers programs from kindergarten through high school. The schools now operate from a state-of-the-art facility with 33 classrooms, cable and video systems, a library, a science lab, music rooms, and a large gymnasium.

Atheneum School
1920 West Dimond Boulevard
Anchorage
(907) 344–2533
www.atheneum.org
A small, private college-prep school with no religious affiliation, Atheneum uses Socratic seminars and classic texts in a curriculum model that mirrors that of St. John's University's Great Books approach. In addition to its middle and high school programs, Atheneum publishes a semi-annual journal of student work and offers summer programs that are open to the public. The school emphasizes lifelong, relevant learning in a spirit of inquiry.

Heritage Christian Schools
Abbott Campus
9521 Lake Otis Parkway
Anchorage
(907) 349–8032
Since the 1970s, Heritage Christian Schools has maintained an emphasis on quality education, moral character, and academic excellence. With a mission to promote a Christian worldview in a post-modern culture, Heritage

operates kindergarten and elementary programs at their Abbott Campus while offering secondary programs at their Sentry Campus. Homeschool and pre-kindergarten programs are also available.

CHILD CARE

Private and home child care programs in Anchorage are licensed through the municipality's Child and Adult Care Program, which conducts an average of three inspections per year on licensed facilities in addition to monitoring complaints. For a list of licensed child care providers in the city, go to www.thecityof anchorage.com/childcare/index.html.

Child Care Connection, Inc.
P.O. Box 141689
Anchorage, AK 99514-1689
(907) 563–1966
www.childcareconnection.org/ccc/
contact.htm
For child care services and information in Anchorage and throughout Southcentral Alaska, the Child Care Connection is an excellent resource. With a mission of promoting quality early education and child development, this nonprofit works with parents and communities as well as providing learning opportunities for child care professionals. In addition to staffing offices in Valdez, Kenai, Anchorage, and the Mat-Su Valley, the Child Care Connections runs an online referral network

HEALTH CARE
Hospitals
Alaska Native Medical Center
4315 Diplomacy Drive, Anchorage
(907) 563–2662
www.anmc.org
One of the premier medical facilities in the state, this Alaska Native–owned hospital serves members of the 229 Native groups in Alaska. Located off Tudor Road near Providence Hospital, the Alaska Native Medical Center (ANMC) has 150 beds plus an outpa-

ℹ️ When traveling in Alaska, keep emergency preparedness in mind. Cell phone coverage can be spotty even on parts of the road system, so it's a good idea to have a first-aid kit handy. Satellite phones can be rented for remote trips, but they aren't cheap.

tient clinic. It has the only Level II Trauma Care Center in the state, offering round-the-clock attention for trauma cases. Primary-care services focus on patient relationships, prevention, and wellness. Native art adorns the walls of the medical center, which fosters a "gathering place" atmosphere for the Native community. ANMC is a teaching facility for the University of Washington Medical School, and the center has received awards from the Institute of Health Care Improvement, the American College of Physicians, the Emergency Medical Services system in Alaska, the U.S. Indian Health Service, and the American Nurses Credentialing Center.

Alaska Regional Hospital
2801 DeBarr Road, Anchorage
(907) 276–1131
www.alaskaregional.com
This 238-bed hospital provides a full range of health care services, with a commitment to superior technology and expertise. With its own landing strip, Alaska Regional is the only hospital in the state that has front-door access for fixed-wing aircraft for medevac (medical evacuation) services. They offer a free physician referral service, and they are the first hospital in Alaska to provide robotic-assisted surgery for delicate operations.

Central Peninsula General Hospital
250 Hospital Place, Soldotna
(907) 714–4404
www.cpgh.org
Accredited by the Joint Commission on Accreditation of Healthcare Organizations, Central Peninsula is a full-service 62-bed facility. The 32-person medical staff includes seven emergency room physicians who provide

round-the-clock care. Medical services at the hospital include cardiac health and rehabilitation, diagnostic imaging, a family birth center, an oncology center, surgical services, and the Serenity House Chemical Dependency Treatment Center. Community outreach programs at Central Peninsula include Prepared Childbirth classes, Safe Sitter training, the Safe Kids Program, and Dine & Discuss health care information forums. The hospital is a borough-owned, nonprofit entity governed by an all-volunteer board of directors.

Mat-Su Regional Medical Center
2500 South Woodworth Loop, Palmer
(907) 861–6000
www.matsuregional.com
The first hospital serving the Mat-Su Valley dates from 1935, when the first colonists arrived under Roosevelt's New Deal package. When the original hospital burned in 1947, services were spread among a variety of facilities until the current state-of-the-art medical center opened in 2006. This new 74-bed hospital with all private, single-bed rooms overlooks the Valley on a 30-acre site off the Palmer-Wasilla Trunk Road. The third floor is shelled in for expansion to include 52 additional beds plus acute care and ancillary services. The new facility also includes a Cardiac Catheterization Laboratory, a fast-track emergency room, four operating rooms, and one C-Section operating room.

Providence Alaska
3200 Providence Drive, Anchorage
(907) 562–2211
www.providence.org/alaska
From the time that the Sisters of Providence brought health care services to Nome in 1902, Providence has been the leading name in medical services throughout most of Alaska. Providence Alaska in Anchorage is now the largest hospital in the state, with a comprehensive range of services, medical equipment, and treatment options. The hospital operates a 24-hour nurse advice line (907–261–2945) and physician referral serv-

ice (907–261–2945). Lifeguard Air Ambulance Service transports patients with critical needs from around the state. Providence has specialty clinics for cystic fibrosis, diabetes, occupational therapy, family medicine, sleep disorders, sports medicine, and a wound center. They also offer behavioral health services and a crisis line.

Providence Seward Medical and Care Center
P.O. Box 365
Seward, Alaska 99664
(907) 224–5205
www.providence.org/alaska/seward/default
.htm

Services at this medical facility include emergency care, in-patient hospital care, radiology, lab facilities, speech therapy, physical therapy, respiratory therapy, nutrition counseling, home health care, and long-term care. Registered nurses staff the emergency department around the clock, and Lifeguard Air Ambulance service can transport patients to Providence Alaska in Anchorage as needed. Though far from a full-fledged hospital, the Seward center does have two rooms for short-stay patients. On weekdays, board-certified family practice doctors see patients by appointment. The 40-bed Providence Wesley facility offers long-term care and rehabilitation services.

Providence Valdez Medical Center
911 Meals Avenue, Valdez
(907) 835–2249
www.providence.org/alaska

Physicians, nurses, and support staff treat a wide variety of medical conditions at this facility with 10 long-term-care beds and 11 short-term-care beds. In addition to 24-hour emergency services, the center offers diagnostic services such as X-rays, ultrasounds, and CAT scans; a variety of laboratory services; physical, speech, and occupational therapy; and outpatient health clinics.

South Peninsula Hospital
4300 Bartlett Street, Homer
(907) 235–8101
www.sphosp.com

A recent expansion project created this 25,000-square-foot facility with 47 beds, including 8 acute-care rooms. This small hospital offers diagnostic imaging services, a surgery department, emergency facilities, and a sleep lab. Community health and rehabilitation services also are available through South Peninsula. The hospital's mission is to promote health and wellness through cost-effective, locally managed, holistic health care.

Clinics

Alaska Health Care Clinic
3600 Minnesota Drive, Anchorage
(907) 279–3500

Offering comprehensive family care at affordable rates, this clinic is open weekdays from 8:00 A.M. to 7:00 P.M. and Saturday from 10:00 A.M. to 4:00 P.M. Patients may be seen by appointment or walk-in, and waiting times are minimal. The staff includes one medical doctor, five registered nurses, and one family nurse practitioner. Home visits may be arranged for those unable to get to the clinic.

Alaska VA Healthcare System and Regional Office
2925 DeBarr Road, Anchorage
(907) 257–4700, (888) 353–7574

From their facility within the Alaska Regional Hospital, the Alaska VA System offers outpatient services to qualified veterans within a large service area. Inpatient services for veterans are provided through a cooperative agreement with Elmendorf Air Force Base and other local hospitals.

Anchorage Native Primary Care Center
4320 Diplomacy Drive, Anchorage
(907) 729–3250
www.southcentralfoundation.org/pcc.cfm

Under the management of Southcentral Foundation, this clinic offers a wide range of serv-

Emergency Services

Fire, Police, Ambulance, Search & Rescue	911
Anchorage Police	(907) 786–8500
Alaska State Troopers	(907) 269–5511
Search and Rescue Civil Air Patrol	(907) 272–7227
Coast Guard Emergency	(800) 478–5555
Suicide Intervention	(907) 563–3200
Abused Women's Aid in Crisis	(907) 272–0100
Child Abuse Hotline	(907) 269–4000
Rape & Assault Hotline	(907) 276–7273
Pet Emergency Hotline	(907) 274–5636
Poison Control Center	(800) 222–1222
Road Conditions	(907) 272–6037, (800) 478–7675

ices as part of the Alaska Native Medical Center. Audiology, a children's clinic, family medicine, maternal-child health, radiology services, women's health services, and urgent care are among the specialties of this Native health organization.

Anchorage Neighborhood Health Center
1217 East 10th Avenue, Anchorage
(907) 257–4686
www.anhc.org
With a mission of providing quality, compassionate health care for all, the Anchorage Neighborhood Health Center offers a wide range of medical services on a sliding-fee basis. The clinic provides family practice serv-

ices to more than 13,000 people a year, including those with private insurance, the uninsured, and Medicaid/Medicare recipients. Dental services, prenatal care, chronic disease management, school and sports physicals, prenatal and well child care are among the wide range of services provided. The Center also operates a facility at 3521 Mountain View Drive (907–792–2300).

Sunshine Community Health Center
Mile 4.2 Talkeetna Spur Road
Talkeetna
(907) 733–2273
Open Monday through Saturday from 9:00 A.M. to 5:00 P.M., this clinic provides a wide range of family-care services, including dental care, behavioral health, family planning, immunizations, chronic disease management, school and sport physicals, well child care, and urgent medical care. Diagnostic services and periodic specialty clinics also are available. The health center, which has been providing health care in the Upper Susitna Valley since 1987, also operates a clinic in Willow.

RETIREMENT

It's far from the Sun Belt, but in 2005 Anchorage was selected by CNN Money as one of the best places to retire. The number of Anchorage residents older than age 50 has increased by more than 100 percent in the past several years, though the median age is still 32. The Mat-Su Borough also reports a large influx of senior citizens, with the number of residents age 65 and older increasing by 150 percent during a recent five-year period. Some retirees come from the Lower 48 to be closer to children and grandchildren, while some Valley seniors migrate north from Anchorage for a more laid-back lifestyle in smaller communities such as Willow. Homer, with its relatively temperate climate and easy access to the ocean, is another popular choice with retirees.

Although Alaska's Longevity Bonus Program paying a monthly stipend to the state's senior citizens fell victim to budget cuts a few years ago, the state-run Pioneer Homes remain, supplementing a handful of private retirement communities and assisted-living options.

Anchorage Pioneer Home
923 West 11th Avenue, Anchorage
(907) 276–3414
Conveniently located in the city's downtown core, this five-story building looks over the Delaney Park Strip. More than 200 residents enjoy mountain and city views from the home, which has a fifth-floor dining room as well as five smaller dining areas in various parts of the complex. Like other Pioneer Homes throughout the state, this assisted-living facility offers a variety of services depending on the needs of individual residents, with recreational and social activities designed to promote independence and fulfilling relationships. Residents include many of the pioneering folks who came north during the homesteading era and lent their energies and talents to bringing Alaska into its own. The Anchorage Pioneer Home is an official "Eden Alternative" home, designed with a home-like atmosphere in mind. This government-owned facility has 78 private rooms and 228 semiprivate rooms, with a minimum age of 65 for residents.

Anchorage Senior Center
1300 East 19th Avenue, Anchorage
(907) 258–7823
For a nominal fee, seniors can enjoy lifetime memberships with a variety of services and activities at this nonresidential community center. Located on nicely wooded acreage, the center offers preventative health services as well as assistance with insurance, housing, home care, and money management. Arts and crafts, games, and a library are among the programs here. Classes at the center include fitness, hiking, skiing, dancing, and computer instruction. There's live music every Friday night and a social hour every Wednesday, plus the Arctic Rose Restaurant is open on weekdays.

Cook Inlet Housing Complex Retirement Homes
9131 Centennial Drive, Anchorage
(907) 338–2211
Established by the Alaska State Legislature in 1974, the Cook Inlet Housing Authority (CIHA) is charged with providing housing opportunities for those living at or below 80 percent of the area's median income. CIHA is affiliated with the Cook Inlet Region Native Corporation but serves a culturally diverse clientele. Retirement home options include 75 continuing-care units and 120 apartments, with a minimum resident age of 62. The 20-unit Knik Corners Apartments, the 53-unit Kenaitze Point project, and the 75-unit Chickaloon Landing have earned awards for their fresh and appealing architecture and layout. All three buildings, along with the newer Tyonek Terrace, are located in a secluded campus in East Anchorage, with nice views of the Chugach Mountains.

Friendship Terrace
250 Herndon Avenue, Homer
(907) 235–6727
www.alaskais.com/homerseniors
This assisted-living facility features private apartments that overlook the waters of Kachemak Bay, dining in a common area, and round-the-clock assistance as needed. Laundry and housekeeping services are provided, as is access to social and recreational activities. An enclosed walkway connects Friendship Terrace with the neighboring Homer Senior Center, where residents can participate in a variety of activities. Short-term respite care also is available

Mountain Rose Estates
(907) 746–1493, (907) 262–2493
www.mountainroseestates.com
Offering private housing for active seniors through new developments in Palmer, Soldotna, and Eagle River, Mountain Rose Estates includes yard care, snow removal, exterior maintenance, and insurance as part of the Home Owners Association dues. The projects

are designed for a small-town lifestyle with distinctive new homes that promote energy-efficient living, comfort, and security.

Palmer Pioneer Home
250 East Fireweed Lane, Palmer
(907) 745–4241

Built in 1971 on the site of the former Alaska State Fairgrounds, this state-run assisted-living facility offers spectacular mountain views as well as access to shops and restaurants in the quaint downtown section of Palmer. In keeping with the Valley's historical link to agriculture, staff and residents tend a large garden that is harvested for meal preparation at the home. Like its sister property in Anchorage, the Palmer Pioneer Home is an Eden Alternative Home, dedicated to the concept of de-institutionalizing long-term care with a structure that replicates resident neighborhoods. Its 79 residents range from those living with complete independence to those with chronic but stable medical conditions. In 2006, a major remodeling project merged a Veterans facility into the home. State statute sets the admission requirements for the Pioneer Home at one year of residency and a minimum age of 65.

Soldotna Senior Center
197 West Park Avenue, Soldotna
(907) 262–2322

The Soldotna Senior Center has come a long way since 1986, when the project opened with noon meals served at the Sports Complex. Now the center has its own new facility where you can have lunch, visit with friends, and participate in a variety of activities. The senior center van provides rides to the center and to medical appointments as well as delivering meals to the homebound.

WORSHIP

Alaska's history with regard to organized religion dates back more than two centuries, when Russian settlers in Southeastern Alaska and on Kodiak Island brought the Russian

Orthodox faith with them. Though most of Southcentral Alaska was not impacted by Russian settlement, Russian Orthodox churches dot the landscape today, with the Orthodox Diocese of Alaska located next to the St. Innocent Orthodox Cathedral (907–333–9723) in Anchorage.

After the Russians came waves of Protestant and Catholic missionaries. The state was more or less divided up for mission activity, so in rural areas you'll find enclaves of Catholic, Moravian, Methodist, and Russian Orthodox influence. Anchorage is more eclectic in terms of religion. Surveys conducted by the American Religion Data Archive show that of those claiming a religious preference from the choices offered, most Anchorage residents chose "other," with Catholic, Baptist, Mormon, and Lutheran faiths claimed in descending order.

More than 325 religious organizations can be found in Anchorage. While the vast majority of them represent either Christian denominations or nondenominational Christian groups, other faiths are represented in the Anchorage Zen Community (907–566–0143), the Baha'i Center (907–349–1844), and the Islamic Center of Alaska (907–562–4241). The Congregation Beth Shalom (907–338–1836) serves believers committed to Reform Judaism.

The Catholic Archdiocese of Anchorage was established in 1966 to serve what is now more than 400,000 people, or more than two-thirds of the state's population. An estimated 8 percent of those living within the service area of the diocese are Catholic, with the largest parish, St. Elizabeth Ann Seton, serving 1,500 families in South Anchorage, and the smallest parish, St. James in Seldovia, with five members. The Holy Family

i The Russian Orthodox church uses a calendar that's slightly different from Catholic and Protestant calendars. Holidays such as Christmas, New Year's, and Easter typically fall a week later for adherents of the Orthodox faith.

Cathedral (907–276–3455) in downtown Anchorage hosted Pope John Paul on his visit to Alaska in 1980.

Among the Protestant churches in Anchorage, the Anchorage Baptist Temple (907–333–6535) and its longtime pastor Dr. Jerry Prevo have a large presence. The largest congregation in the state is at Changepoint (907–344–7780), which was established in 1989. Changepoint recently moved from three services at Dimond High School into a huge facility near the end of Raspberry Road. The new church incorporates a themed environment for Sunday school and public-use rooms, with a full-size private plane hanging from one ceiling and a replica of the Alaska pipeline-turned-slide in another area. The 202,000-square-foot building can hold 1,600 people per service. Small groups help folks feel at home, and the church also maintains an emphasis on community service with a downtown soup kitchen, Christmas backpacks for the homeless, and Right Way Automotive, providing car repair for the needy at little or no cost.

In the Mat-Su Valley, the Rally Point Teen Resource Center on Knik-Goose Bay Road has made a big splash. Operated by the Wasilla Assembly of God (907–376–5732), it offers classes in writing, barista training, and multimedia. Tutoring is provided, and the hangout includes plasma televisions and new computers for kids to use.

MEDIA

Covering the large geographical area of Southcentral Alaska are several newspapers, radio stations, and television stations. Many newspapers have online editions with select articles available to nonsubscribers. Magazines focusing on life on the last frontier are another good way to keep up with what's happening in the state.

NEWSPAPERS

Anchorage Daily News
1001 Northway Drive, Anchorage
(907) 257–4200
www.adn.com
Though its primary market is in Anchorage, this paper's daily circulation of more than 71,000 reflects a statewide readership. Issues of the paper may be delivered to readers in far-flung parts of the state by small plane, snow machine, or boat. In both 1976 and 1989, the *Daily News* garnered Pulitzer Prizes for public-service features on the Alaska Teamsters and the perils facing Native Alaskans. The paper, owned by the McClatchy Company since 1979, maintains a full-service Web site that averages seven million page views per month. If you want to get a taste of the daily news in Anchorage, you can sign up for free e-mail links to the top stories of the day. The Web site also offers helpful links to keep you up-to-date on the arts and entertainment scene through their "Play" section, which presents features from the Friday entertainment section of the paper.

Anchorage Press
540 East Fifth Avenue, Anchorage
(907) 561–7737
www.anchoragepress.com
A popular weekly with a fun, independent slant, the *Anchorage Press* is distributed free throughout the city. Billed as "Anchorage's most widely-read weekly newspaper" and "Alaska's Hardest-Partying Newspaper," the *Press* is chock-full of great updates on the arts, dining, entertainment, and recreation in the Anchorage area. Regular features such as "Savage Love" and "Freewill Astrology" draw readers, as do a mix of news and features on life both inside and outside of Alaska. Book reviews, music reviews, and a calendar of arts, entertainment, and other events make this a great publication for keeping in touch with the pulse of what's happening in the area. The newspaper's Web site is updated every Thursday with lots of links to recent articles as well as "Eating Briefs," featuring local dining tips. The *Press* also maintains an online hotel booking service.

Frontiersman
5751 East Mayflower Court, Wasilla
(907) 352–2250
www.frontiersman.com
Published and distributed throughout the Mat-Su Valley by Wick Communications, this local paper comes out on Tuesday, Friday, and Sunday. By visiting their Web site, you can read abbreviated versions of select news and feature articles.

Homer News
3482 Landing Street, Homer
(907) 235–7767
www.homernews.com
This weekly paper, owned by Morris Communications, comes out every Thursday with local news, sports, features, and opinions. At the *Homer News* Web site, you can view recent news stories as well as classified advertisements. There's also an online order

form for a free visitor's guide to Homer and the South Peninsula region.

Peninsula Clarion
150 Trading Bay Drive, Suite 1
Kenai
(907) 283–7551
www.peninsulaclarion.com

From its humble beginnings in 1970 as a weekly paper that was published in cramped quarters in Old Town Kenai, the *Clarion* has grown to five issues per week, published Monday through Friday. Local owners sold the paper to Morris Communications in 1990. The Web site, which first went online in 2000, offers links to current and archived stories. The *Clarion* publishes a free ad-and-features edition called the *Clarion Dispatch* on Wednesday.

Valdez Star
P.O. Box 2949
Valdez, AK 99686
(907) 835–2405
www.valdezstar.net

A quintessential hometown weekly, the *Star* has been known to run front-page news with such headlines as "Animal Control Seeks Identity of Biting Dog." A detailed police blotter and lots of classifieds add to the local flavor. At their Web site, you can read a couple of local stories and browse the classifieds.

MAGAZINES

Alaska Business Monthly
501 West Northern Lights Boulevard,
Suite 100
Anchorage
www.akbizmag.com

Written and published by Alaskans with the goal of promoting economic growth in the state, *Alaska Business Monthly* analyzes business trends and features key industries from all around the 49th state. Each monthly issue focuses on a different aspect of the business climate in Alaska. In print since 1986, *Alaska Business Monthly* features a nice mix of coverage including everything from multinational corporations to sole proprietorships.

Alaska Magazine
301 Arctic Slope Avenue, Suite 300
Anchorage
(800) 288–5892
www.alaskamagazine.com

Since 1941, readers of *Alaska Magazine* have been fueling their interest in the 49th state by devouring the 10 annual issues of this general-interest magazine. Columns and feature articles by popular Alaskan writers Nick Jans, Sherry Simpson, Ned Rozell, and Andy Hall keep readers coming back for more, as evidenced by sales rates that top 200,000 copies per month. In addition to monthly articles on intriguing aspects of life in the far north, you'll find regular features and columns including On the Edge, Alaska Traveler, From Ketchikan to Barrow, and My View North.

Alaska Men
205 East Dimond Boulevard, Suite 522
Anchorage
www.alaskamen-online.com

It's not every state that can boast its own matchmaking magazine, but thanks to the vision and efforts of publisher Susie Carter, *Alaska Men* has been promoting eligible Alaskan bachelors since 1987. The mainstream media ate up the concept, and after appearing on several high-profile television shows, Carter created a steady stream of interest in this more-or-less annual publication that profiles Alaskan men and invites women from around the world to contact them in hopes of igniting those proverbial sparks. Never mind the quintessential Alaskan saying about our men, "The odds are good, but the goods are odd." Susie's guys are keepers.

RADIO

In a state where people are spread out far and wide, radio has played an important role over the years, conveying not only top news stories but also broadcasting personal messages to family and friends in remote areas. Public radio has a big presence in the state, especially in the more rural areas, as does local Christian radio. Anchorage stations have a decidedly urban flair, playing everything from the usual talk radio to alternative and music mixes.

Alternative

KRUA 88.1 FM   Anchorage

Christian

KATB 89.3 FM   Anchorage

Classical/Jazz

KLEF 98.1 FM   Anchorage

Country

KASH 107.5 FM   Anchorage

Music Mix

KMXS 103.1 FM   Anchorage
KQEZ 92.1 FM   Houston

News/Talk

KENI 650 AM   Anchorage
KFQD 750 AM   Anchorage

Public Radio

KSKA 91.1 FM   Anchorage
KBBI 890 AM   Homer
KTNA 88.5 FM   Talkeetna

TELEVISION

Television isn't something that longtime Alaskans take for granted. Not so many years have passed from the days when there were only a couple of channels available and sports fans had to watch their favorite teams in tape-delayed matches that were broadcast well after the final score had been decided. That has all changed thanks to satellite and digital technology. Rural communities that once had access to only one station through the now-defunct Rural Alaska TV Network now have broader access to programming through commercial satellite television. Cable service is available in most towns and cities through a handful of different providers.

For uniquely Alaskan programming, *Alaska Magazine* has produced a series of 52 half-hour travel-adventure-lifestyle shows about life in Alaska featuring honest-to-goodness Alaskans. Though the magazine's offices are based in the Lower 48, this programming is produced in Alaska, by Alaskans. Footage from the archives of the former statewide television network is incorporated into the shows. To access copies of these broadcasts, visit www.alaskamagazinetv.com.

TV Channels

KIMO (Channel 13)   ABC
KTVA (Channel 11)   CBS
KTBY (Channel 4)   FOX
KTUU (Channel 2)   NBC
KAKM (Channel 7)   PBS
KYES (Channel 5)   UPN

INDEX

ABOUT THE AUTHOR

DEB VANASSE, a former teacher and real estate broker, has lived in Alaska since 1979. She has traveled extensively throughout the state, including remote areas of Southwestern Alaska, where she lived and worked for eight years. Her two children were born in the Bush, where riverboat, snow machine, and small plane are the only ways to get from one village to another. During her years in rural Alaska, she made frequent trips to Anchorage to pick up groceries and enjoy some of the luxuries of city life. Eventually she moved to Fairbanks and then to Anchorage.

A graduate of Bemidji State University in northern Minnesota and California State University at Dominguez Hills, Deb is the author of several books set in Alaska, including *Under Alaska's Midnight Sun; Alaska's Animal Babies;* and *A Totem Tale: A Tall Story from Alaska.* She was also a coeditor of *The Cama-i Book,* a collection of interviews, stories, and photographs from Southwestern Alaska.